Empire and Tribe in the Afghan Frontier Region

Empire and Tribe in the Afghan Frontier Region

Custom, Conflict and British Strategy in Waziristan until 1947

Hugh Beattie

I.B.TAURIS
LONDON • NEW YORK • OXFORD • NEW DELHI • SYDNEY

I.B. TAURIS
Bloomsbury Publishing Plc
50 Bedford Square, London, WC1B 3DP, UK
1385 Broadway, New York, NY 10018, USA
29 Earlsfort Terrace, Dublin 2, Ireland

BLOOMSBURY, I.B. TAURIS and the Diana logo are trademarks of
Bloomsbury Publishing Plc

First published in Great Britain 2019
This paperback edition published in 2021

Copyright © Hugh Beattie 2019

Hugh Beattie has asserted his right under the Copyright, Designs and Patents Act, 1988, to be identified as the Author of this work.

Cover design: Adriana Brioso
Cover image: Waziris tribesmen of Waziristan, North West Frontier Passage, early twentieth century. (© Culture Club/Getty Images)

All rights reserved. No part of this publication may be reproduced or transmitted in any form or by any means, electronic or mechanical, including photocopying, recording, or any information storage or retrieval system, without prior permission in writing from the publishers.
Bloomsbury Publishing Plc does not have any control over, or responsibility for, any third-party websites referred to or in this book. All internet addresses given in this book were correct at the time of going to press. The author and publisher regret any inconvenience caused if addresses have changed or sites have ceased to exist, but can accept no responsibility for any such changes.

A catalogue record for this book is available from the British Library.

A catalog record for this book is available from the Library of Congress.

ISBN: 978-1-8488-5896-1
PB: 978-0-7556-4372-1
eISBN: 978-1-8386-0084-6
ePDF: 978-1-8386-0085-3

Series: Library of Middle East History

Typeset by Deanta Global Publishing Services, Chennai, India

To find out more about our authors and books visit www.bloomsbury.com and sign up for our newsletters.

Contents

List of Illustrations	vi
Acknowledgements	vii
Introduction	1
1 Waziristan and early British contacts	5
2 Britain and Waziristan 1870–93	19
3 The Durand Line and Mullah Powindah	33
4 Mullah Powindah, suicidal attacks and British responses	55
5 Death of Mullah Powindah and the First World War	71
6 The Third Anglo-Afghan War, the 1919–20 expedition and the early 1920s	89
7 British policy in Waziristan and the Razmak base	109
8 The 1920s and peaceful penetration	129
9 Regime change, Congress and Waziristan and Anglo-Afghan relations	145
10 Mirza Ali Khan's Insurgency, Mullah Sher Ali and the Shami Pir	165
11 Mirza Ali Khan, the Second World War and British withdrawal	183
12 Summary and conclusion	201
Appendix 1: Timeline	209
Appendix 2: Brief relevant details of some personalities mentioned above	213
Appendix 3: Some genealogical links between Mehsud and Wazir lineages	218
Notes	220
Glossary	282
Sources and bibliography	284
Index	296

Illustrations

Map

1 Waziristan in relation to western Pakistan and eastern Afghanistan (c.1935) viii
2 Central and South Waziristan (c.1935) ix
3 North Waziristan (c.1935) x

Figures

1.1 Houses at Kot Handgar (Langar) Khel village, Waziristan, 1930. Their defensive towers are clearly visible. Holmes, Randolph Bezzant (1888–1973). Credit: British Library, London UK@British Library Board. All Rights Reserved/Bridgeman Images 7
6.1 Tractor and six-inch howitzer near Razmak, Waziristan, Pakistan, dated 1890 but in fact probably early 1920s. Photo by Mela Ram/Royal Geographical society/Getty Images 99
7.1 The burning of 'Makin' from air and land – Waziristan, Pakistan, dated 1890 but in fact probably early 1920s. Photo by Mela Ram/Royal Geographical society/Getty Images 119
7.2 Daily convoys for Razmak, showing a long camel train proceeding through the snow to Razmak. Holmes, Randolph Bezzant (1888–1973). Credit: British Library, London UK@British Library Board. All Rights Reserved/Bridgeman Images 123

Acknowledgements

I would like to thank the Open University for allowing me to have the time to undertake research for this book and to write it up. It is also a pleasure to thank the staff at the British Library, Cambridge University Library and South Asian Studies Library for their help with locating official records, private papers, books and photographs. I would also like to thank the editors at I.B. Tauris, Maria Marsh, Thomas Stottor and Sophie Rudland, for their patience and advice, as well as the two anonymous readers for their helpful comments and suggestions. I am most grateful to Louisa Keyworth for preparing the maps and Jennifer Nesbitt for her work on the charts. I am as always indebted to my wife, Claire, for reading and commenting on successive drafts.

Maps

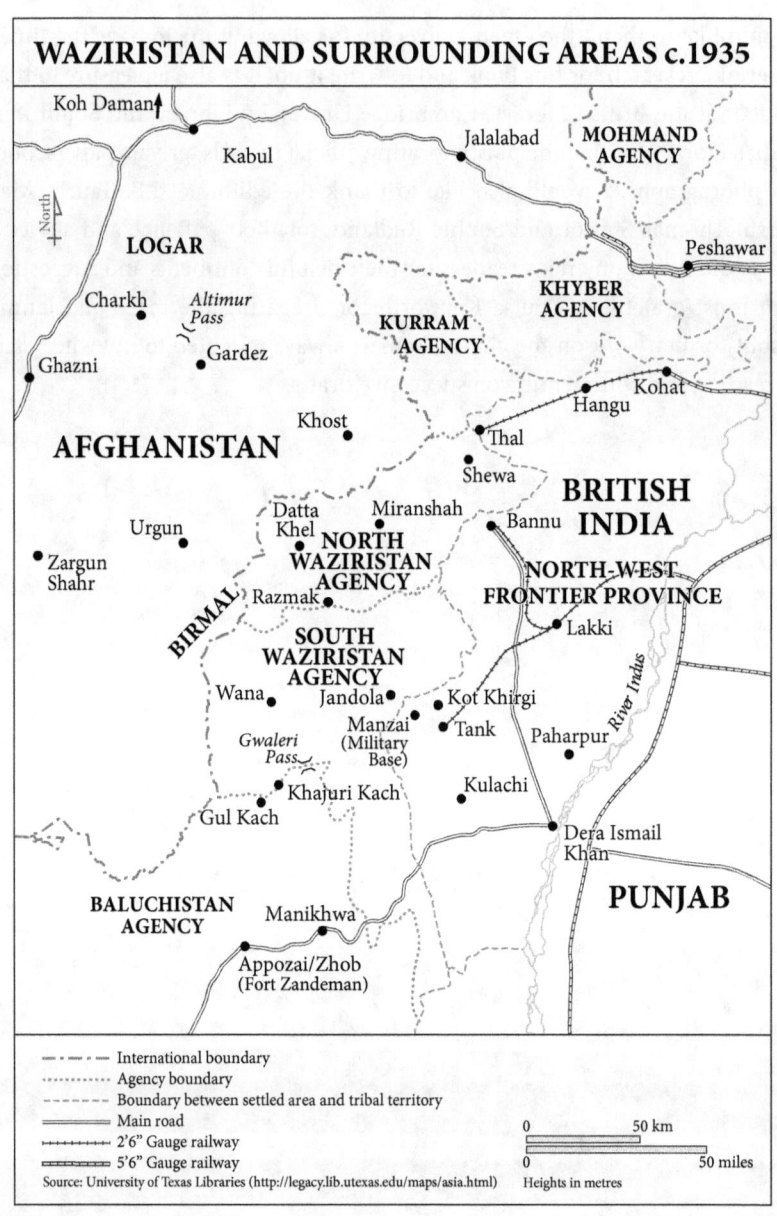

Map 1 Waziristan in relation to western Pakistan and eastern Afghanistan (c.1935).

Maps

Map 2 Central and South Waziristan (c.1935).

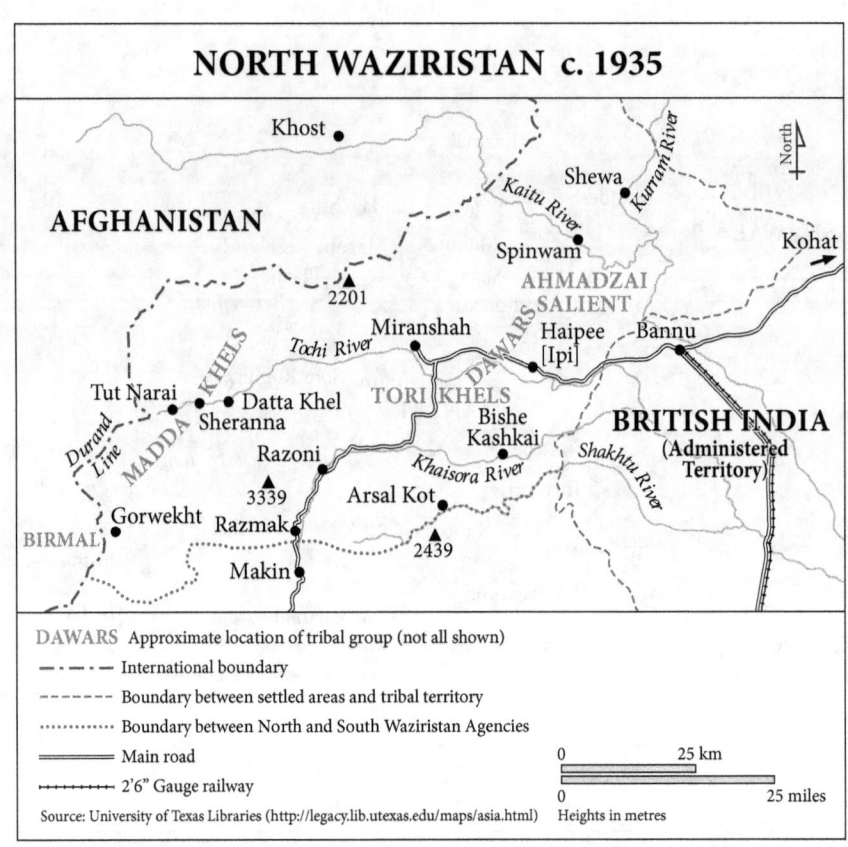

Map 3 North Waziristan (c.1935).

Introduction

Waziristan, a mountainous region in western Pakistan, was described by former American president Barak Obama as 'the most dangerous place in the world'; it has endured a number of invasions since the mid-nineteenth century and remains an unsettled borderland. This book explores its history from the early nineteenth century to the present day, and in doing so sheds light on the reasons for its continuing volatility. The principal focus is on the efforts the British made to gain control of it from 1849, when they arrived on its eastern border, until the creation of Pakistan in 1947.

British interest in Waziristan reflected what they took to be its strategic significance. As they saw it, to protect their Indian empire they needed to keep Russia out of Afghanistan, and this meant controlling Waziristan. In 1849 the region was more or less independent. By 1914 a combination of force and bribery had enabled the British to establish a tenuous control of it. This weakened during the First World War and largely broke down in the early summer of 1919, when the outbreak of the third Anglo-Afghan war led to the collapse of the militias the British had set up to help them manage it. In response, at the end of the year a large British force began to fight its way into central Waziristan, and a few years later the British established a large military base at Razmak. During the interwar period they tried to open up Waziristan and extend their control of it by pursuing a policy of what they called peaceful penetration: sending regular troops and irregular scouts to visit as many parts of it as possible, coupled with limited efforts to provide education, health care and economic assistance. This was not very successful either, and it was much more expensive than the previous strategy; a major insurgency broke out in 1936, and the costs of trying to control Waziristan continued to rise. By 1947 raiding from Waziristan into the towns and villages to the east was worse than it had been in 1849.

Why did Britain fail to get a firm grip on it? This book attempts to answer that question. There were several reasons. In the first place financial constraints limited the amount that could be spent both on the use of force and on more peaceful means of winning its people over. Second, there was Waziristan's location on the border with Afghanistan. Afghans thought they had a stronger claim to it. Even after the demarcation of the Durand Line in the mid-1890s divided the North-West Frontier into British and Afghan spheres of influence, the Afghan government continued to maintain and develop links with people whose homes were on the British side of the line. Third, the region's mountainous topography made it difficult to access. The culture of its 'tribal' inhabitants, who greatly valued their independence and their individual autonomy and were reluctant to submit to any authority, whether internal or external, was also very important. In addition to exploring these issues, the book examines the roles played by poverty and religion in the encounter, including the importance of suicidal violence, looks at some British and North-West Frontier understandings of violence, and draws some comparisons between aspects of British and French colonial strategy. In shedding light on Britain's experience of Waziristan, this book engages with some significant aspects of British imperial history. It also contributes to our understanding of subsequent developments along this frontier, because, although much has of course changed since 1947, there are some significant continuities.

Earlier scholarly discussions of Waziristan's recent history consisted of chapters in books dealing with the British period on the North-West Frontier as a whole, and they tended to concentrate on shifting British policy and on the military encounters. Examples include William Barton's *India's North-West Frontier* (1939, London), Sir Olaf Caroe's *The Pathans 550 BC.-A.D.* (1957, Oxford), Colin Davies's *The Problem of the North-West Frontier 1890-1908* (1932, Cambridge), Major-General James Elliott's *The Frontier 1839-1947: The Story of the North-West Frontier of India* (1968, London), and James Spain's *The Pathan Borderland* (1963, The Hague). *Frontier Legion: With the Khassadars of North Waziristan* (Ferring, 2003), written in 1950, by Frank Leeson, describes his experiences as a tribal police officer in northern Waziristan in 1946-7.[1]

Brian Robson's *Crisis on the Frontier: The Third Afghan War and the Campaign in Waziristan 1919-20* (2004, Staplehurst) is a more recent study that also focuses on military history. Books that deal specifically with Waziristan include Alan Warren's *The Faqir of Ipi and the Indian Army* (2000, Karachi) and Andrew Roe's *Waging War in Waziristan* (2010, Lawrence, Kansas); Warren's study in particular contains much original research. Other recent work that has some discussion of Waziristan includes David Omissi's *Air Power and Colonial Control: The Royal Air Force 1919-1939* (1990, Manchester).

Researchers have also begun to go beyond the military aspects of the encounter to explore the changing nature of the British frontier administration and British imperial culture. Their publications include *The Edge of Empire: The British Political Officer and Tribal Administration on the North-West Frontier 1877-1947* (2011, Farnham) by Christian Tripodi and Brandon Marsh's *Ramparts of Empire: British Imperialism and India's Afghan Frontier, 1918-1948* (2015, Basingstoke).[2] When security was less of a problem, social anthropologists carried out field research in several frontier locations, and their work has informed subsequent scholarship. These include several publications by Akbar S. Ahmed, notably *Millennium and Charisma among Pathans* (1976, London), *Pukhtun Economy and Society: Traditional Structure and Economic Development in a Tribal Society* (1980, London) and *Resistance and Control in Pakistan* (1983, London). Fredrik Barth's study of political organization in Swat, *Political Leadership among Swat Pathans* (1959, London), has become a classic. Among other valuable contributions are David Edwards's *Heroes of the Age: Moral Fault Lines on the Afghan Frontier* (1996, Berkeley) and Charles Lindholm's *Generosity and Jealousy: The Swat Pukhtuns of Northern Pakistan* (1982, New York) and *Frontier Perspectives: Essays in Comparative Anthropology* (1996, Karachi).

More recently, there has been a renewed interest in the history and culture of the frontier people and religious and political developments in the North-West Frontier Province in the British period, as researchers have begun to investigate a range of archival sources.[3] For instance in my earlier study *Imperial Frontier: Tribe and State in Waziristan* (2002, Richmond), I looked in detail at the first thirty-five years of the British relationship with Waziristan, exploring not only the ways in which the British tried to manage relations with it but also the ways in which people responded to them, showing how in this early period there was much more to British strategy on the Waziristan border than simply the use of force. Other examples include Robert Nichols's *Settling the Frontier: Land, Law, and Society in the Peshawar Valley 1500-1900* (2001, Karachi), Sana Haroon's *Frontier of Faith: Islam in the Indo-Afghan Borderland* (2007, London) and Mukulika Banerjee's study of the Khudai Khidmatgaran, *The Pathan Unarmed: Opposition and Memory in the North-West Frontier* (2000, Oxford/Santa Fe). Benjamin Hopkins and Magnus Marsden's *Fragments of the Afghan Frontier* (2012, London) covers aspects of the modern history and society of the frontier and Afghanistan, as does their edited volume *Beyond Swat: History, Society and Economy along the Afghanistan-Pakistan Frontier* (2013, London). Elizabeth Leake's *The Defiant Border: The Afghan-Pakistan Borderlands in the Era of Decolonization, 1936-1965* (2017, Cambridge) breaks new ground in exploring in depth the relationship between developments along the frontier and in Afghanistan and Pakistan from the mid-1930s to the 1960s.

In this book I have drawn on some of the work on the frontier that has been published since the turn of the century, as well as on the records and personal correspondence in the British Library, the Cambridge University Library and the Cambridge South Asian Studies Library, to discuss developments in Waziristan over the whole period from the early 1880s to 1947 in more detail than any previous studies. I have tried to read the sources 'against the grain', but of course they have their limitations, not just because of their inherent bias but because they focus on some aspects of the encounter at the expense of others. Nevertheless, in going beyond 'state-centred national histories', the book is a contribution to the kind of 'connected history' advocated by Potter and Saha and the study of borderlands and their characteristic features.[4] Chapters 1 to 4 look at the geography, society and culture of Waziristan and review the wider political context in the early nineteenth century before the British arrival in 1849, going on to examine some of the key developments during the second half of the century. These include the impact of the Second Anglo-Afghan War, reactions to the implementation of the forward policy and the demarcation of the Durand Line, and the new approach introduced by the viceroy, Lord Curzon. Chapters 5 to 8 take the story up to the early 1920s, looking at the part played by an influential mullah, Muhiy-ud-Din, the so-called Mullah Powindah, the deteriorating British position during the First World War, and developments after it. Chapters 9 to 11 explore the policy of peaceful penetration and its failure, the insurgency led by Mirza Ali Khan (the 'Faqir of Ipi') and the recrudescence of raiding along the border, British withdrawal and the challenges posed by it and the partition of India. The final chapter reviews the key points that emerge from the discussion as a whole.

1

Waziristan and early British contacts

Waziristan

Waziristan, 'land of the Wazirs', is part of what came to be called by the British the North-West Frontier, and most of it is now in Pakistan. To the west this rugged mostly mountainous region borders the Afghan provinces of Paktika and Khost; to the east is the Derajat.[1] Southern Waziristan has the higher mountains (to the west rising to 3,513 metres – approaching 11,000 feet), as well as deep valleys and narrow gorges cut by rivers flowing east to the Indus. In northern Waziristan, the mountains are lower and valleys are more open. Some parts are still forested, others arid and treeless. The climate is harsh with cold winters and hot summers.

In 1849 when the British arrived on its eastern border, rivers, gorges and mountains and its highly independent people made travelling through it difficult, but it was neither insulated from external influences nor very far from major urban centres. Makin in central Waziristan, for example, is about 140 miles from Kabul, and about the same distance from Peshawar. In modern times the North-West Frontier has not always been a political border. During the seventeenth century, for example, Waziristan and the rest of the mountainous area between the Kabul River to the north and the Gumal River to the south formed a semi-independent enclave encapsulated within the Mughal Empire. Similarly in the later eighteenth and early nineteenth centuries the Durrani rulers, initially based in Kandahar and then in Kabul, had ruled much of the territory along the borders of Waziristan, but not Waziristan itself. It was the rise of the Sikh kingdom in the early nineteenth century and its conquest of the Punjab that began to turn the region into a frontier zone.[2]

The people

In the mid-nineteenth century the majority of those living along the North-West Frontier were Pashtuns, who belonged to descent groups 'composed of lineages (Pashto – *zai* "sons of") that traced their origin to Qais Abdurashid, the putative common ancestor of all Pashtuns'.[3] The British generally regarded these groups as 'tribes' (or sometimes clans).[4] In Waziristan they included Darwesh Khel Wazirs, Mehsuds (or Mahsuds), Dawars and Bhittanis. Bhittanis were supposedly descended from Qais's second son, Bitan, while one version of the origins of the Darwesh Khel Wazirs, Mehsuds and Dawars was that they were descended from Karlanri, an adopted son of Qais's third son, Ghurghusht. Mehsuds and Darwesh Khel Wazirs (as well as the Gurbaz Wazirs) however were believed to share a common ancestor in Karlanri's grandson Sulaiman, while the Dawars traced their origins back to another grandson, Shitak.[5]

The Darwesh Khels (referred to from now on simply as Wazirs) inhabited an arc of territory extending from Wana in the south-west to the Kurram River and Upper Miranzai in the north-east. They were further divided into Utmanzais and Ahmadzais. The Mehsuds were divided into three main groupings, Alizais, Bahlolzais and Shaman Khels. They lived in the centre and south of Waziristan, but apart from the Manzai Alizais these larger groupings did not have separate territories of their own.[6] To the east of the Mehsuds, between them and the plains (the Derajat) lived the Bhittanis. To the north the Dawars lived in the Tochi valley. To the south-west, around Wana, lived Dotani Ghilzais. There were also small colonies of Hindu and Sikh traders and moneylenders. In addition at Kaniguram there was a settlement of people known as Urmurs, or Barakis, who spoke a separate language, Urmuri.

To the east of Waziristan lay the Bannu district whose inhabitants were mostly either Pashtu-speaking Bannuchis (Karlanri Pashtuns) or Punjabi speakers known as Jats. Between Bannu and Tank lived Pashtu-speaking Lohani Marwats (who also claimed descent from Qais's second son, Bitan). Most people in the Tank district to the south of Bannu were Marwats and Kundis (also Pashtu-speaking Lohanis). To the south of Waziristan itself was the Gumal River, and south of it lived Miani and Sherani Pashtuns. To the south-west and west the population consisted mostly of Ghilzai Pashtuns (also claiming descent from Bitan), including Dotanis and Kharoti and Suleiman Khel Ghilzais. To the north-west, in Khost, lived other Pashtun tribal groups; the Mangals and the Zadrans were the largest; others included Gurbaz Wazirs, Tannis and Muqbils. To the north were Zaimukhts, Turis, Bangash and Khattaks (all supposedly descended from Karlanri).[7]

Settlement and economy

Some Mehsuds were transhumants, some nomadic, but the majority appear to have been settled and lived in small settlements. The better-off lived in walled compounds with defensive towers, the poorer in scattered huts or caves (Figure 1.1).[8] Mehsud occupations were diverse, and included agriculture, horticulture and pastoralism, as well as mining, small-scale industry and trade. For example, they mined and smelted iron near Makin and Kaniguram and sold it in the Tank market. In the mid-nineteenth century there were also a number of workshops, mainly at Makin and Kaniguram (and also some at Shakai and Babar) where agricultural implements, knives and cooking utensils were made. Waziristani people also sold timber, nuts, wool, skins, honey and charcoal in Tank and Bannu. Some areas, Manzai for example, were less agriculturally productive than others, and those living in them were often very poor. They included some of the Shingi, Abdur Rahman Khel and Jalal Khel Bahlolzais, and men from these sections sometimes raided the settled areas to the east or attacked the caravans of the trading nomads (Powindahs) in the Gumal Pass

Figure 1.1 Houses at Kot Handgar (Langar) Khel village, Waziristan, 1930. Their defensive towers are clearly visible. Holmes, Randolph Bezzant (1888–1973). Credit: British Library, London UK@British Library Board. All Rights Reserved/Bridgeman Images.

to the south.⁹ Nevertheless, it seems that few if any Mehsuds (or Wazirs) relied solely on raiding to help them survive.

As regards the Wazirs, many of them were pastoral nomads who moved from summer pastures to winter ones in the autumn and back again in the spring. Their summer pastures and cultivation included the Shawal and Shakai valleys in the mountains of western Waziristan near the present-day border between Afghanistan and Pakistan. In the winter they moved with their flocks to several different places including the Wana district, Birmal, Baddar, Spinwam, Shewa, Miranzai and Bannu. Some lived in tents all year round, and others spent part of the year in houses. Often they grew a spring crop before leaving for higher ground in the early summer. There were permanent villages, for instance in the upper Tochi valley, the Shaktu valley and Dawar; the largest Wazir settlement appears to have been the Madda Khel settlement of Sheranna in the upper Tochi. Some Wazirs were traders and carriers. The Manzar Khel Wazirs, who lived to the north of Miran Shah, mined iron ore in the Ghoreshti Nala behind the Darweshta Sar mountain from which they manufactured horseshoes and nails for sale.[10] Dawars were mostly farmers and horticulturalists. Bhittanis, some of whom were also nomadic, combined pastoralism and agriculture. They also traded in Bannu, Kulachi and Tank. Nowadays Waziristan's population is estimated at over 800,000.[11] It is very hard to say with any certainly what it might have been in the mid-nineteenth century, but it was probably less than 100,000.[12]

Political and social organization

Wazirs and Mehsuds are or were often thought of as typical *nang* Pashtuns (*nang* meaning honour) who were able to live according to supposedly traditional Pashtun values, by contrast with those living in the plains, who paid land revenue to the state, whom Ahmed calls *qalang* Pashtuns – from *qalang*, meaning rent or tax.[13] Traditional values included upholding honour; individuals, families and groups had to maintain their honour and avoid anything which could lead to them being shamed. This was central to Pashtun custom (*riwaj*) or Pashtunwali. Men were supposed to be as self-reliant and independent as possible and not to take orders from others, or allow any challenges or insults to go unanswered. Male honour depended partly on women behaving modestly and avoiding all contact with men other than their close relatives. Hospitality was also highly valued.

From the point of view of both the British and the rulers of Afghanistan, Waziristan was 'a recalcitrant landscape' with 'fugitive, resistant inhabitants': 'mob rule prevails', as one official put it.[14]. It makes more sense, however, to envisage it not as a violent free-for-all, but as a society in which there were no strong leaders and no hereditary leadership, and in which social order was maintained in other ways, including the threat of retaliation and the availability of customary procedures for mediation and reconciliation – among them tribal councils or jirgas and appeal to the authority of religious intermediaries. There were men referred to as maliks (from the Arabic *malik*, king or prince) among all the different groups, who had some influence. But particularly among the Mehsuds this influence was usually limited, and not inherited: 'any man through the display of courage or wisdom may become a Malik irrespective of birth', it was reported.[15] Decisions affecting the group as a whole were usually reached in these jirgas, which could appoint men to act as a kind of police force and enforce their decisions, or call for men to fight against enemies (known as *chalweshtis*).[16]

So far the people of this stateless region, Mehsuds, Wazirs, Dawars, Bhittanis and so on, have been referred to as if they were straightforwardly divided into distinct tribes or tribal groups that predated the encounter with the British and Afghan states. In fact things were more complicated. It seems that people did identify themselves as belonging to different groups on the basis of what was understood to be shared patrilineal descent. At the same time this shared descent was potentially the basis for a whole range of groups of different sizes, depending on how far back up the genealogical tree one went. It appears therefore that people identified with different groups according to the circumstances. It was not necessarily clear to outsiders which the important level or levels were, and exactly what their importance was.

In addition there were factions and networks which crossed genealogical boundaries. According to segmentary lineage theory members of the same genealogical segments should form political groups to compete with distantly related segments, but this does not appear to have happened very often in Waziristan. This was partly due to the existence of an institutionalized rivalry between patrilateral first cousins (*tarburs*), known as *tarburwali*. In the case of the Mehsuds in particular it was also due to the fact that members of different sections sometimes lived together in the same area, rather than having a distinct territory of their own. Other factors which influenced people's social and political behaviour and identities included generational tensions (between *mashars* – elders, implying better-off and *kashars* – young men, the poor) and matrilineal kinship. It is an obvious point, but it would be wrong to think of any of these groups as comprised of people who all thought and behaved in the same way. As everywhere, there appears to have been in Waziristan 'a multiplicity of inconsistent voices and values, varying according to gender, class, age, ideological persuasion and so on'.[17]

The resulting lack of cohesion was particularly noticeable among the Mehsuds. At the same time, however, both Wazirs and Mehsuds did see themselves as sharing an identity. This was based on the idea of a thread or link – *sarishta* – connecting them, which was associated with the concept of *nikat* (from the Pashtu word for grandfather – *nika*). *Nikat* was a tariff according to which both benefits acquired from outsiders and losses suffered at the hands of outsiders were to be shared in fixed proportions, first between the Mehsuds and the Wazirs, and then in the Mehsud case, for example, between the three main divisions – Alizais, Bahlolzais and Shaman Khels – and then between the smaller ones.

Religion

Apart from the Hindu and Sikh traders and moneylenders, the people of Waziristan were Muslims, usually Sunnis. Men with religious authority included mullahs (Persian, from the Arabic *mawla* – someone educated in theology and Islamic law), who had acquired some knowledge of the Qur'an and the hadiths in a local seminary or *madrasah*, led prayers and performed rites of passage for the villagers among whom they lived. Sometimes they helped mediate conflicts. They may have represented a different source of authority to that of the maliks but were not usually outsiders. There were many small *madrasahs* in Bannu, Dawar and Kaniguram.[18]

There was some overlap between the ordinary mullahs and various Sufi or quasi-Sufi figures, whose authority was based mainly on the spiritual power they were believed to develop through prayer and meditative exercises and self-discipline, including fasting and periods of retreat (which could last up to forty days) known as *chillas*. This enabled them to look beyond the veil of ordinary existence into the unseen or unknown (*al-ghaib*) and perform miraculous feats (*karamat*) (strictly speaking God was able to perform these feats through them). So, for instance, they could control the behaviour of birds and animals, feed large numbers of people, cure illness, render enemy bullets harmless and influence the weather.

Some Sufis were wanderers. Others settled down and established permanent bases, lodges referred to as *khanaqas*. Traditionally the Sufi master (*pir*) had disciples who took an oath of allegiance (*bai'at*) and entrusted themselves, body and soul, to him. He would preside over a mosque, where visitors and followers could sleep, and a *langar*, or kitchen, where they would be fed. Famous examples from the frontier during the British period included the Akhund of Swat (1794–1878) and the Hadda mullah (d.1902). Well-known Sufi teachers attracted disciples – *khalifas* and *sheikhs* (deputies), *murids* (disciples), and *talibs* or *taliban* (from *talib-ul-ilm* – seekers after knowledge). As we shall see, these *talibs* were to be a problem for the British. One report referred to them as 'half students, half secular priests, [who] swarm in the mosques leading an idle life and ever ready to incite their clansmen to mischief. They are ignorant and fanatical in an extreme degree.'[19]

Religious authority could be inherited as well, and there were also sacred lineages, for example of Sayyids, whose authority was based on their sacred descent (initially from the Prophet Muhammad himself). They sometimes had hereditary links with particular tribal sections, whose members made regular offerings to them (*shukrana*) in return for the blessings they were believed to bestow. They might, for example, heal the sick by reciting verses from the Qur'an over them. Examples in Waziristan included the so-called Kaniguram Sayyids, who lived at Kaniguram, the Shondakas and the Michan Khels (they were referred to as pirs rather than mullahs). During the later nineteenth century the Kaniguram Sayyid Sultan Akbar Shah, for instance, had links with the Shaman Khels, and another Kaniguram Sayyid, Rahmat Badshah, with the Bahlolzais.[20]

The political position in 1849–50

We have seen that in the early nineteenth century Waziristan was more or less independent, inhabited by stateless people. The founder of the Durrani Empire, Ahmad Shah Durrani (c.1722–72), had established his authority over much of the territory surrounding Waziristan (including Bannu and Tank) in 1748. Waziristan was thus largely encapsulated within his empire, but Dawar seems to have been the only area over which he had some control. His successors continued to claim authority over it, and they did have some limited influence because they shared a religious and to some extent a cultural identity with its inhabitants and had links with some of the leading men.

British contacts with Waziristan began before the annexation of Punjab in 1849. After the British had defeated the Sikh state in 1846, they sent a resident to the court at Lahore to supervise the administration of the Sikh empire.[21] The resident dispatched several ambitious young British army officers to the north and west of it to supervise the collection of revenue. Among them were Herbert Edwardes, who was sent to the Derajat, and Reynell Taylor, who went to Peshawar. When the Second Anglo-Sikh War began, following a rising in Multan in April 1848, anti-British Sikh troops took control of the forts at Bannu and at Lakki between Bannu and the Indus. In October 1848 Reynell Taylor besieged the Lakki fort, which surrendered on 10 January 1849 (as did the Bannu fort a few days later).

After they had annexed Punjab in 1849, the British incorporated Bannu into the new administrative structure they created, and it initially formed part of what was called the Leia Division (Leia is a town to the south-east on the east bank of the Indus). They based a deputy commissioner there, who was responsible to the commissioner in Leia, who in turn answered to the Board of Administration in Lahore. They also set up the Punjab Irregular Force to police the frontier, and along the southern part they built cantonments at Kohat, Bannu, Dera Ismail Khan, Asni and Dera Ghazi Khan, with outposts near the border. They also raised several police regiments and recruited irregular levies.

Tank, however, retained some independence. The British appointed Shah Nawaz Khan, the grandson of its former ruler, as its tax farmer, and left him in charge of that section of the border. Shah Nawaz Khan had connections in Waziristan. His mother was a Mehsud, and he was married to the sister of an influential Mehsud, Yarik Khan Langar Khel Alizai.[22] He not only faced the problem of dealing with the Mehsuds but also encountered opposition from an influential group living in British territory. These were referred to by the British as the Multani Pathans, and the British appointed some of them to posts in the new frontier administration, particularly in Bannu.[23] As a result after 1849 two factions, one associated with the Multanis and the other with Shah Nawaz Khan, competed for influence in the administered areas along the Waziristan border. Each was ready to try and use its links with the transborder tribes to discredit the other. This sometimes involved misrepresenting British intentions to the tribes, even colluding with them to arrange raids and robberies.[24]

Waziristan and the British in the 1850s

In January 1849, just before Taylor arrived there, one of the Afghan amir Dost Mohammed Khan's sons, Sardar Muhammad Azem, the governor of Khost, had briefly occupied Bannu. The amir himself had occupied Peshawar in December 1848, and in February 1849 he had sent his cavalry to join the forces of the

Sikh general, Chattar Singh, in fighting against the British at the Battle of Gujrat.[25] They were defeated, and apprehensive that the British might punish him for his involvement, in 1850 the amir and Sardar Muhammad Azem wrote several letters to Taylor, in which they tried to sound out British intentions towards them.[26] The governor general, Dalhousie, instructed Taylor that he should tell them that they should write to him if they wanted to know, and the correspondence petered out. After that, there do not appear to have been any more contacts with Kabul until 1854 when the Peshawar commissioner, Herbert Edwardes, with Dalhousie's permission, began informal talks. In 1855 Edwardes and another of the amir's sons, Ghulam Hyder Khan, held formal negotiations in Peshawar that resulted in a treaty. After this the British were allowed to appoint an Agent at Kabul; the first was one of the Multani Pathans, Nawab Foujdar Khan.[27] A second treaty was negotiated in 1857, and there was some cooperation between the local British officials and their Afghan counterparts along the border in Miranzai and the Kurram district to the north of Waziristan.[28]

Border or frontier situations

During the 1850s British resources were severely stretched by the task of establishing an administration in Punjab. Any threat to India from Russia (or Afghanistan) seemed to have evaporated, and they did not regard the Waziristan frontier as having any strategic importance. Besides there was the difficult terrain and the independent ethos of Waziristan's people. The policy pursued until the later 1880s was therefore one of relatively limited interference with it, often described as the close or closed border policy. This meant that, at least in theory, only in exceptional circumstances were British officials allowed to cross the border into independent territory. At the same time, however, the fact that some transborder tribesmen carried out plundering raids along the border meant that the tribes could not simply be ignored. Moreover, to a greater extent than the Durrani and Sikh rulers, the British believed that they had a duty to maintain security throughout their territory and were convinced that failure to do so would be seen as weakness by their imperial subjects. They could not simply leave the border villages to defend themselves but had to assume responsibility for them and try to keep them safe. This meant that they had to begin to grapple with the problem of establishing a relationship with Waziristan.

One way empires have responded to challenging borders and frontiers has been to create and support client states to manage independent peoples beyond them – a form of indirect rule. The Roman and Sassanian empires, for example, had maintained client kingdoms on the northern borders of Arabia partly to help them manage the Bedouin Arabs.[29] On the North-West Frontier, where possible, the British did rule indirectly through client states, such as the Khanate of Kalat in Baluchistan. To the north of Peshawar the British began to support the nawab of Dir in the late nineteenth century and in the twentieth century recognized the grandson of the Akhund of Swat as the ruler of Swat.[30] They also supported the Mirs of Chitral. Indeed Afghanistan itself under Abdur Rahman and Habibullah had some features of a client state. The appointment of Shah Nawaz Khan as tax farmer of Tank (he was made a nawab in 1859) is an example of this strategy.

Another approach taken by empires was to try and turn looser associations into political units by organizing them into more formal groups.[31] In much of Algeria, for instance, the Ottomans consolidated smaller groups into larger ones and appointed local chiefs as leaders. In some regions they allowed local chiefs, sometimes Sufi *pirs* or *sheikhs*, to retain some autonomy and in return for their cooperation rewarded them with administrative appointments, honours and money. Another strategy was actually to move difficult groups from one place to another; in early modern Iran, for example, rulers or would-be rulers wanted to control people as much as they did territory.[32] The Safavids for instance moved Kurdish tribes from the border of western Iran to the east.[33] They also appointed chiefs and constructed tribal confederacies, thereby indirectly creating 'the whole tribal system by controlling its terms of existence through print and propaganda'.[34] Similarly during the late nineteenth and early twentieth centuries the Afghan government (GOA) moved Pashtun groups (including both Ghilzai farmers and pastoral nomadic Durranis) from eastern Afghanistan to the north, to help consolidate its control there.[35] As regards Waziristan the British were never strong enough to move people by force in any numbers. Instead they tried either to turn the loose groupings they encountered, in theory at least based on shared patrilineal descent, into more organized groups, or to create leaders or a stratum of more influential men who could manage these groupings for them.

Other ways of controlling recalcitrant border populations included the construction of defensive barriers. The question of building a wall along the frontier was raised during the early twentieth century, but never taken very seriously. Another possibility was the use of force, and it was often used by the British. It was deployed in various ways, usually accompanied by the imposition of some sort of collective 'tribal' responsibility. As well as punitive expeditions, it included *barampta* – finding and seizing in British territory men, animals and property belonging to a group on which it was desired to put pressure. Another technique was to bar people living across the border from visiting British territory (a kind of reverse blockade known as *bandish*). In time this could reduce people to starvation. The British usually imposed fines before lifting blockades or releasing the men, animals and property they had seized.

Forms of soft power have played an important role too. We have seen that some at least of the transborder people were accustomed to trading in British territory. The British did their best to encourage this along the Waziristan border. They hoped that it would increase people's dependence on British territory, and by exposing them to the 'civilizing' influences they would encounter there, encourage them to become more peaceable and productive.[36] Later they began to provide land for them to settle on. Another possibility would have been to pay the Mehsuds and others protection money, 'blackmail', to keep out of British territory.[37] In their early years on the frontier, however, the British refused to consider this; payments were only be made to transborder people in return for service, for example by providing irregular soldiers.

Relations with the Mehsuds

For the first few years after the annexation of Punjab, British officials themselves did not have much contact with the Mehsuds. On the Tank border, Shah Nawaz Khan was left to manage relations with them. His principal Mehsud contacts were two Alizais: his brother-in-law, Yarik Khan Langar Khel Alizai, and Jangi Khan Salimi Khel Alizai (who was referred to in contemporary British reports as their leading man). Although he maintained friendly relationships with some Mehsud men, the nawab also had to deal with raiding by others. It seems to have been Bahlolzais who were mostly responsible, principally Mamia Khel Shingis, Abdur Rahman Khel and Jalal Khel Nana Khels, and Abdullai and Malikshahi Aimal Khels. Some raids were almost certainly provoked by the Multani Pathan faction to discredit the nawab and show that he could not manage the border properly.

The first British punitive expedition into Mehsud territory took place in March 1860. As many as 1,500 Mehsuds had tried to invade British territory in February. British cavalry intercepted them and drove them back, killing many of them. To punish them, the governor general, then viceroy, Lord Canning, decided that a punitive expedition should take place as soon as possible. Led by

Brigadier Neville Chamberlain, commander of the Punjab Irregular Force (1854–63), nearly 7,000 troops left Tank on 16 April 1860 and moved into Waziristan, halting at Palosina, about 20 miles from Tank. Here Mehsuds attacked them killing sixty-three soldiers.[38] In retaliation the troops destroyed some villages in the Khaisara valley, returning to Palosina before moving up the Tank Zam to Makin, which comprised four large villages and several small ones and a large number of defensive, mud-brick towers. They set fire to and blew up many of the houses. Taylor commented that 'this was probably the first page in the chapter of Muhsood civilisation'.[39] In mid-May the troops moved out of Mehsud territory and returned to British territory via the Khaisora valley to the north.[40] After British troops left their territory, the Mehsuds remained blockaded in their hills and banned from visiting British territory. They were able to hold out for some time and continued to carry out minor raids along the border.

The difficulty of controlling Waziristan in the absence of any institutionalized political authority has already been mentioned. British officials saw that people identified themselves as Wazirs, Mehsuds, Bhittanis and Dawars on the basis of supposed patrilineal descent from a common ancestor. In the absence of a leader or leaders, this 'tribal' identity seemed to offer a way of getting a grip on them, by making those who shared it collectively responsible for each other. But this kind of accountability was not something to which the Mehsuds themselves were necessarily accustomed; in 1860 Reynell Taylor, for instance, commented that they were 'unused to the idea of being bound to control every member of the tribe and be responsible for his acts'.[41] Their usual response was to try and limit responsibility to as few people as possible ('dividing in order not to be ruled').[42] In June 1861, therefore, when they tried to reach a settlement with the British, the Mehsud representatives would not accept that all the Mehsuds should be responsible for each other, only members of the subsections, Shingis for example. Negotiations broke down on this point, and an agreement was not finally reached until the autumn, when the Mehsuds agreed to widen this collective responsibility to include at least those who belonged to the same main sections (Alizais, Bahlolzais and Shaman Khels).[43]

During the mid-1860s the Mehsuds continued to carry out raids. Frederick Graham, the deputy commissioner, believing that this was mainly due to their poverty, proposed a small settlement and militia scheme for them. After difficult and lengthy negotiations twenty families were given land in British territory, and twenty-five men were given service in the frontier militia. Ultimately the scheme did not achieve very much. This was partly because it was on such a small scale, although Graham intended to give the Mehsuds more positions in the militia when the opportunity arose. Relations with the Mehsuds remained difficult in the later 1860s. In 1867 there was a recrudescence of raiding, kidnapping of Hindus and murder.[44] In 1868, for example, Shaman Khels and Zilla Khels massacred some sixty Hindu pilgrims from Tank at a shrine of Shiva near Murtaza in the Gumal Pass. In response new military posts were built nearer the border, but it remained vulnerable to raids.[45]

The Wazirs and North Waziristan

At the end of the 1860s the position on the North Waziristan border with Bannu was also precarious, but to understand this we need to return to 1849 when Bannu, unlike Tank, came under direct British rule and Reynell Taylor was appointed its first deputy commissioner. We saw above that some of the Wazirs, both Ahmadzais and Utmanzais, had begun to spend the winter in Bannu and grow crops and pasture flocks there.[46] The Punjab Board of Administration instructed Taylor to do his best to maintain good relations with them, and he was largely successful in doing so and persuaded them to pay revenue on the land they were occupying in Bannu.

Edwardes and Taylor even tried to persuade a Sudan Khel Ahmadzai Wazir malik, Swahn Khan, to act as the official representative of the Wazirs who were using land in Bannu, and manage them on their behalf. But Swahn Khan was well aware that other men would object if he cooperated with the British; if he did, he said, they would kill him, and he refused to take on the role. A small Ahmadzai Wazir group, the Umarzais, provided the only real problem for the British on this part of the border during the first few years after annexation. Following a dispute over payment of revenue, they attacked one of the Bannu villages in 1849. They killed six people and damaged property worth three or four thousand rupees. They were barred from British territory but stayed in the hills north of Bannu, in what the British came to call the Ahmadzai salient, a rugged desolate area to the north of Bannu and a traditional outlaw hideout, for more than three years. Reynell Taylor's successor, John Nicholson, attacked them in December 1852, and in 1853 they were allowed to return to British territory and resume cultivation of their land.[47]

After this the Bannu border was relatively quiet until November 1859 when a gang of Kabul Khel and Hatti Khel outlaws killed a British officer, Captain Robert Mecham, travelling from Bannu to Kohat. They fled into the hills and took refuge with some Kabul Khels, who were camped in an area in the north-east of Waziristan not far from Upper Miranzai. The British demanded that the tribe surrender the actual murderer and the leader of the band to which the murderers belonged. They refused to do so. In response the British dispatched an expeditionary force to try and capture the wanted men. The troops spent nearly three weeks in independent territory, killing twenty or thirty men and seizing a large number of animals (many of which they slaughtered and ate on Christmas Day 1859). But they did not catch the wanted men. Taylor persuaded the Bannu Ahmadzai Wazirs that they should take action themselves. In mid-January as many as a thousand of them, mostly Hatti Khels, set off to capture them, and one of them was caught and hung.[48]

To have induced these Wazirs to take this kind of action shows how much influence Taylor had been able to build up in Bannu. It is clear that the policy of encouraging the pastoral nomadic Wazirs to spend the winter with their flocks in the Bannu district had been relatively successful. Minor raiding continued to occur, and to try and improve security along the Bannu border, during the 1860s Taylor's successors began to emphasize a form of collective responsibility they called pass responsibility. Some of these Wazir groups usually spent the summer in or round the entrance to one of the passes that led into Waziristan from Bannu. In return for ensuring the security of 'their' pass, their maliks were given the right to nominate some men to serve in the frontier militia, and their land in Bannu was subject to a lighter revenue assessment.[49]

In the later 1850s and for most of the 1860s the arrangements seemed to work reasonably well, but a crisis blew up in 1870. Men from the small Muhammad Khel tribe were failing to uphold their pass responsibility. The local officials (some of them Multanis) responded by imposing unusually heavy and frequent fines on them. They also treated the tribe's elders disrespectfully. On 13 June 1870, without any warning, Muhammad Khels attacked a detachment of ten men from the Fourth Sikh Infantry on the way to the Kurram outpost to the north-west of Bannu. They shot and killed six men and wounded a seventh before cavalry drove them off. The Wazir maliks in Bannu handed in a petition to the authorities complaining about the way they had been treated by the officials. All the Wazirs with land in Bannu seemed discontented, and the arrangements for managing them that had been in operation since 1849 seemed about to collapse. However, the local officials were able to play on the rivalries between the different Wazir groups and factions, and the crisis passed. The Muhammad Khels remained in the hills across the border, and by the summer of 1871 they were starving and in September they surrendered.[50]

2

Britain and Waziristan 1870–93

To try and prevent any recurrence of the problem experienced with the Muhammad Khels, the Government of India (GOI) introduced some changes to its frontier administration. It was decided that British officials should take more responsibility for managing the border and rely less on intermediaries. To help them they were to be given extra staff and left in their posts for longer; they were also required to learn Pashtu.[1] The introduction of the Frontier Crimes Regulations in 1872 was another important development. In 1861 the GOI had promulgated a new Indian Penal Code and in 1866 had introduced a chief court in Punjab to take on the role performed since 1849 by the judicial commissioner. After the Muhammad Khel difficulties, the officials decided that these legal changes had adversely affected law and order along the border, and that the Indian Penal Code and the Chief Court's procedures were not suited to a frontier district like Bannu. As a result they introduced a set of special rules in the border areas, known as the Frontier Crimes Regulations. These legalized the use of several traditional methods of tribal management such as *barampta* (seizing some people and their property to put pressure on others) and *bandish* (blockade). They also introduced new arrangements for the trial of alleged offenders in cases in which it was difficult for the prosecution to provide evidence of a sufficiently high standard for an ordinary court. They could be tried by a jirga of local men selected by the official responsible.[2] These rules remained in force more or less unchanged in Pakistan's Federally-Administered Tribal Areas (FATA) after 1947. British officials also set up a separate border police under the control of the civil officers. Finally, they reviewed arrangements for the security of the passes leading into the Bannu district and introduced some modifications to them.[3] After this relations between the Wazirs wintering in Bannu and the government improved.

The Nawab's party, Afghanistan and the 1879 Tank raid

As well as their links with influential men and faction leaders in British territory, some Mehsuds had connections with different members of the Afghan ruling family. As a result rivalry in Kabul came to be linked with rivalry in Waziristan. The Mehsud Umar Khan Salimi Khel Alizai was in touch with Sher Ali Khan, while Nabi Khan Shingi Mehsud had links with Dost Muhammad Khan's son, Azem Khan, who had, it will be recalled, briefly occupied Bannu in January 1849 and corresponded with Taylor in 1850.

Amir Dost Muhammad Khan died in 1863. He had designated a younger son, Sher Ali Khan, to succeed him, but Sher Ali's half-brothers Azem Khan (and Azem's son Abdur Rahman Khan) and Afzal Khan resisted him.[4] In 1865 Sher Ali drove them out of Kabul, and they took refuge in Waziristan with Nabi Khan Shingi. In 1866 Afzal Khan expelled Sher Ali and took over as amir, and Azem Khan invited Nabi Khan to Kabul and found work for him there. Afzal Khan died in 1867, and Azem succeeded him, but Sher Ali regained the throne and retained it until 1878 when he was forced out by the British. Azem Khan tried to escape to Iran but died on the way.[5] Sher Ali imprisoned his rivals' protégé Nabi Khan, but he escaped and returned to Waziristan.[6]

In the early 1870s the relationship between the Mehsuds and the British remained difficult. Many British officials argued that the Tank border was much more violent than anywhere else along the frontier, and that this was unacceptable.[7] In 1872 the government took responsibility for security in Tank away from the nawab and gave it to the new Dera Ismail Khan deputy commissioner, Charles Macaulay, and he set up a new police force for the Tank district.[8] Macaulay regarded the Shaman Khels and the Bahlolzai sections as more troublesome than the Alizais, and in 1873 he successfully negotiated agreements with representatives from both, based on paying hostages to live in British territory.[9] He also reached a settlement with the Bhittanis in 1876 and persuaded them to take on responsibility for the security of the passes running through their hills. In return they were given paid service in the frontier militia. He made similar arrangements with other tribes living along or near the Tank border, the Mianis and Gorezais, as well as the Shahur Shaman Khels and Zilla Khel Ahmadzais. One important outcome of the negotiations with the Bahlolzais was that two men in particular began to play a more prominent role in dealing with the Mehsuds. One was Nabi Khan Shingi, whose relationship with Afzal Khan and Azem Khan has just been mentioned. The other was a landowner living in British territory, a Kundi also named Azem Khan. He had taken part in the negotiations for a settlement after the 1860 expedition and begun to set himself as a rival to the nawab of Tank in dealing with the Mehsuds. Azem Khan Kundi was, Macaulay later commented, 'a man of little prejudice and strong reason', who belonged to 'a class of men who have gained and not lost by British rule'.[10] As Azem Khan Kundi's influence grew, the nawab's influence declined, as did that of his principal Mehsud contact, the late Jangi Khan's son, Umar Khan Alizai.

Some Mehsuds were unhappy with the rise of Nabi Khan and Azem Khan Kundi. Nabi Khan had rivals among the other Shingi Bahlolzais, and some of them formed a network whose members tended to support the nawab rather than Azem Khan Kundi; they were often referred to as leaders of 'the nawab's party'. It is possible that the nawab conspired with them to try and discredit Nabi Khan and Azem Khan Kundi, and by doing so undermine Macaulay himself.[11]

To help him cope with the nawab's party, in the same year Macaulay was given permission to impose tribal responsibility on the Mehsuds as a whole, including the Alizais, although he had had relatively few problems with them.[12] This meant that the Alizais had to accept responsibility for the activities of the nawab's party and to pay a share of any fines the British imposed on the Mehsuds for raiding. Umar Khan and Yarik Khan, and other leading Alizais, resented this. They tried to persuade Macaulay to change his mind, but were unsuccessful. We saw that Graham had introduced a small settlement scheme for some Mahsuds in the mid-1860s. At this point Macaulay was working on a much more ambitious plan to link a new settlement scheme with the pacification of the Gumal route that led into Afghanistan, used by thousands of trading nomads (Powindahs) each autumn and spring. In return for receiving land to settle on in the Tank valley, the Mehsuds would supply levies to keep the Gumal free from raiders.[13]

By the early 1870s, British's relations with the Afghan amir Sher Ali Khan were beginning to deteriorate. Fearful of another British invasion, he had begun to try and build up his influence with the frontier people. He invited the Wazir maliks with land in Bannu to visit him in Kabul and received them in some style, giving them ceremonial robes, and appointed a special officer, Mufti Shah Mahmud, to look after them. The mufti himself visited Birmal in western Waziristan later in 1875. The amir began to pay allowances to some of the Wazirs (indeed he may well have been doing so already).[14] In 1876 the amir also invited some

Mehsuds to visit Kabul. By then some British politicians and strategists were raising concerns about a renewed Russian threat to Afghanistan and thereby to India, and beginning to call for a more assertive policy towards Afghanistan. The viceroy, Northbrook, was concerned by this and resigned in 1875. His departure enabled the secretary of state for India, Lord Salisbury, to appoint Lord Lytton as the viceroy, with instructions to increase British influence over it. In 1877 Robert Sandeman, agent to the governor general in Baluchistan, negotiated a treaty with the ruler of Kalat (in Baluchistan) providing for the establishment of a British garrison at Quetta on the Shal plateau. This strengthened the British position in relation to Afghanistan and alarmed the amir.[15]

The situation became more complicated when in the summer of 1878, without authority from St Petersburg (or an invitation from the amir), Constantine von Kaufman, the Russian governor general of Turkestan, sent a mission to Afghanistan led by General Nikolai Stolietov. It arrived in Kabul in July. Von Kaufman may have hoped in this way to involve the British in another Afghan campaign at a time when Russia was at war with Ottoman Empire, at this point Britain's ally.[16] If so his tactic worked. The viceroy informed Amir Sher Ali Khan that he must accept a British political agent in Kabul. The amir refused. Lytton responded by demanding that he receive a British delegation. The amir refused that request as well. Lytton dispatched a mission to him in September, but the amir would not allow it to enter Afghanistan. At the beginning of November Lytton sent a letter reiterating the demand that the amir accept a British agent in Kabul, and giving him just under three weeks in which to reply. No reply had been received when the deadline expired on 20 November, and the next day Lytton ordered three columns of British troops to move into Afghanistan.[17]

It was unfortunate for Macaulay that the implementation of his settlement scheme overlapped with the introduction of this more aggressive British policy. In an effort to increase British influence over the Mehsuds at this critical moment, Macaulay hurriedly put his settlement scheme and Gumal pass pacification plans into operation. In November 1878 the Mehsuds began to gather in Tank, ready to occupy the land, and all seemed to be going well. But some of the more influential Mehsuds did not take part; they included Umar Khan, Azmat Shingi, Mashak Abdur Rahman Khel and Boyak Abdullai who in October had visited Kabul again at the invitation of the amir.

The amir and Mullah Adakar, a religious leader who had links with Waziristan, encouraged Umar Khan to lead an attack on British territory. He returned to Waziristan with Yarik Khan, and Matin (another influential Langar Khel Alizai), and in December collected a lashkar of nearly 2,000 men. The majority were Alizais but several hundred Bahlolzais and some Shaman Khels joined them too. On 1 January 1879 they came down into British territory, passed the British outposts without meeting any resistance, reached Tank and plundered the bazaar. They were unable to break into the fort, and withdrew towards midnight, but their incursion encouraged widespread disorder. On 4 January, Zilla Khel Wazirs persuaded the militia in the Jatta post to surrender; they burned the post and plundered the Gumal bazaar. During the next few days Wazirs, Bhittanis and Powindahs attacked and burned eleven villages.

The principal reason for the Mehsud incursion was the British invasion of Afghanistan.[18] It was no coincidence that the raid occurred at the point when British forces were in the country. The fact that Umar Khan resented the imposition of tribal responsibility, and was unhappy about the way that the nawab had been sidelined in favour of Azem Khan Kundi, played a part too. Religious loyalties were also significant; Muslim territory was under attack, and the conviction, stirred up by the Mullah Adakar and other preachers, that it was the Mehsuds' duty to support its ruler undoubtedly went into the mix.

Because technically Tank belonged to the nawab and was not part of British India, the British did not regard the raid as requiring an immediate military response. They decided to demand the surrender of six men whom they regarded as ringleaders – Umar Khan, Yarik Khan, Mashak, Boyak, Azmat and Matin. They also demanded that the tribe as a whole pay a fine and compensation totalling Rs.117,000, and in the meantime barred its members from visiting British territory. They also called on the Bhittanis, some of whom had taken part in the looting, to pay a fine of Rs.7,000, and took away their militia appointments, which were worth Rs.12,000 p.a.

The wanted men did not surrender. In April 1881, following the withdrawal from Afghanistan, the British assembled troops at Tank. Four of the men gave themselves up, and a hostage was given as security for the fifth, but Macaulay and his superior, Alexander Munro, the Derajat commissioner during the 1870s, thought this was not enough. Macaulay wanted to take the opportunity to assert his authority over the Jalal Khels and Abdur Rahman Khels, and the other Nana Khel Bahlolzais, even though not many of them had taken part in the Tank raid. The troops therefore moved into Waziristan, and as in 1860 they destroyed property and crops and killed men who resisted them. At this point the Mehsuds had little access to modern weapons, and mostly still relied on flintlocks, matchlocks and swords. They did not put up much resistance; Yarik Khan surrendered in the autumn of 1882 and Mashak was handed over by other Mehsuds.[19]

Return to the close border

In 1882 Macaulay revived his hostage arrangements and the settlement scheme. As noted in Chapter 1, traditionally the Mehsud jirgas had been able to appoint *chalweshtis* as a kind of police force to carry out their decisions; because they were acting under the jirga's orders there should be no retaliation against them if injury or death occurred during their operations. This time Macaulay aimed to use his hostages as *chalweshtis*.[20] He also secured an additional 5,000 acres in a tract of uncultivated land belonging to the Gandapurs (another Pashtun group living to the south of Tank), called Niskor, on which Mehsuds were to settle.[21]

Not long after this he resigned, having served as the deputy commissioner of the Dera Ismail Khan district almost continuously since 1873. Septimus Thorburn, who had been deputy commissioner in Bannu in 1869–70, took over. Waziristan remained unsettled. This was partly because of the activities of Amir Abdur Rahman Khan, who with British support and a British subsidy, was building a stronger state in Afghanistan. One feature of this was an effort to assert his authority in the areas along the frontier with India. For example he occupied Kunar, along the Kunar River to the north of Jalalabad, in 1883, and Asmar, further up the Kunar River, in 1888. He also began to try and extend his influence in Waziristan. In 1883 he invited Wazir, Dawar and Mehsud maliks to Kabul again, and some of them accepted the invitation. In addition he sent emissaries to different parts of Waziristan who tried to persuade people to allow the amir to establish military posts in them.[22] During the winter of 1883–4 he dispatched officials to the Wana district, and they started to collect revenue there (in the form of produce rather than cash).[23]

The amir was not sure how the British would respond, but it was most unlikely that they would support his efforts to extend his control into the frontier areas. The lieutenant governor, Sir Charles Aitchinson, instructed the new Derajat commissioner (1880–8), Edward Ommanney, to tell the Kabul officials that the GOI meant to maintain its right to deal directly with the tribes.[24] Lytton's successor, Ripon, commented that 'it would create constant complications between us the amir, and be a fertile source of irritation, if every time that a frontier raid took place we had to make a complaint to the amir instead of settling our quarrel directly with the offending tribe'.[25] In the meantime Yarik Khan and Azmat had died in detention. In 1884 the British released the other Mehsud prisoners, Umar Khan, Matin, Boyak and Mashak, and allowed them to return to Waziristan. The amir gave up his attempt to establish his rule there for the time being, but his agents remained at Wana exercising 'the most shadowy and remote' authority.[26]

In 1884 the GOI wrote to the local officials ordering them to report on any measures taken 'for reclaiming the predatory Mahsud tribe'.[27] The letter referred to Graham's settlement scheme and raised the question of whether anything else could be done to win over the Mehsuds. Thorburn did not reply until 1886. The Mehsuds, he reported, had begun to take an interest in using the land Macaulay had given them, but there was not sufficient land or money available to settle many of them, certainly not enough to persuade them to give up raiding.[28] Other local officials did not agree. In 1887, the deputy commissioner, George Ogilvie, who had taken over from Thorburn in 1885, reported that the Mehsud settlement schemes had had some good results and recommended that the exemption from paying rent on their land in British territory should be extended for another five years, provided they remained peaceful and worked the land themselves, and this was sanctioned.[29]

Thorburn also criticized Macaulay's *chalweshti* experiment. He found he could not use the *chalweshtis* as a kind of tribal police, as Macaulay had intended.[30] Instead, when a raid took place, he imprisoned the men from the raiders' section, and if necessary reduced their pay.[31] In any case, he thought, living in British India was not exerting a 'civilizing' influence on them and suggested a change.[32] Currently, about half the money paid to the *chalweshtis* was divided among the sections from which the hostages came.[33] He suggested halving the number of *chalweshtis* and paying the money saved directly to the sectional jirgas. The commissioner approved of this plan, but the lieutenant governor rejected it. Paying the Mehsuds directly without demanding some service in return would be 'to introduce a fresh and inexpedient departure in the policy of Government on the border'.[34]

By the mid-1880s, however, the wider strategic context was changing again. In spite of the establishment of the Afghan buffer state under the rule of amir Abdur Rahman Khan, some influential British strategists remained concerned about the potential Russian threat to Indian security.[35] Already in the 1870s some strategists and politicians had begun to talk about introducing what they called a 'scientific frontier', which would make it easier for Britain to defend India's north-western border. In the autumn of 1878, for instance, the P.M., Benjamin Disraeli, had claimed that the invasion of Afghanistan would facilitate this.[36] General Frederick Roberts, the British hero of the Second Anglo-Afghan War, who in 1885 was made the commander-in-chief in India (1885–93), became one of the scientific frontier's most important proponents.[37] The consensus came to be that it should be envisaged as a line running from Kandahar to Kabul via Ghazni. Although the British would not actually occupy the line, should a Russian force advance into Afghanistan, they would be ready to respond by quickly sending troops into the country to meet it. To facilitate this, the advocates of the scientific frontier argued both that troops should be stationed as near as possible to it and that the routes they would use to move up to it should be brought under British control.[38]

The forward policy

In 1884 the Russians took control of the Merv oasis, 200 miles north of Herat. They pushed on towards the Amu Darya and in March 1885 clashed with and defeated Afghan troops at the most northerly Afghan outpost, Panjdeh. British diplomats persuaded the Russian government not to advance any further and to agree to the joint demarcation of the border between Russia and Afghanistan. The crisis gave more weight to the views of the advocates of the scientific frontier policy, even though introducing it would mean more interference with the independent areas between India and Afghanistan.[39] In 1884 the secretary of state, Kimberley, sanctioned the construction of new roads and railways along the border with independent territory.[40] In 1885 an Imperial Defence Committee was set up to determine frontier policy.[41] It was decided to introduce

> a fresh departure in our policy towards the frontier tribes, in order that when the time for a formal movement arrives they may identify themselves with us and assist us not only with supplies and transport but by sharing in the maintenance of our lines of communication.[42]

In Waziristan the British identified two routes as being of strategic importance. These were the Tochi route through northern Waziristan and the Gumal one on its southern edge. In 1885 the Imperial Defence Committee recommended among other things that the Gumal route should be surveyed and a strong fortification should be built along it connected by road to Dera Ismail Khan.[43]

A Conservative government had taken office in 1885, and the new P.M., Salisbury, was sympathetic to the ideas of the advocates of the forward policy.[44] In January 1887 Cross, the secretary of state, ordered the GOI to arrange for a survey of the Gumal route and construction of the proposed fortification.[45] On 17 August 1887 the GOI wrote to the Punjab government that it was time to 'bring under our control and, if possible, to organise for purposes of defence against external aggression' the independent territory on the North-West Frontier.[46] The Punjab government should start by opening the important routes into Afghanistan, including the Gumal and the Tochi.[47] As they had done with the groups living along the Khyber Pass, British officers would raise irregulars from the groups living along the routes through Waziristan and pay them to protect these routes. This would give people an incentive to support the British and 'familiarize them with the presence of our officers in their midst, and it is to be hoped that from the beginning thus made a general improvement in our relations may before long result'.[48] As far as possible allowances would only be paid for actual services, and not become 'political subsidies'.[49]

In 1887 George Ogilvie, the deputy commissioner, escorted by police, Mehsud maliks and Powindahs, made a preliminary inspection of the Gumal route as far as the junction of the Gumal and Zhob rivers at Khajuri Kach without any difficulty. He tried but failed to carry out a more detailed survey early in 1888, mainly thanks to problems with the 800 or so Mehsuds who accompanied him, most of them uninvited. To punish them, their rent-free land was confiscated and the hostages were sent home. They responded by carrying out a number of raids.[50]

The viceroy, Dufferin, wrote to Amir Abdur Rahman in May 1888 informing him that the GOI intended to open the Gumal route and maintain direct relations with the Wazirs, but that it did not plan to occupy Wana.[51] The amir was unhappy about this and continued to try and cultivate support in Waziristan. For example, when in July 1888 Mehsud men gathered at Kaniguram, he sent letters to representatives of each of the three main sections inviting them to visit Kabul. He sent a similar message to the Zilla Khel Wazirs. An influential anti-British Mullah, Mullah Gulabdin, who lived in Dawar, visited Kaniguram and urged the Mehsuds to take up the amir's invitation.[52] The jirga decided to send a deputation, and 154 men went to Kabul in August. Reportedly they asked the amir to send them some troops and a governor. Ogilvie (by now the commissioner) reported that they were not representatives of tribal opinion as a whole.[53]

Ogilvie's successor as deputy commissioner was Richard Bruce, who had previously worked with Robert Sandeman in Baluchistan. At this point the British mostly regarded the Mehsuds and Wazirs as 'democratic or anarchical', and essentially leaderless.[54] The Mehsuds especially were seen as being 'extremely democratic in their ways … they like to assert their equality'.[55] We have seen that in the absence of leaders, British officials had tried to work with Mehsud jirgas, and Ogilvie commented that one major problem had been that so many men would turn up to take part in them that they became unmanageable.[56]

Bruce argued that he could manage the Mehsuds more effectively by taking a different approach.[57] In Baluchistan Robert Sandeman had extended British control by paying allowances to selected chiefs and backing them up with force when members of their tribes refused to follow their orders.[58] Bruce was convinced that this would work with the Mehsuds. He agreed that at present they lacked any kind of institutionalized authority, but argued that British policy was responsible for this. Before 1849, he maintained, the Mehsuds had had leaders, and it would be possible to recreate them. It is true that earlier British reports did sometimes refer to Jangi Khan and Umar Khan as leading men.[59] But their authority was always limited. Bruce was exaggerating when he claimed that 'the main difficulty will be to undo the evils we have ourselves done. By ignoring the headmen and working through go-betweens we have raised up a multitude of nobodies in the tribe until their jirgas have become a perfect rabble. These men have pushed themselves to the front either by sharp practice or in the general scramble.'[60] He aimed therefore to develop a kind of oligarchy of maliks who would form what he called a 'manageable representative jirga'.[61]

In June 1888 he held a meeting attended by some 400 Mehsuds.[62] It was agreed that the money the British had been spending on the *chalweshtis* (Rs.1,000 p.m.) and the employment of Mehsuds in the Border Military Police (Rs.264) would be paid to fifty-one maliks who would nominate sixty-one men for irregular military service on the border.[63] These levies were to comprise thirty-seven Bahlolzais (thirteen Nana Khels, including four Abdur Rahman Khels) and only twenty-three Alizais and twenty-one Shaman Khels, so Bruce did not keep to *nikat*, the tribal charter for profits and losses.[64] Bruce explained that the Abdur Rahman Khels were one of the sections most dependent on raiding and had caused most problems, so he had tried especially hard to accommodate them.[65] Ogilvie agreed that the policy of trying to manage the Mehsuds through jirgas had not so far been very successful, but had reservations about the new approach.[66] Sixty-one levies were, he thought, not enough. Employing a relatively small number of men would not do much to increase British influence over the Mehsuds as a whole. Nevertheless it was worth a try; giving the maliks the right to nominate the service holders should help to build up their influence, and the scheme was comprehensive enough 'to enable us to test the feasibility of forming a jirga of the kind described'.[67]

Some years later another frontier official, Frederick Johnston, commented that the maliks had been 'chosen in the most slip-shod fashion': 'a small clique, headed by Azem Khan Kundi, nominated its friends as Maliks', he suggested, 'and their pay was fixed on the most arbitrary scale'; they were not representatives of

Mehsud opinion in general.[68] A good opportunity had been wasted, he thought. Bruce himself later admitted that he had not chosen the maliks very carefully. But perhaps the real problem was that Mehsud men valued their independence so highly that they were very reluctant to accept anyone else's authority, however influential they supposedly were.

Opening the Gumal

In June 1889 the Viceroy's Council formally agreed that the close-border policy should be abandoned, and in November Lansdowne, the viceroy, Sir James Lyall, the Punjab lieutenant-governor, and Roberts, the commander-in-chief, accompanied by Robert Sandeman, visited the Derajat and held meetings with the local officials.[69] It was decided to make agreements with the leading men from groups living near the Gumal pass and in the Zhob valley to guarantee the safe passage of British troops and officials travelling through them.[70]

Sandeman and Bruce invited representatives from various Mehsud sections, as well as Zilla Khel, Tazi Khel and Sirki Khel Wazirs, and Dotani Powindahs, Sheranis (who lived south of the Gumal) and Mando Khels (who lived in Zhob), to a jirga to be held in January 1890 at Appozai (Fort Sandeman) in the Zhob valley. Macaulay's former go-between, Azem Khan Kundi, continued to play an important role. The negotiations went well, and in return for service payments the tribal representatives agreed to supply levies to man the small posts which would be built along the Gumal route to prevent raiders attacking travellers.[71] Again Bruce did not keep to Mehsud *nikat* in distributing the appointments. With Rs.9,996 now allocated for the maliks, and Rs.20,460 for service pay, total expenditure went up to Rs.30,456.[72] For the next two years or so the new arrangements seemed to work well. Levies from all the different groups were posted at Spinkai, Nili Kach and Khajuri Kach, and troops and civil officials travelled safely through the Gwaleri pass.[73] From the British point of view things looked promising.

But there was one critical question to which different British officials gave different answers. Were British aims to be restricted to opening the pass and establishing good relations with the tribes? Lyall, the lieutenant-governor, thought they were. There was no political or military case for doing more, and there should be no attempt to extend British authority into Waziristan. He thought that the amir would probably accept the Appozai agreement, if it was made clear to him that there was to be no interference with tribes' independence.[74]

Bruce and Sandeman had a different answer. Sandeman thought that the Zilla Khels and Mehsuds 'must hereafter all come more directly than at present under British influence', while Bruce presumed that the government's aim was

> to open out the entire country, reclaim it from anarchy, and render it safer for all comers, develop its resources, so that its supplies, transport, &c., may be available for the purposes of Government, and in short bring it into line with its southern neighbours, in whose territories commerce and agriculture are now carried on without interruption, and the roads ... can be traversed in safety by night or day without the protection of armed escorts.[75]

The Appozai settlement and Bruce's evident intention to extend British authority into Waziristan alarmed the amir. In 1890 he proclaimed that the Gumal and Waziristan were Afghan territory, and in 1892 he wrote to the GOI asserting this.[76] In May he sent Sardar Gul Muhammad Khan, with 100 cavalry and 100 infantry to Wana to try and persuade the Mehsuds and Wazirs to accept his authority and break off relations with the British (he also sent some men to Gul Kach south-east of Wana).[77] In addition he dispatched Qazi Khalifa Nur Muhammad from Margha in Birmal to Jandola on the eastern edge of Waziristan with the same message. With eight copies of the Qur'an spread out in front of him the qazi preached to a gathering of Mehsud and Bhittani men, urging them not to support the British government. The Sardar also wrote to Mullah Gulabdin in Dawar to try and persuade him to support him.

Lansdowne told the amir that his claim to Waziristan could not be accepted and that the GOI had always dealt directly with the Wazirs and intended to continue doing so.[78] Some of the maliks asked for British support, and in August the government sent troops up to Khajuri Kach and Jandola.[79] The viceroy wrote to the amir informing him that if he did not withdraw his troops, they would be driven out. The amir did recall them, but he and Sardar Gul Muhammad Khan continued to keep in touch with Mehsuds and Wazirs and encourage them to repudiate the Appozai agreements. He invited Mehsuds and Zilla Khels to visit Kabul again; Badshah Khan and Badr Din Alizai, and Juma Khan Nekzan Khel Bahlolzai were among the Mehsuds who accepted the invitation.[80]

Like Bruce's agreement with the Mehsuds in 1889, the Appozai agreement seems to have been made in a hurry and to have been based on unrealistic expectations about how far other Mehsud men would accept the maliks' authority.[81] During 1892 the situation began to deteriorate. Mehsuds and Zilla Khels carried out several attacks both on the Powindahs' caravans in the Gumal and on troops and levies in Zhob.[82] They aimed to get hold of British rifles, while some other men who had not been awarded a service allowance at Appozai, the Mehsud Shahir Abdullai for example, hoped to get one by showing that they should not be ignored. Shahir encouraged three Abdullais, Shahzar, Namdar and Narga, to resist and they murdered a cavalry sowar near the Zam post. Bruce imposed fines on Zilla Khels and Mehsuds.[83]

In July 1893 Jambil and Karram Abdur Rahman Khel, who had been included in the 1889 list of maliks, murdered Kelly, a Public Works Department official, in Zhob. Bruce responded by seizing some sixty men from the sections concerned, with their caravans and cattle, and called on the maliks to secure the surrender of the men responsible. Unlike Sandeman in Baluchistan, Bruce had no troops to back him up, but he was still able to persuade the maliks to bring the wanted men into Dera Ismail Khan for a trial by jirga. The maliks had arranged for the jirga to find them innocent, but Azem Khan Kundi bribed its members to find them guilty, and they sentenced Jambil and Karram to seven years imprisonment. They also sentenced Shahzar, Namdar and Nargai to two years and a fine of Rs.5,000, but it seems that nothing happened to Shahir Abdullai. The men were imprisoned in Peshawar jail. Until then Mehsuds living outside British territory had not been formally tried, sentenced and imprisoned in this way, so this was an important development. Some, including the men's relatives, were unhappy about it, and they arranged for the murder in 1894 of three of the maliks who had helped to surrender the men (Abdur Rahman Khels killed Dawagar and Abdullais killed Karim Khan and Chaprai). For their own safety two of the other maliks involved left for British territory.[84]

The maliks needed more support if Bruce's policy was to have any chance of succeeding, so the Punjab government recommended a punitive expedition. The GOI refused to allow this, arguing that it would interfere with the demarcation of the frontier which, as we shall see in Chapter 3, they had undertaken to carry out by the terms of the agreement reached with the amir in November 1893.[85] Sandeman's 'system' of tribal management depended on the ability to use force to back up the maliks, so in practice this was the end of the attempt to apply it in Waziristan. Bruce was ordered to continue working with the tribal jirgas and persuade them to surrender the murderers or deal with them themselves. The maliks meanwhile began to be more cautious and tried to avoid antagonizing their fellow tribesmen, while anti-British Mehsuds continued to carry out attacks, killing twenty-seven people during the first six months of 1894.[86]

3

The Durand Line and Mullah Powindah

The Durand Line

The British had rejected amir Abdur Rahman's claim to Wana, but he continued to try and push forward into other areas of the still largely independent frontier region between Afghanistan and India, such as Bajaur (to the north of Peshawar). He was unhappy about the British attempt to extend their influence into the Gumal as well as by other forward moves such as the opening of the railway to New Chaman on the Afghan border between Quetta and Kandahar in 1891. After some diplomatic manoeuvring he and Lansdowne were persuaded to agree to the joint demarcation of a border between British and Afghan spheres of influence along the frontier. In the autumn of 1893 Sir Mortimer Durand, the GOI's foreign secretary, was sent to Kabul to negotiate with the amir, and an agreement was reached in November. As regards Waziristan, the amir was persuaded to give up his claim to it, apart from the western district of Birmal.[1] Agreements were signed on 12 November 1893, and demarcation began in 1894.[2]

The demarcation of the Durand Line was an enormously important development. The line has come to be seen as an international boundary between two states, but it had not necessarily been envisaged as such when it was originally marked out. Its original purpose was to demarcate Afghan and British spheres of influence – areas in which one government would be dominant and the other would not interfere.[3] Some argued that 'it leaves the border tribes in the same independent position that they occupied before the settlement was made'.[4] People living along the proposed borderline, however, anticipated that demarcation would result in more British interference.[5] The fact that the line divided the territory of some groups was also to cause problems. In Waziristan these included the Madda Khels, Kabul Khels and Gurbaz.[6] To the north the new frontier divided the Mohmand area to the north-west of Peshawar (the Mohmands having previously been mainly under Afghan influence).

Bruce meanwhile continued to press for the establishment of a permanent British military presence in Waziristan (he suggested that people would welcome this), proposing the establishment of a 'strong military station' in or near Wana as well as a number of outposts. He also asked for additional troops and called for the opening of the route between Jandola and Wana via the Shahur valley.[7] In making a case for all this, he contrasted the situation in Waziristan with that in the Khyber Pass, where a strategic route also passed through independent territory. Along this route, he said, there was no need for a British military presence, because the Afridis were the only tribal group involved, and they did not want the government to intervene. In Waziristan, he argued, things were more complicated. The three main groups, Wazirs, Dawars and Mehsuds, were 'hereditary enemies … whose interest are diametrically opposed and in conflict'.[8] On the Tochi side to the north the Dawars wanted protection from the Wazirs and Mehsuds, and the Wazirs from the Mehsuds. On the Gumal side to the south, the Zilla Khel Wazirs wanted protection from the Mehsuds and the Powindahs. Moreover, habitual Mehsud raiders would need to be restrained, and this was not something, he now accepted, that the other Mehsuds could do.[9]

Lyall had been critical of Bruce's aims in 1890. His successor, Sir Denis Fitzpatrick, was even more doubtful. In 1892 he had deprecated any attempt to pacify Waziristan as a whole, and he did so again in 1894.[10] To try and keep the peace among the different groups living there, as Bruce proposed, would be expensive.[11] In particular, there were no maliks or *tumandars* (local leaders) strong enough to control the Mehsuds, and the maliks therefore had to volunteer to pay fines themselves. 'A really powerful headman of a tribe is a natural growth having its roots lying very deep,' Fitzpatrick argued, 'and if the tribe does not produce such a headman we can scarcely hope to make it produce one by any amount of top-dressing.'[12]

Nor was the comparison with the Khyber helpful, he thought. The Afridis were also disunited, and other tribal groups lived near them and had to be accommodated as well.[13] The reason the present arrangements worked in the Khyber was that people clearly understood that what the British wanted was to keep the road open, not to encroach on their territory. Fitzpatrick commented on the way Bruce always played down potential difficulties. There were in his letter, he noted, passages which taken on their own could give the impression that the proposed demarcation and the location of troops in Waziristan 'would be so popular with the Waziris that we might undertake them with a light heart'. But, he said, 'this, as we all know, is merely Mr Bruce's way of writing'. On this frontier, he thought, and 'wherever there are wild tribes distracted by internal feuds, there are always two sets of people pressingly inviting us to interfere, namely, the classes who are for the time being getting the worst of the struggle, and the classes who hope to profit by getting service under us in the event of our interfering'.[14] He did not believe that the majority of Mehsuds wanted the British to take over their country, quite the contrary; any attempt to do so would therefore be difficult and expensive.[15] But there would be no need for a military presence at all if people could be reassured that the British were only interested in keeping the Tochi and the Gumal roads open and would not interfere elsewhere in Waziristan.[16]

Lord Lansdowne's viceroyalty ended in 1894. The new viceroy, Lord Elgin, a Liberal, tried to find a middle way.[17] He rejected Bruce's ambitious plans, but did not agree with Fitzpatrick that Waziristan could be left to its own devices as long as the Gumal and Tochi routes into Afghanistan remained open. He argued that the GOI had assumed 'a measure of responsibility for the peace of the Afghan border which has not hitherto been ours, and which, under present arrangements, we have no adequate means of discharging'.[18] The people of Waziristan were, he said, mostly farmers who were prevented from cultivating their lands properly by 'petty rapacious chiefs' (as we have seen it was not quite as simple as that), and Britain had a duty to improve their condition.[19] The idea that Britain had a moral obligation towards Waziristan is not one that any previous viceroy had articulated so explicitly. His aim was to 'bring the tribes whom this settlement concerns further within our influence', but not to interfere widely or undertake local administration.[20] Those living along the frontier were to be informed by proclamation that a Commission would be appointed to demarcate the new boundary line, and that a political officer would be appointed to arrange for the pacification of the country and the preservation of order, and to open roads. He also recommended the establishment of a permanent garrison at Spin, to the south of Wana, to protect the Gumal route, and the secretary of state gave permission for this.[21] In spite of all this, Elgin said that he wanted 'to interfere as little as we can with … [the people's] internal affairs, provided only that our obligations are discharged'; it is difficult to see how these goals could have been achieved without considerable interference.[22]

Mullah Powindah

Increasing British interference in Waziristan encouraged the emergence of a religious leader, Muhiy-ud-Din, a Sultanai Shabi Khel Mehsud, known as Mullah

Powindah. For the first forty or so years after the British arrived on Waziristan's eastern border, religious leaders and loyalties seem to have played a relatively minor part in its inhabitants' response to them. Islamic loyalties were only one among several influences, except during the Second Anglo-Afghan War when Muslim territory was under direct threat. From the later 1880s, however, growing pressure from the British began to give religious leaders the opportunity to present themselves as defenders of Waziristan and play a more important role, reducing such limited authority as the maliks possessed. In the 1890s Mullah Powindah began to play a prominent role in Waziristan.[23] As we have seen, many Mehsuds were unhappy about recent developments and reluctant to accept the maliks' authority, and the mullah became their leader against the latter.[24] 'A large handsome man of dignified and respectable bearing', he had attended a *madrasah* in Bannu, and he described himself as *badshah* (king) of the *taliban*.[25] He was one of a number of men who drew on their religious training and supposed miraculous powers to build up followings of *sheikhs* (deputies) and *taliban* (plural of *talib-ul-ilm*, seeker after religious knowledge) and acquire influence among the frontier people during the British period.[26] They often led militant movements of opposition to the British presence, which in some respects anticipate for instance the movement of the Tehrik-i-Taliban that emerged in the 2000s.

Many mullahs were associated with the network originally established by Abdul Ghaffur, the Akhund of Swat, who had been influenced by the revivalist understandings of Islam percolating from northern India during the nineteenth century (in particular from the seminary founded at Deoband in northern India in 1867). Reportedly the Akhund himself had had considerable influence in Waziristan at one time.[27] After his death in 1878 his *murid* (disciple), Najmuddin, known as the Hadda mullah, inherited much of his spiritual and political authority, and consolidated and extended part of his network.[28] As well as Mullah Powindah, its members included several men who lived in neighbouring Khost, Mullah Hamzullah (a Bizan Khel Ahmadzai Wazir), Mullah Sayyid Lal Shah, known as Lala Pir, and Mullah Karbogha, who had some influence in northern Waziristan among the Kabul Khels. Mullah Karbogha had been Hamzullah's teacher, but the two men were on bad terms with each other by the 1890s.[29]

In the meantime the British decided that Wana, in southern Waziristan, would be a better place for a garrison than Spin, and in accordance with Elgin's instructions, on 19 October 1894 Bruce held a large jirga at Khajuri Kach. At this he announced that he was about to begin the demarcation of British and Afghan spheres of influence along the Waziristan border, that troops would be stationed permanently at Wana, and that Wana, Spin and the Gumal road would be 'protected areas' in which the GOI would keep the peace.[30] But he had overestimated the Mehsuds' willingness to accept the growing British presence. Mullah Powindah wrote to him objecting; undeterred, Bruce and his military escort reached Wana on 25 October.[31] The mullah called for a lashkar to assemble at Torwam in the Khaisara (about halfway between Wana and Kaniguram), and in the small hours of 3 November, with the mullah himself beating a drum in the rear, around 2,000 men attacked Bruce's camp.[32] They were almost entirely Mehsuds, mostly Shabi Khels and Abdullais, with some Abdur Rahman Khels and Garrerais and Langar Khel Alizais.[33] The mullah had promised his follower that British bullets could not harm them, and they were only driven back with some difficulty, getting away with some rifles, horses and cash. The British lost twenty-two men (including two officers) and forty-three others were wounded, while according to British reports as many as 300 or 400 Mehsuds were killed.[34]

In response Bruce demanded that by 1 December 1894 the Mehsuds surrender eighteen men who had played a leading role in the attack and return the stolen cash as well as the horses and rifles (or pay Rs.500 for each). The men whose surrender was demanded included four Abdullais, three Abdur Rahman Khels, one Shingi, one Langar Khel, two Shabi Khels and two Garrerais. Among them were Shahir Abdullai, and a number of men whose names crop up in later reports, including Jaggar and Mianji Abdur Rahman Khel, and Pashakai Shabi Khel Alizai.[35]

The Mehsuds held a large jirga at Torwam attended by several thousand men, including the mullah and representatives from most groups, to decide how to respond to the British demands. By 12 December some of the men whose surrender was demanded had still not done so.[36] Almost immediately the British sent troops into Mehsud territory (for the third time since 1849) with the aim of punishing those regarded as chiefly responsible for the attack Bruce's camp, especially the Shabi Khels from Torwam, where the lashkar had assembled. This time, under the overall command of General William Lockhart, the Punjab commander-in-chief, three columns took part, one moving north from Wana via the Tiarza and Shorawangi *algads* (ravines) to Kaniguram, the second north-west from Jandola to Makin via the Tank Zam and the third west from Bannu via the Khaisora to Razmak. A number of Mehsud maliks accompanied the troops, among them Muhammad Afzal Khan, whose father, Dawagar, had been one of the maliks killed by Abdur Rahman Khels after the surrender of Kelly's murderer. They reached their objectives without much opposition, attacking any men who did resist, and as usual destroying their houses and defensive towers, and their crops, and seizing their livestock.

The British called the Mehsuds to a meeting on 21 January 1895. It was attended by 272 men, representing all the sections except the Shabi Khel Alizais and Abdur Rahman Khel Bahlolzais. The British announced that they must hand over the men who had not yet surrendered (to be kept as hostages in Dera Ismail Khan), pay a fine and surrender fifty breech-loading rifles. By the end of January most of the wanted men had given themselves up, and the Mehsuds had restored most of the stolen property and agreed to pay a fine of Rs.13,000 to settle outstanding claims for raiding.[37] They also agreed that Mullah Powindah would leave Mehsud territory while the Waziristan portion of the Durand Line was being demarcated. We noted above that Bruce had requested permission to open the Shahur route to Wana from Jandola, as it was more direct than the Gumal one. General Lockhart now insisted on this, and the government and the Mehsuds agreed. To help secure the Shahur troops were left encamped at Barwand in Mehsud territory; it was the first time that a permanent British military presence was established in it. Garrisons of regular troops were also retained at Wana and Jandola.[38]

The Tochi valley and the maliki policy version two

The Tochi valley runs through the north of Waziristan. As we have seen, at this point British strategists regarded it as one of the routes into Afghanistan that troops could use to move up to the scientific frontier, and therefore argued that agreements should be reached with its inhabitants too. In 1894 the secretary of state had sanctioned a policy of 'more effective protection and closer relations with the headmen of the Waziri tribes'.[39] In April 1895, 394 Dawar maliks and *mohtabars* ('elders') and 142 Wazir maliks and *mohtabars* from the Tochi and other parts of Waziristan petitioned to be brought under British rule and applied for service and allowances.[40]

Fitzpatrick and the civilian members of Elgin's council were sceptical about their motives, and the majority of the secretary of state's council objected to the move into the Tochi.[41] Sir Donald Stewart (who had been the commander-in-chief for much of the 1880s and was now a member of the Viceroy's Council) referred scathingly to

> irresponsible and ambitious soldiers ... who would support and applaud any scheme that is likely to bring them the chance of active employment and distinction ... and the philanthropist who believes the border tribes are savage

barbarians ... and who would be tickled with the idea of Mr. Bruce's system of civilization and ... would probably be of the opinion that the end justified the means though the means involves the expenditure of a good deal of powder and shot in the process.[42]

Nevertheless, the GOI decided to accept the Wazirs' petition and to establish an outpost in the Tochi valley and declared the route through it a Protected Area, along which robbery and murder would not be permitted.[43] With regular troops in the Tochi and at Jandola and Wana the British thought that it would be possible to dominate the whole of Waziristan, and in particular, with troops to the north and south of them, to get a grip on the Mehsuds (this came to be called 'external control').[44] The GOI also decided to take direct control of Dawar and to set up the North and South Waziristan Agencies, and appoint British political agents to manage relations with Waziristan's inhabitants (based in the south at Wana and to the north at Miranshah in the Tochi).[45] The agents' job was to ensure that people kept the peace in the Protected Areas in Waziristan itself and did not raid outside it, and make them pay compensation for any breach of the rules. Outside the Protected Areas the position was less well defined; political officers were permitted to give assistance and advice, but not arrest and try offenders, nor adjudicate in any disputes except in a friendly capacity.[46] In 1896 the British began to set up military posts in the Tochi valley – at Miranshah, Datta Khel, Boya, Idak and Saidgai.[47] Over the next year or two the GOI established a basic administration in Dawar and began to levy a light revenue. This was another significant extension of British influence.

After the attack on the camp at Wana in 1894 Bruce had cancelled the Mehsud service payments. He admitted that his original choice of maliks had not been very representative and that he had left out several important sections and individuals. He claimed that this time he could establish who the really influential men were and reach an agreement with them. He was given permission to try again, and the money available was raised by around Rs.10,000 to Rs.61,548. This time he awarded subsidies to a much larger number of maliks, 270 in all, dividing them into five classes, each class being paid at a different rate, according to how much influence he judged them to have. The maliks themselves were to receive Rs.28,488 p.a. Levies were to be posted in the Shahur, and Rs.33,060 were to be distributed as service allowances and shared between them and the maliks. In return the maliks agreed to prevent raids into British India and the Protected Areas, including Gumal, Wana, Spin and Zarmelan, and surrender for trial and punishment any men guilty of offences against the government. In addition officials were to be allowed to go everywhere in Mehsud country on government business, and the maliks would provide escorts for them. This would have meant significant interference with the Mehsuds' cherished independence.[48]

In any case, the new allowances were not going to bring stability. There was not enough money to give a service payment or allowance to all the men who wanted one, and as we have seen the have-nots sometimes resorted to violence to show that they should not be ignored. But even if there had been enough money to give everyone something, they would still have competed to get larger shares than their rivals. Moreover, as we have seen, it was really impossible to identify men who remained sufficiently influential in the longer term; as Hubert Watson, the South Waziristan political officer at the turn of the century, put it,

> The tribe is so *democratic*, and members of it attain to prominence and notoriety so rapidly, that it is quite possible that a year or two later men without allowances will have risen whose recently acquired influence makes itself felt in their sections and who will commit offences until their claims are satisfied, as their predecessors did.[49]

In fact it appears that Bruce's second, third, fourth and fifth grade maliks were nominees of the first grade ones and had little influence.[50] The really meaningful distinction it would appear was that between a small number of men with wider but still limited influence, and a large number of elders or *mohtabars*, as many as 2,000 of them, each of whose influence was restricted to 'the half dozen or so families' living in one of the 'small kots or towered villages in which the Mehsud sections are scattered over the country'.[51]

Bruce also called for a further extension of the British military presence in Waziristan. He argued that the fact that the Mehsuds had come to terms so quickly after the third punitive expedition showed that if the maliks were properly supported they could exert real influence. Optimistic as ever, he was convinced that most people would welcome an extension of British authority, and the time had come to consolidate the gains made so far and lay the foundations for a peaceful tribal state.[52] Troops should remain at Barwand, or somewhere nearby, and a large cantonment should be built in central Waziristan (he suggested Razmak on the border between the Tori Khel Wazirs and the Abdullai Mehsuds), with outposts at Wana and Sheranna. In this way it would be possible to dominate Mehsuds, Wazirs and Dawars.[53] The government rejected these proposals and told Bruce he must not visit Mehsud country even with a tribal escort.[54] The government also turned down his proposal to establish an additional military post in the Khaisara valley at Narai Raghza or Torwam.

This did not mean the end of British interference; it meant continuing to encourage the maliks to deal with problems on the government's behalf. In 1896 the British built posts for levies in 1896 at Haidari Kach, Sarwakai and Narai Oba and moved the Barwand military post to the edge of Mehsud territory at Sarwakai.[55]

For a year or two after the 1894–5 expedition Mehsudland was relatively quiet. Mehsuds did not take part in the frontier-wide risings of 1897. As we have seen, British officials had already made efforts to pacify them by giving them land to cultivate in British territory. Bruce originally argued that this was pointless, but changed his mind during the 1890s; one reason why the scheme set up the early 1880s had not worked, he thought, was that most of the land set aside for the Mehsuds lacked a permanent water supply.[56] Before he left the frontier in 1896 he sorted this problem out and produced a new scheme for distributing all the available land in three roughly equal proportions among the three sections. Mehsud tenants were to cultivate the land, and it was not to be alienable by sale or mortgage.[57] This is not the only example of him changing his mind, and his overconfidence, carelessness even, is striking. As we have seen, having claimed that his 1888 settlement had included every Mehsud of importance, he admitted in the mid-1890s that he had got things wrong and embarked on a new and much more complicated distribution of allowances to the supposedly influential men. Another example is the way that in the Memorandum he had written in the late 1880s he criticized Macaulay for relying too much on Azem Khan Kundi to help him deal with the Mehsuds and Zilla Khels, but in the 1890s began to make considerable use of Azem Khan himself.[58]

Madda Khels and 1897

The Madda Khel Utmanzai Wazirs lived along the Tochi River eastwards from Sheranna towards the Durand Line, and along the Kazha River, which joins the Tochi, and its tributaries. They were divided into two groupings, Ger (or Gor) and Kazha.[59] The former lived along the Tochi River and the latter on the Kazha. The significance of this division is not very clear, but it was not based primarily on descent, as the same subsections were found among both. Most of their territory lay just on the British side of the Durand Line, next to that of the Zadrans on the Afghan side, but a few Madda Khels lived on the Afghan side too.[60]

Since 1849 some of the Madda Khels had maintained links with the government in Kabul and been hostile to the British; for many years their leading man had been Adam Khan (one of the men who had sheltered Mecham's murderers in 1860). But by the 1890s both Ger and Kazha Madda Khels were reported to recognize Sadde Khan as their head malik and his family as the leading Madda Khel family. His uncle, Ayub Khan, was reported to be an influential man too, while another close relative, Ayambe Khan, led an anti-British faction.[61]

As we have seen, following the demarcation of the Durand Line in the mid-1890s, the British decided to establish a permanent military garrison at Miranshah in the Tochi, as well as smaller outposts, to employ Dawar and Madda Khel, Manzar Khel and Tori Khel Wazir levies at a cost of Rs.63,736 and to levy a light revenue in Dawar itself, which became a Protected Area.[62] They began to distribute allowances on 5 November 1895.[63] Work began on the military posts early in 1896.[64]

However, during the winter of 1896-7 Madda Khels (as well as Manzar Khels and Khizr Khels) from the Upper Tochi carried out 'numerous acts of lawlessness' and began to show signs of being dissatisfied with recent developments.[65] During the Eid il-Fitr at the end of Ramadan, the Madda Khels customarily assembled near Sheranna at what were referred to in one report as 'the ancestral tombs' of Malik Sadde Khan's family. At the gathering (on 16 March 1897) some of the mullahs and religious students (*taliban*) made impassioned speeches in which they condemned the maliks for cooperating with the British and tried to encourage anti-British resistance.[66] Sadde Khan and other leading maliks were able to calm things down. However, in early April they met the Derajat commissioner, Henry Anderson (he had worked with Bruce on the demarcation of the Durand Line and succeeded him as commissioner in 1896), and asked for various written assurances. These included an undertaking that the government would not take revenue from them, that their *jangal* (jungle) and grazing grounds would not be interfered with, that they would retain ownership of their mines, that offenders would be kept in jails in the Tochi not in British territory and that cases in which women were involved would be decided according to their own customs.[67] Obviously the maliks were concerned about the British move into the Tochi and anxious lest it upset the rest of the Madda Khels. In June a Madda Khel named Waris Khan murdered Honda Ram, the clerk at the Sheranna post, and fled to Afghanistan, in order it seems to discredit Sadde Khan. In July 1896 leading Madda Khel maliks, including Sadde Khan, were among the men from Waziristan who went to Urgun to meet Sardar Gul Muhammad Khan.[68]

The way that the British distributed responsibility for payment of the fine imposed for Honda Ram's murder between the different subsections also upset the maliks. In the early summer of 1897 Major Herbert Gee, the political officer, announced that he intended to visit Maizar, a group of Madda Khel settlements about eleven miles west of Datta Khel and not far from the Durand Line, in order to select a site for a new military outpost. The maliks were unhappy about this and held a meeting on 8 June. They may have thought that troops were coming to collect the fine. By the time Gee and his escort arrived on 12 June they had worked themselves up into 'an excited state of mind', and without any warning, some Madda Khel men attacked him and his military escort, killing Lieutenant-Colonel A. C. Bunny and two Artillery officers (women joined in throwing stones and also reportedly firing guns).[69] Some of the soldiers retreated to a position on a hill three miles away and held out there until they were relieved by troops sent from Datta Khel.[70]

Initially some British officials attributed the attack to fanaticism, and the influence of Mullah Powindah.[71] Gee and Anderson thought the attack had been premeditated, but Fitzpatrick referred to what he called 'the sudden gusts of feeling to which Pathans are only too prone';[72] the first shot might well have been fired 'by some ruffian who wanted to commit his tribe to the attack at the height of their excitement'.[73] In the end the British decided that the attack had been more or less spontaneous. Some men were unhappy with the increasing British encroachment and were anxious about what was to come, and were therefore easily provoked.[74] Anger about the allocation of the fine for the murder of Honda Ram played a part, as did rivalries within the Madda Khels between Sadde Khan and Ayambe's factions.

After the attack the Madda Khels retreated into the mountains, many of them crossing the Durand Line into Afghanistan, and in July British troops commanded by Major-General Wilkinson Bird destroyed their settlements at Sheranna and Maizar. The allowances were stopped, and terms were announced at a meeting on 17 August. The Madda Khels were to hand over seventeen maliks and pay a fine of Rs.1,200 for the murder of Honda Ram, and another of Rs.10,000 for the attack at Maizar.[75] Mullah Powindah and Mullah Hamzullah wrote to the commissioner offering to mediate in order that as they put it, 'the spit and roasted meat may not both end in destruction'.[76] Afghan officials also appear to have become involved, among them Sardar Sher Dil Khan, 'one of the principal officials of the Kabul Government'.[77] The troops remained at Sheranna; the maliks did not surrender (in September two of them had taken refuge in Afghanistan). Bird argued that there was nothing to be gained by insisting on their surrender and that it would sufficient reparation if the other men paid Rs.1,000 for each man who had not given himself up.[78] This was agreed, and after some negotiation Sadde Khan himself surrendered on condition that he was not put to death nor sent anywhere outside India. The Madda Khels returned to their villages, and the British began paying their allowances again.[79]

After the attack on Gee and his escort at Maizar, there were several major risings in areas to the north of Waziristan. They began in Swat late in July 1897 and were followed by outbreaks in the Malakand, the Mohmand area, the Khyber and the Samana range. They were the most serious challenge to British authority along the frontier since Britain had annexed Punjab in 1849. The British launched seven extensive military operations involving the deployment of 70,000 troops, and they did not completely crush the risings until the following year.[80] Waziristan remained relatively quiet.[81]

Mehsuds and Mullah Powindah

We have seen that Bruce had made a new settlement with the Mehsuds in 1895 and that the Barwand military post had been moved to Sarwakai and levy posts had been established there and at Haidari Kach and Narai Oba. Robberies and raids became more frequent later in the decade; for example a group consisting mainly of Guri Khel men carried off a large number of Jani Khel animals from the Bannu District on 3 September 1898 and in February 1899 Shingis killed four Suleiman Khel Powindahs and seized 1,200 of their goats and sheep near Nasran.[82] In 1899 Anderson and the other local officials managed to induce the Mehsuds to pay fines totalling Rs.30,000 for the raids and various other robberies, thanks to 'several surprises of villages', the seizure of Mehsud convoys in Bannu and Tank, the blockade of various sections and the efforts of the maliks, who paid some of the fines themselves.[83]

Mullah Powindah had returned in May 1895 and resumed his efforts to promote himself as the Mehsuds' leading man. In 1896 he went to Afghanistan with a large party of Dawars and Mehsuds. They asked the amir for land and money to live on, but he did not offer them anything, and they came home. The mullah also made various approaches to the local British officials, who had been instructed to ignore him.[84] In 1898 the amir wrote to him via Sardar Gul Muhammad Khan, assuring him that he was welcome to return to Kabul whenever he wished.[85] The British position began to deteriorate. On 20 July 1899 a Tori Khel man, assisted by some of Mullah Powindah's *sheikhs*, actually tried to kill Watson, the South Waziristan political agent; they failed, killing his messenger boy instead.[86] On 15 December 1899 Mehsud gangs carried out two attacks on Border Military Policy in which they killed six sepoys and took away five rifles. On 9 January 1900 as many as forty men, led by some of Mullah Powindah's *sheikhs*, attacked the Zam post. They killed two border policemen, three Bhittani levies and a landowner and stole four rifles. By now people living along the border with Waziristan were reported to be more frightened of the Mehsuds than ever. They had been disarmed, but the Mehsuds took their guns into the settled areas and intimidated the landowners and the Border Military Police, and the Indian officials were too frightened to take action against them.[87] Some years later Deane, the chief commissioner, referred to 'the system of Mehsud terrorism under which that frontier has suffered for some time past, described and complained of by the Chiefs and British subjects as well as Bhittanis and Waziris'.[88] A serious drought affected the district in the 1890s, and the resulting scarcity of food and fodder contributed to the unsettled situation.[89]

When Bruce's maliki policy was introduced, officials had largely abandoned the practice (introduced by Macaulay) of making all the Mahsuds collectively responsible for any difficulties caused by individual Mehsuds or small groups of them. Instead, in return for allowances and service appointments, the maliks were supposed to sort out any problems. In practice they were simply too weak to do so. Divided among themselves they found it difficult to cooperate, especially as competition for allowances had become a new feature of Mehsud politics.[90] Those who had not been given an allowance arranged raids to show the government that they should get them, and those who did might encourage raiding in the hope of obtaining larger ones.[91]

The lieutenant-governor, William Mackworth-Young, who visited Waziristan in the autumn of 1899, decided that the policy of imposing sectional blockades and *baramptas* had not worked; instead he suggested a blockade of the Mehsuds as a whole. First, however, the local officers should assemble a Mehsud jirga, comprising not just the men who received allowances (the maliks), but 'all the grey-beards, elders and persons of influence who sway the tribal councils' and demand that they agree to pay compensation for the raiding.[92] Anderson arranged for the jirga to meet at Tank in March 1900 and presented them with a bill for Rs.35,000. The maliks suggested various ways in which this could be paid; Anderson accepted them and went on leave, handing over to William Merk.[93] In his final report he stated that the jirga displayed a very friendly attitude. He did not agree that the current approach had failed. As he saw it, the maliks, whom he described as 'sensible and responsible men', had been able to increase their influence and had been helpful to him in managing the tribe.[94] For him and the other local officers, most of the Mehsuds were not giving much trouble; the real problem was the activities of mullah Powindah and his followers, and the maliks could not control him.[95]

Anderson did not accept Mackworth-Young's claim that tribal blockades were the best way of dealing with the Mahsuds. He admitted that trying to 'enforce the graded responsibility of sub-sections, sections, and finally the tribe' was a slow process.[96] On the other hand it was 'a much less primitive system' than the previous practice of imposing tribal responsibility straightaway.[97] Indeed, during the past year, he said, personal responsibility had been successfully imposed more than once, and it was, he thought, correctly no doubt, far more popular with the Mehsuds themselves. Tribal responsibility was 'repugnant to them, because the weak and innocent are forced to share the punishment with the strong and the guilty'; they were, he said, 'sufficiently civilized to appreciate the ethical superiority of the one system to the other'.[98] The imposition of tribal responsibility, in his view, was more likely to lead to punitive expeditions precisely because it involved the whole tribe.[99] The lieutenant-governor did not agree. He thought that the imposition of this 'graded responsibility' from the actual offender through subsections to the 'whole body of the clan is no doubt excellent in theory', but in practice did not work. When the maliks did not surrender offenders promptly, it was more effective to impose tribal responsibility immediately.[100] This was not the first time that the officials had disagreed about how widely collective responsibility should be shared. In any case perhaps Anderson had painted too rosy a picture. Mehsud robberies and cattle lifting continued to occur after the March jirga; the maliks were still failing to prevent raids and offences in British territory, or get hold of wanted men for the British.[101]

Following the 1897 risings the British had reassessed their approach to the frontier, and Elgin's successor as viceroy (1898–1905), Lord Curzon, introduced a new policy. He insisted that officials should not take on any new responsibilities or annex any more territory, partly because of the expense, and also because there was also some concern that it might provoke resistance on the frontier that could spread into India itself.[102] Most of the garrisons of British troops that had been established in independent territory were withdrawn and replaced with militias. The military strategists also decided that after all maintaining the scientific frontier did not require control of the Gumal and Tochi routes into Afghanistan, and the strategic emphasis shifted to the Khyber Pass to the north and the Bolan Pass to the south.[103] As regards Waziristan Curzon insisted that regular troops were withdrawn from Miranshah and Wana. He was particularly critical of British policy in the Tochi; as he put it, 'We have to pay large annual sums to the tribes, who desire to be protected, for the privilege of protecting them.'[104] Another very important feature of his viceroyalty was the separation of the districts to the west of the Indus and north of the Gumal (and Hazara which was on the east side of the Indus) from Punjab to form a new North-West Frontier Province.[105] In charge of the new province he placed a chief commissioner and agent to the governor general, based in Peshawar, who was to be directly responsible to the GOI.[106]

Curzon was also willing to consider a change of policy towards the Mehsuds. We have seen that the lieutenant-governor, Mackworth-Young, was concerned by developments in Waziristan. At a meeting with Curzon at Dera Ismail Khan in April 1900, he and the new commissioner, Merk, argued that paying the maliks to keep the Mehsuds in order had not worked. The 277 men in receipt of British allowances were not 'the government of the tribe ... though with our help they have been able to pose as such'.[107] Merk also suggested that the ordinary people did not benefit from the allowances. A question they often asked was, 'We see nothing of what the Maliks get; why should *we* be held responsible and they get the money?'[108]

We saw in Chapter 2 that Bruce had, not very convincingly, argued that the problem the British faced in Waziristan was not the same as that in the Khyber Pass to the north. Merk also compared the Mehsuds with the Khyber Afridis, but reached a rather different conclusion.[109] Originally he thought the Afridis had been just as democratic as the Mehsuds, but successive governments, the Mughals for example, had paid subsidies to the leading Afridis as well as to the others to ensure safe travel through the Khyber Pass. As a result hereditary authority had developed. But nothing comparable had happened in Waziristan; 'in a democratic republic, like that of the Mehsud community', it was only through the old tribal jirga that order could be maintained.[110] Contact with the British had weakened the tribe's political organization and led to 'political paralysis' within it; they no longer appointed *chalweshtis* (tribal militias) to enforce the tribal will, nor did they hold jirgas with representatives from the whole tribe.[111] Bruce's maliki system was responsible, he said. The Mehsuds formed 'an independent little republic', in which some men (i.e. the maliks) had some influence but 'little real power', and Bruce had failed to understand that behind them were the 'many yeomen who constitute the real republic, and with whom obviously the ultimate power rests'.[112]

Harold Deane, the first chief commissioner of the North-West Frontier Province, agreed that the Mehsud society was divided into 'innumerable petty groups which admit the leadership of no single large Malik, [which] itself necessitates representation by numerous smaller men'.[113] Merk thought therefore that by distributing the allowances more widely to the heads of families, it would be possible to gradually rebuild the overall sense of community, strengthening what he called 'internal self-government', and so revive the Mehsuds' ability to run their own affairs; 'The little Mahsud Republic shall be in future a kind of Nation State', he commented optimistically.[114] Some money might however still be set aside for a small number of influential men in particular, provided they made themselves useful.[115] The levies would be disbanded, and allowances of Rs.61,548 – Rs.28,000 to the maliks and Rs.33,000 for militia service – would in future to be distributed to the Mehsuds as a whole.[116] As we shall see, the question was how this was to be managed.

Blockade

Merk called on Mehsud representatives to meet him at Tank in November 1900.[117] In spite of continuing raids, the jirga went ahead.[118] Against the wishes of the majority, the maliks again requested the British to take over their country.[119] Merk told the men attending that to clear the slate the Mehsuds should pay a fine of one lakh (Rs.100,000), and they left to consult the others. No agreement had been reached by 1 December 1900, and Merk barred them from visiting the administered areas.[120] The local officials distributed arms to the border villages to help them defend themselves.[121] The Mehsuds did pay part of the fine and handed over animals and rifles and revolvers as security for cash payments, by May 1901 to the value of Rs.67,500, but the blockade remained in force.[122]

We saw earlier in this chapter that Mullah Powindah appeared to be playing a double game, making approaches to the British while encouraging his *sheikhs* and other Mehsuds to launch attacks on the police and the posts. Towards the end of the decade, however, senior officials had decided to reopen communications with him and try to win him over by secretly offering him an allowance of Rs.100 per month (more than twice as much as any of the maliks received). In 1900 he had agreed to accept this. The news leaked out somehow and became widely known; it was seen by most Mehsuds as endorsing the mullah's status as their leading man. Things had been 'shockingly mismanaged', Curzon commented.[123] During the blockade the mullah interfered with the efforts the maliks made to resolve the situation, while they spoiled his attempts to do so.[124] As in 1860 and at various points since, the Mehsuds were incapable of united action; by the early summer they were reported to be dressed in ragged clothes with 'sickly faces' and 'suffering from dyspepsia'.¹²⁵ Merk called a jirga of some 1,500 men at Jandola early in May. It met

> in a large circle on the stony plain; [the Mehsuds] ... would listen to the representations of the British officers; they would storm and abuse each other and all shout at once; maliks would fling stones at one another and even shake each other in their rage; the assembly would break up into little sections, sitting apart, each deaf to the petty concession or compromise which alone offered a way out. For four long days they wrangled in the plain.¹²⁶

The Punjab government and the GOI agreed that the Mehsuds must pay the money still owing in cash, rather than guns or animals, before the blockade could be lifted; on 28 May the jirga accepted this.¹²⁷ The maliks and the other Mehsuds continued to argue about who should pay it and in what proportions.¹²⁸ Raids continued too; for example Nabi Bakhsh, a former malik from the Bannu district, attacked the village of Attar Singh in the Derajat. Attar Singh was a Hindu moneylender and landowner and had acquired Nabi Bakhsh and his brother's property (presumably because they could not repay money borrowed from him).¹²⁹ After this Nabi had moved into Mehsud territory. On 3 September 1901 he and his gang attacked the village in which Attar Singh lived, twenty-five miles into administered territory, killing him and his son and daughter and four other people.¹³⁰ In another incident, on 3 November 1901, near Khuzhma Khullah in the Gumal, the Mehsuds attacked a survey party escorted by a small detachment of the 17th Bengal Infantry. They killed twenty-nine men in all and stole thirty rifles. Meanwhile in September and October 1901 Abdullai Mehsuds managed to drive the Tori Khel Wazirs off some land in Baddar and take possession of it themselves.¹³¹

The insurgency was becoming serious. Because the blockade had failed to induce the Mehsuds to accept the terms offered to them, rather as in 1894–5 the British resorted to brief but destructive incursions. On 25 November 1901 four small columns, each about 1,000 strong, went into Mehsud territory and destroyed towers and mills, took prisoners, drove off animals and ruined or took away as much grain and fodder as they could. In the fertile Khaisara valley for instance the roofs were piled high with jowar (Indian millet) straw. The troops set light to this, and fire spread to the buildings below.¹³² Further incursions followed in which troops visited many different parts of Mehsud territory, including Shahur, Splitoi, Inzar, Shinkai, Shuza and the Shaktu valley. They attacked and partly destroyed Makin again.¹³³ The Mehsuds did not put much resistance, although at Kotkai in the Tank Zam some men opposed the troops sent up from Jandola.¹³⁴ The troops killed some 130 men in all. Merk thought that they inflicted more damage to property than in the three expeditions of 1860, 1881 and 1894 put together.¹³⁵

By the end of 1901 the Mehsuds had had enough. On 16 January their jirga sent a deputation of Kaniguram Sayyids to offer submission; negotiations continued until 10 March when the blockade was raised.¹³⁶ The jirga paid the fine and surrendered sixty-five rifles; it also undertook to surrender wanted men and return stolen flocks. As security it gave ninety-three hostages or 'jirga prisoners', and despatched *chalweshtis* to arrest Mianji, Barak and the other Mehsud outlaws, and seized their property, but they had already fled to Birmal, on the Afghan side of the Durand Line.¹³⁷ It seems that by now the Afghan authorities had given some of them land to cultivate at Ghozba near Ghazni.¹³⁸ On 29 March the chief commissioner, Deane, accepted the Mehsuds' formal submission and told them their allowances would be restored.¹³⁹

Merk thought that there was now some hope of as he put it 'reforming' the tribe. This would be accomplished, first, by enlisting Mehsuds in the militia and the army and employing them on the Wana road and other public works. Second the allowances would be redistributed and paid to the real holders of political power, and the officials would manage the Mehsuds 'by and through the whole jirga, ignoring individuals, whether they be Maliks or Mulla Powindah'.¹⁴⁰ Merk planned to distribute Rs.54,000 to 1,565 men, drawn equally from the three sections – Alizais, Bahlolzais and Shaman Khels, each of whom should receive the allowances on behalf of several families besides their own. An additional Rs.7,000 was to be reserved for those he judged to have some special influence.¹⁴¹ In this way he hoped that he could develop the capacity of the Mehsuds as a whole to manage their own affairs and deal with raiders and outlaws.

The problem of the Mehsud bandits (or rebels) had not been solved. They had links with some Wazir outlaws, and they sometimes joined forces with them. Early in April 1902, for example, a band consisting of Barak and Mianji Abdur Rahman Khel and Zariband Malikshahi (Bahlolzais), Ashiq Palli Khel Manzai Alizai, and Bostan Madda Khel attacked a party of the 27th Punjabis between Toi Khulla and Khajuri Kach, killing eight soldiers and taking their rifles. The British imposed fines on both the Mehsuds and the Saifali Kabul Khels who had sheltered the outlaws.¹⁴² This was the first time that the British records mentioned Mehsud outlaws living on the Afghan side of the Durand Line in Birmal and attacking troops on the British side.¹⁴³

Meanwhile, in October 1901 the Afghan amir Abdur Rahman Khan had died, and his eldest son, Habibullah Khan, succeeded him. Habibullah continued his father's policy towards Waziristan. He paid subsidies to selected men and invited tribal deputations to Kabul to receive gifts and *khillats* (robes of honour).[144] Curzon wrote to the new amir asking him to expel the raiders; he did so, and they returned to Mehsud territory. Mehsuds surrendered some of the men involved in the Toi Khulla attack to the British, including Ashiq, who was tried and convicted. They tried to hand over Mianji and Guldad (another outlaw) too, but only a few miles from Sarwakai both men tried to escape. Mianji got away and went to Kabul, but Guldad was killed. Barak was killed in another fight not long afterwards. The officials suspected Mullah Powindah of having instigated the Toi Khulla attack and persuaded him to come in for a trial by jirga at Sarwakai. He did so, and not surprisingly he was acquitted. Towards the end of the year he helped to catch and surrender an Urmur who had been sentenced to three years imprisonment but had escaped.[145]

The GOI ordered that deductions should be made from the Mehsud allowances to compensate for the Toi Khulla raid and their failure to keep various promises.[146] By this time Frederick Johnston had taken over as political officer. He found that *nikat* continued to be a major problem, because those sections which had relatively little land or property and had more of a tradition of raiding, like the Abdur Rahman Khels and Garrerais, were not paid as much money per head as the more prosperous and less numerous Shaman Khels. Moreover he noted that Merk had left the more influential men, the 'old maliks' (men like Badshah Khan Salimi Khel, Badrudin Umar Khel, Shah Salim Jindi Khel and Jaggar Abdur Rahman Khel), as well as the elders or small maliks (*mohtabars*), out of the scheme.[147] As a result the men through whom the allowances had been distributed had little influence and had not been of much use. As he put it, it was like the House of Commons trying to carry out the work of the Cabinet. Although the old maliks and the *mohtabars* had been helping him, he feared that in future they might not be willing to do so. Therefore he recommended that they should be formally involved in the distribution of the allowances and should help the officials with managing the rest of the tribe, and to reflect this additional responsibility the total *maliki* allowances should be increased to Rs.16,000.[148] Second, the arrangements for distribution should be changed. Each small subsection would choose representatives (*wakils*) from among the old maliks and *mohtabars*. In future the tribal or *tumani* allowances of Rs.54,000 would be distributed through them. In return for this, and for helping to manage the rest of the Mahsuds, these men would also receive a share of the Rs.16,000.[149]

Deane supported Johnston's recommendations. Curzon was concerned that the officials wanted to introduce further changes so soon, but gave his permission. Johnston announced them in February 1903 at a jirga held at Jandola and attended by Mullah Powindah and all the other influential men.[150] The 1,565 householders present selected 1,334 *wakils*, and each of the *wakils* (representatives) also received a share of the *maliki* money, in theory for helping Johnston to manage the Mehsuds. Although some new names were added to the list, the new *wakils* were in many cases the same men through whom the allowances had been paid according to the original arrangements, and the number of recipients was only reduced by 231. Howell commented that Merk's 'utterly impracticable plan of dealing only with the "great jirga of the Mehsuds" perished still born'.[151] In fact it looks as though Merk's scheme was modified rather than completely abandoned.[152] The system was still based on many small payments to a larger number of men and remained one of tribal responsibility, although, as Merk himself had intended, it still had some *maliki* features.

Mullah Powindah himself said the new arrangement was 'fair, just and generous'.[153] He announced that in future he would cooperate with the government; 'his presence [at the jirga] … meant the beginning of a new era' in Mehsud relations with the British government, Johnston thought.[154] During the summer of 1903 Captain J. B. Bowring took over from him as South Waziristan political agent. In the same year the Anglo-Afghan Commission went down the Durand Line from the Kurram to the Gumal settling cases between tribes living on either side of it.[155]

As we have seen, one of the principal features of Curzon's modified close-border policy was the replacement of regular troops in forward positions by locally recruited militias. The British had begun to set up North and South Waziristan militias at the end of the 1890s. About half the men in the South Waziristan militia were recruited from elsewhere along the frontier, while the other half consisted of three companies, one from each of the Alizais, Bahlolzais and Shaman Khels. In all nearly 400 Mehsuds served in the South Waziristan militia and about 120 in the North Waziristan one.[156] Men from different Wazir groups served in the latter; Madda Khels supplied the largest single contingent. During 1903 and 1904 the militias took over all the posts in Waziristan which had previously been held by the regular army, except Jandola.[157] At around this time Mehsuds were also recruited into the Indian army. In 1898 a Mehsud company (114 strong) was formed in the 124th Baluchistan Infantry, and in 1903 the 130th Baluchistan Infantry raised another one.[158]

We have seen that there was raiding by Mehsuds based in Afghanistan. In addition men from Khost began to use the Kabul Khel country between Thal and the Tochi to carry out raids into the Bannu and Kohat districts, and from 1898 to 1902 the Bannu border also remained in a very disturbed state.[159] In February 1899 troops attacked Kabul Khel raiders holed up in a tower at Gumutti a few miles to the north of Bannu. The defenders killed six soldiers and wounded thirteen and remained in possession of the tower.[160] Not until 1902 were the British able to take and demolish it and establish a military outpost there.[161]

4

Mullah Powindah, suicidal attacks and British responses

Following the lifting of the blockade and the redistribution of the allowances, relations between the Mehsuds and the British appeared to improve, but nothing had been done to restrain Mullah Powindah, who remained determined to maintain and develop his influence. His main aim was to have the Mehsuds accept him as their leading man, and therefore he had to convince the *tuman* (the Mehsuds as a whole) that he was determined to stand up for their interests. As Leslie Crump, who became the political agent in 1905, saw it, after 1902,

> To control the fanatical elements in the tribe, whom he could no longer permit to raid openly, and to gratify his own fanatical hatred of Government, he preached that fear of the power of Government alone made him keep the peace but that at heart he hated the Kafir [disbeliever] and was a true Ghazi, and this is undoubtedly his real attitude.[1]

He also wanted both the British and the Afghans to recognize him as the Mehsuds' leader. He had to convince the British officials that his influence over the Mehsuds meant that it would be a mistake to ignore him, but reassure them that he was willing to cooperate with them.[2] At the same time he had to show the Afghan government that he was a useful ally who was worth supplying with arms and money that he would use against the British and their supporters.

It was a difficult task, but he was a skilful political operator. To keep the British happy, now and again he handed over one of the many wanted men he sheltered.[3] When the Mehsuds criticized him for being too friendly with them, he arranged some sort of anti-British demonstration.[4] Typical of his methods was the way that he reacted to the creation of the new militias. He saw that there was a danger that he might lose his influence over the Mehsuds who joined them. Nevertheless he encouraged them to do so, but at the same time he sent warning letters to the political agent, advising that the new recruits were untrustworthy but not explaining why.⁵ He would also tell other mullahs that they should not perform the usual funeral rites for men who died or had been killed while working for the British.

In order to maintain his influence the mullah also had to ensure that no other religious leaders could emerge to challenge him. He therefore tried to have any mullah who dared to oppose him killed; for instance he 'repeatedly sent men to kill his own *Ustad* [teacher], the Wazir Mullah Hamzullah, for opposing him on religious questions'.⁶ At Marobi, where he had a mosque, he maintained a *langar* or kitchen and dining room. Around him he collected a following of men referred to as *talibs*, *khalifas* and *sheikhs*. Money for food and the upkeep of the mosque came from a sort of tithe, *shukrana*, which the mullah and his followers would travel round the country collecting. Wherever he went he was accompanied by a retinue of followers, often armed, who carried flags and beat drums. In the evening his followers would sing songs of jihad, which might include praise of the mullah as a *ghazi*, a fighter for Islam.⁷

As well as having his own followers, he had links with the Mehsud outlaws living in Afghanistan and sometimes encouraged their raiding and murder. One British source described them as 'a gang of cut-throats of whose character and exploits he cannot well have been ignorant. Indeed, whenever any of them made a successful coup he took a share in the proceeds.'⁸ The plundering and raiding that he encouraged was obviously motivated by a desire for money and loot, but it also had a political aspect. Although they feared the raiders, many people also admired them for their daring.⁹ Some of them at least were 'social bandits' or 'bandit rebels' – robbers and outlaws seen by public opinion not as simply criminals but as avengers or resistance fighters.¹⁰ The mullah also continued to visit Kabul, and the Afghan authorities sometimes gave him money, guns and ammunition. He also ran his own communications network which kept him in touch with adjacent areas of the frontier as well as with Lahore, Peshawar and Kabul.¹¹

For a few years in the early 1900s therefore, by playing his cards carefully the mullah succeeded in selling himself to both the British and Afghan governments as a man worth cultivating, while maintaining his position as the most influential man among the Mehsuds.¹² The British officials did not see him as complicit, for instance, when in July 1904 a gang led by Mianji attacked the Khuni Burj post in the Zhob Agency, killing the jemadar and a sepoy, and wounding another, and made off with all the arms and ammunition. Nor did they blame the Mehsuds as a whole; officials thought that most of them gave no trouble, though it was clear that some men, including in particular some

Abdur Rahman Khel, Nekzan Khel and Abdullai Bahlolzais, and some Shabi Khel Alizais, remained difficult to control.[13]

Suicidal attacks

Meanwhile Lieutenant Colonel Richard Harman had not found it easy to find reliable recruits for the South Waziristan militia; he was unable to persuade the tribal jirgas to put men forward and give guarantees for them. Instead he had to enlist individuals directly, after making enquiries about them himself.[14] It came as a shock nevertheless when, during the evening of 19 September 1904, Kabul, a young Abdur Rahman Khel recruit to the South Waziristan militia, stationed at the post at Sarwakai, without any warning, attacked and killed a British official. Earlier that day he had bought some clothes and coloured handkerchiefs from the militia shop, explaining that he was about to go on leave. Later in the evening he dressed in the new clothes and blackened his eyes with antimony: such preparations were 'not uncommon in the case of fanatics contemplating outrages'.[15] At 2 o'clock the next morning he shot and killed Captain Bowring, the political agent, as he lay sleeping on the roof of the post. Kabul then rushed to the top of the keep from where he began to fire at anyone he could see. In the morning his uncle, Kastor, jemadar of the South Waziristan militia, was sent to negotiate with him. He agreed to come down from the keep and allow himself to be killed by a firing party of men from his own section, on condition that his body should be handed over for proper burial. When he eventually came down the men fired at him. The first volley missed him completely, but he was wounded in a second. He begged the men to finish him off, but they refused. He was taken to hospital for a few days, tried under the *Punjab Murderous Outrages Act* and executed at Dera Ismail Khan. Rather than burning it, the British allowed his relatives to have his body, and his tomb became 'a shrine to Mehsud patriotism'.[16] Kabul knew that he would almost certainly be killed as a result of murdering Bowring, so that his attack was in effect a suicidal one.

At this point it will be helpful to say something about what were usually referred to by the British as 'fanatical outrages' – suicidal attacks by small groups of or individual Muslims on colonial officials, and those regarded as collaborating with them. Such attacks occurred in several areas of South and South-East Asia during the colonial period, including Mindanao and Sulu, Atjeh (Sumatra), and Kerala in southern India; there they were carried out by the minority Muslim Mappilas (the British called them the 'Moplah Outrages'). Along the North-West

Frontier, as the secretary to the Punjab government, Lepel Griffin, explained, resentment of colonial rule and 'the belief that the assassination of an infidel was a sure passport to paradise' led to a number of surprise attacks on British and Indian officers and officials.[17] In fact such attacks began even before Britain had formally annexed Punjab in 1849. One was carried out, for example, against the young Herbert Edwardes, who, we saw in Chapter 1, had been sent in the autumn of 1847 to Bannu to collect the revenue owing to the Sikh government. Towards the end of the year a *shahid* attempted to assassinate him. As Edwardes described it,

> The would-be assassin proposed the question to his religious adviser in the village 'whether anyone killing a Feringee would become a Shaheed or blessed martyr?' The Moolah replied, 'Decidedly, and a very meritorious act it would be'. ... The same priest seems to have put an extraordinary prayer before his congregation, appropriate to the dreadful calamity which had fallen upon Bunnoo in the arrival of the zalim [oppressive] Sahiblog, and implored the help of God in the crisis. It is not wonderful therefore that the prisoner, who is but just full grown and full of all the pride of youth, should have brooded over these matters, till, as he says, on the day of the murder the fixed determination came into his heart immediately after saying his noontide prayers to go and kill the Sahib. Taking his sword therefore in his hand he went to the camp, and gave away a spare pair of paijamahs on the road to another Moolah who was at prayer! 'Take these', he said, 'in the name of God'. The Moolah replied 'Kubool! Your prayer is accepted!' Drawing near the camp he had his sword in his clothes and found myself and General Cortland in the latter's tent. On hearing that the Sahib was unlikely to come out until the evening he made up his mind to force his way in, and cut down the sentry, but fled and was captured when others came up.[18]

Another unsuccessful attempt was made on Edwardes's life a few weeks later (20 January 1848). This time Edwardes shot the would-be assassin dead.[19] In 1856 John Nicholson, the deputy commissioner of Dera Ismail Khan, was attacked in similar circumstances. According to his account he was standing at the entrance of his compound at noon when a man armed with sword rushed towards him 'in an excited manner'. Nicholson shot and killed him. He discovered that his attacker was a man of 'good family and an extremely comfortable circumstances' from a village in the district;

> He would appear to have become religiously insane some months ago, entirely neglecting his business, and spending his time in devotional exercises and reading his Koran. Before leaving Murwut he gave away all his property to

different people. His last night, he spend in the village of Gurzye, about 10 miles from this, on the Bunnoo and Murwut border, in company with a theological student 'talib' which whom he occasionally associated, and who having since disappeared, was very probably his prompter.[20]

Other attacks like these took place elsewhere along the frontier at this time. In 1853, for instance, the newly appointed Peshawar commissioner, Frederick Mackeson, was killed by an assassin. He was hearing petitions on his veranda when a man he supposed to be a petitioner approached and stabbed him in the chest; reportedly he had for some time been a disciple of one of the 'fanatical "moolahs"' (mullahs) in Kabul. Mackeson died a few days later from the wound.[21] The Punjab chief commissioner, John Lawrence ordered the murderer's body burned and the ashes scattered in a river. This meant that his grave could not become a shrine, and a focus for resistance.[22]

Other recorded attacks included the murder in October 1865 of Major R. P. Adams by a 'Kandahar fanatic' in Peshawar, and, in January of the same year, of Lieutenant A. Ommanney at Mardan by a man who had recently visited the Mujahidin (or as the British referred to them 'Hindustani fanatic') colony at Malka in the mountains north of Peshawar. The colony had originally been established by Ahmad Shah Bareilly (1786–1831) in 1826, as a place where, on the model of the Prophet Muhammad's hijra to Medina and his victorious return to Mecca, South Asian Muslims could establish themselves securely, before returning to India and expelling the British.[23] Indeed the attacks became so frequent that in 1867 the British had introduced the *Punjab Murderous Outrages Act*. This regularized the 'punishment of fanatics murdering or attempting to murder' with the aim of preventing 'the occurrence of the murderous outrages which have so frequently of late been committed against Englishmen and others, by fanatics on the frontier'.[24] It made it legal for assassins to be put to death immediately, without recourse to the Chief Court. Since martyrdom was usually their goal, it is difficult to see that this can have made much difference.[25]

To return to Captain Bowring's death in 1904, his murder seems to have shared some features with the earlier attacks. His assassin, Kabul, made sure that he was as well dressed and groomed as possible. When last home on leave, he had talked about killing a British official, and although his parents had tried to dissuade him, he had gone to Marobi to see Mullah Powindah and obtained his blessing before carrying out his mission. Soon after that he returned to Sarwakai, and only two days later shot Bowring. British officials, however, did not initially suspect Mullah Powindah of being involved. He was later reported, however, to have declared that the killing of British officials was lawful and that their killers would go to paradise and have houris to serve them. He was heard to praise Kabul openly in his mosque, and on other occasions to declare that Kabul had become 'a lord in Heaven (*da Jinnat Sardar*)'.[26]

In the meantime British concerns about Russian influence had resurfaced. Amir Abdur Rahman had reluctantly accepted that he should not have diplomatic relationships with any country other than Britain. After his death in 1901 the Russian government began to press the Afghan government to allow it to deal with it directly.[27] The viceroy, Curzon, was concerned by this and in 1902 demanded that the new amir, Habibullah, come to India to discuss the situation.[28] He was unwilling to do so, and Curzon stopped the subsidy that had been paid to his father. He even recommended another invasion, but the government in London did not agree. While Curzon was on leave in 1904, the amir announced that he would be willing to receive a British mission in Kabul, and the GOI's foreign secretary, Sir Louis Dane, was sent to negotiate with him. Negotiations began in December 1904, and in the end the amir was able to persuade the British to accept a renewal of the arrangements reached with his father, and they resumed payment of the subsidy.[29] As regards the frontier, he undertook not to interfere on the British side of the Durand Line. The treaty was signed in March 1905.[30] However, the relationship remained a difficult one. The secretary of state, Morley thought it was unsatisfactory that the amir was paid a large subsidy, but he could not check his subjects' anti-British activities.[31]

More attacks on British officials

As we have seen, the British were beginning to experience difficulties with the South Waziristan militia; by late 1904 the South Waziristan militia commandant, Colonel Harman, was aware that all was not well with it and was trying to weed out any men whom he did not trust. Mullah Powindah was anxious to get rid of him and arranged for Sabir, an Astanai Shabi Khel, to try and kill him.[32] During the evening of 10 February 1905, while the British officers were eating in the mess at Sarwakai, Sabir came into the room holding his rifle with bayonet fixed. Harman and Plant, the second in command, leapt up from the table and rushed at him; Sabir stabbed Harman through the heart and he died shortly afterwards. His last words were the following: 'They've got me, I knew they would.'[33]

The other officers disarmed Sabir, and then the other Mehsuds in the militia, and sent most of them back to their homes next day. Sabir was hanged a few days later, but before his death he made a full statement. He said that at the Jandola jirga in December 1904 he had decided to kill Colonel Harman, but did not do so then for fear of making things difficult for the other Shabi Khels. So he enlisted in the militia and waited for two months for his chance to kill Harman and as many others as possible:

> His special desire was to show himself a better man than Kabul, the Bahlolzai who killed Captain Bowring in September. Like Kabul he was an ignorant impressionable lad of about eighteen, and his object does not appear to have been any more pure fanaticism than a vain desire for notoriety to pose after death as the hero of ballads in the hills. He was tried and executed on the 13th February and his body buried secretly near the Wana Post in a place where there is no probability of a *Ziarat* [shrine] being erected over his grave.[34]

'He met his death', Howell records, 'in a resolute spirit. Indeed he was exultant and spent his last half-hour in the cell blackening his eyelids with collyrium [probably kohl] as young bucks do amongst the Mehsuds, to adorn himself for the houris of paradise.'[35]

Some officials thought that Harman's murder was part of a wider conspiracy in the Mehsud ranks to murder all the British officers at Wana and hand the fort and its contents over to Mullah Powindah. It could even have been part of a wider plot involving some of the Wazirs as well, the Madda Khels in particular.[36] At the time there was considerable excitement in the Upper Tochi where a mullah had been claiming as an ally a supernatural being known as a *shahpirai* (literally 'king of the fairies'). Some Madda Khels, it was reported, believed that the *shahpirai* had an army of jinns or genies at his disposal, who were ready to support the mullah in attacking the British.[37] However, the British could find no proof of any conspiracy, and although twenty other Mehsuds were arrested and sent to Dera Ismail Khan for trial, only seven were convicted on comparatively minor charges and imprisoned; the other 400 in the militia were discharged. As for Mullah Powindah, the investigators found no evidence that he had been directly involved, and no action was taken against him.[38]

Other attempts to assassinate British officers at this time included an attack on 18 January 1905 on an officer from the 59th Sind rifles, Captain Browne. He was playing golf within the boundary of the cantonment in Bannu, when a young Sardi Khel Jani Khel Wazir attacked him with an axe, but was overpowered before he could kill him. The Wazir explained that a few days ago a mullah living in his village (in British territory some miles south of Bannu) had encouraged him and some others to murder any Englishman (*sic*) they might meet and that that was why he had come to Bannu.³⁹

In spite of these attacks Deane thought that as a whole the Mehsuds were reasonably contented and wished to remain on good terms with the government. Since the end of the blockade in spring 1902, they had given little trouble. Some of them were dissatisfied, he admitted. First, there were men who had been dismissed from the militia. Second there were Bruce's 'old Maliks'. Although they were now receiving a special additional allowance, they did not think it was enough and were 'talking among themselves of seceding en masse to Kabul'.⁴⁰ He doubted that they would do so, but the fact that they blamed the mullah for the reduction in their allowances meant that they might try and make trouble for which he could be blamed. Third there was Mullah Powindah himself. Deane thought he had behaved well since his trial in 1902, surrendering criminals and deserters who sought shelter with him, exerting a peaceful influence and at times sending useful advice to the Wana officials. But he accepted that the mullah was an ambitious man, who might resort to anti-British activities in order to retain his influence.⁴¹ Presumably in the hope of retaining his goodwill, in 1905 the local officials told the mullah that they would present him with a tent and a gun.

Crump and the Mullah

In May 1905 Leslie Crump replaced Johnston as Political Agent at Wana (he had stepped in again after Bowring's murder). At the Mehsud allowance jirga in October he presented the mullah with the promised tent and gun. Other Mehsuds accused him of being too friendly with the government and said he was a *kafir*. The mullah decided to show that they were wrong by arranging another assassination. The victim was another army officer, Captain Donaldson, the Brigade Major at Bannu. His assassin was Gullajan, a Sultanai Shabi Khel Mehsud, a close relative of Mullah Powindah and an ex-militiaman. His motive was 'fanaticism and revenge', Crump reported.⁴² In mid-November 1905 Gullajan swore on the Qur'an in the presence of a mullah named Ikhlas at Hassu Khel in Dawar that he would kill 'a Sahib'.⁴³ He went down to Bannu, accompanied by Kalagai Patanai Shabi Khel, one of his uncle Pashakai's servants.⁴⁴ On 16 November he lay in wait behind a low wall just outside the cantonment and shot Captain Donaldson as he rode by. He died some hours later. Gullajan was arrested and executed under the terms of the *Murderous Outrages Act*. Kalagai returned home.⁴⁵

In the autumn of 1905 Minto replaced Curzon as the viceroy. In a farewell letter Curzon claimed that his frontier policy had worked well. The frontier was quiet; frontier expenditure had been considerably reduced, and no punitive expeditions had been undertaken on his watch. This was not quite true; for example, as we have seen, there had been a number of destructive incursions into Mehsud territory in 1901. His successor was not convinced. He even went so far as to say that 'official reports had been ... had been deliberately slanted to throw a favourable light on the Frontier situation'.[46]

As regards responsibility for the suicidal attacks, Crump blamed Mullah Powindah for Donaldson's murder, and for Bowring and Harman's deaths too. He wanted the government to demand the surrender of five of Gullajan's relatives, confiscate the Sultanai Alizais' land in British territory, stop the Shabi Khels' and Garrerais' allowances and impose a fine of Rs.25,000 on the Mahsuds as a whole. If the Mehsuds did not hand the relatives over within a month, the British should take over their country. Deane agreed, and Minto accepted that any military action should 'take the form of military occupation of the Mehsud country (lying as it does within the Durand line, the term annexation scarcely applies)', but did not think there would be any need to do more than establish a loose control of it.[47] The secretary of state, Morley, on the other hand, would not commit himself to permanent occupation, but was willing to sanction an expedition.[48] As a result there was no military response.

The British announced their terms to the Mehsuds at a jirga held at the end of February 1906.[49] These included the surrender of Umar Khan (one of Gullajan's maternal uncles), his paternal uncles (Dalagai, Narmi Khan and Pashakai) and Pashakai's servant Kalagai, who had accompanied Gullajan on his murderous visit to Bannu. Mullah Powindah was married to Pashakai's niece.[50] Another paternal uncle, Mekan Khan, was a mullah who lived in Bannu, and he was arrested on 13 January 1906 (he died in prison). Mullah Powindah arranged for Dalagai, Narmi Khan and Kalagai's surrender; he brought them in himself with their hands tied together. He also surrendered one of his own sons and three of his nephews, as well as Pashakai's three-year-old son (with their hands bound too). Narmi Khan was an elderly man who did not actually live in the same house as Gullajan, and he was soon released (as were the children). One of the maliks, Mir Dil Mal Khel Manzai Alizai, surrendered Umar Khan on 2 April. In the meantime Crump had even suggested he might visit the mullah at his home in Marobi, but Deane would not allow this.[51]

Only Pashakai remained at large. He was a relative of the mullah and had taken part in the 1894 attack on Bruce's camp at Wana. He was described as 'an old ally in evil and a man capable of the bitterest revenge'; even the mullah seems to have been frightened of him.[52] A jirga was held at Kaniguram at the end of May to discuss the situation, and the consensus was that he should turn himself in. He was almost certainly still hiding at Marobi (in a cellar under his house), and the jirga sent men to find him. He was warned and escaped. At a second jirga a few days later Mullah Powindah was made to take an oath on seven copies of the Qur'an that he had not concealed him and did not know where he was. Everyone else took the oath as well, and a deputation was sent to the political agent. They offered to burn Pashakai's house and arrest him and his sons if they found him in Mehsud territory. In fact Pashakai was still there, moving from place to place to avoid capture. In May a tribal force burned his house, destroyed his crops and scattered stones over his fields. Crump and Deane agreed that there was no point in taking things any further and that payment of the Mehsud allowances should resume in October. In October Dalagai, Kalagai and Umar Khan were tried by jirga in Dera Ismail Khan for Captain Donaldson's murder. Dalagai was acquitted, and the other two were each sentenced to fourteen years imprisonment.[53] Pashakai never surrendered.

At about this time, Crump also made two other recommendations. First, since the government was unwilling to annex Mehsud territory as he had advocated, he revived the plan of giving Mullah Powindah land in British territory. There was no point in a 'half-and-half policy', he said: either we should be friends with him or not. Since 1902 the Mullah had managed to prevent organized raiding, and he could equally well stop the suicidal attacks on British officers and officials if he tried. Such a gift might encourage him to do so. Moreover, changing tack, Crump thought it would diminish his influence. It might even encourage the mullah's enemies to try and kill him (perhaps he was hoping that this would be the outcome).[54]

By then Deane had changed his mind about the mullah and objected to the land grant. Because he had been involved in the murder of two British officers, as well as other 'fanatical movements', giving him land would be a bad precedent and betray an undignified 'desire for peace at all costs'.[55] Minto, however, thought it worth trying. Mullah Powindah was 'one of those friends, of whom there have been examples in the history of British rule, whose services are worth buying', he wrote; breaking with him altogether might have serious consequences.[56]

In this connection one issue that arose for frontier Muslims was whether it was acceptable for them, and especially mullahs, to accept allowances from a non-Muslim government, like the British one. It was one of several questions that came up during a public debate between the Mullah Hamzullah and his former teacher, the Karbogha Mullah, who belonged to different mullah factions, held in May 1906. It took place in independent territory along the Kurram River. It was a substantial gathering that continued for several days and was attended by several hundred men. There was 'much involved' theological discussion in which, according to one report, Mullah Hamzullah demonstrated his superior understanding of Islam, and the Karbogha Mullah was discredited.[57]

Further changes to the allowances

Crump's second suggestion was that allowances should be redistributed again, this time in favour of the 'old maliks'. These men were, he suggested, the government's friends in the tribe, and 'when called upon to act for Government by leading the tuman against the Mullah at Kaniguram, they responded whole-heartedly'.[58] He referred to the election of the *wakils* in 1903 as a farce and argued that the changes Johnston had made to Merk's original plan had not achieved the aim of bringing the old maliks and other influential men who had been left out in 1902 into the system. Those who received the special maliki allowances were still those through whom the *tumani* (tribal) allowance was paid. Moreover names had been added to the list in the meantime, and it had grown to 1,558. Consequently, he claimed, the old maliks were 'discontented, the jirga ... as unwieldy as ever and expensive as ever and there [was still] ... no regular machinery for dealing with the tribe'. As a result, officials found that when an issue involving the whole tribe came up, they had to deal with Mullah Powindah and pay the old maliks extra to deal with 'matters concerning the sections'.[59]

Crump argued that Merk's 1902 settlement had been based on a misunderstanding of Mehsud political organization; in fact the old maliks were the 'natural leaders of the tribe', just as Bruce had claimed.[60] Crump planned to continue paying Rs.54,000 p.a. through the *mohtabars* at the half-yearly jirgas, but in order to strengthen what he called 'the oligarchy of really efficient maliks', he intended to reduce the number of men who received a share of the Rs.16,000 maliki money; the recipients would only include men who were reliable and helped him to manage the Mehsuds, and they would form what he called 'a wieldy jirga for working purposes'.[61] He intended to continue paying Rs.54,000 p.a. through the *mohtabars* at the half-yearly jirgas.

Deane objected to this as well. Although disillusioned with the mullah, he thought that the way that the majority of Mehsuds had behaved since 1902 showed that the current distribution of allowances was achieving its purpose, and he could see no reason to change it.⁶² There was nothing wrong with the way the maliki allowances had been reallocated in 1903.⁶³ No one of importance (whether old malik or *mohtabar*) had been left out. He admitted that the number of *wakils* to whom allowances were paid was larger than had originally been anticipated, but they were 'the real heads of the little groups which constitute Mehsud society'; the current arrangements enabled minor problems to be sorted out with these men.⁶⁴ Without them this would be more difficult. Nor were the old maliks dissatisfied, as Crump claimed. The 1903 arrangements had been a success. Apart from the murders of British officers, for which Mullah Powindah was responsible, they had worked well. The relationship with the Mehsuds as a whole was as good as could be expected under the circumstances, he concluded, and he was probably right.

In spite of Deane's opposition, Crump was given permission to introduce the changes. He actually asked the mullah to help the political tehsildar draw up the new list of allowances, presumably hoping to make him share responsibility for their redistribution. The mullah saw the danger. He agreed to help but did his best to ensure that the new arrangements left as many men dissatisfied as possible.⁶⁵ The new list was given to the various Mehsud sections to look at and approve in consultation with him at a jirga held at Sarwakai in October 1906.⁶⁶ At the jirga Crump announced that he intended to reduce the number of recipients of maliki allowances from 1,588 to about 300. He also said that from now on the *tumani* allowances would be paid to the Alizais, Bahlolzais and Shaman Khels separately at sectional jirgas; gatherings of thousands of Mehsuds would no longer be needed.⁶⁷ At the jirga Crump also announced the grant of land to the mullah. It caused some surprise, and particularly annoyed Kalagai's relatives. (He had been surrendered by the mullah after Donaldson's murder.)⁶⁸

In practice the changes were a step back in the direction of Bruce's maliki system, and they were unpopular with many Mehsuds. More than a thousand men lost their extra allowance. The payments were not generous, but being in receipt of one was regarded as a mark of status, and it was humiliating to have it taken away. The new arrangements sent them 'straight into opposition', Johnston reported.⁶⁹ Nor did Crump keep to *nikat*, the tribal tariff for the distribution of rewards and allowances in reallocating the maliki allowances. Instead he fixed different levels of allowance for different maliks according to 'the same arbitrary system' as that adopted by Bruce in 1894. This made them less likely to cooperate with each other, 'as each man refused to admit the superiority of another drawing larger allowances, especially when, as was frequently the case, the superiority was not a fact'.[70] Indeed, in spite of their favourable treatment, at the jirga the maliks still refused to take responsibility for the remaining Mehsuds in the South Waziristan militia (the Shabi Khels had all been dismissed), who were discharged. It was, Deane thought, a sign of the maliks' weakness.[71] Disappointed, the viceroy wondered whether it was too late to withhold the grant of land.[72]

In the meantime the relationship with Afghanistan remained difficult. This was partly because Amir Habibullah had less control than his father over the anti-British group at the Afghan court, led by his younger brother Sardar Nasrullah Khan. Nasrullah was a *hafiz* (someone who has memorized the Qur'an) and 'extremely Anglophobic'; unlike his brother, Habibullah, who wore western-style clothes, he wore traditional dress.[73] This group gained some influence in Kabul and did its best to support the anti-British frontier mullahs, including Mullah Powindah, Mullah Hamzullah, the Lala Pir and Mullah Karbogha.[74] Around 1906 Nasrullah, together with his protégé, the Andar Ghilzai Haji Abdur Razaq, and a man referred to as Safar the Nazir, devised a scheme for 'co-ordinating all anti-British elements among the tribes on the British side of the Durand Line and for converting them into a first line of offence and defence for Afghanistan'.[75] Nasrullah instructed Lala Pir to use his influence to encourage his Wazir and Mehsud contacts to promote anti-British activities, such as raiding by the Khost outlaws and other men from Waziristan.[76] The Afghan government had recently given some Mehsud outlaws, including Mianji, land at Ghozba in Afghanistan, and it continued to invite Mehsuds and Wazirs to settle there. Jaggar, who had taken part in the 1894 attack on Bruce's camp at Wana and was by now a well-known raider, joined the Ghozba settlers in November 1906.

In the autumn of 1906 the mullah himself went to Kabul where he was made welcome. Amir Habibullah praised him to his face; he was referred to as 'Ghazi Mullah' and given several thousand rupees.[77] Nevertheless it did not all go his way. As noted above, many Mehsuds were upset by the announcement that the British were giving him land, and several attempts on his life followed. For instance, to repay the mullah for surrendering Kalagai to the British, his cousin, Nazar Din, shot and wounded him in his mosque at Marobi. Nazar Din lived in Raji Gul Shabi Khel's house, and in retaliation the mullah's Shabi Khel supporters burned it down.[78] Raji Gul's family fled to North Waziristan, where in turn they looted a convoy coming from Kabul with supplies for the mullah.

The failure of Crump's strategy

Crump reported in January 1907 that few people were visiting the mullah and that his influence was declining. In April the Mehsuds came in and accepted their allowances.[79] Deane doubted that the mullah had suffered a knock-out blow. He was right.[80] The mullah was down but not out, and in the spring of 1907 he began to preach jihad and *ghaza* again. In April he sent out five *sheikhs* to kill British officers, and in May he began to work actively against the maliks.[81] Thanks partly to the readjustment of the allowances, majority Mehsud opinion was beginning to swing round in his favour again, and there were more raids, kidnappings and attempts to kill Britons. The British officers were reported to be 'practically prisoners in the Militia forts.'[82]

'The Mulla', Crump complained, 'is frankly impossible; if he has full power in the tribe, he retains it by instigating fanatical murders: if he has not, he discredits his rivals by instigating raids'.[83] The attempt to discredit him by giving him land had failed. Redistribution of the allowances had not made the maliks strong enough to deal with him, and the Mehsuds remained divided between his supporters and those of the maliks.[84] Part of the answer, Crump thought, was for the government to find work for the Mehsud men. It should give them more land in the administered areas and employ more of them in the militias and the regular army. It should also put pressure on the amir; as long as he encouraged Mehsuds and Wazirs to move to Afghanistan, giving 'land and honour to these pilgrims from the country of the Unbelievers' as Crump put it, it would be impossible to stop the raiding.[85]

The situation was also affected by international developments. Early in 1907 the amir had visited India. The amir had been pleased with his reception, and the visit had gone well, but the signing by Britain and Russia of a Convention in August upset him. The Convention delineated British and Russian spheres of influence in Persia, Tibet and Afghanistan. Russia recognized Afghanistan as outside its sphere of influence, while the British undertook not to interfere in its internal administration nor annex any part of it. The amir's approval was supposedly required for it to come into effect, but he was not consulted during the negotiations, and he refused to give it. The British decided to ratify the Convention anyway. Habibullah responded by allowing Sardar Nasrullah and his agent, Haji Abdur Razaq, to step up their anti-British activities along the frontier.[86] In August Lala Pir visited Waziristan, passing through the mullah's village of Marobi on his way to Shakai. The Wazirs mostly remained faithful to Mullah Hamzullah and did not take much notice of him. He returned to

Marobi where many Mehsuds gathered, and according to Crump, 'the usual lies were repeated, drums were beaten and songs of *ghaza* and *jehad* sung'.[87] Mullah Powindah sent out two more assassins, but they were both intercepted.

In fact the amir's call to jihad proved so popular that the British put pressure on the amir to suppress the movement. In 1908–9 Habibullah did reign it in, and arrested and executed some of those responsible for inciting the border mullahs and their anti-British activities, and largely withdrew his support for them (although his brother continued to keep in touch with them and invite them to Kabul).[88] Meanwhile Crump had written a long report in which he gave his reasons for thinking that the Mullah was at least partly to blame for the murders of the British officers in 1904–5, and for other difficulties. Again he and Deane recommended a punitive expedition.[89] Because the Anglo-Russian Convention had only recently been signed, the viceroy and Lord Kitchener, the commander-in-chief in India, were anxious to avoid one. Violence on the frontier might create difficulties for the amir.[90] Minto suggested again that if and when it did come to the use of force, rather than sending another expedition, it would be better to occupy Mehsud territory properly and establish military posts and improve roads. Morley, the secretary of state, continued to oppose occupation and refused to allow it. Crump was informed that he should stop the allowances and take away Mullah Powindah's land grant and have no contact with him.[91]

The mullah continued to despatch 'fanatical emissaries'.[92] One of them was Gulband, a Langar Khel Alizai from Kot Langar Khel, who had previously served in the militia as well as taking part in raids. The Mullah summoned him and a fellow raider, Muhammad Akbar Shaman Khel, to meet him in Marobi. He took them into his mosque, closed the door and placed a copy of the Qur'an before them. He explained that Kabul, Sabir and Gullajan had been his *sheikhs*: 'You cannot see,' he said, 'but I see them now, living in paradise, tended lovingly by the houris and they are masters of the dainty fruits.' He went on to say that he was particularly anxious to have Crump murdered. This would help him to re-establish his authority in the hills and make the government take him seriously. He had twice sent his sheikhs and nephews to do so, but they had failed. Now it was up to Gulband and Muhammad Akbar. They should try and kill Crump or some other sahib or the Political tehsildar. Here is part of the translation of Gulband's revealing statement:

> The Mullah said that, if this was done, the kingdoms of both the worlds would be ours; I said that I was a lonely man, having no parents alive, no house or other relations, except a brother named Gulaband who four years ago had been

imprisoned for seven years. Pray for us to crown our efforts with success as I preferred death to life. The Mullah said – 'If you die the houris will serve you and if you return alive then consider me your father; I will arrange for your marriage and maintenance and my sons and nephews will love you as their brother and better than their lives. In addition to these you will make a name amongst the Pathans for taking the revenge of your brother Gulaband. I have a great confidence in your bravery and am sure that you will be successful.'[93]

Gulband found work as an escort for a Mehsud contractor and went to Wana, where he was arrested and imprisoned before he could kill anyone. The fact that he was a lonely man with no family, apart from a brother in prison, probably made him more susceptible to the mullah's manipulation.[94] Whereas the first Mehsud suicide attacks had been carried out by young men in their late teens or early twenties, it seems that older men who were described by the British as common cut-throats and professional criminals also began to participate.[95] They all seem to have been inspired by a mixture of motives. They almost certainly wanted to express their opposition to the British presence in their homeland. Sometimes they wanted to demonstrate their courage and uphold the reputation of the particular group to which they belonged and hoped to leave behind a name for their bravery. If the contemporary British reports are to be believed, beliefs about the sexual satisfaction that they would enjoy in paradise also played a part. Dale suggests that psychological and sociological factors have to be taken into account in order to understand why some individuals take part in suicidal attacks. But at the same time, he suggests, it would be wrong to see all the attacks as having been carried out by 'psychologically aberrant or sociologically marginal individuals ... for ultimately they were religious acts and were thought to serve the interests of the community'.[96] This may well have been the case in Waziristan too.

5

Death of Mullah Powindah and the First World War

We saw in Chapter 4 that Kalagai's relatives blamed Mullah Powindah for surrendering him to the British. In the autumn of 1907 the mullah reached a temporary settlement with them. They 'did nanawatai'; following the established procedure for reconciliation and pardon, they sent eight sheep, seven women, seven copies of the Qur'an and Rs.1,000 to the Shabi Khel jirga. Under safe conduct, the jirga took them to see the mullah. The women begged him to forgive the men who had shot at him. The mullah agreed, returned the women and the Qur'ans, had the sheep killed and held a general feast of reconciliation. 'So this chance of the tribe getting rid of their evil adviser seems to have finally ended,' as Crump put it.[1] The family was able to return to Marobi. However, the feud was not over and further killings took place on both sides. Raji Gul and his family fled again and did not return until after the mullah's death in 1913.[2]

Meanwhile, in October 1907 Mullah Powindah sent a petition addressed to the viceroy asking for Crump to be removed. If he stayed, he would 'bring about a war between the British and the Mehsuds for nothing'; 'for the sake of God and Christ the Innocent', it continued, 'do not wage war against us'.[3] In November the mullah went to Kabul again; this time he returned with Rs.7,000 and 2,000 cartridges.[4] He continued to send out suicide attackers. The Mullah's *sheikhs*, and some Abdur Rahman Khels, also carried out a number of raids into the Tochi and Dera Ismail Khan districts. Some were very profitable; in one case the raiders got away with as much as Rs.30,000.[5] In October the mullah tried to get one of Crump's escorts, an Abdur Rahman Khel named Brag, to kill him, but failed.[6]

Raiding continued during the spring of 1908. It was very difficult to deal with. The raiders 'lie hid by day; they move with extreme caution at night; they are popular heroes, and information is not willingly given; they are feared for their weapons, their skill, and their ruthlessness, and the penalty for informing against them is mutilation or worse'.[7] In March 1908 they made another attempt to kill Crump. They found out that he and the political tehsildar would be travelling from Sarwakai to Murtaza on 13 March through the Khuzma Nullah. In fact only Crump's bearer and the tehsildar's *muharrir* made the journey on that day. The bandits intercepted them. They shot the bearer, who was recovering from pneumonia and still very weak, several times, stripped him naked and disembowelled him. They shot the *muharrir*, a Pashtun, in the thigh, and he bled to death. Crump ordered an immediate *barampta* of Mehsuds, and 379 men and 1,854 head of cattle were seized. Morley seems to have been more shocked by the *barampta* rather than the actual attack; it savoured, he said, 'unpleasantly of the forward frontier school'.[8]

Deane held a jirga of maliks at Tank in April 1908 and told them that the allowances would be withheld and those for 1908–9 cancelled. Once again he requested permission for a punitive expedition. This time Minto agreed, but Morley did not.[9] Mullah Powindah held a counter-jirga at Kaniguram and called on the Mehsuds not to make any agreements with the government except through him. In June 1908 Deane collapsed and died after a short illness and was succeeded by Sir George Roos-Keppel. By this time Crump was thoroughly disillusioned. Frustrated by his experience with Mullah Powindah, he wrote that 'no Mulla of Islam as interpreted on the North-West frontier of India can be a sincere friend of a Christian Government'.[10] He went on leave and was replaced by Captain R. A. Lyall. Roos-Keppel created a new post of resident in Waziristan in order to improve the British management of it; John Donald, who had first served in Waziristan during the 1890s, was the first incumbent.[11]

Ignoring Mullah Powindah again

Following Donald's appointment as resident, British officials returned to the policy of ignoring Mullah Powindah as far as possible. Some Mehsuds continued to make things difficult for them. In 1908 Mianji and his band played a leading role in three serious attacks. In one they killed twelve soldiers and in another looted property worth around Rs.50,000.[12] During the third attack Mianji was killed, and raiding became less frequent. Donald did not invite the mullah to the large jirga he held at Sarwakai in August 1908. In December he instructed the Mehsud maliks to hand in sixty rifles as security, and they did so in January 1909. In March he held another very large jirga at Tank, this one attended by more than 7,000 Mehsuds. At this he paid the allowances, allowed the rifles to be redeemed at Rs.250 each and settled various outstanding cases.[13] These jirgas were tricky affairs. According to one account, for example,

> Some 2 years ago [1907] the then PA [Captain Patterson] was holding a jirga at Jandola for the discussion of affairs and the transaction of business. All was going well and everyone appeared happy. Suddenly some man rushed up shouting that the Sahib had arrested the Mulla [Powindah]. In a moment all was changed. The jirga rushed for their rifles, the troops in the fort and on the PA's side stood to their arms, and for a few seconds both sides faced each other with loaded rifles and fingers on the triggers. One shot fired on either side and there would have been a general blaze and enormous loss of life.[14]

Nevertheless Donald appeared to be regaining the initiative, and the mullah's next move was to arrange an attack on the Bhittani village of Khecha near Jandola. He also promised the former *wakils* (who had lost their allowances as a result of Crump's intervention) that he would have these restored; the maliks actually offered to give theirs up. The mullah visited Kabul in August 1909 and continued to try and persuade the resident to reply to his messages, without success. In November 1909 he tried but failed to convene a jirga at Kaniguram. His influence appeared to be declining again.[15]

By this time the British were spending about Rs.1,800,000 a year in Waziristan, in addition to expenditure on the military.[16] Commenting on the British position on the frontier as a whole, the new commissioner, Roos-Keppel, referred to three unwelcome developments. In the first place, he thought, Afghan intrigue had increased, with the local Afghan authorities along the border giving asylum to 'outlaws' from the British side and encouraging them to raid on the British side of the Durand Line. Second kidnapping, especially of Hindus, had grown more frequent. Third, access to modern rifles sourced from the Persian Gulf greatly increased the frontier peoples' ability to resist British forces. Since the turn of the century the Mehsuds had reportedly acquired more than 8,000 breech-loading rifles.[17]

The changes to the distribution of the allowances that Crump had introduced in 1907 had not improved the British position. Some Mehsuds suggested that the problem was not just the allowances, but the whole direction of British policy.[18] In June 1909, for example, some maliks told Donald that their country was

> now a regular hell and in utter chaos and confusion; that British occupation of Wana had done them no good, and had indeed tended to increase the lawlessness in their country; he begged ... that Government would adopt one of the following courses: (a) occupy their country and establish good rule; (b) withdraw from Wanna (*sic*) altogether and leave them alone; or (c) allow the amir of Afghanistan to occupy and rule.[19]

In spite of Donald's efforts, the Mehsuds continued to cause problems. A large, mainly Mehsud, gang carried out several raids in 1909–10; a real battle took place near Lakki in March 1910 when Border Military Police and troops engaged with thirty-two Mehsuds. They killed Captain Stirling and six soldiers, losing eight men themselves, including one of the mullah's *sheikhs*, Kamil Shabi Khel.[20] The British were able to use sectional *baramptas* to impose some control.[21]

The extension of British influence along the Tochi River in northern Waziristan had brought British outposts much nearer the district of Khost, on the Afghan side of the Durand Line, and references to it in the British records began to increase.[22] The GOA's hold on Khost was weak, and raiding from it into the Tochi Agency and the Bannu district grew after 1907.[23] In 1910 Mangals and other inhabitants of Khost rose against the GOA, and the British were concerned that they might cross over to the British side of the Durand Line. They stationed regular troops in the Lower Tochi posts and moved the militia to Spinwam and Shewa (between Thal and Idak), where they were able to intercept raiders.[24]

Towards the end of 1910 one of Mullah Powindah's sons, Sahib Din, came in to see the political agent. He said that his father wanted to resume his friendship with the British government and to prove his willingness to cooperate had stopped all raiding by Mehsuds for the previous five months. But late in the same year a large party of Mehsuds also went to Kabul, bringing a letter from Mullah Powindah to Sardar Nasrullah. The Sardar arranged for some Wazir families to settle in Khost and receive an allowance.[25]

New allowance arrangements

In the autumn of 1910 many crops in Waziristan failed again and harvests were poor.[26] Officials were already discussing proposals for improving the British position. One suggestion was that they might recruit large numbers of Mehsuds as levies or khassadars (tribal police). This was rejected, but as we shall see it was revived in the 1920s. Merk, who was the acting chief commissioner for a time in 1910, suggested that thanks to the gradual establishment of British control over the territory around the Mehsuds' homeland,

> the natural process by which the tribe obtained a vent for its surplus population and energies has been stopped. The Mehsud allowances no doubt represent roughly what the tribe used to make out of the six-monthly Powindah loot;

but, as Mehsuds have often told us, it does not compensate for the loss of the fun and excitement of the attacks on the great Powindah caravans as they struggled through the Pass. There is no doubt that the tribe feels itself hemmed in much as if emigration were forbidden in a European country.[27]

Like Crump, he recommended further recruitment of Mehsuds for the British army. He accepted that the policy of taking them into the South Waziristan militia had not worked well, but he pointed to the progress that, thanks to the recruitment of 3,000 or 4,000 men for government service, had been made with the Afridis. Without this, he asserted, the government would have had no choice but to occupy their homeland in Tirah. He also asked if in addition the Mehsuds could be given more land in British territory, this time along the Paharpur Canal (recently opened to the north of Dera Ismail Khan, about fifty miles east of the Waziristan border). If 1,000 Mehsuds could be recruited for the army and 1,000 families settled along the Canal, he argued, the problem would be solved.[28]

The Mehsuds were not given more land, but the Indian army raised its Mehsud contingent from 2 to 10 companies, each 114 strong, distributed between 4 battalions, more than a thousand men in all.[29] Mehsuds were also given temporary work on the Khuzma road in the Gumal and the Mughal Kot road in Zhob which had been damaged by flooding; the work was allocated according to *nikat*. In addition they were employed on the narrow-gauge railway that was built at this time from Lakki, on the Kalabagh-Bannu railway line, to Tank.

Because Crump's changes to the allowance arrangements had failed to bring peace, the British officials decided to make a further change in December 1910, by increasing the number of elders or *mohtabars* who received an allowance, which meant a return to something like the system established after the Mehsud blockade.[30] Donald and his team redistributed the Rs.16,000 service allowances at an enormous and 'absolutely representative' jirga attended by 7,000 or 8,000 men.[31] In the meantime Mullah Powindah visited Kabul again, and in May 1911 Major George Dodd took over as political agent in South Waziristan.[32]

By then Hardinge had succeeded Minto as viceroy. Thanks to the Anglo-Russian Convention he felt that the Russian threat to India had largely evaporated, but he thought that what he called 'religio-national feeling' in the subcontinent was a growing danger and that an uprising on the frontier was a definite possibility. The Italian intervention in Ottoman-ruled Libya in 1911 was unpopular with Muslims in India and Afghanistan and was discussed on the frontier.[33]

As we have seen, a striking feature of British policy towards the Mehsuds since the 1880s had been its inconsistency, and it is worth asking why this was the case. Changing ideas about imperial strategy and how best to keep India secure were important. Concern over Russia's advance towards Afghanistan led to the introduction of the forward policy in the later 1880s and the demarcation of the Durand Line in the 1890s. This was the main reason for the risings of 1897 which provoked a return to a modified form of the earlier close-border policy. The death of Amir Abdur Rahman and the succession of Habibullah was another factor. Habibullah was not as ruthless as his father, nor as secure on this throne. The anti-British faction at his court, led by Sardar Nasrullah, grew stronger, and it was able to give the Mehsuds and Wazirs more support than before, making intermittent payments of money, arms and ammunition to men like Mullah Powindah, Mullah Hamzullah and Lala Pir.[34] But if the broad parameters of British policy were dictated in London and Calcutta, the frontier officials were able to play a significant role in devising ways of trying to control it. New officers were often anxious to show that they could succeed where others had failed. As we have seen, Bruce, Merk, Johnston, Crump and Donald all made changes to the arrangements they inherited from their predecessors.

1911–13 and the death of Mullah Powindah

In July 1911 Donald assembled another Mehsud jirga at which some minor changes were made to the allowances.[35] While it was being held, the mullah went back to Kabul. This time Sardar Nasrullah was not so welcoming. Muhammad Akbar Khan, the governor of Khost, accused the mullah of not having done enough to resist the rail and road development on the Waziristan border and the recent reoccupation of the posts between Thal and Idak by the Tochi militia.[36] Nevertheless the Sardar gave the mullah Rs.7,000.[37]

On his return to Waziristan he made a more determined effort to make things difficult for the British. He called on Mehsuds to stop working on building the new railway, and in February 1912 he and his followers tried unsuccessfully to organize an attack on the Sarwakai post. They managed to do some damage to the Khuzma road; a fine of Rs.10,000 was imposed and paid by the maliks.[38] Abdur Rahman Khels, Nekzan Khels and Abdullais launched some destructive raids, and the British officials continued to use sectional *baramptas* to keep them under control. In addition, they set up Conciliation Committees, composed of leading men from both sides of the administrative border. These enabled outlaws to reach settlements with the families of men they had killed or wounded and return to their homes in the administered districts; they were spared confiscation of all their property under the provision of Sections 87–88 of the Criminal Procedure Code.[39]

In March 1912 Muhammad Akbar Khan's mismanagement in Khost provoked the Mangals to revolt again. They captured several forts, defeated Afghan troops in the Altimur Pass near Gardez on the route from Kabul and besieged the governor at his headquarters in Matun.[40] The GOA removed Muhammad Akbar Khan, and the rising petered out.[41] Mullah Powindah visited Kabul again in 1912; he was given Rs.1,000 in addition to the regular allowance he was now receiving. By then the GOA was reported to be paying Rs.38,000 a year to men living in South Waziristan, most of it going to the mullah and his *sheikhs* and anti-British maliks and elders.[42]

Sardar Nasrullah continued to encourage raiding, which took on an increasingly political character. In 1913 for instance the Abdur Rahman Khel outlaws based in Ghazni carried out several raids, in all killing eight soldiers and capturing seven rifles.[43] Men living in Khost continued to cross the Durand Line and kidnap Hindus in Kohat and Bannu; in one encounter with British troops they killed Major Chrystie and two sepoys. To obtain the release of the kidnapped men, the British authorities arrested some 500 people from Khost living in British territory. The move was successful; the Hindus were recovered and the Khost men were released.[44] In June 1913, to try and enhance his authority over the Mehsuds and Wazirs, the mullah took a number of Mehsuds with him to visit the Wazirs. On the way back some Tori Khels ambushed them at Razmak and about twenty men were killed on each side.[45]

Later in October the mullah fell ill and he died on 2 November 1913. Many Mehsuds believed he had been poisoned, supposedly by his elder son, Sahib Din, at the instigation of one of the political tehsildars. To some the fact that Sahib Din fled to Tank immediately afterwards was proof of this, but there was no hard evidence. The Mehsuds held a jirga at Kaniguram, presided over by Mullah Hamzullah. Mullah Powindah's confidential secretary, Mullah Abdul Hakim, a Malikdinai Manzai Alizai, read the mullah's farewell out aloud to the gathering.[46] In it he 'exhorted [the assembled Mehsuds] … to hold their nationality intact and allow neither the British Government nor the Amir to encroach upon their country, to compose their internal differences and to give up raiding, so as to deprive Government of a convenient excuse for occupying Mehsud country'.[47] The mullah had nominated his second surviving son, Fazal Din, who was only fourteen years old, as his heir, rather than the elder son, Sahib Din, whom he regarded as being pro-British, and for the time being Mullah Abdul Hakim acted as regent.

Before looking at developments after Mullah Powindah's death, we should briefly reflect on his methods, aims and achievements. Curzon referred to him as a 'first class scoundrel', and Kitchener called him a 'pestilential priest'. Not all British officials took this view. Merk described him as 'according to his light ... what we would call a patriot',[48] and Evelyn Howell thought that his character 'cannot be judged by any standards current among Englishmen' and that 'given more malleable metal to work upon than the Mehsuds have ever afforded, and a more fortunate setting in time and place, he might well have ranked with many who are accounted great men'.[49]

The mullah was undoubtedly a charismatic personality and a talented political operator, able to convince British officials to let him take part in their negotiations with the Mehsuds at several points, and twice to persuade them that he was worth buying off with an allowance and a grant of land. As we have seen, on a number of occasions the Afghan government gave him money and arms. In competition with the maliks for influence within Waziristan, he tried to build up influence by acting as a mediator in feuds between different tribal groups (particularly between Mehsuds and Wazirs) and worked hard to create coalitions between them. He was not particularly successful in this. Nevertheless he remained the single most significant leader of Mehsud resistance to the British (and the Afghans) for more than twenty years and did more than anyone else to undermine the efforts of a series of able British officials to get a grip on the Mehsuds.

His objections to the extension of British influence into Waziristan were partly religious. However, the mullah's cause was not just a religious one. He was almost as keen to prevent the encroachment of the Muslim Afghan government as he was British intrusion, and he succeeded in keeping it at a distance while accepting support from it.[50] Some of his methods were deeply reprehensible, in particular the way he encouraged young men to carry out suicidal attacks on British officials, but he does seem to have been dedicated to the cause of preserving Mehsud independence as well as increasing his own influence. He played a significant role, but his authority was largely confined to the Mehsuds, and he lacked the wider appeal of some other more or less contemporary religious leaders on the frontier such as the Hadda mullah.[51]

After the mullah's death, Mehsuds and Wazirs continued to attack British officials and officers. In January 1914 a sepoy in the South Waziristan militia killed the second in command, Captain Butler.[52] Two months later, on

12 April 1914, there was a particularly serious incident. A Mehsud, Sarfaraz Malikshahi Aimal Khel Bahlolzai, shot dead three British officers and three men from the Frontier Constabulary as they sat in the garden of the political agent's bungalow in Tank. The British victims were the political agent, Major Dodd, Captain Brown, second in command of the South Waziristan militia, and Lieutenant Hickie of the Royal Artillery. Sarfaraz was almost immediately shot dead in turn. The gun he used had been a gift from Dodd himself.

Since 1910 Sarfaraz (from a 'good family') had been one of Dodd's orderlies.[53] While on leave in 1913 and early in 1914, he had spent some time with Fazal Din and Abdul Hakim, suggesting that religious motives played a part in the murders. Fazal Din might have arranged it in order to show that he deserved to inherit his father's authority. But there is another possible explanation. As well as being Dodd's orderly, Sarfaraz was a road-building contractor. He had arranged for some work to be done on the Gumal road. Dodd suspected that the workmen were involved in sheep stealing and had recently stopped a cheque for Rs.339 in payment. Sarfaraz did not find out until he came back to Tank on 11 April. The next day he tried unsuccessfully to persuade Dodd to allow the cheque to be cashed. This may have provoked his murderous attack.[54] Some Abdur Rahman Khel men were probably involved in setting it up as well. They wanted to take revenge for the murder of a former Abdur Rahman Khel raider, Muhammad Jan, in suspicious circumstances.[55]

The political tehsildar seized four Malikshahis who happened to be at Sarwakai when the shooting took place – Sarfaraz's eldest brother, Silla Khan, and three influential men. Two others were arrested at Wana. They were all sent to Dera Ismail Khan as hostages.[56] The arrests gave Donald (at this point the acting chief commissioner while Roos-Keppel was on leave) a certain amount of leverage. He met the Mehsud jirga in May and demanded that they surrender for trial by jirga three of Sarfaraz's other relatives – two of his brothers, Markai and Mobin, and a cousin, Nambai, as well as three Abdur Rahman Khels – Brag, Mirza Khan and Sherdad, all suspected of involvement in the murder. The jirga asked for time to consider their response. In the meantime the Mehsud allowances were suspended. At a follow-up meeting with Donald in August the Bahlolzais said they would not give up any of the wanted men.[57]

Once again British officials raised the possibility of sending troops into Waziristan, but the viceroy, Hardinge, and the secretary of state, Crewe, did not think that an expedition was the right response. Donald agreed; he thought it would be very difficult to attack the Malikshahis and Abdur Rahman Khels without provoking the Mehsuds as a whole. The Malikshahis were too scattered and there would be no way of attacking the Abdur Rahman Khels without warning, and they would be able to retreat to the Baddar Algad in western Waziristan near the Afghan border.[58] It has been suggested that if the British had promptly avenged the murders in Tank, they might have saved themselves a great of trouble in future.[59] Given the deteriorating international situation it is not clear that the British had the resources to do so; moreover a punitive expedition just before the First World War would have made it more difficult for the amir to ensure that Afghanistan stayed neutral during it.

Waziristan and Afghanistan during the First World War

As noted above, in 1910 the Mehsud quota in the Indian army had been raised from 2 to 10 companies, each 114 strong; mainly to make them easier to manage, they were distributed between 4 battalions.[60] Mehsuds were quick to enlist. The results were mixed. There was a serious incident on 20 November 1914. The Mehsuds in the 130th Baluchis were upset because Hayat Khan Manzai Alizai had been passed over for promotion to Subahdar Major in favour of an older man, an Afridi, and another Mehsud shot and killed their commanding officer on the quayside in Bombay. The regiment was diverted to Rangoon, where there were more problems, and three Pashtun companies were disarmed.[61] Other Mehsuds, those who served with the 124th and 129th Baluchis for instance, fought bravely in France and then in East Africa, but there were many desertions. All the Mehsuds were discharged at the end of the war and no more were recruited for some years.[62]

In September 1914 a large Mehsud deputation went to Kabul; it was probably not a coincidence that at the same time a number of Ahmadzai Wazirs led by Mullah Hamzullah also visited the city. Sardar Nasrullah welcomed them and gave them far more money than ever before – Rs.21,500. When they returned, a meeting was held at Kaniguram attended by Lala Pir at which he and Fazal Din's party tried to persuade the Mehsuds to lead a lashkar against the British. However, Lala Pir upset them by encouraging them to petition the amir to take over Waziristan, and the jirga took no action.[63]

In November 1914 the Ottoman sultan, Mehmed V, had proclaimed a jihad and entered the war on the German side. Many Sunni Muslims had come to regard the Ottoman sultan as the caliph and as such having authority not just over those in his empire but all Muslims. The sultan wrote to the amir to encourage him to join the war. Some members of the Afghan ruling elite believed the government should do so, and a majority of Afghans agreed with them.⁶⁴ The amir's view was that that to join the Ottomans would encourage Britain and Russia to invade Afghanistan. He had made an agreement with the British, he said, and it would be a breach of his religious duty to renounce it.⁶⁵

At this point, men from some Bahlolzai sections, Abdullais in particular, were preoccupied with the struggle with the Tori Khel Utmanzai Wazirs, and they continued to encroach on the latter's land around Razmak. Later in 1914 Lala Pir tried to mediate between them, but without success; early in 1915 Mehsuds reaped the Wazirs' spring crops and sowed an autumn one.⁶⁶ Afghan mediation prevented fighting between the two groups, and a peace agreement was reached, according to which the Tori Khels would reoccupy Razmak and five towers that the Mehsuds had built at Spinkamar would be destroyed. Meanwhile Nana Khel Bahlolzais and Shabi Khel Alizais continued to raid into the administered areas.⁶⁷

The amir's brother Sardar Nasrullah, as we have seen, had built up connections with a number of leading frontier mullahs and maliks, periodically giving them money and ammunition and encouraging them to resist British influence along the border. After the Ottomans joined the war, he stepped up his efforts. In 1915 for instance he gave Lala Pir Rs.30,000 to be distributed among Wazirs and Mehsuds.⁶⁸ Raids continued and became more frequent, with attacks extending nearly as far as the Indus.⁶⁹ The Mehsuds were reported to be 'harrying [the] Dera Ismail Khan [District] to an extent never known before'.⁷⁰

Throughout the war the amir continued to face considerable pressure from various quarters to join the Ottomans and Germany. But he kept his nerve and did not give in. He had some stressful moments, particularly after the arrival in Kabul in October 1915 of a German mission led by an army officer, First Lieutenant Oskar von Niedermayer and a diplomat, Werner Otto von Hentig. They stayed there for eight months, hoping to persuade the amir to give up his neutral stance and sign a treaty of friendship, and encourage anti-British activity along the frontier if not to attack India.⁷¹ The amir was in a difficult position. On 24 January 1916 he did actually sign a draft treaty with the Germans, but it was a delaying tactic, and on 29 January he held a durbar with tribal chiefs and representatives from across Afghanistan in which he announced that the country would continue to remain neutral.⁷² News of the surrender of the British force at Kut on the Euphrates in Iraq in April 1916 worried him too. The British raised his subsidy by two lakhs, and King George V wrote him a personal letter in which he said how gratified he was by the amir's attitude.⁷³ In the end the members of the German mission left Kabul in May 1916, having failed to win him over.

Men from India itself were also ready to take advantage of the opportunities the war seemed to offer.[74] Some anti-British Muslims in India had a rather romantic and idealistic view of the frontier as a place where Muslims were free to practise Islam properly. The Deobandi scholar, Maulana Husain Ahmad Madni, for instance, described frontier society as 'the ideal of a religiously observant society because mullas were part of their institutions of justice and social order'.[75] Two leading Indian nationalists who had links with the mainly Sikh anti-British Ghadar (meaning 'rebellion') party had accompanied the German mission. They were Muhammad Barakatullah and Rajah Mahendra Pratap. In October 1915 Obeidullah Sindhi, a Sikh convert to Islam, joined them in Kabul. They set up a provisional government of India, and they stayed there after Niedermayer and Hentig left.[76] Obeidullah and Maulana Husain Ahmad Madni, in cooperation with the chancellor of the Deoband seminary, Maulana Mahmudul Hasan (also known as Sheikhul Hind, d.1920), devised a plan to liberate India from the frontier. Reprising Sayyid Ahmed Bareilly's earlier initiative, their aim was to re-establish Mujahidin bases at Chamarkand in the Bajaur area and Asmast in Buner as 'political and military centres for the organisation of the religious warriors, or ... Jamaat-i-Mujahidin'.[77] Maulana Mahmudul Hasan had gone to the Hejaz in 1915 and obtained a proclamation of jihad from the Ottoman governor, Ghalib Pasha, and copies of the document, known as the *Ghalibnama*, were widely distributed along the frontier as well as in India itself.[78] But plans for a widespread anti-British conspiracy (known as the Silk Letter conspiracy) were undermined when messages between Obeidullah and Maulana Mahmudul Hasan and Maulana Madni came to light in August 1916. The British arrested the two Maulanas and two of their associates and sent them to a prison camp in Malta.[79]

To return to the Waziristan border, at the beginning of the war, the British experienced some difficulties with men from Khost. In the autumn of 1914 they had tried to close the border with it. Encouraged by a mullah known as the Lewanai Faqir, Zadrans and other men from Khost formed a lashkar, crossed the Durand Line and looted and partly burned the Miranshah bazaar in the Tochi on the night of 28 November, before being driven off.[80] In January 1915 as many as 10,000 men from Khost, mainly Zadrans but also Tannis, Mirzais and others, crossed into the Tochi valley. In fact, rather than fighting, some of them may have hoped to bring pressure on the government to open the border by entering British territory en masse; some members of the lashkar referred to practical grievances including the fact that they could no longer visit the Tochi. But the younger men provoked a clash with the militia, which drove the lashkar back across the border (as many as 200 members of it were killed).[81] Late in March the British repulsed a third incursion.[82]

The British still wanted the Mehsuds to surrender the three Abdur Rahman Khels and three Malikshahis suspected of having been involved in Dodd's murder. But they had few troops to spare at this point, and none trained in mountain warfare. In fact the government was concerned that there might be a full-scale Mehsud invasion and was anxious to avoid provoking one. This was probably the reason why Donald decided against imposing a full-scale *barampta* on the Mehsuds.[83] Some additional troops were sent to Tank, but their commanding officers adopted what Hardinge referred to disparagingly as 'a lenient policy of passive defence'.[84]

During the winter of 1914–15, one of the wanted men, Brag Abdur Rahman Khel, was killed in a quarrel.[85] In July 1915 the Mehsuds surrendered three of the others – the Malikshahis, Mobin, Markai and Nambai – perhaps in the hope that this would encourage the government to restart the allowances.[86] In October 1915 a jirga of the whole tribe met at Kaniguram. They sent a petition calling for this and the release of various prisoners, including the men interned after the problems with the 130th Baluchis in Rangoon.[87] The British answer was that they would have to stop raiding before there could be any negotiations.[88]

Partly in response some Mehsuds launched several serious attacks.[89] On 18 November 1915, for example, a large group, mainly Abdur Rahman Khels and Shabi Khels, attacked a picket of the 45th Sikhs near Khajuri Kach, killing a British officer and five sepoys, and wounding nine. The British finally imposed a tribal *barampta* and blockade, and in December 1915 more troops were sent to Tank, but Roos-Keppel complained about what he saw as the British failure to challenge the Mehsuds along this section of the border. He thought that the general in charge of this section was reluctant to do anything 'except on the strict defensive' and made no effort to intercept raiders.[90]

Encouraged by the mullahs and Afghan agents, during 1916 large bands of Mehsuds continued to raid along the Waziristan border. In April there were seventeen raids in the Dera Ismail Khan District alone. One raiding party was successfully intercepted, and several raiders were killed, but in the most serious incident, in the Zarwani Pass near Manjhi, seven Frontier Constabulary sepoys were killed, two wounded and seven rifles taken. Another *barampta* was ordered. This time it was more successful, and a settlement was reached with some of the sections, and their members were permitted to trade across the Waziristan border in the settled districts again. In the autumn of 1916 a jirga refused to recognize Fazal Din's right to speak for them and informed the Afghan government of this.[91]

The 1917 insurgency

In December 1916 a British force moved north from Basra and in March 1917 entered Baghdad. Amir Habibullah was relieved, reassured that in staying neutral during the war he had made the right choice. In theory success in Iraq should have strengthened the British position in Afghanistan and along the frontier, but it may have stimulated resistance because some men may have felt that they should support the sultan in his hour of need. Early in 1917 Fazal Din resumed the struggle. In February he produced a letter, supposedly from Kabul and signed by Sardar Nasrullah, but probably a forgery, encouraging the Mehsuds to 'unite and rise and promising help'.[92] Fazal Din and Mullah Hamzullah wrote to the maliks claiming that the British were planning to break a promise they had supposedly made not to repair the Spinkai-Madh Hassan road. They succeeded in persuading about 1,500 Mehsuds, mainly Nana Khels and Shabi Khels, to attack Sarwakai.[93] They surrounded the post and subjected it to heavy sniping from a nearby hill. In the fighting that followed they killed a British officer, Major Hughes, two Indian officers and eighteen sepoys, wounded ten, took eleven men as prisoners and seized thirty-eight rifles. Reportedly they cut off Hughes' head and placed it on Mullah Powindah's tomb at Marobi.[94] The British relieved the post, and the lashkar moved away. The troops returned to Tank. Representatives from some of the Mehsud sections met the political agent, James Fitzpatrick (who had taken over from Theodore Copeland) at Wana, and things seemed to be settling down.[95] In response to a request from the viceroy, the amir ordered his officers in Khost not to allow any Afghans to join the Mehsuds.[96]

But the Mehsuds were not finished yet. Emboldened by their success at Sarwakai and encouraged by Fazal Din and Hamzullah, the anti-British men carried out further attacks. On 9 April they ambushed two pickets between Khajuri Kach and Nili Kach in southern Waziristan, and killed twenty-four soldiers, wounded fifteen and captured fifteen rifles.[97] The troops returned and camped at Tanai, from where they could quickly move to the Sarwakai, Wana and the Gumal posts. They had to be supplied by camel convoys, and on 1 May the insurgents attacked another convoy in difficult terrain in the Gwaleri Pass. They killed four officers (two British and two Indian), and fifty-one men of other ranks, wounded fifty-three, and seized sixty-four rifles. Only one attacker was killed and one wounded.⁹⁸ Meanwhile raiding parties continued to move out of Waziristan, for example attacking a gathering of Hindus in Drakka, a settlement fourteen miles north-east of Tank, and killing two of them and a (Muslim) *chaukidar*.⁹⁹

The British position was rapidly deteriorating; the pro-British maliks announced that they could not continue to support the government without a guarantee that they would be protected from reprisals. The new viceroy (Chelmsford) decided that a forceful response was required.¹⁰⁰ On 10 May troops moved out from Sarwakai to attack the Mehsuds encamped between Sarwakai and the Khuzhma Sar and killed seventy men, including their leader Sher Dil Abdur Rahman Khel and the nephew of the anti-British mullah Gulabdin Shabi Khel; two British officers, one Indian officer and thirty-six rank and file also died, and 120 rifles were captured. 'Thus although our casualties have been heavy', it was reported, 'the Mahsuds too have been hard hit and there is weeping in almost every encampment throughout their country'.¹⁰¹

Towards the end of May, the amir wrote to the viceroy explaining that he did not object to the British government taking steps to punish the Mehsuds and that he had issued orders to the Afghan authorities not to allow Afghans to join them. He undertook to inform the Mehsuds that they would receive no allowances from him while they were at war with the British, but at the same time counselled conciliatory measures.¹⁰² The commander-in-chief kept back two Indian battalions due to sail for East Africa and organized a field force.¹⁰³ To begin with aeroplanes were sent out to attack Mehsud camps in Splitoi, initially with Lewis guns and then with bombs. It was one of the first occasions on which air power was used in this way on the frontier. 'Good political effect' was reported, but attacks continued. The military posts at Khajuri Kach, Wana and Sarwakai were effectively cut off.¹⁰⁴ To the north some of the Mehsuds living nearer the Tochi also joined in.¹⁰⁵ On 31 May Musa Khan Abdullai and six other Mehsuds, two of them former members of the North Waziristan militia, dressed up and made up to look like young women, inveigled their way into the Tut Narai post. They killed six of the small garrison and wounded eight ('an exploit worthy of Robin Hood').¹⁰⁶ Joined by a lashkar waiting nearby they escaped with 59 rifles and 8,000 rounds of ammunition.

The viceroy explained to the secretary of state, Austen Chamberlain, that the government needed to respond effectively to this, or trouble might well spread to other frontier areas, and Chamberlain agreed.¹⁰⁷ Troops were to carry out 'a retaliative raid' as soon as possible.¹⁰⁸ Time was of the essence because one aim would be to destroy crops, and by mid-June it was thought the Mehsuds would have threshed all their grain and hidden it in caves. In early June therefore a British force set out commanded by Major-General G. W. Benyon. Two brigades strong and supported by aircraft fitted with Lewis machine guns, it advanced to Torwam in the Khaisara, destroying crops and a number of villages at Nano and elsewhere in the valley.[109]

The Mehsuds sued for peace on 25 June, and the next day hostilities were suspended. The British demanded that they return 386 rifles that had been captured since 1 March 1917 and surrender all their prisoners and all the outlaws they were harbouring; they also demanded that the Mehsuds hand over for trial by jirga Mirza Khan and Sherdad Abdur Rahman Khel, whose surrender had first been demanded in 1914 for involvement in Major Dodd's murder. The Mehsuds accepted the terms, and in August 1917 at Sarwakai a peace agreement was concluded. Mirza Khan and Sher Dad surrendered themselves; they were given a jirga trial and acquitted. The Mehsuds handed over 291 rifles and gave hostages for the remainder. In return the government undertook not to build any new roads or posts in Mehsud country, to release many of the Mehsud political prisoners and to restore all allowances.[110] It seems that many Mehsuds particularly welcomed the undertaking not to build any new roads or posts in their territory, and the number of robberies and murders declined substantially.[111] The British employed some men in road construction in the Gumal. However, in March 1918 the Abdur Rahman Khels demanded an extra Rs.6,000 in allowances (1/42 of the whole) to compensate them for the loss of their income from raiding. This was referred to the tribe as a whole, and the other Mehsuds agreed to pay it for one year from the money they earned on road contracts.[112]

The peace settlement in August 1917 removed the immediate threat to the British position in Waziristan. The maliks argued that it was mainly thanks to them that a settlement had been reached and suggested to Fitzpatrick that their allowances should be raised. They were not paid nearly enough, they said, to work for the government and thereby incur the hostility of the rest of the tribe. Fitzpatrick and Roos-Keppel had some sympathy for them. Fitzpatrick pointed out that their allowances were much smaller than those paid to the Afridi maliks (a maximum of around Rs.220 p.a. compared with Rs.600 to Rs.1000 p.a.).[113] Although the *tuman* would not agree to give up any of its share to the maliks, there were gaps in the lists due to the deaths of a number of men. Fitzpatrick thought this would enable him to increase the amount paid to the maliks and *wakils* as well as the *tuman* (who were paid through the *wakils*), in the hope that with the tribe's consent 'a body of really influential allowance holders' would evolve.[114] 'Much has been written on the pure democracy obtaining in the Mehsud polity,' Fitzpatrick wrote, 'but the fact remains ... that, as with every Pathan tribe on this frontier, the democracy is unable to carry on work with government without its representative Maliks.'[115] Like his predecessor, Johnston, he drew attention to the practical impossibility of negotiating with gatherings of five or six thousand men; instead he divided them into eleven separate sectional groups. At this point Waziristan was reasonably quiet, although the fact that the Mehsuds had inflicted some serious losses on the British troops and raided widely during the war may well have encouraged some of them to think of further resistance. The most important reason for the troubles that followed was the assassination of Amir Habibullah in February 1919. Sardar Nasrullah proclaimed himself his successor, but Habibullah's son Amanullah seized the initiative and Sardar Nasrullah had to give way.[116] For the British the situation rapidly deteriorated again.

6

The Third Anglo-Afghan War, the 1919–20 expedition and the early 1920s

The new amir, Amanullah Khan, decided that Afghanistan should take control of its own foreign affairs and appointed his father-in-law Mahmud Tarzi (1866–1935), a modernist writer and Afghan nationalist, as foreign minister. He proclaimed a war of independence against Britain (the Third Anglo-Afghan War), issuing a call for jihad to the frontier people, and his officials contacted leading Mehsuds and Wazirs, including the Wazir officers of the North and South Waziristan militias. He gave Sardar Nasrullah's principal agent, Haji Abdur Razaq, money and sent him to Waziristan to mobilize anti-British resistance there.[1]

The war began on 6 May and lasted until 3 June 1919. The Afghans dispatched several columns towards the frontier. Only one created serious difficulties for the British, mainly because of its impact on the militias. The Afghan commander-in-chief, General Nadir Khan (from a collateral branch of the same family as the new amir), moved south-east from Matun in Khost down the Kaitu River to the north-east of Waziristan on 22 May, and by 24 May his troops were near Spinwam. Many British-side Wazirs joined them, and on 25 May the British responded by withdrawing the militiamen from the Upper Tochi posts – Datta Khel, Tut Narai, Spina Khaisora and Boya – and just in time from Spinwam and Shewa. The Spinwam militiamen had a particularly close shave; by the time they left the post the Afghan and Wazir *lashkar* were 300 yards away.[2] This was a serious mistake, although it made sense in military terms, because it encouraged the militiamen to think that the British position was weaker than it really was (the officer responsible came in for a great deal of criticism subsequently).[3] The jemadar, Tarin Tori Khel, and the subahdar, Abdur Rahman Macha Madda Khel, who had won the Croix de Guerre fighting in Europe during the First World War, were able to persuade the 600 Wazir militiamen in the Miranshah fort, mostly Madda Khels, to desert, taking their rifles with them. Hostile lashkars gathered near the Lower Tochi posts – Dardoni, Miranshah and Idak – too, anticipating that they would also be evacuated. However in June the Dardoni militia made a successful sortie, and on 4 June a relief column arrived from Bannu.[4]

In the meantime Nadir Khan's force had moved on towards Thal to the north of Waziristan and laid siege to it, but British troops commanded by General Reginald Dyer arrived on 1 June and drove him back.[5] British troops also captured the Afghan fort at Spin Boldak on the road between Quetta and Kandahar at the end of May and advanced a little way into Afghan territory on the western side of the Khyber Pass.[6] British aeroplanes bombed Jalalabad, and one plane reached Kabul and attacked the amir's palace, an armaments factory and Abdur Rahman's tomb.[7] The GOI declared an armistice on 3 June.

To the south things went very badly for the British; Haji Abdur Razaq had had some success in encouraging resistance among the Zilla Khels in the Wana area.[8] When they heard of the Upper Tochi evacuations, the five British officers present at Wana decided to abandon the South Waziristan militia posts. The Sarwakai and Nili Kach garrisons withdrew eastwards to Murtaza without much difficulty. But on the evening of 26 May some men in the Wana garrison mutinied and seized the keep. They allowed the British officers and about 290 militiamen, with 150 followers, to leave; harassed by Zilla Khels, it took them until late on 30 May to cover the 75 or so miles to Appozai (Fort Sandeman).[9] In June Afghan troops arrived in Wana.[10]

This and the evacuation of the Upper Tochi Posts meant that British authority in Waziristan had evaporated except in the Lower Tochi ('there had been nothing like this since the Indian Mutiny,' Chevenix-Trench suggests); it was a serious blow to British prestige.[11] Four British officers and the Indian assistant political agent had been killed; 'Two British officers were wounded; the militia practically ceased to exist; 1,200 .303 rifles and 700,000 rounds of ammunition fell into the hands of the tribesmen.'[12] To the south in Baluchistan most of the Zhob militia companies also mutinied, and at Kapip a lashkar of Zilla Khels, Sheranis and Suleiman Khels attacked a British supply convoy and its escort. The attackers included Subahdar-Major Asmat Khan, son of Malik Banochai, one of the leading Yarghul Khel Zilla Khels, who had previously been orderly to various political agents at Wana.[13] They killed four British officers and forty-nine other ranks, wounded seventy-one and seized all the carts and two guns.[14] At the beginning of June a Mehsud lashkar led by Fazal Din besieged Jandola (garrisoned by regular troops), and it was not relieved until 9 June. Even though Nadir Khan and his troops had retreated from Thal and an armistice declared, many people in Waziristan had been persuaded that the British had actually agreed to transfer it to the amir, and were about to do so, and that there would be an amnesty for all who had supported him, a belief which Nadir Khan may have encouraged.[15]

The British had imposed another blockade on the Mehsuds after the attack on Jandola, but it was not very effective.[16] In the meantime the Afghan government had sent Colonel Shah Daula, who had previously commanded a cavalry regiment in Khost, to South Waziristan. He arrived in Wana in June 1919 with 2 guns and 200 men and took over the abandoned keep; Haji Abdur Razaq joined him there.[17] In July Shah Daula attended a Mehsud jirga at Kaniguram, and the two men continued to encourage the Mehsuds to resist the British, supplying them with money and ammunition. Mehsuds, Zilla Khels and other Wazirs and Sheranis, often in large numbers, carried out more than 100 raids into the administered areas from May to October 1919, causing many deaths and injuries.[18]

At the end of July 1919 the GOI invited an Afghan delegation to Rawalpindi to discuss a peace treaty. The Afghans asked if they could take over Waziristan and the other frontier areas and be given a subsidy for doing so.[19] There was no chance of this, but an interim treaty was signed on 8 August 1919. It provided for another Afghan mission to visit India in six months' time to discuss matters of common interest and re-establish friendly relations so long as 'the Afghan government had shown by its acts and conduct that it was sincerely anxious to gain British friendship'.[20] After the peace treaty had been signed, Shah Daula continued to insist that it only meant a ceasefire for six months. Rumours that the British had would hand over the border region to Afghanistan in a few months' time continued to circulate.[21]

The breakdown of British authority meant that Shah Daula was also able to visit Sarwakai and the Gumal and install volunteers in some of the former British posts. He styled himself Waziristan's minister of war; Haji Abdur Razaq called himself its *rais* or ruler. In September 1919 Shah Daula invited some prominent men (including Marwat Shaman Khel, Mehr Dil Mal Khel Manzai Alizai, Hayat Khan Michi Khel, ex-subahdar of the 130th Baluchis [also Manzai Alizai], Aziz Khan Shingi, and Mullahs Fazal Din and Abdul Hakim) to accompany him to meet Nadir Khan in Matun. In October Nadir Khan himself took sixteen Mehsuds and Wazirs to Kabul, where they were 'liberally rewarded' and had an audience with the amir.[22] Afghan officials in Khost enlisted many of the Madda Khel men who had deserted from the North Waziristan militia in May, in a militia of their own (referred to in British reports as the Khost or Urgun militia). This was commanded by Abdur Rahman Madda Khel (referred to in the reports as 'Pak').[23]

The occupation of 'Mehsudland'

The British were determined to reassert their authority over the Mehsuds and repay them for all the trouble they had given during the war, and by the autumn of 1919 they had assembled enough troops to be able to go on the offensive. They offered terms to the Mehsuds at a jirga held at Kot Khirgi on 3 November. The Mehsuds were to surrender the rifles, ammunition and equipment stolen since 1 May 1919 and 200 other rifles, and pay a small fine of Rs.10,000. In addition they were to accept the government's right to build roads, station troops and build posts anywhere in the Protected Area, which would be extended to include land west of Jandola along the Shahur Zam as far as the Tiarza Pass and then north-westwards to link up with Wazir territory. This would have meant a significant extension of British influence, and not surprisingly the Mehsuds rejected the terms on 11 November 1919.[24] At about this time Maulana Bashir, a son of the Haji of Turangzai, and a member of the Jamaat-i Mujahidin, moved to a settlement near Makin, where he began publishing a newspaper called *Ghazah* (religious war).[25]

In the meantime the British had presented their terms to the Tochi Wazir jirga on 9 November (Madda Khel men, and men from two small Kabul Khel subsections in the Kaitu valley between Datta Khel and Khost in Afghanistan, the Manzar Khels and the Khizr Khels, did not attend). These included the surrender of rifles, ammunition and equipment stolen since 1 May 1919 and the surrender of 200 other rifles, payment of a fine (from the different sections) of Rs.50,000 and acceptance of the government's right to build roads and station troops wherever there had previously been posts.[26] On 17 November the jirga accepted the British terms. On 18 November the RAF bombed some of the Madda Khel villages, and they gave in and agreed to pay a fine of Rs.10,000. The Kabul Khel subsections were bombed some weeks later, and they submitted too; the Manzar Khels agreed to pay a fine of Rs.1,500 and the Khizr Khels Rs.1,000.[27] The British raised the overall Tochi Utmanzai allowances to Rs.72,000 p.a.[28]

Bombing failed to persuade the Mehsuds to accept the British demands. By now the British were moving troops up to Jandola. They anticipated a short campaign which would be over by the end of March 1920 at the latest, after which they could deal with the Wana Wazirs. If we include the punitive incursions in 1902 and 1917, it would be the sixth British invasion. The British chose to approach via Jandola and the Tank Zam. It was a more difficult route, running through two narrow defiles, the Barari and Ahnai Tangis, and would be easier to defend. Some British officers actually hoped that this would encourage the Mehsuds to resist the advance and lead to them suffering more casualties. No agreement was reached at a meeting with the Mehsuds on 12 December. On 18 December, commanded by Major-General Andrew Skeen, 29,000 troops and nearly 34,000 non-combatants and tens of thousands of animals set off towards Mehsud territory. This substantial force camped first at Palosina where Chamberlain had camped during the first British invasion fifty-nine years earlier.

The Mehsuds had been told that the Afghan government would support them, and led by Musa Khan Abdullai and Fazal Din, they put up a much more sustained and coordinated defence than ever before. For some weeks Skeen found it very difficult to establish pickets to cover his advance from Palosina; he even asked for permission to use poison gas, but did not get it.[29] Not until the end of December was he able to advance slowly but surely in the face of determined opposition through the Ahnai and Barari Tangis, and the troops reached Ahmadwam on 28 January 1920. The next day Shah Daula, with a contingent of Wana Wazirs and two six-pounder mountain guns, joined the Mehsuds, but the guns proved to be useless, and the troops were able to move on, often by night, in spite of very cold weather at the beginning of February. Some Mehsuds and Wazirs had already started to return to their homes and resistance gradually weakened; by 6 February the troops had reached Piazha Raghza between the Barari Tangi and Marobi, where they remained for a week. The Mehsud representatives were informed that there could be no negotiations until all fines had been paid and the rifles surrendered. This was hard for them to accept. A rifle was needed for self-defence, and owning one was a mark of status; some rifles were jointly owned.[30]

The troops began to demolish nearby villages, looting the houses before blowing them up. On 15 February they began to move forward again, and next day they camped on the west side of the Tauda China stream. On 20 February alone they destroyed 17 towers, 160 houses and many retaining walls in the fields, and they continued to demolish buildings and agricultural infrastructure; among the settlements destroyed were Marobi, the late Mullah Powindah's home, where Fazal Din now lived, and Makin. On 1 March the troops withdrew from Makin and moved south to Ladha on the Baddar river and then on 6 March to the vicinity of Kaniguram. They destroyed more settlements, but left the mainly Urmur town of Kaniguram alone. By now most of the Mehsuds living along or near the Takki Zam (Shingi Bahlolzais, Shabi Khel Alizais and Shaman Khels) had stopped fighting. They now brought in 148 government rifles and 178 locally made ones and paid much of the fine. Others, including many of the Abdullais living in Spinkamar and the Dashkai algad (which runs into the Darra algad to the north-west of Makin), the Haibat Khels, the Abdur Rahman Khels and the Jalal Khels (all Bahlolzais), still did not surrender. Living in remoter areas with more difficult terrain they were beyond the reach of British ground forces.[31]

On 21 March 1920 the British officers called a jirga and told the Mehsuds that the troops would remain in their territory and that they might attack sections that had not submitted without warning. Early in April the British sent a force to deal with the Abdur Rahman Khels and Giga Khels who lived at the head of the Baddar valley on the borders of Shakai. They resisted strongly, and the troops were not able to do much damage. Their camp at Kaniguram was some distance from the administered areas, and it would have been difficult to support them had the Mehsuds renewed the struggle. Skeen therefore returned to Ladha at the beginning of May. The Derajat Column was disbanded, but around 15,000 soldiers remained at Ladha and at Piazha Raghza and Sora Rogha, along what was called the Ladha line; two brigades also stayed in the Tochi valley.[32]

The campaign had not crushed the Mehsuds; as Fitzpatrick later put it, 'though we have taught the Mahsuds a severe lesson … they are not by any means on their knees.'[33] The historian James Spain exaggerates when he says the campaign was a fiasco.[34] But there had been many British casualties; the number of men killed, missing, or dying of wounds or sickness has been estimated at least 2,500. It had been expensive too – Robson put the cost at £1,350,000.[35] As many as 1,400 Mehsud and Wazir men had been killed in battle or died of wounds. (There are no figures on the number of non-combatants who died from bombing, starvation and illness, but it is likely to have been several hundred.) Nevertheless the British had succeeded in establishing for the first time a commanding position in Mehsud territory. The viceroy, Chelmsford, argued that it would be a mistake to give it up.[36] It was decided that the troops should stay at Ladha permanently.[37]

In May 1920 Fitzpatrick returned from leave, and taking on the roles of resident and political agent, replaced Major Crosthwaite as political adviser to Wazirforce. By then the cost of the occupation was beginning to cause concern, and his brief was to try and conciliate the Mehsuds so that fewer troops would be needed and a civil administration could take over. In July 1920 Major-General Torquil Matheson replaced Skeen in command of Wazirforce. The chief of general staff wrote to him emphasizing the desirability of 'the pacification as opposed to the mere cowing of Waziristan'. This was to be achieved not by force but 'by gradually associating [the Mehsuds] … in our administration of their country, the first step being the introduction of a system of Khassadars enlisted through the tribal elders'.[38]

Fitzpatrick held a jirga at Ladha on 28 May 1920 at which he announced that the blockade would be lifted for the sections that had complied with the terms.[39] This encouraged some of the other sections to do so over the next few months, including the Haibat Khels, who paid their share of the fine in July.[40] He went on to introduce the 'policy of conciliation, meeting the tribe in a friendly spirit, paying for their local produce instead of taking it, listening to their grievances and remedying them when reasonable and generally showing that we wished them well and bore them no ill will for the fight they had put up in defence of their homes'.[41] The atmosphere improved somewhat, but the British found Mehsud sniping between Ladha and Piazha Raghza sufficiently troublesome to send troops back to Makin in July 1920 to destroy more houses and crops; as they withdrew they were attacked and the 4/39th Garhwal Rifles suffered sixty casualties.[42]

As we have seen, the GOA had already given members of some of the anti-British Mehsud sections land in Afghanistan. In particular since the early 1900s up to fifty 'houses' or extended families of Abdur Rahman Khels had settled in Ghozba, Logar, Charkh, Bek Samand and near Ghazni. They mostly spent the summers there and wintered in Waziristan.[43] In the meantime Haji Abdur Razaq moved for a time to Shakai, on the British side of the Durand Line, taking over from Shah Daula as leader of the anti-British resistance in Waziristan. He tried to put into operation a plan to provide houses and irrigation in Birmal on the Afghan side, aiming to persuade British-side Ahmadzai Wazirs to settle there and intending to recruit them as khassadars and use them for anti-British activities.[44]

Some Mehsuds continued to carry out attacks along the British supply line in Waziristan itself, while raiding into the administered areas along its eastern border actually grew worse.[45] Encouraged by Haji Abdur Razaq, large gangs, mostly Mehsuds and Wazirs, went on raiding and kidnapping.[46] To deal with the continued difficulties, the British recruited levies along the border with the tribal areas, and in August 1921 introduced new tactics. They mounted additional patrols along the border and inaugurated a more active policy of counter-raiding into tribal territory to seize men and property; in October 1921, for example, troops and levies attacked two villages in Kabul Khel territory, captured a number of wanted men and released fourteen kidnap victims.[47] Village pursuit parties (*chighas*) were given better arms, encouraged to pursue and attack raiders and rewarded for doing so. The legal position of outlaws from British territory living in Waziristan was also changed. We saw above that since 1913 British officials had begun to arrange Conciliation Committees, which made it easier for outlaws to return to the administered districts; they were also spared confiscation of their property. These concessions were withdrawn. The British insisted on full tribal responsibility too, with the Bhittanis for instance. They imposed territorial responsibility on their villages in administered territory and located Bhittani khassadars in posts along the routes most often used by raiders.[48]

In the meantime, in the spring of 1920, the GOI had invited Afghan representatives to India to discuss a treaty. The negotiations were held at Mussoorie and continued from 17 April to 24 July 1920. The Afghan negotiators continued to assert Afghanistan's interest in Waziristan, but the British were unwilling to make any concessions. Sir Henry Dobbs, the GOI's foreign secretary, produced a draft treaty, but the viceroy did not approve it and decided to end the negotiations for the time being.[49]

Wana Wazirs

While the Mahsud invasion was taking place, Wana remained independent.[50] Haji Abdur Razaq moved back there from Shakai, accompanied by his son, Abdul Rahim, and Shah Daula and his guns. They aimed to stop the Wazirs reaching a settlement with the British and 'hoisted their Red Crescent flags' over the keep. These were, they said, 'the emblems of Afghanistan, Turkey and Germany' and would make the buildings that flew them safe from attack.[51] The British were anxious to remove them and make the Wana Wazirs, particularly the Zilla Khels, pay for their behaviour in May 1919.[52] They assembled a force at Jandola early in October and summoned the Wana Wazirs to a jirga at Murtaza on 10 October, but they did not attend. Abdur Razaq tried to occupy the fort at Sarwakai, but the Manzai Mehsuds of Nano and the Khaisara drove him out. The British began to attack the Wazirs from the air on 11 November, and on 12 November the troops moved to Sarwakai.[53] The Wazirs surrendered fifty-one government and eighty-seven tribal rifles, but the British did not think that this was good enough, and the troops moved forward again on 16 December. The Wazirs tried to resist them at Karab Kot, but were easily dispersed. Abdur Razaq and Shah Daula left Wana, and the British force arrived there on 22 December

1920. Some of the Wazir sections submitted, others did not. It was difficult to coerce the latter because being semi-nomadic they had neither houses nor crops to be destroyed. All that could be done was to try and destroy their flocks. Nevertheless by the spring of 1921 the Wazirs had handed over most of the remaining rifles and paid much of the fine. In March John Maffey took over from Alfred Hamilton Grant as the chief commissioner; 'the outstanding Frontier officer of his generation', Maffey had been the private secretary to the viceroy, Lord Chelmsford.[54]

Continuing resistance and further pressure

By the autumn of 1920 most of the important Mehsud sections had given up fighting and had begun trading with British territory again. In December a number of maliks submitted a petition; it was clear that they accepted that occupation of their country was likely to be permanent and were ready to take advantage of any economic opportunities that it might offer. But men from some other sections, mainly Abdullai, Jalal Khel and Abdur Rahman Khel Bahlolzais, continued to resist. The Makin area in particular was reported to be 'the headquarters of hostile intrigue, and the source of a perennial stream of ammunition, cash and propaganda in opposition to the measures of government'.[55]

In the early autumn of 1920 Amir Amanullah invited a British mission to Kabul to resume negotiations for a treaty. The GOI wanted to accept the invitation and hoped for a treaty of friendship. The government in London had misgivings, partly because the Afghans had signed a draft treaty with the Soviet Union in the late summer; it suspected that this authorized the Russians to set up consulates in Kandahar, Jalalabad and Ghazni, which would bring them closer to the frontier.[56] Nevertheless the GOI sent a mission to Kabul in January 1921; it was led by Sir Henry Dobbs.[57] There were four phases in the negotiations that followed. These were from 20 January 1921 to 9 April; from 9 April to mid-July; from mid-July to 18 September and from 18 September to December.[58]

One of the main issues to be resolved was the future of Waziristan.[59] Although the GOI was becoming increasingly desperate to reduce its expenditure there, it was very reluctant to abandon the 'tribal pacifications and annexation in the Waziristan area'.[60] In any case it was not thought safe to withdraw troops until an agreement had been established with Afghanistan.[61] It has been suggested that the British reluctance to make concessions in Waziristan at this point made good relations with Afghanistan impossible in the future.[62] It certainly contributed to the difficulties faced by the negotiators.

The progress of the negotiations had an impact in Waziristan and vice versa. The British originally proposed to announce their plans for Waziristan to the Mehsuds in April 1921. Dobbs, the chief British negotiator, thought it would strengthen his hand if this could be delayed until an agreement was reached, and it was postponed. At an unofficial meeting in May, the Afghan foreign minister, Mahmud Tarzi, said that if the Afghans were given Waziristan, they would be willing to conclude an anti-Russian alliance with Britain. This was out of the question, but Dobbs suggested that after the British had re-established their authority in Waziristan, they might withdraw regular troops from Wana. But he wanted the Afghans to break with the Soviet Union first. This they would not do. The atmosphere worsened. At one point Dobbs requested permission to close the passes from Afghanistan into Punjab, should he judge it necessary.[63] The British Foreign Office's attitude was unhelpful. For example, in March 1921 Amanullah had sent a mission led by General Muhammad Wali Khan to visit various countries to encourage foreign trade and investment in Afghanistan. The general had some success in Italy, and it was arranged that an Italian mission would set out for Kabul on 3 July. The British Foreign Office put pressure on the Italian government to delay it, and it was abandoned. This upset the Afghans and made things more difficult for Dobbs.[64]

In the meantime some Mehsuds continued to resist the British occupation. The RAF had supported Skeen's advance to Makin, and in February 1920 the British constructed a landing ground at Sora Rogha. Aerial attacks had initially helped to weaken Mehsud resistance, but they found ways of coping. For example, they would stay in the shadow of rocks when they heard aeroplanes; they also took refuge in caves and dug cellars in which to shelter during raids. Casualties were often fewer than expected.[65] The British therefore tried a new tactic. Their camp at Ladha was in a commanding position and many of the Mehsud settlements in this part of Waziristan, including Makin, were visible from it.[66] Late in 1920 the troops used teams of horses to drag two six-inch howitzers up to the camp. In the following spring the British warned the Mehsuds that women and children should leave the area and began to use the howitzers to shell Makin's fields and grazing grounds. This continued for some weeks, following which they made another attempt to persuade the hostile Mehsuds to come to an agreement.[67] This failed, and from June to September 1921 the howitzers continued to shell Makin 'daily and intermittently and wherever movement was observed' (Figure 6.1).[68]

Figure 6.1 Tractor and six-inch howitzer near Razmak, Waziristan, Pakistan, dated 1890 but in fact probably early 1920s. Photo by Mela Ram/Royal Geographical society/Getty Images.

Violence

It still seems shocking that the British were prepared to use this tactic given the risk of harming women and children, and men who had not resisted them. This is a good point at which to put the narrative aside briefly and look at the question of violence and cruelty in relation to the British encounter with Waziristan and the frontier as a whole. The British usually regarded readiness to resort to violence as central to frontier culture and frequently drew attention to this. As far back as the 1860s Taylor had commented that 'the way in which they [the inhabitants of Peshawar] butcher each other is something awful'.[69] In the early 1920s the NWFP chief commissioner, John Maffey, referred to the border region as 'this great blood-sucking frontier'.[70] The British tended to regard Pashtun men as being addicted to murdering each other in revenge and feud (and always ready to cut off their wives and daughters' noses, if not kill them, on the slightest suspicion of 'dishonourable' behaviour). The prevalence of feuding was often blamed for Waziristan's poverty; it was argued that the prevailing insecurity made men wary of investing labour and money in productive enterprise and meant that money that could have been spent on productive resources was spent on weapons.[71]

It is true that in a more or less stateless society like that of Waziristan, men usually had to be prepared to use violence to defend themselves and their families. They did sometimes use extreme violence against outsiders, for example the GOI and its servants. Men (and sometimes women) might castrate wounded soldiers before killing them. There are also many reports of the killing of grass-cutters, coolies and others working for the British, for instance the murder on the night of 29 August 1919 by a raiding party, consisting mainly of Shaman Khels, of twenty-six unarmed coolies and the wounding of twenty.[72] Howell suggested that this threw some light on 'Mehsud psychology and their occasional fits of blood lust'. He also referred to the Mehsuds and Wazirs giving way to what he called 'senseless ferocity' during an attack on a British military labour camp at Kaur Bridge, when they killed thirty-seven camp followers and labourers, two British soldiers and a British officer.[73]

This characterization of frontier Pashtun society as a highly violent one, characterized by feud and vendetta, casual aggression and pointless brutality, served to justify the British presence. In practice British officials were equally ruthless when they thought the occasion demanded it.[74] Reynell Taylor and John Nicholson, for example, had no scruples about ordering summary executions, and the Murderous Outrages Act made these legal in the case of murderous attacks on British officials.[75] During the late nineteenth century Britain and the other colonial powers tried to impose some rules on the conduct of war in Europe, with, for example, the signing of the Geneva Convention; elsewhere it was often different.[76] Some military men began to talk about 'savage wars' and 'irregular wars' as 'small wars' – a separate category to be distinguished from 'civilized' conflict.[77] Hugh Trenchard, who played a prominent role in the creation of the Royal Air Force, for instance, said that 'in warfare against savage tribes who do not conform to codes of civilized warfare, aerial bombardment is not necessarily limited in its methods or objectives by rules agreed upon in international law'.[78]

We have seen that Skeen was not allowed to use poison gas in 1919, but the British did not usually hesitate to employ the latest military technology against the frontier people, in 1897 for instance using 'shrapnel shells, a forerunner of the modern-day cluster bomb, which fired hundreds of bullets at the enemy on impact'.[79] Matheson's resort to using howitzers developed during the First World War to attack Makin is another good example. The same is true of the use of aircraft. We have seen that bombers were used during the 1917 Waziristan expedition, and bombing of settlements as well as irregular forces began to play an important role after the First World War on the North-West Frontier (as well as in other parts of the Empire including Aden, Egypt, Iraq, Somaliland, the Sudan and Palestine). In these cases it seems that techniques developed in Europe, the bombing of civilians for instance, were exported overseas, rather than the other way round (as has been argued, for example, with the German repression of the Herero and Nama people in Namibia and the Holocaust).[80] There were claims and counterclaims about the extent to which it was possible to avoid collateral damage. There was no such thing as precision bombing some said; there could be no question of it when delayed action bombs were used.[81] It is true that at least on the North-West Frontier advance warning was usually given, but the message did not always get through because most people were illiterate, and there were often some who for whatever reason found it difficult to leave their homes.[82]

In fact colonial war often consisted precisely in 'persuading or coercing an irregular enemy to come out and fight so that he could be duly slaughtered in satisfactorily large numbers'.[83] As John Lawrence, the Punjab chief commissioner, had argued in 1855, there was no point in an expedition against the Mehsuds if their men would not stand and fight; 'To make the punishment effective, it must consist in our killing and wounding a good number of them.'[84] To take a different example, in parts of Algeria where pastoral nomads preferred not to resist the French conquest directly and had no houses or fields that could be destroyed, the French commander-in-chief and governor general in Algeria in the later 1830s and 1840s, Marshal Thomas-Robert Bugeaud, encouraged use of a form of surprise attack, the *razzia*, and observers noted what was described as the great 'moral effect of a well-executed *razzia*'.[85]

If ideas about when and how violence may legitimately be used differ between and within societies, it remains the case that violence is a 'cultural performance', 'a discursive practice, whose symbols and rituals are as relevant to its enactment as its instrumental aspects'.[86] Violence always has meaning.[87] European colonialists often justified it by claiming that it was the only language that 'the savage understands'.[88] Sometimes it seems to have been the only one they shared.[89] On the frontier British violence was communicative.[90] So punitive expeditions, for example, were sometimes justified on the grounds that they sent the message, not just to those on the receiving end, but along the frontier as a whole, that raiding and resistance did not pay and encouraged them to take up more peaceful pursuits.[91] Such expeditions probably did discourage raiding in the short term, but do not appear to have significantly changed attitudes in the long run. Somewhat similarly Marshal Thomas-Robert Bugeaud defended the ruthlessness of his army in Algeria in the mid-nineteenth century by arguing that violent tactics were in fact 'the most humanitarian' because they would persuade others not to resist.[92]

Nor was the message of violence just for nearby neighbours. Punitive expeditions, for instance, conveyed the message not only in India and Afghanistan but also around the world that the British Empire remained resolute and powerful. For Mehsuds too violence certainly sent a message – along the Waziristan border with British India showing, for example, that its perpetrators should not be ignored when the government was allocating allowances or arranging for the appointment of khassadars. Arguably even the Mehsud attacks on unarmed labourers were 'like so much violence ... in a sense, communicative; and for the oppressed or disenfranchised, as much as for the oppressor, [might] ... represent an alternative "political language"'.[93] As a form of terrorism, they maintained the reputation of the Mehsuds as people to be afraid of and weakened the government's authority by showing it could not defend its subjects properly.

To return to the howitzers, it is difficult to judge their impact; Fitzpatrick thought that although the shelling did not cause serious damage to houses and agricultural infrastructure, it did have an effect on the Mehsuds' morale.[94] Nevertheless the Mehsuds carried out a number of well-planned attacks on the troop convoys. In April 1921 for instance with 300 or 400 men Musa Khan ambushed the up and down convoys at Janjal, killing three officers and ten other ranks, and a large number of camels and getting away with their loads. In July Abdullais and Jalal Khels attacked a convoy in the Shahur Tangi and killed sixteen soldiers.[95]

At a jirga held at Makin on 3 September 1921 Maulana Bashir reportedly distributed more money (Rs.2,500). But later in September the Makin Abdullais, the Band Khels and the Warza Shingis sued for peace. Musa Khan left for Kabul.[96] The Afghan government undertook to pay allowances to him and some other Mehsuds.[97] In the meantime the British announced terms at a jirga on 27 September 1921; these included the surrender of more rifles.[98] Early in October the Mehsuds agreed to hand over twenty rifles immediately, but insisted that after that each subsection would have to be dealt with separately and that they could not be held responsible for each other. Matheson refused to accept this because several men (possibly from different sections) might share ownership of a single rifle, and the Abdullais stopped cooperating in the surrender.[99]

Meanwhile the negotiations continued in Kabul; the Foreign Office in London was still unhelpful. When General Wali Khan reached the UK in August, the foreign secretary, Curzon, refused to recognize him as an official representative of the Afghan government and insisted that negotiations could only be conducted through the secretary of state for India and the GOI.[100] Afghan relations with the Soviet Union continued to improve, and in the same month the Soviet-Afghan treaty was ratified. Dobbs feared that Soviet influence was increasing and became more anxious to reach an agreement; he persuaded the GOI that a less comprehensive treaty would be better than no treaty at all. Among other benefits, he said, it should calm the situation along the frontier.[101] Negotiations continued through the autumn. The Afghans continued to assert their claim to Waziristan and call for an amnesty for its people and tried to use their influence there (and elsewhere along the frontier) as a bargaining counter with the British. In the end they dropped the Waziristan claim, but it was important for them not to be seen to be too obviously abandoning the Mehsuds and Wazirs because it was in their interests to do so. They pressed at least for the British troops to be withdrawn from Wana. Dobbs agreed to this but thought it should wait until the treaty was signed.[102]

While Musa Khan was away in Kabul, on 5 October 1921 Fitzpatrick held a jirga at Jandola to discuss the completion of the road from Kotkai to Ladha and the possibility of awarding contracts for work on it to Mehsud contractors. He summoned 100 men, but as had so often happened in the past, far more men than expected turned up (between 1,500 and 2,000, including all the maliks and *tumani* leaders of the friendly sections). He told them that the road would be pushed forward with or without their help, and the speakers at the jirga said that they would cooperate if some concessions could be made. A list of these was drawn up.[103] Fitzpatrick thought they all were reasonable, but that one in particular – that the maliki and *tumani* allowances might be increased and that they might be 'granted chairs [presumably to sit on during meetings], etc, just like other tribes' – would require further discussion.

Fitzpatrick divided the work on the road up into a large number of small contracts worth Rs.1,000 each and distributed them equally between the three main sections. This should, he thought, solve what he thought were the Mehsuds' serious economic difficulties. The agreement showed, he commented, that they had come to terms with the British government's intention to occupy their country permanently and more or less accepted it. The question of the allowances remained to be sorted out; hitherto, he suggested, it had been, 'easily the most thorny one in their politics and is that on which successive Mehsud settlements have come to grief'.[104] This is a revealing comment, given that the allowances were supposed to have made relations with the Mehsuds easier, not complicate them further. As we have seen, he argued that they were inadequate, especially those paid to the maliks, and should be increased. There would be, he promised the Mehsuds, further discussion of these.

The relative success of these negotiations vindicated the more conciliatory policy he had introduced since his return. From the British point of view the overall Mehsud situation continued to improve slowly, thanks to the road-building contracts (and the employment of Mehsuds as escorts and khassadars) and efforts to make the presence of the troops less irritating, and the decline of active Afghan interference. All the Mehsud sections had now submitted, apart from the Jalal Khels, some Abdur Rahman Khels and a few Nekzan Khels and Band Khels. The Jalal Khels and the Abdur Rahman Khels posed the greatest challenge. The Jalal Khels lived in caves and grass huts; they spent the summer in the hills facing Sora Rogha and the winter in the Shuza: both areas that were difficult to access. As for the Abdur Rahman Khels, a good number were now living with their families in Afghanistan, reportedly only visiting Waziristan to raid. Some still lived in Baddar and Splitoi, but they had no government rifles to return. Meanwhile on 20 October 1921 the Afghans were reported to have given Maulana Bashir (as we have seen, then living at Makin), 3,000 rounds of ammunition and 2,000 rupees.[105] On the following night Mehsuds and Wana Wazirs attacked a military labour camp at Kaur Bridge. They killed a British officer, two British soldiers and thirty-seven camp followers and labourers and carried off twenty-six rifles and a number of horses and mules. Mehsuds also continued to snipe at troops moving along the road between Ladha and Piazha Raghza.[106]

The British had already postponed the announcement of their plans for Waziristan twice because the negotiations in Kabul had not been concluded. Fitzpatrick thought it was time to end the uncertainty and recommended that the British should announce formally that they intended to occupy the Mehsud country permanently, and Dobbs agreed.[107] On 5 November 1921, the British informed the Mehsuds that the government intended to remain in occupation of the Mehsud country 'for so long as it pleases', but that it had no intention of introducing 'the regular administration of a settled district' and would 'administer it on tribal lines in accordance with tribal customs and usage'. Allowances would be paid 'having due regard to services rendered and especially to the degree in which the co-operation of Maliks and tribesmen is forthcoming for the restoration and maintenance of law and order'.[108] As for Wana, it was agreed that regular troops would would be withdrawn as soon as possible.

Fitzpatrick judged that most of the Mehsuds were ready to accept the occupation, although it would be unpopular and that some would look for opportunities to continue resisting it. 'It is perhaps not realised', he said,

> what an advance is marked by tribal acquiescence in our new policy, but care and above all sympathy is needed, if we are not to relapse: to the Mehsud, the loss of his independence which he has cherished is a matter of overwhelming importance, for he is sensitive beyond words and dreads the sneers of other tribes; and we can only make our occupation the success it can and ought to be by making allowances, where allowances are to be made, and punishing with discrimination, where public opinion and custom will support us.[109]

The GOI's foreign secretary during the 1920s, Sir Denys Bray, called on Fitzpatrick to be cautious when deciding on the allocation of the subsidies or allowances to the Mehsuds, because 'so many different methods of distribution have been tried without success'.[110] Fitzpatrick proposed to proceed with the scheme he had outlined in 1918. It seems that he wanted to pursue a kind of middle way between Bruce and Crump's *maliki* policies and Merk's *tumani* one. 'We got very poor value for our money', he wrote, 'in frittering it away in sums of a few annas of rupees in the system of automatic distribution by houses, and I want to see every man possessing influence in his section, given a financial interest in controlling it and preserving order'.[111] But this would take time. The maliks were not very powerful and must be 'built up and strengthened gradually'. This could be achieved, he thought, by involving both maliks and *wakils* (or *mohtabars*) in choosing and paying the khassadars. Their roles would gradually coalesce, producing 'a body of men admittedly the leaders of the tribe and drawing generous allowances in return for definite responsibilities whose interest is one with the interest of Government'.[112]

In November 1921 the negotiators finally agreed on the terms of a neighbourly treaty between Britain and Afghanistan. Legations would be established in London and Kabul, and Afghanistan would be granted 'tax exemptions on materials designed to help modernize the country'.[113] The British had feared that the Afghans might yield to Soviet pressure to allow the establishment of Soviet consulates in eastern Afghanistan, too near the Indian border for comfort, but they did not. Dobbs had been instructed that he could not sanction a tribal amnesty and that there could be no change in Britain's Waziristan policy, but he made some face-saving concessions.[114] These included the insertion of an article (XI) in the treaty in which Britain and Afghanistan each undertook to 'inform the other in the future of any military operations of major importance which may appear to be necessary for the maintenance of order among the frontier tribes residing within their respective spheres before the commencement of such operations'.[115] In addition, in a letter to be annexed to the treaty, Dobbs stated that 'as the conditions of the frontier tribes of the two governments are of interest to the Government of Afghanistan, I inform you that the British government entertains feeling of goodwill towards all the frontier tribes, and has every intention of treating them generously, provided they abstain from outrages against the inhabitants of India'.[116] On 22 November 1921 the treaty was signed. As we have seen, Dobbs had also given an undertaking that regular British troops would be withdrawn from Wana. The political agent, Major Arthur Parsons, objected to this; he wanted to facilitate what he called 'peaceful penetration' by keeping troops there and constructing outposts, a telegraph line and roads. But he was overruled, and on 1 December 1921 the British withdrew the troops, and khassadars took over, at a cost of Rs.21,096 p.a.[117]

Although the treaty had been signed, a misunderstanding over Arnawai on the Chitral border to the north (which had been occupied by the Afghans in May 1919) nearly upset everything. Dobbs thought that the amir had agreed to surrender Arnawai in return for Torkham in the Khyber Pass. Amanullah, however, denied this and told him that if he insisted on Arnawai's return, the treaty would have to be cancelled.[118] The amir had recently settled some Wazirs, mostly Zilla Khels, at Shahjui. At this point they carried out a major raid into Baluchistan, killing two British officers and forty soldiers, and burning some villages and destroying the fort at Barshor some twenty miles from Pishin.[119] The amir was reported to be 'genuinely horrified and upset', and to make amends, he withdrew his objections to the return of Arnawai.[120]

British influence in Afghanistan remained substantial, even though it had begun to conduct its own foreign relations, and the amir no longer received a British subsidy. After the agreement had been reached in November 1921, rather than being represented in Kabul by an Indian Muslim Agent, the GOI was allowed to appoint a British representative. A large legation was built for him on an extensive plot in the Karte Parwan district on the edge of Kabul. Not surprisingly, however, relations between Britain and Afghanistan continued to be difficult.

British officials tended to dislike and mistrust Amanullah and his policies. They resented the attack that he had launched in 1919 and the way he had interfered in Waziristan, and they were annoyed by his links with the frontier people. Moreover, they were concerned by his apparent willingness to have good relations with the Soviet Union.[121] They thought that the Soviets might encourage tribal opposition along the border. The Afghans for their part were anxious about British intentions towards Afghanistan. Amanullah saw the British move into Waziristan in the winter of 1919 and the continuing presence of the troops at Ladha as an indirect threat to Afghanistan itself. With some justification, he was also concerned that if the British re-established their influence over the tribal groups living along the border, they would be able to use them against him if they wanted.[122]

7

British policy in Waziristan and the Razmak base

Haji Abdur Razaq and Wana

Haji Abdur Razaq, it will be recalled, had been sent to Waziristan by Amir Amanullah in May 1919: he remained there after the signing of the Anglo-Afghan Treaty in November 1921. On 18 January 1922 he sent a long letter to the North Waziristan political agent, signing himself 'Ghazi Haji Abdur Razaq Rais [chief, leader] of Waziristan'. In it he drew attention to 'the piteous plight of the Musalman world and the pernicious diplomacy of England all over the world', and said that he was following the guerrilla tactics of the Boers in the Transvaal and the Russians during Napoleon's retreat. He also issued a proclamation at around this time in which he said that 'the oppressed tribes of Waziristan ... have selected a tribal Government as a centre to collect all their martial and tribal power and have appointed me as President by a majority of votes'. He said he was declaring a holy war against the British which would continue until they left Waziristan. 'What a monstrous shame it is', he said, 'that for 1 ½ years by day and night air-raiding has been carried on against women and children while the British claim to be the most merciful and just and civilised nation in the world'.[1] In February 1922 he issued a proclamation in which listed the ways in which the British had broken the promises they made when they declared war on the Ottoman Empire on 1 November 1914.[2]

In March he wrote to the South Waziristan political agent, saying that the tribes of Waziristan disliked the new treaty and would continue to resist and that there would be no peace until the British had gone.[3] He also issued a proclamation of jihad in which he stated that it was a Muslim's duty to obey the [Ottoman] caliph and imam, and any Muslim who fought against him, or those fighting for him, 'is considered to have drawn his sword against God and the Prophet' and is not a Muslim even if he prays, keeps fasts and thinks he is one. When Muslims are under attack it was their duty to fight, he said, referring to some of the hadiths that have traditionally been used to support the lesser jihad.[4] He also emphasized that Hindus, Sikhs and other non-Muslims were sympathetic to the Muslim cause; they are 'being locked up in prisons, looted and disgraced but they do not give up the help of the Moslems and are shouting "Moslems are being subjected to cruelties"'. Indeed, he said, 'Mahatma Gandhi is moving from house to house and city to city with the Koran in his hand and is preaching the commandments of the Shariat.' In spite of all this Muslims were failing to support each other. What will they say, he asked rhetorically, when on the Day of Judgement God asks them what they were doing at a time when even the Hindu Mahatma Gandhi 'preached the commandments of the Koran and helped Islam'.[5]

He also referred scathingly to Muslims who supported the British, although they may 'have long beards, say prayers punctually, read beads and when anybody calls them, keep silent for some minutes to denote that they are reading Wazifa [prayer offices] in order that people may say that such and such a Mulla or Maulvi, or Mirza is always engaged in reciting the name of God'.[6] Inconsistently it seems, he also said that a secret understanding existed between the amir and the British, according to which the British would shortly leave Wana, and allow it to become independent.[7] At this point some British officials thought that he was getting money from the Russian embassy in Kabul, but there is no evidence of this.[8]

Around this time some of the Shahjui Wazirs returned to Wana.[9] They may well have been among the Zilla Khels who, encouraged by Abdur Razaq, captured a convoy proceeding to Wana from Tank on 22 March 1922, and then on the night of 4 April surrounded the fort at Wana itself. This was now held only by khassadars.[10] The besieged and besiegers spent the next two days talking to each other, and early on 7 April the Mullah Hamzullah arrived with 100 men from Shakai to join the latter. There was some firing but no one dared to shoot to kill for fear of starting a blood feud.

Not long before, Sir Francis Humphrys, who had previously served as an assistant political officer in Waziristan, had been appointed as the British representative in Afghanistan.[11] He was instructed to demand that the GOA order Haji Abdur Razaq to leave Wana.[12] The RAF bombed villages around it. Reportedly, 'practically all the damage fell on the friendlies but the effect on the situation was equally good'.[13] One plane had to make a forced landing, owing, many of the Wazirs believed, to Mullah Hamzullah's prayers.[14] The Afghan government did recall Haji Abdur Razaq, and the lashkar dispersed.[15]

Early in May 1922 two British Officers and 500 South Waziristan Scouts arrived in Wana. They rounded up four villages in the neighbourhood and arrested fifteen outlaws.[16]

This incident was to influence policy in Waziristan. Sir Henry Rawlinson, the British commander-in-chief in India, argued the Wana khassadars' failure to shoot to kill showed that khassadars could not really act as police; the consensus came to be that it would be a mistake to give them too much responsibility. More Shahjui Wazirs returned to the Wana area during 1922.[17] The British commander in Waziristan, Matheson, wanted to retain a presence there to ensure that it did not become 'a happy hunting-ground for all disturbing elements, i.e. Afghan adventurers, Bolshevist emissaries, Indian revolutionaries, etc'.[18] He recommended that it should continue to be occupied by Scouts. Pears (who had taken over from Fitzpatrick as the resident in January 1922) and the chief commissioner agreed with him. Nevertheless the Scouts were withdrawn in April 1923, and for some years it was left in charge of the khassadars.[19]

Less than three weeks after the signing of the Anglo-Afghan treaty, there had been another incursion from Afghanistan. In November 1921 British troops had reoccupied Datta Khel in the Upper Tochi.[20] Presumably in reply, on 11 December 1921, between 400 and 500 men attacked British troops escorting a convoy at the eastern entrance to the Spinchilla Pass between Datta Khel and Miranshah. The lashkar was led by ex-jemadar Tarin, a Tori Khel deserter from the North Waziristan Militia and consisted of Afghans and other Tori Khel and Wazir deserters from the North Waziristan Militia who were employed as levies by Afghan officials and garrisoned near Matun. They killed three officers and thirty-nine other ranks, while suffering many casualties themselves, Tarin among them. British officials blamed the Afghan officials for inciting the attack and accused them of receiving a share of the plunder from the convoy.[21]

Continuing Mehsud resistance

Although many Mehsuds had surrendered and the British had started building the road, some were still not reconciled to the new order. It was probably some Jalal Khels who killed N. S. Woodhouse of the Frontier Constabulary near the Zam post on 17 April 1922. In May a large Mehsud group attacked a patrol of the 101st Grenadiers at Shinkai, killing 21 men and wounding 4, and taking away 22 rifles and 800 rounds of ammunition.[22] In July Pears and Parsons held another large jirga, this time at Ladha. They reached agreements with representatives drawn from all sections except the Abdullais, Jalal Khels and Abdur Rahman Khels. Pears insisted on the importance of both territorial responsibility and what he called tribal or community responsibility. As he saw it, the main principle of what he called 'Pashto' (by which he meant Pashtun customary law or *pashtunwali*) was the joint responsibility of the community.[23] It is revealing that the British were still having to insist on tribal responsibility after so many previous attempts to force the Mehsuds to accept it.[24] As regards territorial responsibility, Parsons commented that it would in practice be new, and most unwelcome to the Mehsuds, but that it must be enforced.

Pears told the men that the allowances would be raised from Rs.70,000 p.a. to Rs.108,000. Rs.60,000 would comprise the *tumani* portion and be distributed among the maliks and representatives from subsections according to *nikat*. The remaining Rs.48,000 would be maliki, or *khidmati* (for service), and it would be distributed among the maliks and sub-sectional representatives for 'special services rendered – or any other factor meriting special adjustment'.[25] In addition the British would recruit Mehsud khassadars. The maliks would suggest suitable men, who would be paid directly; thus 'by providing grants to the elders, and government service to the younger tribesmen, it was hoped to bind both adult generations to the government'.[26] These khassadari wages were in addition to the maliki and *tumani* allowances, so there was a substantial rise in payments to the Mehsuds.

The strategy suffered from the problems that had experienced with previous distributions. First, it was impossible to allocate the allowances in such a way as to please everybody. Second, there was the fact that the number of people in each of the three main sections bore little relation to their respective *nikat* shares. In particular, although the Shaman Khels were only about one-sixth of the total Mehsud population, they received the same *nikat* share as the more numerous Alizais and Bahlolzais. Third, although the allowances were supposed to be given for service, recipients quickly came to regard them as personal possessions to be handed on to their heirs when they died, whether or not they did anything useful for the government.[27]

Some Abdur Rahman Khels reacted by attacking a picket near Ladha on 28 July 1922, killing three soldiers and wounding three others. A few hours later they sent a message to explain that this had been done to persuade the other Mehsuds to accept that their special additional payment of Rs.6,000 should be reinstated. They were instructed to pay a fine and surrender six more rifles. After further bombing, the pro-British men met these terms, and the blockade was raised early in September 1922.[28] Only the Abdullais and the Jalal Khel remained unreconciled. In November 1922 some Jalal Khels actually tried to kidnap the chief commissioner, John Maffey, while he was on tour in the Dera Ismail Khan district. In a daring move they held up the motor vehicle in which they thought he was travelling, shot the driver and kidnapped seven passengers, including Extra Assistant Commissioner Khan Sahib Muhammad Hayat Khan. Presumably because the chief commissioner had not been among them, they quickly released them.[29]

British policy in Waziristan

The British had to decide on the policy to be pursued in Waziristan in the longer term. Their options were limited by the deteriorating financial climate. They could have withdrawn the regular troops and restored the arrangements which Curzon had introduced at the beginning of the century. These, it will be recalled, had consisted of two widely spaced lines of posts, held by militias, stretching towards Datta Khel in the north and Wana in the south, with garrisons of regular troops just outside Waziristan. Some argued that the rapid collapse of this system after the Third Anglo-Afghan War in 1919 showed that it was not worth reviving it, though others disagreed.

In developing policy, the viceroy, Chelmsford, was influenced by the opinions of his senior military advisers – the commander-in-chief, Henry Rawlinson, the deputy chief of the general staff, Archibald Montgomery, and Torquil Matheson, the commander of Waziristan district. All had played major roles on the western front during the First World War, but had no experience of the frontier.[30] Rawlinson argued that continuing military occupation offered the opportunity to settle the Waziristan problem once and for all.[31] To withdraw the troops would be taken as a sign of weakness and encourage Afghan, even perhaps, Soviet interference. Nor would it save money in the long run: the situation in Waziristan remained unsettled, and unless it was properly pacified further costly military intervention would be needed in the future. Others were concerned about possible Soviet interference too. The 1907 Anglo-Russian Convention had helped to allay British concerns about Russian interference in Afghanistan, but the collapse of the Tsarist government and the establishment of the revolutionary Soviet regime in 1917 revived them. Although the Afghan-Soviet treaty had been signed in August 1921, the British were worried about the possibility of growing Bolshevik influence along the frontier ('world-wide possibilities made the acceptance of Waziristan as a perpetual source of trouble inadvisable', the secretary of state, Lord Peel, later commented).[32] Some civil officers had also argued for Waziristan to be brought under full British control. They included Roos-Keppel and his successor, Hamilton Grant. The latter actually wanted disarmament, the introduction of 'civil administration on rough lines', the levying of nominal revenue and the general improvement of communications.[33]

This was out of the question, while, as we have seen, a return to the Curzon policy was unlikely. Chelmsford agreed that lines of outposts had been too vulnerable to Afghan attacks and that they had not done enough to restrain the Mehsuds. He wanted a 'policy of stringent control over predatory tribes'; this he thought would be popular in India itself – some Indian politicians and the Indian vernacular press had complained vociferously about the attacks by men from Waziristan on Hindus living along the Waziristan border and wanted a vigorous response.[34] Following Bruce and Crump, Chelmsford proposed 'the permanent occupation of a position in central Waziristan'. This he thought should be in the neighbourhood of Makin. In addition he suggested 'a chain of Militia posts along the Gomal to Wana, and a series of strategic roads, including a central road for motor vehicles connecting the Tochi with Kot Khirgi via the new base at Makin'.[35]

By now the military occupation of Waziristan was making a major contribution to the Indian Imperial Budget deficit – in 1921–2 approximately £22 million; the London *Times* suggested that what it called the 'imprudent attempt to occupy Central Waziristan' was largely responsible for excess military expenditure of £1,750,000.[36] Economies could not be avoided. Most members of the Viceroy's Council were civilians, and mainly because of the cost they wanted regular troops to be withdrawn as soon as possible. In particular Sir Malcolm Hailey, the finance member, argued that Waziristan was becoming 'a bottomless well down which India's revenue is disappearing'.[37]

The British began to look for cheaper alternatives. Chelmsford's successor was Lord Reading, who arrived in India late in 1921. He arranged for a committee presided over by the commander-in-chief, to review the Waziristan situation.[38] It reported in January 1922. Its members agreed unanimously that, although 'permanent occupation and domination' up to the Durand Line was the only real answer to the Waziristan problem, the financial situation made it impossible. They suggested that regular troops should be withdrawn during the summer of 1922 to the Manzai base and Tank to the south-east and Dardoni near Miranshah to the north. Hailey put forward a plan to withdraw the troops altogether and replace them with 3,500 khassadars and 1,000 Scouts (distributed at various different points).[39] The majority, however, agreed that the garrison should be withdrawn from Ladha and that a new base should be established at

Razmak, just north of Mehsud territory. This would be held by 500 Scouts; a road would be built to it from Idak in Dawar, to be protected by Scouts located in towers and by khassadars, and regular troops would be located in the Tochi and at Bannu to support it.[40] Having a presence adjacent to the Mehsuds, they said, would make it easier to put pressure on them when necessary and help to keep them in line. The chief British negotiator in Kabul, Dobbs, had also argued that it was important to maintain a presence in Waziristan; without it there would be renewed Afghan encroachment that would make relations with Afghanistan difficult. The viceroy, therefore, asked the secretary of state, Lord Peel, to approve this.[41]

He would not do so. As we have seen, the commander-in-chief, Rawlinson, wanted to keep troops in central Waziristan. He was able to exert effective influence in London by playing a double game: appearing to go along with the consensus in the Viceroy's Council, but also writing to his friends at the India Office and the War Office, asking them to pressure Peel into insisting on the deployment of regular troops at the proposed new base at Razmak. Although the two situations were so different, another argument that he and others deployed was that the GOI's failure to allocate sufficient resources to the Mesopotamian campaign during the First World War had been to blame for the humiliating British surrender at Kut in 1916. Such a mistake, they said, should not be made again.

In his telegram of 22 February 1922 Peel insisted on a more expensive and intrusive policy. He agreed that a base should be established at Razmak, but, influenced by Rawlinson, he stipulated that it should be garrisoned by regular troops, not Scouts. In addition he wanted a 'mechanical transport road' to be constructed through Waziristan from Kot Khirgi (east of Jandola on the edge of Waziristan) to Idak via the Ahnai and Barari Tangis and Razmak, and another from Idak to Thal (to the north of Waziristan in the Kurram Agency). This was referred to in the correspondence as the '469 lakhs scheme'.[42] Peel accepted that this would involve extra expenditure in the short term, but claimed that over time it would save money. Not to occupy Waziristan properly now would mean further punitive expeditions in the future and affect relations with Afghanistan. Moreover, 'the Mehsuds were told that we should occupy their territory and they will never believe again that we shall be able to maintain this threat if we now go back on it'.[43]

Reading was doubtful and objected. (He visited the frontier himself in April 1922.)[44] A subcommittee of the Committee of Imperial Defence in London looked at the question and advised the secretary of state to ignore his objections.[45]

Differences of opinion between the GOI and the Home Government were becoming serious.[46] Towards the end of April Reading telegraphed Peel, drawing attention to the mounting financial difficulties of the Indian government and to the fact that relations with Afghanistan appeared to be improving. He accepted, he said, the need for the Razmak base and the mechanical transport road from Idak to Razmak, but thought that there was still scope to cut costs. He and the council were not convinced, for example, that it was vital to complete the remaining section of the Tank Zam road from Sora Rogha to Razmak, or upgrade the Idak-Thal road so that it could be used for light mechanical transport. They also thought that the proportion of regular troops vis-à-vis scouts and khassadars to be stationed at Razmak could be adjusted.[47] Even Rawlinson agreed that there was some scope for modification of the 469 rupees scheme.[48] Reading suggested to Peel that a final decision on these questions should be postponed for two or three months and that in the meantime work could start on constructing the Idak-Razmak road and improving the Idak-Thal one. Towards the end of June, however, he was persuaded to withdraw his opposition to Peel's plan, and this was sanctioned on 7 September 1922.[49]

Some British officials continued to be in favour of withdrawing many if not all the regular troops. In the summer of 1922, the new chief commissioner, Maffey, influenced by Hailey, decided that they were right. He wrote a memorandum to Reading in which he made a compelling case for it. Continuing to maintain a permanent military presence in Waziristan, he argued, far from exerting a pacifying influence, would merely antagonize its inhabitants, encouraging them to intrigue with the government in Kabul and respond to the mullahs' calls for jihad. In fact, 'the more you are involved in the tribal area the greater will be your difficulties when the hour of greater danger strikes'.[50] If regular troops were withdrawn from most of Waziristan, security could still be maintained along the border with the help of the RAF.[51] Better roads along the border would mean that intensive patrolling and aerial reconnaissance would make it possible to detect and head off raiding parties. If they did get through, redress could be sought through the traditional techniques of frontier management – such as arresting tribesmen and seizing their property, and barring them from British territory. If it came to it, there could be quick 'cutting-out' expeditions to seize property from villages in tribal territory, and as a last resort artillery bombardment and air attack.[52] Maffey was therefore advocating a return to something closer to a real close-border policy – keeping Waziristan quiet by reducing interference with it to a minimum, even though he thought that on this part of the frontier the Lower Tochi and Miranshah should be retained on strategic grounds.[53]

Because, as the chief commissioner, Maffey would be the man responsible for making the policy of military occupation work, Reading thought that his objections to it could not be ignored. In the early autumn of 1922 he sent two members of his council, Sir William Vincent and Sir Muhammad Shafi, to Waziristan to ascertain the views of the local officials.[54] The Mehsuds had their own sources of intelligence in British India and were well aware of the mission. Its arrival may have led them to think that the British had not after all made up their minds about Waziristan and that further resistance might encourage them to withdraw. In late November and early December anti-British Mehsuds were able to halt British efforts to establish Mehsud khassadar posts at Sarwakai, Haidari Kach and Dargai Oba.[55] Musa Khan was also able to stop Mehsud khassadars setting up posts near Makin, and they were dismissed on 13 December 1922. The day before some Abdullais had killed Lieutenant Dickson in Mohmit Khel limits while he was surveying the Sora Rogha-Razmak road, and work on it was suspended.[56] Garrerais and Guri Khels of Ahmadwam in the Inzar Valley, other Manzai sections and Jalal Khels mounted raids and carried out minor attacks on troops. The British had to admit that the hostile Mehsuds had successfully defeated their attempts to establish 'a system of tribal administration in Mehsud country'.[57] There was also further Afghan interference; in December Brigadier Adam Khan went to Shakin and summoned the hostile Wazirs and Mehsuds who belonged to Haji Abdur Razaq's levies, ostensibly to pay their wages and allowances.[58]

In November 1922 Reading had tried to reopen the question of policy in Waziristan. He wrote to Peel suggesting that a commission be appointed to examine it. Peel insisted that it was too late.[59] He was very critical of the Vincent/Shafi mission and 'the manifest hesitation of your Government to carry out the policy which HMG have approved', because, he claimed, they had encouraged further Mehsud resistance.[60] In his reply Reading explained that a few months ago it had seemed that the Sora Rogha-Razmak road could be built under the protection of khassadars with Scouts in support. Renewed Mehsud resistance now meant that regular troops would have to remain to protect the men working on it. This would impose a serious additional financial burden, he said, and might lead to the Indian legislature trying to reverse the whole Waziristan policy. There were further discussions in the council, during which opponents of the Razmak policy, especially Hailey, continued to put their case.[61]

In the meantime Matheson and Pears thought that bombing would bring the Makin Abdullais and other Mehsuds who would not surrender to heel, and 'air operations on a scale previously unknown on the Frontier' were conducted against them and others during the winter of 1922–3.⁶² When it seemed likely that Makin would be bombed, women and children were usually sent out to the surrounding mountains. During these air raids, *Al-Mujahid* ('The One Who Strives for God'), the paper produced by the Mujahidin at Chamarkand from 1922 to 1940, reported that a number of children were lost 'wandering in the hills in cold and snow'.⁶³ But still the Mehsuds did not submit. Details of the quantities of bombs dropped were released by the RAF to the press in India. The secretary of state was unhappy about this bad publicity; in future such detailed reports were not to be issued.⁶⁴ Matheson also used the howitzers again to shell Makin and the surrounding villages.⁶⁵ In January an aircraft crashed in Darra Toi in Abdullai territory and another in Jalal Khel country and caught fire. In both cases the Mehsuds captured and released the crews.⁶⁶

Matheson had requested that he might delay the withdrawal from Ladha for another month, and this was sanctioned.⁶⁷ Because air operations had not succeeded in crushing the Mehsud resistance, he organized a series of punitive raids, sending troops into the Makin villages to carry out the usual destructive operations and remove stores of grain and other reserves of food. Musa Khan's settlement at Mandesh was one of the principal targets. The British had intended to demolish the settlement of Dinour, but as a result of the previous bombing and shelling there was only one house left to destroy.⁶⁸ The anti-British groups finally submitted in February 1923. The fact that the military felt compelled to send troops into Makin again, just two years after the last attack, suggests that the whole approach was flawed.⁶⁹ We might recall that sixty-three years earlier in 1860 Taylor had confidently predicted that burning Makin was the 'first page in the chapter of Muhsood civilisation', but it had been attacked again in 1894 and 1901 (Figure 7.1).⁷⁰

At the end of 1922 the Mehsuds had sent a large deputation to Kabul to complain about the bombing and shelling. Reports of this in Indian newspapers had already upset the amir, and he and the Afghan Foreign Office protested to Humphrys, the British minister in Kabul, that the operations were in violation of Article XI of the 1921 treaty and its appended letters. In January 1923 the Afghans protested again about the renewed military operations against the Mehsuds, arguing that according to the treaty they should have been given prior warning of them.⁷¹ When Amanullah and Humphrys met on 2 February, the amir requested that the road-building south of Razmak might be suspended. The tribesmen, he said, blamed him for not supporting them, and the arrival of refugees from Waziristan put him in an awkward position.⁷² A number of articles appeared in the Afghan press drawing attention to this; for example the *Ittihad-i-Mashriqi* ('Union of the East'), a newspaper published in Jalalabad,

Figure 7.1 The burning of 'Makin' from air and land – Waziristan, Pakistan, dated 1890 but in fact probably early 1920s. Photo by Mela Ram/Royal Geographical society/Getty Images.

published several very anti-British pieces early in 1922; among other things the British were accused of committed atrocities worse than those resulting from the German air force bombing of London and Paris during the First World War.[73] During 1923 the GOA continued to complain about British activities in Waziristan in the Afghan press and through its representative in London, Abdul Hadi.[74]

The amir had been keeping in contact with the frontier mullahs who had been cultivated by his uncle, Sardar Nasrullah. He invited some of them to attend the state jirga in Kabul in August 1922.[75] He also invited men from the British side of the Durand Line to a jirga held in Jalalabad in February 1923, while Matheson's troops were carrying out their destructive activities in and around Makin, and he gave money and encouragement to influential anti-British men from the Indian side of the Durand Line.[76] In March 1923 thirty men from the Mujahidin bases north of Peshawar went to Makin, where they remained under Maulana Bashir's direction to encourage opposition to the British; the Afghan government sent them some money.[77] In August 1923 Mullahs and other men from the British side of the Durand Line attended Afghan Independence Day celebrations and paid their respects to the amir. They were given money, horses, guns and carriages. The GOA also made endowments to support the establishment of mosques and schools along the border.[78] Some frontier mullahs, however, were not opposed to British efforts to increase their authority over the frontier.[79] They accepted that these would continue and wanted to ensure that the groups with which they were connected received a fair share of the allowances.[80]

On 3 and 4 April 1923 Lala Pir held a jirga at Kaniguram which was attended by about 2,000 men. He promised generous allowances and compensation for the damage caused by the British air raids. As usual there were differences of opinion, in particular between Musa Khan and his supporters and 'the discontented maliks of the Khaisora', Hayat Khan Michi Khel Manzai Alizai, and Qutab Khan Salimi Khel Manzai Alizai (Adam Khan's nephew) and their followers. Lala Pir had instructed them not to do so, but Qutab Khan and Hayat Khan with around 200 less influential Alizais and Shaman Khels went to Urgun; Qutab Khan and Hayat Khan went on to Kabul.[81] It appears that the GOA also paid Rs.20,000 to the Wana Wazir jirgas though Adam Khan.[82]

By this time the amir had recruited his own Mehsud and Wazir khassadars.[83] He was now maintaining his own militia in Waziristan and was still making payments to anti-British men on the British side of the Durand Line, reportedly Rs.70,000 a year to Mehsuds and Rs.20,000 to Wazirs.[84] British officials objected to this, ignoring the fact that Article XI of the 1921 treaty and the attached letter admitted 'an Afghan interest in the welfare of the tribes on the Indian side of the Durand Line' and 'gave as it were a certain legal basis to Afghan interference across the line'.[85] As Fraser-Tyler put it, until 1947 the British government kept trying to 'induce the Afghan Government to recognize the illegality of action, which they themselves had by implication sanctioned'.[86]

The Razmak policy

To return to British activities, apart from the C. in C. Rawlinson, the members of the Viceroy's Council still wanted to defer construction of the Sora Rogha-Razmak road. On 29 and 30 January 1923 Peel telegraphed to insist it went ahead (a slap in the face for Reading, Rawlinson commented happily).[87] In his reply Reading pointed to the additional costs that would be incurred because of the recent deterioration in the Waziristan position, which would mean that troops would be needed to protect the workers. He asked for a postponement, but Matheson insisted that the road could be finished in nine months.[88] The majority of the members of his council continued to oppose this, but Reading himself finally withdrew his objections and agreed that the road should be built as soon as possible and that military occupation should continue until it was finished.[89] Work on the new Razmak base began in January 1923, and at the beginning of February the British began to withdraw troops from Ladha, but troops did not leave the Tank Zam until November 1923, following the road's completion.[90] In a speech to the Indian Legislative Assembly in the same year, Sir Denys Bray, the foreign secretary, described the new policy as aimed at 'the control of Waziristan – through a road system … and the maintenance of some 4,600 Khassadars and of some 5,000 irregulars' [the Scouts].[91]

It is easy to see why, after fighting so hard to establish a strong position in it, the British generals were reluctant to withdraw from central Waziristan, but they may well have exaggerated the risks of withdrawal and failed to take the possible benefits fully into account. Maintaining the new garrison at Razmak was expensive. Some local contractors aside perhaps, people did not like it, and as we shall see, having troops based inside Waziristan did not always make it easier to repress outbreaks of resistance. Robson suggests that withdrawal would have meant ignoring Waziristan's economic problems. But in practice the new modified forward policy did not do much to address these either, although as we shall see road building and the Razmak base did offer employment, and there were some efforts to improve agriculture in the later 1920s and 1930s. There would still have been difficulties after withdrawal, but Bray's claim that a closed-border policy would 'leave [the tribesmen] … in their devil's kitchen of mischief to brew incalculable trouble for us' was a rhetorical flourish.[92]

The British regarded Amanullah's frontier policy as an aggressive one. In fact, by doing what he could to maintain his influence in Waziristan, the amir was trying to make himself more secure. Britain had already invaded Afghanistan twice, so it is not surprising that he worried that they might do so again. Anxious about British intentions, he regarded the frontier areas as a 'prickly hedge' of tribal defence against possible attack.[93] If Britain had withdrawn regular troops from Waziristan, given Amanullah's evident interest in it Afghan influence there would almost certainly have grown. But the amir had little control of those living on his side of the Durand Line; as we shall see, it was very difficult for him to establish his authority over areas such as Khost. Just as people whose homes were on the British side of the Durand Line could easily cross into Afghan territory, so people living in Khost could cross into British territory in order to escape Amanullah's unpopular programme of modernization and centralization.[94] There would have been definite limits to what he could do in Waziristan.

It is possible therefore the British might have found that a return to something more like Curzon's policy worked reasonably well. Even at the time some had argued that Curzon's policy had not been given a fair trial because no attempt had been made to support the Upper Tochi Valley outposts when the Afghans attacked in 1919. Had they been reinforced by just a small force of regular troops, it was suggested, they might have held out, and then the South Waziristan militia would almost certainly not have collapsed in turn.[95] By the 1920s, given the availability of air power, better ground transport and radio, it might have been possible to rely mainly on Scouts and khassadars to maintain a presence in Waziristan and prevent raiding.

By the end of 1922, the two civilian officials primarily responsible for Waziristan, the chief commissioner, John Maffey, and the resident, Stuart Pears, could not agree on the policy to be pursued towards it. Pears supported the establishment of the Razmak base and its garrisoning by regular troops, Maffey did not. He used his contacts to try and encourage support for his point of view. For example he was in touch with the editor of the London *Times*, and in January 1923 the paper published an article advocating that troops should only be kept in the Lower Tochi and that otherwise Waziristan should be evacuated.[96] But Maffey was fighting a losing battle, and in 1923 he resigned, and with his resignation 'went the last chance of a radical solution to a problem which continued to bedevil the British administration down to 1947'.[97] He was succeeded as the chief commissioner by Norman Bolton.

In addition to establishing the new Razmak garrison, making new roads and raising allowances, the British had made some changes to the security forces. In 1913 they had created the Frontier Constabulary to replace the Border Police, and in the early 1920s they raised two new irregular corps, the Tochi Scouts and South Waziristan Scouts. Recruited from loyal elements of the disbanded North and South Waziristan Militias and the Mohmand Militia, the Scouts came under the authority of the political officers. No Mehsuds were enrolled in the South Waziristan Scouts because they were thought to be unreliable on their home ground (though Pashtuns from other areas were not necessarily much more popular in Waziristan than the British themselves). Finally, as we have seen, in the early 1920s the British began to employ large numbers of tribal police known as khassadars, who were untrained and supplied their own weapons.[98] The khassadar system provided employment and encouraged men to identify themselves to a certain extent with British interests. However the fact that the appointments quickly became hereditary made them less useful, as did the khassadars' reluctance to kill other men because it might lead to blood feuds.[99]

Nor could they always be entirely relied on. In 1924, for example, British officials congratulated themselves on the way that in February the Manzai khassadars had managed to obtain the release without ransom of three Hindus kidnapped from Manzai by Karim Khan Guri Khel. But in the same year, they had to disband a company of Tazi Khel khassadars because they had killed a Naib Tehsildar whom they were escorting to Wana and dismiss half a company of Band Khel Bahlolzais because they murdered two Gurkha soldiers with whom they were on picket duty at Tauda China. Khassadars came to be used mainly for protecting the roads which ran through their own territories (Figure 7.2).[100]

Meanwhile in January 1922 the resident, Pears, had put forward new proposals for the payment of additional allowances to all the Waziristan groups in return for khassadar service. The British authorities had quickly approved these. As we have seen, they raised the Tochi Utmanzais' allowances to Rs.72,000, and in May 1922 the Tori Khels agreed to the establishment of a British garrison on the Razmak plateau, which lay in their territory just to the north of Mehsud territory. In January 1923 British troops began to establish themselves and create one of the largest garrisons in the whole of India.[101] In the end 'as many as 15,000 regular troops, British as well as Indian, thousands of horses and mules, a fleet

Figure 7.2 Daily convoys for Razmak, showing a long camel train proceeding through the snow to Razmak. Holmes, Randolph Bezzant (1888–1973). Credit: British Library, London UK@British Library Board. All Rights Reserved/Bridgeman Images.

of transport vehicles, and an armoured car company sat behind a triple circle of barbed wire with artillery pieces pointed out in all directions, while batteries of floodlights kept the perimeter bright twenty-four hours a day'.[102] Razmak acquired a bazaar, a cinema, a roller skating rink and various clubs to keep the troops amused in what was described as the world's largest monastery.[103]

Relations between Britain and Afghanistan had improved somewhat after the signing of the treaty in 1921, but the British still mistrusted Amir Amanullah. They disliked the fact that he had been paying allowances to, among others, Musa Khan and other Bahlolzais – in 1922 for example about 60,000 Kabul rupees in all.[104] This was, as we have seen, a development of existing practice. Since the early 1870s, if not before, the government in Kabul had invited men from Waziristan to visit it, and by the late nineteenth century it was giving arms and ammunition and money to men from the British side of the Durand Line, including Mullah Powindah.[105] What was new was the way that the amir had recruited some deserters from the North and South Waziristan Militias into a militia of his own and enlisted several hundred Mehsuds and Wazirs as khassadars.[106] The British also blamed him for encouraging some Mehsuds and Wazirs to continue their resistance in 1922 and 1923 and put pressure on him to reduce his support for them.[107] They wanted him to dismiss the deserters from the North and South Waziristan Militias who had joined his militia and not to employ any men from the British side of the Durand Line as khassadars. They also wanted him to stop paying allowances to men living on the British side of the Durand Line.[108]

Several murders in 1923 made relations between Britain and Afghanistan even more difficult. In revenge for the hanging of a relative by the British in 1909, on 8 April two Shinwari men from the Afghan side of the border, Ardali and Daud Shah, killed two British officers near Landi Kotal in the Khyber. A few days later a gang led by an Afridi, Ajab Khan, kidnapped a young British woman, Molly Ellis, and murdered her mother. In 1920, 120 rifles had been stolen from the cavalry magazine in Kohat, and the officials suspected that Ajab Khan had been responsible for this. In 1923 forty-four more rifles were stolen from the Kohat police magazine; troops searched his village and found some of the missing weapons. During the search they insisted on looking into the faces of all the women to make sure that there were no men among them dressed as women. Ajab Khan was shamed by this, and in response, during the night of 14 April 1923 he and his gang tried to kidnap Mrs Ellis, the wife of Colonel Ellis, in their house in the Kohat Cantonment. She woke up, and Ajab's brother, Shahzada, killed her, and the gang kidnapped her daughter Molly instead.[109] One of the nurses at the Church Missionary Society Medical Mission in Peshawar, Lilian Starr, courageously went into Afridi territory to negotiate for her release, and with the help of a local mullah, Mullah Mahmud Akhundzada, she was freed. Ajab Khan and his band fled to Afghanistan. The British representative in Kabul, Francis Humphrys, demanded his surrender, and that of Ardali and Daud Shah as well. Such a surrender would have been unprecedented, but the amir had Daud Shah and Ardali arrested and issued orders for the arrest of Ajab Khan and his gang should they be found in Afghanistan. In fact they remained on the British side of the Durand Line, and in November 1923 they tried to abduct Mrs Watts, wife of Captain Watts of the Kurram militia from Parachinar in Kurram. She and her husband woke up, and the gang killed them both.[110]

Two other British officials were murdered in the same month. Some Zilla Khels, led by Misri Sheikh Bazid Khel, shot and killed Major Finnis, the Zhob Agency political agent, and his driver as his car was passing through the Hasuband Pass on its way to Manikhwa in the Zhob Agency.[111] Misri was the brother of Angur, who had taken part in an attack on the Tiarza Militia Post in 1909 and had been given the rank of Firqa Mashar by the GOA. Another Zilla Khel man, Shahi Khan Masti Khel, shot the (Naib) Tehsildar while travelling by car through the Hinnis Tangi from Kot Khirgi to Jandola, and he died from his wounds.[112]

Humphrys continued to raise these issues with the Afghan government. In June 1923, for example, he had a meeting with Nadir Khan, now the minister of war, who had recently returned from northern Afghanistan. Nadir expressed his concern about Soviet activities along the border, said that he wanted good relations with Britain and reminded Humphrys of the various steps that the GOA had taken to meet recent British demands. As well as arresting Daud Shah and Ardali, he pointed out that orders had been issued for the arrest of Ajab Khan and Shahzada and the rest of their gang. Moreover, he said, his government had sacked the editor of the anti-British *Ittihad-i-Mashriqi*, recalled Brigadier Adam Khan from the Waziristan border, abandoned Haji Abdur Razaq's Birmal settlement scheme and issued orders for the dismissal of the Wazir khassadars, and the amir had told a Mehsud deputation to go home and make peace with the British.[113] It is clear that the GOA was making some effort to meet British demands.

Two months later, in July 1923 three Mehsuds shot Lieutenant Webster, a Royal Engineers officer supervising work on improving the road through the Tank Zam near Piazha. Some British officials suspected Musa Khan of arranging this to disrupt the khassadar arrangements, but Harap Khan, a wealthy Astanai Shabi Khel road and railway building contractor, had fallen out with Webster over a contract and may well have been responsible.[114] By this time support for Musa Khan and Mullah Fazal Din was falling. The resident reported in September 1923 that the hostile Mehsuds and Zilla Khels were now convinced that the British meant to stay and that there was no point in further resistance. At a jirga held towards the end of the month British officials reached a settlement with many of the Garrerais. They agreed to pay a fine of Rs.3,000 and accept responsibility for their outlaws. Some of the Guri Khels still refused to comply with the terms offered to them and the RAF bombed their villages in the Ahmadwam area.[115]

In spite of Humphrys' representations, in October 1923 Afghan officials in Khost paid allowances to Musa Khan and a group of his supporters. The resident, Richard Bruce's son Lieutenant-Colonel Charles Bruce, did not think the British could afford to match these; if it did, other Mehsuds would demand higher allowances too. In spite of the payments from Kabul, it seems that Musa Khan had reluctantly come to the conclusion that there was no more to be done about the British occupation of Razmak. The resident suggested that he should be left alone if he kept quiet.[116] By then the so-called 'hostiles', including Musa Khan, were not necessarily actively hostile. They were men who had not settled with the British and had no British allowances or khassadar service. Some gave no trouble, while 'many so-called friendlies did all the harm they could'.[117] If the hostiles came to terms, the British would not need to rely so much on the friendlies, so the friendlies sometimes actually encouraged the hostiles to engage in anti-British activity.[118] In spite of Webster's murder, work continued on the roads, and by the end of 1923 the whole of the Kot Kirghi to Razmak road was completed; by September 1924 a road from Jandola to Sarwakai was finished as well.

In the meantime Ardali and Daud Shah had been imprisoned in a jail in the Arg fortress in Kabul, but in August 1923 they escaped.[119] In September arms and supplies that Amanullah had purchased from Europe had arrived in Bombay, and the British decided not to allow it to be sent on to Afghanistan until they had been recaptured.[120] In the autumn, to apply further pressure, Humphrys's wife and the other women living at the British Legation were sent back to India. Early in 1924 the GOA arranged for Ardali and Daud Shah to give themselves up, but the surrender went wrong. Daud Shah escaped and Ardali was killed. In January Ajab and his group had finally surrendered to the governor of Jalalabad, and they and their families were exiled to Mazar-i-Sharif in northern Afghanistan. In

March 1924 the British released the Afghans' arms from Bombay and the British women returned to Kabul.[121]

British policy continued to be to maintain Afghanistan as a stable and effective buffer between Russia and India. Many Afghans did not like the amir's modernizing and centralizing policies and disapproved of the efforts he had made to please the British by arresting outlaws and controlling raiding gangs operating from within Afghanistan.[122] Pressuring him to adopt a more pro-British stance simply made him more unpopular. In March 1924 Mangals and Ahmadzai Ghilzais living in Khost rebelled against the amir, and anti-Amanullah religious leaders took refuge in Waziristan.[123] Nadir Khan, the minister of war, had a good relationship with the Pashtuns living on both sides of the Durand Line. He had advocated a less confrontational approach to the Afghan ones; he declined to act against the Khost rebels and resigned, becoming the ambassador in Paris.[124] Amanullah sent Haji Abdur Razaq back to Waziristan to try and recruit men to fight for him. Lashkars drawn from various tribal groups, including Madda Khel and other Wazirs and Mehsuds, including Musa Khan, but mainly men who were living in Logar, as well as some Khugianis, Shinwaris and Mohmands joined the fighting and helped to put down the rebellion.[125]

If his frontier policy had been partly dictated by anxiety about British intentions, by now the amir was becoming more concerned about the Soviet Union. In spite of the friendship treaty of 1921, the Soviets reneged on some of their commitments. They had undertaken to respect the freedom and independence of Bukhara and Khiva, but had annexed them and incorporated them into the newly created republics of Uzbekistan and Turkmenistan.[126] As a result Amanullah gradually reverted to 'the traditional [Afghan] policy of seeking a balance of power in the area', which meant 'a rapprochement with Great Britain', and he reduced his support for anti-British activities in Waziristan.[127]

8

The 1920s and peaceful penetration

The Mehsuds and the RAF

Although British relations with the Mehsuds and with Afghanistan were improving, Waziristan had not settled down. During the first few months of 1924 the British continued to experience problems with some Mehsuds, particularly some of the Abdur Rahman Khels, though bands of Jalal Khel Bahlolzais, Faridais, Maresais and Guri Khels also carried out some serious attacks.[1] Following a raid in May 1924, the RAF bombed the Abdur Rahman Khels living in Splitoi.[2] Bombers were also in action against the contractor Harap Khan Shabi Khel towards the end of 1924 because he and other Astanais had been involved in raiding. In this operation several aircraft had to make forced landings owing to bad weather, and four crewmen were killed. Harap Khan handed over one of the survivors to the British and paid a fine.[3] In December 1924 Giga Khels killed Lieutenant Tapp who had strayed into their territory with some Scouts during a training exercise; they were made to pay a fine and surrender some rifles.[4] It seems that Harap Khan continued to cause problems. In January 1925 a bridge at Marobi was blown up. Three men gave the British the names of those responsible and were murdered. Harap Khan and three other men were accused of arranging this, tried by jirga in August and found guilty; Harap was fined £1,000.[5]

In the meantime the British relationship with the Abdur Rahman Khels remained difficult. In December 1924 a number of the hostiles and their families returned from Afghanistan to Splitoi and the Dre Algad. British officials assembled a large Bahlolzai jirga at Tank, but could not persuade it to deal with them.[6] On 16 January 1925 the officials held a meeting with the hostiles. They requested an amnesty and a doubling of their allowances, but the officials did not agree to this. In January some Abdur Rahman Khels, accompanied by Guri Khels, Maresais and Faridais, kidnapped four Hindus from Manzai and two more from the coolie camp at Splitoi and then attacked the Gumal Post and stole twenty-seven rifles.[7] The British decided to respond with force. The air vice marshal, Sir Edward Ellington, had suggested that the RAF could carry out punitive operations on its own, and the commander-in-chief decided to see what would happen if for the first time it was given sole charge of a campaign. Wing-Commander Richard Pink established his headquarters at Tank, and three squadrons were moved up to Miranshah and Tank.[8]

Early in March the RAF dropped leaflets advising that women and children should leave the danger zone and warning that long delay-action bombs might be used. Air raids began on 9 March and continued for forty-two of the following fifty-four days. The targets varied from the Faridai and Maresai villages to the 'scattered huts and enclosures' of the Guri Khels and the Abdur Rahman Khels' cave dwellings.[9] By now nearly all the villages had defensive cave systems. The bombers tried to kill livestock, but these were usually driven into caves during the day and fed and watered at night. They only attacked terraced fields once, to show what they could do, because the aim was said to be to intimidate not to destroy productive resources. The bombing was briefly stopped at several points to enable jirgas to be assembled or property collected as security. The Guri Khels surrendered towards the end of March, but the others did not.

The British experimented with different ways of arranging the raids, such as continuous bombing for long periods, and air blockade – when aircraft were sent over at irregular intervals to create 'a general feeling of insecurity, uncertainty and discomfort, and to prevent the pursuit of their normal activities'.[10] On 4 April they began night attacks, using reconnaissance flares to assist the pilots. The aircraft would reach maximum height over the airfields and then throttle down and fly as quietly as possible or even glide as they approached their targets. On 9 April a patrol spotted some Faridai men; it summoned additional aircraft from Miranshah which bombed the group and inflicted a number of casualties.[11] On 15 April planes killed a number of animals belonging to the Abdur Rahman Khel hostiles, who were collecting in Splitoi and the Dre Algad in particular, before moving back to Afghanistan. On 18 April the Maresais and Faridais accepted the government conditions for a settlement. The RAF continued to attack the Abdur Rahman Khels, and by the end of the month most of them had surrendered too.[12]

These were the longest continuous operations conducted by British aircraft since the end of the First World War. Sir Edward Ellington commented that not many people had been killed but that 'losses to flocks had been considerable' and that it would take much time and work to repair damage to property.[13] The commander-in-chief's assessment was that the results of the operations were satisfactory but that if ground forces had been used as well as air attacks, the Mehsuds would have surrendered more quickly; in future it would be better to use both together.[14]

Some British officials, including the commander-in-chief, Rawlinson, did not approve of the use of air power on the frontier, but the RAF continued to argue that aircraft should be substituted for ground troops as the primary instrument of tribal control.[15] At about this time, it should be noted, it carried out an aerial survey of many of the unmapped portions of Waziristan, which the officials found useful. 'On several occasions during the year the fact that detailed knowledge had been obtained of this terra incognita was the deciding factor in bringing recalcitrants to terms', it was reported.[16] Air power continued to play a role. Although some effort was made to avoid casualties among non-combatants, these continued to occur.[17]

From the British point of view the situation in Waziristan continued to improve, partly thanks to the money they were spending there; particularly the substantial increases in allowances – from Rs.130,000 in 1919 to nearly Rs.280,000 by 1925, and the distribution of Rs.1.9 million under the khassadari scheme.[18] Officials also tried to use local contractors for road building and Mehsuds carried out much of the work on the Takki Zam road. By 1924 some men, like Harap Khan Shabi Khel, were prospering from road building and repair. Despite strong opposition, the British threw roadwork on the Tochi road open to public tender. Sorting out the contracts was a demanding business, because the Mehsud men bidding for them continued to insist that when contracts were awarded they should be divided equally between them.[19] Pears agreed that to avoid jealousy it was better to give a share of any contracts to anyone who might be entitled to one, even though this meant much more work.[20]

After 1925 many of the Mehsuds who had taken parts in raids across the Waziristan border over the past fifteen years stopped doing so, leaving the Bannu and Dera Ismail Khan districts largely free from transborder raids.[21] The British officials continued to reach settlements with individual hostiles, such as Qutab Khan and Abbas Khan Salimi Khel Alizai, who were made first-class maliks, though they do not seem to have had much influence in practice.[22] Some men remained discontented, among them Sadde Khan Shaman Khel and his brother Ramzan (nephews of Khan Sahib Marwat Khan Shaman Khel). Reportedly Sadde Khan was annoyed because the British officials would not pay him the allowance that his father had received.[23] In 1927 he tried to persuade other Mehsuds to protest against visits by British officials to Mehsud country and against the pro-British Maliks. They did not have much success, but helped by Abbas Khan Salimi Khel, they did persuade three companies of khassadars to desert.[24]

Violent incidents continued to occur. For instance Shabi Khels murdered three workmen at Piazha in July 1925. The British fined them for this and other offences. They paid most of these in February 1926; the Mirat Khel Jalal Khels also paid their fines.[25] In January 1926 two outlaws, Ali and Faizali, with two other men, killed five men and a woman and wounded five others in an attempt to rob a house in the Dera Ismail Khan District. Pursued by Scouts, Ali and Faizali crossed into Afghanistan, but later returned and took refuge with Kikarai Mehsuds living in the Shaktu. In October 1928, to put pressure on the latter, a party of South Waziristan Scouts surprised the Kikarais and captured seven men and more than a thousand sheep and goats.[26]

British officials continued to be concerned by the payments the GOA was said to be making to men living in Waziristan. For example in 1926 Musa Khan was reportedly paid Rs.100,000, much of which he was to pass on to other Mehsuds.[27] The newly appointed governor of the southern province, Ghulam Nabi Charkhi, told Humphrys that this was not true.[28] Reports like these were, he said, designed to encourage the British officials to be more generous.[29] He may well have been right. Some British officials also objected to the way that the GOA employed men from Waziristan in the Afghan regular army and as khassadars. Others were not so sure that this was reasonable. In 1926 for instance, the chief commissioner, Norman Bolton, pointed out that Hazaras from Afghanistan served in the Indian Army and that therefore there could be no objection to men from the British side of the border serving in the Afghan one. But he did agree that the GOA should not employ these men as khassadars. Rather than asking the Afghans to give this up altogether, however, Humphrys should proceed on 'the basis of previous negotiations and promises, formal and informal', and if the opportunity arose he should request the GOA not to employ near the Waziristan border any Mehsuds or Wazirs whose permanent residence was on the British side of it.[30]

Peaceful penetration

We saw above that in relation to Wana in 1921 Parsons had referred to peaceful penetration. A little background may be helpful here. During the early nineteenth century the French general Thomas-Robert Bugeaud and others began to use the term 'penetration pacifique' during the subjugation of Algeria. Later in the century 'penetration pacifique' came to be applied to what was called a 'new colonial method' that some French military administrators, in particular Theophile Pennequin, Jean de Lanessan, Joseph Gallieni and Hubert Lyautey, are said to have developed in Vietnam.[31] Supposedly Gallieni and Lyautey refined it in Madagascar, and Lyautey perfected it in Morocco, describing it as 'the method of *progressive occupation*' (emphasis in original).[32] The new method had three aspects or 'components: the use of force, political action, and economic-organizational action'. The first two were supposed to apply to 'the first stage of conquest and pacification' and the third to 'the period of development that proceeds from the establishment of peace in a given area'.[33] Gallieni also contrasted *action lente* (slow action) with *action vive* (quick action). *Action lente* was associated with the famous *tache d'huile*, 'oil spot' theory, according to which, having established themselves, the military would spread colonial authority through 'a gradual creeping occupation', involving the progressive creation of secure areas, by protecting and fortifying settlements and arming the people themselves.[34] They would create markets and encourage trade, improve communications, and build schools and hospitals. In this way, like a spot of oil spreading across water, peace would gradually diffuse out from the centre as people began to appreciate the benefits of French rule.[35] This was *action lente* as opposed to *action vive*.[36] *Action lente* was to be the norm, and the use of military force, *action vive*, the exception, though the targeted use of military columns was still available as a last resort. Gallieni thought that political action was the most important factor; this should be based on sound knowledge of how a society was organized. This was called the *politique des races*; in practice it meant a divide and rule policy of setting one group against another. It also meant indirect rule – retaining existing rulers and allowing them to continue to administer their territories, but keeping them under supervision and ensuring that they upheld French interests.[37] The final stage, 'economic-organizational action', was introduced when the country had been sufficiently pacified to allow its economic resources to be properly developed and 'create opportunities for European commerce'.[38] Lyautey referred to this colonial method as 'penetration pacifique'.[39]

There has been much scholarly debate about peaceful penetration. It has been claimed, for example, that the term (almost an oxymoron) had originally been introduced to conceal the destructive nature of French colonial activity in Algeria and the Sahara.[40] But it may be argued that there was more to Bugeaud's strategy in Algeria than merely subduing the people by force. For instance, Bugeaud said that the colonial officer should 'not hesitate by any means to put himself often among the populations: visit the markets, the tribes, and listen to the locals' complaints'.[41] Nor did Bugeaud rely simply on force; he tried to win over the population by political and economic means as well, and he contributed more to the development of Gallieni and Lyautey's method of colonial 'pacification' than is sometimes recognized.[42] Lyautey himself said that Gallieni's method was 'the best of Bugeaud' ('*C'est du meilleur Bugeaud*').[43] As a result, Porch argues, Gallieni and Lyautey's methods were not always as different from Bugeaud's as is sometimes claimed. In practice, he suggests, though they may have sometimes been more discriminating in its application, they had to resort to violence almost as much as had Bugeaud. Nor in practice were they necessarily any more successful. Gallieni did not actually succeed in stabilizing Tonkin, and Lyautey had to resort to 'the exercise of brute force' in pacifying the Middle Atlas in Morocco.[44]

There are some obvious parallels between French efforts to control Algeria, Vietnam, Madagascar and Morocco and British attempts to pacify the North-West Frontier. Like Bugeaud, British officials, Reynell Taylor for instance, also talked about the importance of getting to know people, talking to them and taking an interest in their affairs.[45] British and French administrators shared the ideal of the charismatic official, who won people over by the force of his personality. In addition the earlier British efforts to set up markets and encourage those living across the border to trade in British territory to some extent resemble Gallieni's stage of 'economic-organizational action'. Just as Gallieni and Lyautey tried to use force less often than had Bugeaud in Algeria, the British, partly due to the protests of critics like Sir Bartle Frere, did begin to try and limit the use of collective punishments, particularly punitive expeditions.[46] Comparisons have been drawn in particular between Sandeman's policies in Baluchistan and those that were pursued in the later nineteenth century and early twentieth centuries by French officials.[47] In Baluchistan, Sandeman instituted a form of indirect rule, based on adhering to tribal custom, ruling through existing chiefs, backing them up with military support where required and paying them allowances to recruit local levies. He also took some steps to extend education, medical care and the rule of law, though not to the same extent as his French counterparts. In this way, he argued, people's hearts and minds would be won over by largely peaceful means. His success was partly due to his charismatic personality, however, and his system broke down after his death in 1892. Inter-tribal fighting broke out, and two years later the British had deposed the Khan of Kalat.[48]

After the bloody invasion of Mehsud territory in the winter of 1919–20, officials dealing with Waziristan began to talk about peaceful penetration and refer explicitly to 'nation-building', and the British did begin cautiously at first to extend what was called a policy of 'control, peaceful penetration and elimination of Afghan intrigue' to all the areas along the frontier from the Gumal to the Malakand Pass.[49] In the speech he gave in the Indian Legislative Assembly in March 1923, Sir Denys Bray explained that a 'thorough-going forward policy' all along the frontier was out of the question, but said that there was a need for 'civilization ... to penetrate these inaccessible mountains'.[50] In 1926 the Waziristan resident, Charles Bruce, asked whether a policy of peaceful penetration should be introduced in Waziristan, and if so, what it meant in practice.[51] The GOI confirmed that it was the policy that should be followed, but refused to be specific. It saw 'no advantage and some danger in defining it', commenting that 'this policy and its implications ... not only bear a wide range of meaning in the various parts of the [whole transborder] area but are also in a constant state of change and growth in each'. As regards Waziristan, it pointed out many new responsibilities had been assumed, and 'only cautiously and gradually should any extension of them be made'.[52] In a Legislative Assembly debate in 1940, Major Nawab Sir Ahmad Nawaz Khan, the representative for Dera Ismail Khan, was to refer to peaceful penetration as a third way between the close(d) and the forward frontier policies.[53]

In practice one important feature of peaceful penetration in Waziristan came to be the planting of garrisons of Scouts in many of the places occupied by the militias before the 1919 collapse. In the 1920s forts were built or rebuilt at for instance Datta Khel, Mir Ali and Boya (in the Tochi), Spinwam on the Kaitu, and to the south Jandola, Sarwakai, Shinkai and Khajuri Kach.[54] In addition, troops and Scouts began to use the new roads as much as possible and visit remoter areas.[55] In March 1926, for example, the Razmak Military Column marched to Miranshah, Muhammad Khel and Datta Khel, and back across country from Muhammad Khel to Razoni; the first time troops had done so since 1901.[56] During the later 1920s the political agents and other officials began to make unofficial tours to various out of the way parts of Waziristan.[57] They started to intervene in disputes between tribal groups when they became serious and demarcated boundaries between them.[58] Sometimes their mediation was even requested in intra-tribal disputes, for example in a serious quarrel between two important Mehsud maliks, Khan Sahib Marwat Khan Shaman Khel and Shah Pasand Langar Khel. Mehsud women appreciated this, 'as saving their men-folk from the danger of internal feuds'.[59] Women were, Bruce suggested, no longer 'our worst propagandists [who hated] ... us for the loss of their husbands, sons and brothers and for the damage done to their country. This has now all changed.'[60]

Steps like these might be seen as the equivalent of Gallieni's *action lente*, and the recruitment of Pashtuns from outside Waziristan into the new Scouts regiments as an example of his *politique des races*.

As we have seen, peaceful penetration on French lines also entailed the building of schools, hospitals, improving communications and encouraging trade. The British themselves were ambivalent about education, concerned that it might, for example, contribute to political awareness and activism, both in India and potentially in Afghanistan.[61] Nevertheless during the 1920s a few schools were built in Mehsud territory, and a system of scholarships was introduced to enable Mehsud boys to receive secondary education.[62] This was not popular with everyone. When Captain Mir Badshah opened the first primary school for Mehsud boys in his area at Karama in 1922, Mullahs organized a protest, and a lashkar gathered intending to burn it down. Mir Badshah told the lashkar he would not allow them to do so. Two people were killed in the exchange of fire that followed. The school stayed open, and another was opened at Maidan.[63] By 1928 there were five primary schools in South Waziristan and five in North Waziristan.[64] They also provided some medical services. By the early 1920s the British had opened a civil dispensary at Jandola and a civil hospital in Miranshah, and in 1927 the Razmak Civil Hospital was opened for outpatients and an inpatient ward at the beginning of 1928. In 1928 and 1929 dispensaries were opened at Datta Khel, Khajuri and Spinwam in North Waziristan.[65]

These were limited efforts. If the British no longer conducted punitive expeditions, they continued to rely on the threat (and use) of force. Their strategy in the interwar period was based on the creation of the massive garrison at Razmak and the use of the troops and Scouts periodically to 'show the flag' and move through as many different parts of Waziristan as possible. In this connection, it is interesting to note that the French military command during the French Mandate in interwar Syria considered 'the demonstration of force, rather than its actual employment ... the most effective means of territorial control'.[66] As Neep suggests, 'A key principle of colonial warfare was its dissuasive quality. The conscious and continuous display of military strength was prescribed in order to render the use of this force unnecessary; *montrer la force pour ne pas avoir à s'en servir*, as the slogan would have it.'[67] Similarly, just as the British spent a great deal of money on building roads in Waziristan during the 1920s and 1930s, the French occupation in Syria was initially accompanied by an ambitious programme of road building, which was seen 'as the most efficient means to penetrate the country and facilitate military movements across its surface'.[68] One important difference between British and

French approaches, however, was the greater role of the military officer in the latter. Whereas on the North-West Frontier civil officials directed affairs except in times of crisis, during punitive expeditions for instance, Gallieni and Lyautey preferred to concentrate military and civil responsibility in the hands of one man; the soldier was also the administrator – 'Service in the colonies created a "special being who is neither the *militaire*, nor the civil, but who is quite simply the *colonial*".[69]

Mehsuds and Tori Khels

The fact that the different tribal groups in Waziristan were often at odds with each other was another difficulty the British faced in trying to control it. Probably the best example of this was the struggle between the Abdullai Mehsuds and Tori Khel Utmanzai Wazirs that went on throughout much of the British period. The Tori Khels customarily spent the winter in the Spinwam and Tochi area and between the Tochi and the Shaktu valleys and the summer on the Razmak and Sham plateaux and the upper Shaktu valley.[70] Since the mid-nineteenth century, it appears, the Abdullai Mehsuds had been encroaching on their summer pastures between Razmak and Makin and in Baddar. Partly because they only occupied the lands for part of the year, the Tori Khels were unable to put up much resistance. By the early 1920s the Abdullais had moved up as far north as the Shoran Algad, a stream about a mile and a half south of Razmak.

The Abdullai-Tori Khel conflict only began seriously to affect the British because of the establishment of the Razmak base.[71] One reason why the Tori Khels had agreed to the establishment of the base there was that they hoped that the presence of troops would halt this encroachment and that they might even be able to take advantage of it to push the Abdullais back. In 1923 the Tori Khels raised the issue with the resident, Stuart Pears. He agreed that the land the Mehsuds had taken belonged by rights to the Tori Khels and offered to arbitrate, but they rejected this. In 1924 they tried to drive back the Abdullais but failed.[72] Confrontations between them and the Mehsuds close to the base at Razmak made the officers in charge there anxious. They feared that the base itself might be affected; they were also concerned that other Wazirs, particularly the Madda Khels, might be drawn in.[73]

It was not just a dispute over land. The British had awarded almost all the contracts for the supply of the British garrison at Razmak to the Tori Khels, and the Abdullais wanted contracts too.[74] In February 1925 they began to fortify a position on high ground which overlooked the Razmak base. This alarmed the military, and the Abdullais were made to demolish their fortification. The chief commissioner nominated arbitrators to try and sort out the dispute. They met at the beginning of May and made recommendations, but could not persuade either side to accept them.[75] In March 1926 the government announced that it would pay the Tori Khels Rs.50,000 to compensate them for the loss of their land, and both groups initially accepted this. Bolton thought that 'a very nasty corner in the relations of government with the Wazirs and Mehsuds' had been negotiated.[76] He was too optimistic. The Tori Khels decided after all not to give up their claim.[77] When the viceroy, Lord Irwin, visited Razmak at the end of October 1926, Tori Khels blocked the road and presented him with a petition.[78] For some years the situation remained unresolved.

Zangi Khan and the Madda Khels

As we have seen, the British found the Madda Khel Utmanzais, who formed a sizeable population living up against and across the Durand Line, difficult to deal with. We saw in Chapter 4 that during the later nineteenth century the British had regarded Sadde Khan as their leading man and treated him as such. The fact that he had been present when some Madda Khels attacked the British party at Maizar in 1897 without warning discredited him in British eyes. After things had settled down, they tried to find someone else to take on his role, but were unable to do so, and reluctantly they had to recognize him as the leading Madda Khel malik again. In 1908 and again in 1922 the Madda Khels agreed not to harbour wanted men but continued to do so.[79] Many of them enlisted in the North Waziristan Militia before the First World War; as we have seen, they comprised the largest group from any one tribe in it. Many had deserted in 1919 after the Third Anglo-Afghan War taking their weapons with them and joined Amanullah's Khost Militia.[80] The British had therefore suspended their allowances and tried to get the rifles back.

The fact that some Madda Khel territory lay across the Durand Line made it more difficult to put pressure on them. Before the First World War the Afghan government had paid small annual allowances to some of their maliks, including Sadde Khan, and the British government had not contested this. Sadde Khan died in 1923.[81] His most prominent son was a man called Zangi Khan, but Zangi's authority was definitely limited, and he had a rival in another malik, Arsala Khan, who tended to be pro-Afghan. Some Madda Khels attended a large jirga held at Paghman near Kabul in July 1923, and Madda Khels were among those who helped Amanullah to put down the 1924 Khost rebellion, receiving Rs.20,000 as a reward.[82]

In 1925 the British hold on the Madda Khels remained quite weak, and their tribal allowances remained suspended because seventy-seven of the rifles taken by the deserters in 1919 had not been returned. The officials decided to try and build up Zangi Khan's influence and use him to get a grip not just on the Madda Khels but on the Utmanzais as a whole. So, for example, he was given a bigger allowance and awarded the title of Khan Sahib in 1926 during the viceroy's visit to Razmak.[83] In 1927 it was reported that the Madda Khels had returned as many rifles as could be expected and that relations with them had improved, but in 1928 they were referred to in another report as 'notoriously difficult and independent'.[84]

Although he did cooperate with them over the Mehsud-Tori Khel boundary problem at Razmak in 1925, the local officials did not find Zangi easy to deal with. He was still a young man, and 'his head [was reported to be] … full of wild ideas'.[85] The main problem from the British point of view was that he would not surrender wanted men when requested to do so. Late in 1927 the political agent, Cosmo Edwards, went ahead and changed the arrangements for the distribution of the Madda Khel allowances without consulting him, which seems counterproductive if the aim was to build up his authority. Referring to the Madda Khels as 'an unruly mob', Edwards decided that it would be easier for him to pay the allowances on two successive days (one for the Kazhas and one for the Gers). This would, he maintained, enable him to meet the sectional and sub-sectional maliks and get to know them better. He announced this at the allowance jirga in December 1927. Zangi Khan objected, the allowances were not paid and the relationship with Zangi began to deteriorate; Madda Khels fired at two aeroplanes flying over their territory.[86]

To overawe them, the Razmak column visited Datta Khel from 28 February to 15 March 1928.[87] While they were there, some officers, including General Kenneth Wigram (the commander of the Waziristan District in the later 1920s), expressed a wish to visit the settlement of Maizar where the attack on the troops had taken place in 1897. Zangi Khan invited them to visit his kot at the nearby settlement of Sheranna, from where, he said, he would take them to Maizar.[88] When General Wigram and his party arrived at Sheranna, they sat outdoors within Zangi's walled compound and were given tea followed by a meal. The assistant PA had a meeting with the maliks, while the British officers were introduced to a man they suspected of being an Afghan agent. He was, Wigram reported afterwards, 'courteous almost to the extent of being patronising'.[89] Meanwhile a crowd gathered just outside the main gate of the kot and began to shout and make threatening gestures. Among them the officers saw some outlaws from British territory. After they had finished eating, Zangi told them that he could not take them to Maizar, but did not explain why, and they went back to Datta Khel.

The general and his officers concluded that Zangi had set out to humiliate them and were furious. Wigram wrote to the resident with a revealing example of imperial bombast:

> It seems curious that in the year of grace 1928 an illiterate savage should have the power to refuse British officials wearing the King's uniform the right of visiting British villages in British territory solely that in order that he may enhance his own prestige at the expense of the British, and to prove to our enemies the extent of his power over the British. That his action was dictated by the Afghan Agent and by the outlaws, I have no doubt.[90]

The soldiers wanted to retaliate forcibly for what they saw as a deliberate insult. Bruce even thought that Zangi had actually hoped that the officers would be attacked and had arranged matters in such a way that he could not be blamed for it. Had it not been, he said, for the officers' tact and patience there would have been another 'Maizar outrage'.[91]

The chief commissioner, Bolton, reached a very different conclusion. The fact that local men had gathered outside Zangi's kot and began to shout and gesticulate at the British officers made Zangi realize that if the visit went ahead, he might not be able to guarantee their safety and had therefore cancelled it. By refusing to take them to Maizar, he had actually prevented any repetition of the 1897 outrage.[92] 'The lies and subterfuges incidental to the occasion' might be forgiven, Bolton wrote, as Zangi Khan could not be expected to 'tell the truth and admit his impotence in the presence of his distinguished visitors and his own immediate followers'.[93] It also turned out that the supposed Afghan agent was not actually in the GOA's pay at all.[94]

Zangi and his brother Abdullah Khan were summoned to Dera Ismail Khan to apologize to Wigram and the resident, Charles Bruce, and did so on 17 April 1928. They confirmed that they understood that in return for the allowances and khassadars they were not to harbour outlaws and were responsible for the security of the road between the Tochi and the Afghan border. They also accepted that the government had the right to make roads and build posts in their country and send troops and Scouts patrols into any part of it. When Zangi reached home, however, he told the assistant political officer that he would not honour the agreement.[95] The resident argued that it was time to stop treating Zangi (whom he referred to patronisingly in one report as a 'Jungly savage') as the leading Madda Khel.[96] Bolton did not agree. There was no one else who could take his place he thought, and the foreign secretary agreed that 'it would be regrettable to have to abandon the big experiment of building up a leading hereditary house among the Wazirs'.[97] Bolton offered to meet Zangi to discuss the situation, but he did not respond, and in July 1928 Bolton concluded reluctantly that although he had really done nothing to deserve it, he would have to lose his allowance and title.[98]

In mid-October 1928 Zangi raised a lashkar to try and make those maliks who had taken their allowances or visited the political agent and the resident pay fines. It looks as though the political agent, Edwards, did try to use the pro-Afghan malik, Arsala Khan, against Zangi. But Arsala Khan did not have much support, and most of the maliks regarded him as colluding in a deliberate attempt to divide the Madda Khels. Zangi on the other hand had become something of a hero because he had supported the Tori Khels against the Abdullais over the Razmak boundary, maintained the Madda Khels' right to harbour outlaws and generally resisted British influence. The resident was worried that he might be able to persuade other Wazirs, the Tori Khels for instance, even the Utmanzai Wazirs as a whole, to resist the policy of peaceful penetration. He therefore enforced a *barampta* on the Madda Khels and sent troops to Miranshah and Razoni to impose a blockade on them and prevent them joining forces with Tori Khels.[99]

The officials told the Madda Khel maliks they must recompense the pro-British maliks for any losses they had suffered in the recent dispute and allow khassadar posts to be set up at Sheranna, Maizar, Achar and Sanzalai. The officials also assured them that the government did not intend to construct a new road through their country, or install a garrison of troops, or turn it into an administered district. The maliks agreed to the British terms, and the blockade was lifted and allowances restored. Arsala and Zangi sat together in a jirga in March and appeared to be reconciled. Zangi was anxious to be restored to the government's favour and made efforts to be helpful; for example in August 1929 he suggested that the Mehsuds might pay rent to the Tori Khels for use of the land up to the Shoran, thus recognizing the Tori Khels' title to it.[100] The British gave him back his title and allowances. Bray commented that there had been 'a want of tact at the outset' in dealing with him.[101]

Wana

As we have seen, Zilla Khels had besieged the khassadars in Wana early in April 1922, and the British had to send Scouts to reinforce them.[102] The Scouts were withdrawn in April 1923, leaving Wana in charge of khassadars; later in the year Tazi Khels, led by Shahi Khan, murdered the Naib Tehsildar, Shah Ali Akbar. The Afghan government continued to take an interest in Wana, and Major Finnis's murderers went freely to and fro across the border, as did Shahi Khan.[103] Early in 1926 Scouts patrols began to visit Wana again.[104] Subahdar Major Malik Asmat Khan Yarghul Khel Zilla Khel, who had made peace with the British after 1919, was responsible for security there. In July 1927 his brother, Bat, murdered him because he would not share the money he received from the government. The resident described it as a blow to British's interests.[105]

In 1928-9 the British completed the road to Wana from Sarwakai, making it easier to reach from Jandola. Bray, the foreign secretary, commented that 'the logic of events' showed that Wana, like Razmak, was 'one of those nodal positions in the transfrontier too critical to be entrusted to irregulars'.[106] On 12 November 1929 the British relocated the Manzai garrison to it, built a new cantonment there, and started work on a road that would link up with the Jandola-Razmak road near Kaniguram via Tiarza.[107] It may not have been a coincidence that at this time, as we shall see in Chapter 9, Nadir Shah and his brothers were establishing themselves in Kabul, following the overthrow of Habibullah Kalakani. On 17 November the resident interviewed what was described as a representative jirga from the whole Ahmadzai Wazir tribe; they were reported to be very friendly.[108]

But if some local men may have welcomed the arrival of the troops, this was not true of them all.[109] The British had already experienced some difficulties with the Gangi Khels in the early 1920s. In 1930 Gangi Khel men shot at the political agent when he was out on reconnaissance towards Dahna.[110] This may have been partly an attempt by other maliks, playing on fears that the British were about to extend their authority into Gangi Khel country, to undermine the pro-British Gangi Khel malik, Ajab Khan.[111] The incident gave the British an excuse for constructing a dirt road into the Dahna valley, sending troops into it and carrying out a brigade exercise in the nearby Manra valley, as well as imposing a fine of eight rifles on the Gangi Khels. A foundation had been laid, the PA claimed, for friendly relations in the future.[112]

As regards developments in the rest of Waziristan, some Mehsuds objected to the plan to build the Wana to Kaniguram road mentioned above, among them the anti-British maliks, Sadde Khan and his brother Ramzan Shaman Khel, but their opposition was dismissed as being of no real importance.[113] In 1928 the British experienced further difficulties with men from some other Mehsud sections – Giga Khels, Nekzan Khels and Kikarais, as well as some Shaman Khels and Manzai Alizais, who sniped at pickets and outposts, as well as carrying out kidnaps and murders. As was so often the case, one of their aims was to persuade the government to increase their allowances. Their maliks requested bombing, but, like Rawlinson, the resident, Bruce, was opposed to routine use of bombing to subdue opposition and decided to enforce a blockade instead.[114]

Before this could be introduced, Lieutenant-Colonel Robert Heale took over as the resident. Heale argued that it was vital to support the maliks or trouble would spread. He gave the Nekzan Khel and Giga Khel villages an ultimatum and threatened them with bombing if they did not respond. They did not do so, and they were attacked in November. Bombers badly damaged the villages of two pro-Afghan men, Mirkabul Giga Khel and Miralai Nekzan Khel, destroying stores of grain, cultivated terraces and some livestock.[115] When the bombs caused fires, the inhabitants came out of their shelters and put them out. To stop this, the British fitted some of the bombs with delayed action fuses. The villages surrendered within a few days. Miralai and his family were expelled to Afghanistan, and three 'notorious outlaws' were surrendered.[116] This was one of the relatively few occasions bombing was used in Waziristan in the later 1920s. Some of the local officers might have made more use of it had they been allowed to so do. For instance in 1926 a Hindu girl was kidnapped, and the then resident, Evelyn Howell, wanted to threaten air action if she were not released. The GOI did not approve, commenting that the threat of bombing should only be used in really serious cases, or it would lose its effect.[117]

As regards the Kabul Khel Wazirs, as we have seen, before 1914 they had not always had a very good relationship with the British. Earlier in the 1920s they (and the closely related Malikshahi Wazirs), some of whom lived across the Durand Line, were reported to be the most difficult Tochi Wazirs.[118] During a meeting at Spinwam a Miamai Kabul Khel and some others had fired at the political agent and some maliks. In response early in 1925 officials imposed a large-scale *barampta* on Miamai and Saifali Kabul Khels found in Bannu, and they quickly submitted. In 1926 a report referred to the Kabul Khels as a 'somewhat uncertain factor', but two years later they were described as 'one of the best-behaved tribes'.[119] In 1927 the British began the work on improving the Idak-Thal road they had proposed previously.[120] They had also experienced some problems with the Tazi Khel Ahmadzais in the earlier 1920s, but had settled with them early in 1926. Nevertheless in 1929 some Tazi Khels looted and burnt the hamlet of Darga in the Kohat District and then fired at a Scouts patrol in the Ghoreshta. A *barampta* induced them to pay compensation for both incidents.[121]

In spite of incidents like these, by 1929, Bruce was able to claim that 'we have regained a great deal of our control' in Waziristan and referred to the success of a policy of 'peaceful penetration' and of gradual 'Sandemanization'. (The *Times* commented that 'it seems the Pathan can after all be Sandemanized.')[122] Certainly it was quieter than it had been at any time since 1914. The khassadar scheme with its substantial payments played a part, and towards the end of the decade a considerable improvement in their work was reported. British officials admitted, however, that if the khassadar arrangements were to be successful, they would always need close supervision and encouragement.[123]

9

Regime change, Congress and Waziristan and Anglo-Afghan relations

While the British officials pressed on with peaceful penetration, Amir Amanullah continued with his plans to modernize Afghanistan. Among other things he tried to extend conscription to the army, even in the south and east where the government's control was very weak, as well as introducing higher taxes. All this was unpopular with many Afghans, and in November 1928 the Shinwaris living in Nangahar revolted, attacking the district headquarters at Achin not far from the Durand Line.[1] Soviet pilots in planes supplied by the Soviet Union bombed some villages, and in response a tribal lashkar besieged Jalalabad at the end of November.[2] This sparked off a major insurrection involving much of the rest of the country, led by the Tajik Habibullah Kalakani. (From the village of Kalakan north of Kabul, he has often been disparagingly referred to as Bacha-i-Saqao – 'son of the water-carrier'.) On 14 January 1929 Amanullah left Kabul by car for Kandahar, leaving his elder brother Inayatullah Khan in charge. Three days later Inayatullah abdicated in favour of Habibullah Kalakani and was evacuated to India by the RAF.[3] Security in Kabul deteriorated seriously, and in February 1929 the RAF airlifted the staff at the British Legation and most of the other foreigners in Kabul to India.[4]

From his base in Kandahar Amanullah sent an army north towards Kabul in May, but near Ghazni it was intercepted by a Ghilzai force, and it had to turn back. He made three more unsuccessful attempts to take Kabul in the summer of 1929, after which he was persuaded to leave for exile in Europe. A number of men from the British side of the Durand Line, both Wazirs and Mehsuds, including Musa Khan Abdullai and Sadde Khan Shaman Khel, fought for Amanullah against Habibullah Kalakani. At one point during the crisis Soviet troops actually advanced some way into northern Afghanistan in support of Amanullah's ambassador to Moscow, the former governor of the Southern Province, Ghulam Nabi Charkhi.[5]

In the meantime Amanullah's distant cousin, General Nadir Khan, who had been living in France on the Côte d'Azur, returned to India. He landed in Bombay and arrived in Peshawar on 25 February 1929. He and his brothers Muhammad Hashim Khan and Shah Wali Khan made contact with Humphrys and with the political agent in the Kurram, Richard Maconachie, presumably hoping to gain their tacit support.[6] British officials did not publicly endorse one side or the other, but may well have hoped that Nadir would take over. In March Nadir crossed into Afghanistan, but his efforts to use Afghan tribal irregulars to defeat Habibullah failed.[7] One of the brothers, Shah Wali Khan, recruited as many as 12,000 Mehsud and Wazir levies (Musa Khan and Sadde Khan, and the other Mahsuds and Wazirs switched their support to him) and conquered Kabul in October 1929. Gul Din Zilla Khel is reported to have been Nadir Khan's right-hand man during the advance.[8] The levies proclaimed Nadir king, and rather than restore Amanullah to the throne, Nadir Khan himself assumed power, calling himself Nadir Shah. He issued orders forbidding looting, but the levies took no notice and ransacked the city before returning home.[9] Shodi Khel Hamzoni Bhittani for instance took away 'Persian carpets that were almost priceless, with hangings of royal purple', which he hacked down to fit his house in the Upper Tochi.[10]

It was a change of dynasty. The descendants of Sultan Muhammad Khan (1795–1861) had supplanted those of his brother, Amir Dost Muhammad Khan (1792–1863). Nadir's brother, Hashim Khan, became the prime minister and retained the post until 1946 when he retired because of ill-health.[11] Another brother, Shah Mahmud Khan, became a cabinet minister. Shah Wali Khan became ambassador in London and then in Paris.[12] As for Musa Khan and Sadde Khan, it seems that Nadir did not entirely trust them, although they had switched their allegiance and fought for him, and they returned home.[13]

In mid-November 1929 Britain formally recognized Nadir's government.[14] It is sometimes suggested that because the British had had quite an uneasy relationship with Amanullah, they must have helped Nadir Khan to gain the throne, by allowing, perhaps even encouraging, men from the British side of the Durand Line to support him. It was rumoured at the time that they had actually been responsible for the Shinwari rising that had sparked off the rebellion against Amanullah and that T. E. Lawrence's posting to Miranshah in August 1928, under the name of Aircraftman T. E. Shaw, was more than coincidental. (To try and end such speculation he was sent back to England in January 1929.) It is true that British officials did nothing to help Amanullah when he attempted to fight his way back to Kabul and that they allowed Nadir

Khan to return to India and travel to Peshawar and meet British officials, and cross the border into Afghanistan. If there is no evidence that they took active steps to overthrow him, British neutrality did favour Habibullah Kalakani.[15] It meant, for example, that war matériel purchased in Europe was not sent on to Amanullah when it arrived in India.

Once in power, Nadir Shah and his brothers saw the Soviet Union as a greater threat to Afghan independence than Britain. Nadir was more of a realist than Amanullah and did not share his passion for rapid modernization and Westernization. In any case, his government was not very secure. As well as opposition to it from the late Habibullah Kalakani's supporters in the Koh Daman, north of Kabul, there continued to be significant support for Amanullah in the south and south-east. The British continued to want a stable government and were concerned that unrest in Afghanistan might enable the Soviet Union to increase its influence. More than ever it was in the British and Afghan government's mutual interest to stay on good terms with each other. Maconachie replaced Humphrys as British minister, arriving in May 1930, and in June Faiz Muhammad Zakaria, the new Afghan foreign minister, asked him for help with military supplies. The British agreed to supply 10,000 rifles and ammunition, and a subsidy of £175,000.[16] Some of the rebels from the Koh Daman had taken refuge in India, and the British prevented them, as well as the pro-Amanullah party there from intriguing against Nadir's government.[17]

Nevertheless the problem of the frontier meant that the Anglo-Afghan relationship was still not an easy one. Some British officials found it difficult to accept that things had changed from Amanullah's day and that the new Afghan government was much more willing to cooperate with Britain than its predecessor. Evelyn Howell, now the Indian foreign secretary, for instance, continued to mistrust the GOA and fell out with Maconachie as a result.[18] A particular grievance was the fact that Nadir allowed members of the revolutionary anti-British Ghadr (meaning revolt or rebellion) party, founded in 1913, including Gurmukh Singh and Rattan Singh, to stay in Kabul and maintain contacts with the Soviet Embassy; indeed the British thought of them as Soviet agents. Although Rattan Singh left for Russia in 1931, in the same year another important member of the party, Mitha Singh, was allowed to enter Afghanistan.[19] Mitha Singh and the other Ghadr leaders were subsequently jailed following British representations.[20]

Moreover the GOA did always pursue an entirely pro-British policy along the frontier. Nadir Shah could not afford to be seen to be too accommodating to the British. Pro-Amanullah propaganda represented him as a bloodthirsty and unpopular tyrant, a traitor who had sold Afghanistan to its old enemy.[21] It was therefore very important for his government, and that of his successor, Zahir Shah (1933–73), to portray itself as upholding the country's interests and Islam. Nevertheless he did largely abandon what Richard Maconachie referred to as Amanullah Khan's 'irredentist attitude' to the frontier.[22] Soon after his arrival in Kabul, Maconachie discussed the Afghan government's relationship with men living on the Indian side of the border with the foreign minister, Faiz Muhammad.[23] Faiz Muhammad explained that his government could not give up paying them allowances altogether, but gave him three assurances. First, the GOA would not invite men from the Indian side to meetings in Afghanistan, though if they came, he said, they would have to be 'treated with consideration required by ordinary Pathan custom'.[24] Second, it would not employ men living on the Indian side of the frontier as khassadars, though men from the Indian side might be enlisted in Afghan regular forces and occasionally visit their homes on leave. Third, 'The whole foreign policy of the Afghan Government would be actuated by a desire for peace on both sides of the frontier and a spirit of goodwill towards HM Government.'[25] In August 1930 Maconachie had an audience with Nadir Shah himself, in which the king reassured him that his frontier policy would be different from the late Sardar Nasrullah's.[26]

In spite of Amanullah's departure and the pursuit of a more conservative social policy by the new rulers, the Afghan government remained vulnerable. In 1930, men from some of the same groups that had risen against Amanullah, the Tajiks of the Koh Daman, led by the late Habibullah Kalakani's uncle, Purdel, joined by some Shinwaris, rebelled against Nadir. Nadir called on Pashtuns from along the frontier to crush them.[27] In the summer ill-feeling between the Tokhi Ghilzais and the Shahjui Wazirs led the former to attack government troops, but they were defeated when the government sent reinforcements.[28]

Nadir could not afford to neglect his links with the transborder Pashtuns and exempted some groups living near the Durand Line from military conscription and taxation.[29] Some prominent men in Waziristan, Ramzan and Sadde Khan Shaman Khel, for instance, had been receiving an allowance from Amanullah for some time before his overthrow and had fought for him and then Nadir Khan.[30] After Nadir took power, Ramzan and Sadde Khan, Musa Khan Abdullai, and Khaisor and Nander Langar Khel, among others, continued to maintain links with his government. They do not appear to have formed a cohesive group, though the British tended to refer to them as the 'Kabul party'. In 1930 they were among those who visited Nadir in Kabul, hoping that he would do something for them. He had no money, so he gave them nominal appointments and honorary titles instead; for example Ramzan was made general, Sadde Khan brigadier, Khaisor civil brigadier and Nander colonel.[31]

In 1929 Amanullah's Urgun militia had collapsed, and in 1931 Nadir revived it. The British were unhappy about this, especially as Abdur Rahman Madda Khel, who had deserted from the North Waziristan Militia and taken part in an attack on the Kurram Militia in 1923, enlisted in it.[32] They were also alarmed by the appointment of Shah Daula, who, with Haji Abdur Razaq, had played a prominent role in encouraging anti-British resistance from 1919 to 1921, as governor of Khost, but he seems to have given the British little trouble.[33] The new Afghan government undoubtedly made an effort to pursue a less hostile frontier policy. Though it did not stop doing so entirely, it summoned jirgas of British-side men less often than had Amanullah, and there were no large gatherings of trans-frontier men like the one Amanullah had organized in Jalalabad early in 1923. It also reduced the allowances it paid to men living on the British side of the Durand Line, and once things had settled down, largely stopped giving them honorary titles.[34]

The Khudai Khidmatgaran, Congress and the 1930 crisis

The British themselves faced another brief but serious frontier crisis during the summer of 1930. There were several reasons. The most important was the rise of the nationalist movement in India, which in the North-West Frontier Province was principally represented by the Indian National Congress. The Montagu-Chelmsford reforms of 1919, which led to the establishment of a legislature in most Indian provinces and transferred some powers to the provincial governments, had not been extended to the North-West Frontier Province. Many of its inhabitants, whether Hindu, Sikh or Muslim, resented this and called for their own legislature. The Yusufzai Pashtun, Abdul Ghaffur Khan (known as Badshah Sahib), played an important role here. Born in 1890, he was educated at Edwardes College in Peshawar, after which he opened a school in his home village and began to advocate education for the illiterate villagers. Dissatisfied with British rule, he was in contact with the Haji of Turangzai, visited the Deoband seminary and took part in the Khilafat agitation after the First World War.[35] In 1920 the British imprisoned him for three years. After his release, he and his half-brother, Dr Khan Sahib, who had trained as a doctor in England, founded a party to work for independence and social reform known as the Frontier Congress, or Khudai Khidmatgaran (Servants of God), or from the colour of their shirts as Red Shirts. In 1928 Ghaffur Khan met Mahatma Gandhi and was very impressed by him, and in November 1929 the Khudai Khidmatgaran formally joined the Indian National Congress.[36]

Early in 1930 a serious crisis developed in the Peshawar district. Congress planned to send a Committee of Enquiry into North-West Frontier Province grievances to Peshawar towards the end of April. On 22 April British officials, fearing civil disorder, prevented its members entering the province.[37] Early on 23 April they arrested some nationalist activists, who were taken to the police station in the old city in Peshawar, where a large crowd gathered in protest. In response four armoured cars were sent into the city and ran over at least seven men. The crowd began throwing bricks and stones, and troops and armoured cars fired on the demonstrators; estimates of the number killed vary widely, from 30 to 200.[38] Next day, troops were withdrawn from the city, and it was not retaken until 4 May. Civil disobedience 'plunged much of the Peshawar Valley into turmoil', and unrest spread. Order was restored, but not without further violence.[39]

There was discontent in some of the tribal areas too, thanks partly at least to the policy of peaceful penetration that the British had begun to pursue during the later 1920s. Before the First World War they had usually made *barampta*s, seizures of people and animals, only in administered territory, but in the 1920s they began to make them in Waziristan itself – a significant extension of British influence.[40] Moreover, as we have seen, regular troops had gone back to Wana in 1929, and in 1930 the British were about to begin work on the new road between Tauda China and Wana that would make it easier for the British to access hitherto hard to reach parts of Mehsudland.[41]

There were other reasons for discontent in Waziristan too. Hailstorms and drought seriously affected harvests in 1930.[42] Rumours began to resurface about an imminent British withdrawal from Waziristan, if not actually India itself, adding to the unsettled atmosphere. The *Child Marriage Restraint Act* (or Sarda Act, after the name of its sponsor) which came into effect at the beginning of 1930 also contributed to this. The Act set a minimum age of marriage for girls of fourteen years and for boys eighteen, and some mullahs objected strongly to it because they said it was incompatible with Islamic law and tradition. Moreover, all sorts of wild rumours spread, for instance that it required brides to have a medical examination, which raised concerns about female modesty and family honour.[43] A particularly curious concern that surfaced at this point was that doctors would remove the hearts from corpses.[44] During 1930 many mullahs were giving anti-British and anti-Christian sermons along the border, among them Mullah Kundalai, a *murid* of the faqir of Ama Khel.[45]

In Waziristan some of the more anti-British Wazirs and Mehsuds, perhaps despairing of getting much if any support from the new Afghan government, had been in touch with Indian National Congress members in the administered areas. Early in April 1930 Abdul Ghaffur Khan himself had visited Bannu and Tank.[46] In May 1930 people in Waziristan and along the Waziristan border mounted several challenges to the government's authority. In May the Dawars, who were regarded as being particularly sensitive in religious matters (they were 'a fanatical tribe', the resident, Ralph Griffith, commented; there were a number of madrasahs in Dawar), complained to the resident about the Sarda Act.[47] On 11 May a party of as many as 400 men assembled and fired at the Boya post, halfway between Datta Khal and Miranshah, but one of their maliks persuaded them to disperse.[48] The Mohmit Khel Wazirs also decided to defy the government. On 13 May a large number of them gathered at Shina Starga *ziyarat* (shrine) near Dosalli and decided to refuse further government service and rewards and follow a policy of 'non-violent non-cooperation'.[49] On 14 May some of them looted a lorry and destroyed telegraph and other wires running through their territory, and their khassadars deserted.[50]

More important was the way that Zangi Khan's rival, the pro-Kabul malik Arsala Khan (he had been given the Afghan title Civil Firqa Mashar), encouraged a Madda Khel lashkar to attack the Datta Khel outpost on 11 May. He persuaded Mullah Ghain-ud-Din and his son Muhammad, and other mullahs from Lower Tochi and Bannu to support him.[51] Zangi Khan tried to stop the attack going ahead.[52] On 12 May he persuaded part of the lashkar to withdraw, leaving the field to Arsala Khan and his supporters.[53] The British responded by attacking them from the air that day and the next, and on 14 May they began to bomb the settlements at Maizar and Kazha (Arsala Khan's village), and this was enough to persuade the rest of the lashkar to go home. Next day the Madda Khel maliks went to Miranshah to submit to the government, and on 16 May Zangi and Arsala's brother also met government officials there.[54] The maliks deposited cash and rifles to the value of Rs.15,000, and each of the eight sections gave security of one rifle worth Rs.500 and a bond for a further Rs.500 for the 'good behaviour vis-à-vis government of all members of their tribe and in particular Arsala Khan'.[55] Zangi Khan played the principal role here; having arranged for the production of hostages, he and his supporters also paid the fine.

The Mehsuds in 1930

The difficulties the British were to experience with some of the Mehsuds were not so easily dealt with. At this point, to save them 'the trouble of a wearisome tramp' to Kabul, the Afghan war minister, Shah Mahmud, wrote to the pro-Kabul Mehsuds telling them that the king was too busy to see them.[56] Some British officials suggested that in order to stop Mehsuds and Madda Khels going en masse to Kabul and demanding favours from the government, Nadir Shah ordered the local Afghan officials to distract them by encouraging them to engage in anti-British activity.[57] It is true that men who held Afghan titles and received Afghan allowances, such as Ramzan, Sadde Khan and Khaisor, were to take part in the disturbances that followed, but it seems very unlikely that Nadir would have jeopardized the British agreement to supply with him with arms and money in this way.[58]

In May 1930 the Waziristan resident interviewed jirgas of Mehsud mullahs and maliks. They agreed that no attempt was being made to interfere with Islam and undertook to do their best to make sure that things stayed quiet. They did try, but other men were not so easily restrained. From 16 to 18 May between two and three thousand men held a jirga at Kaniguram.[59] The anti-British mullahs Kundalai and Muhammad Yusuf, the assistant secretary of the Bannu Congress Committee (known as the 'Bannuchi Mullah'), were also present. Muhammad Yusuf sat in the seat of honour in the centre.[60] Around him sat some of the principal members of the 'Kabul Party', among them Sadde Khan and Ramzan, Khaisor, Mullah Gulin Kikarai and Ghazi Mir Jan, one of Mullah Powindah's sons.[61]

Two Hindu Congress supporters from Dera Ismail Khan, Mohan Lal and Chela Ram, also attended.[62] Holding rifles and 'accoutred with bandoliers and ammunition', they addressed the jirga. They referred to the growing anti-British feeling in India, claiming that Indian troops were about to mutiny and called for Muslims, Hindus and Sikhs to join forces to oppose the British. It was announced that a branch of the Congress Committee would be formed in Mehsud territory, that anyone who attacked a Hindu or Sikh working for Congress would be liable to a fine of Rs.15,000 and that cow-killing was henceforth forbidden. Muhammad Yusuf called on the Mehsuds to resolve their internal differences and work with Congress to end British rule. He said it was shameful that they were doing nothing while India was in revolt. On 17 May the meeting discussed proposals for peaceful resistance; RAF planes flew over it and temporarily disrupted it.[63]

As was so often the case, Mehsud opinion was divided. Reportedly three of the Nazar Khel Bahlolzai maliks, Hayat, his brother Subahdar Baluch Khan and Nekarab, argued that the Mehsuds should not allow themselves to be manipulated by Hindu politicians and dragged into a cause which was not their own. Their opponents accused them of being government lackeys.[64] Most of those present were supporters of the former amir Amanullah, and whenever Nadir Shah's name was mentioned they made derogatory comments about him, but when Amanullah's came up they called out approving ones. Mullah Gulin called for armed resistance.[65] Some other mullahs, however, among them Abdul Sarir, reported that the British had no intention of interfering with the practice of Islam and argued against precipitate action.[66]

There was further discussion on 18 May. Mohan Lal and Chela Ram again called for active opposition to the British, and 'shots were fired in the air by the Mehsuds expressing their zeal and excitement'.[67] There was no clear majority in favour of doing anything more than sending a petition containing various complaints and demands to the government. In spite of the objections of the Langar Khel and Shaman Khel contractors who were working on it, the demands included the cancellation of the Wana-Kaniguram road.[68] They also wanted responsibility for offences to be restricted to the actual offenders, suggesting that many Mehsuds continued to resent collective tribal and territorial responsibility.[69] On 19 May they sent the petition to the government.[70]

On 21 May the situation became much more serious when some Garrerais from the village of Sega informed the British authorities that Mohan Lal and Chela Ram, the two Hindus who had delivered the speeches at the jirga calling for the Mehsuds to support the Congress agitation in India, were leaving Kaniguram.[71] Mohan Lal and Chela Ram were arrested at Bibizai and searched. Rs.800 and a letter for the Congress Committee signed by some Mehsud and Wazir maliks were found in Mohan Lal's pocket.[72] Sadde Khan decided to retaliate against the men who had given them away. He organized a lashkar of Shaman Khels from Maidan, Shabi Khels (led by Mullah Nauman) and Kikarai Mehsuds from Shaktu (led by Mullah Gulin). They sent a message to the local British officials informing them that a lashkar was going to attack Sega but that it had no quarrel with the government. The local officials warned them that their villages would be bombed if they went ahead. This did not stop them, and by 28 May the lashkar had assembled outside the village. On 30 May a number of Jalal Khels joined it, and during the night of 30/31 May it got into the village. The defenders resisted vigorously, and though the attackers destroyed the houses of the pro-British inhabitants before withdrawing, fourteen of them were reportedly killed and thirty-five wounded. (One defender was killed and two wounded.) The British responded by sending the Razmak Column to Ladha on 31 May, where it stayed for two months. In addition on 31 May the RAF bombed the village of Kot Langar Khel; it also attacked Sadde Khan and Ramzan's village of Sultana.[73]

Sadde Khan, Ramzan, Mullah Gulin and the others were undeterred and tried to raise more support among the Mehsuds, while Mullah Kundalai and the Bannuchi Mullah did their best to persuade the Utmanzai and Ahmadzai Wazirs to join them. 'Every valley in the Shaktu and Baddar areas ... resounded all day to the beating of drums. Marching and counter-marching of tribal parties induced the impression of a rising tide of warlike preparation.'[74] It was even rumoured that one of Amanullah's sons was about to join them. The RAF bombed Sultana again on 21 and 22 June.[75] At the beginning of July a leading pro-Afghan Mehsud, Miralai Nekzan Khel Bahlolzai (his village had been bombed in 1928) arrived from Kabul, and at a jirga on 3 July he handed out money to the Mehsuds. He claimed that it had come from Nadir Shah, but this seems unlikely. It is possible that Sadde Khan himself supplied the money; he was rumoured to have large quantities of cash hidden away.[76] As regards the funding of the Mehsuds' anti-British activities, Griffith claimed that via Mullah Fazal Din Russian money was reaching them and the Mujahidin colony at Makin.[77] Other officials, including Maconachie in Kabul, were doubtful that these claims had any substance.[78]

The anti-British Mehsuds now raised two fresh lashkars. Mullah Gulin collected one from the Shabi Khels, Kikarais, Nazar Khels and Jalal Khels (among them Khonia Khel).[79] On 6 July his lashkar surrounded the Scouts post at Sora Rogha, smashing the pumps supplying it with water, as well as destroying the khassadar post nearby. In the meantime Ramzan and Sadde Khan had collected a second lashkar, consisting of men from Maidan and Baddar and advanced towards Sora Rogha. On 7 July they attacked the khassadar post at Shamak Raghza and destroyed the bridge above Marobi, cutting communications between Razmak and Jandola. They planned to destroy the bridge below it too, but women from the village came down from shelters in hills and sat on it, making it impossible for the men to do so.[80] 'They would not, they said, have their houses destroyed just to please Gulin.'[81] In fact not very many Mehsuds were willing to support Sadde Khan; Abdullais for instance posted men at Tauda China to prevent him getting into Makin.[82]

This did not stop the lashkar destroying some khassadar posts, while the khassadars at Wazirgai, Langar Khel, Janjal and Piazha demolished their own posts.[83] Official reports, however, commented on the loyalty of most of the khassadars and on the cooperation the government received from friendly sections.[84] The situation remained serious nevertheless.[85] Ramzan and Sadde Khan's lashkar moved on and in the evening of 7 July joined Gulin's force at Sora Rogha.[86] Sora Rogha fort lay 500 feet above the Tank Zam, 'on a plateau amid its wire entanglements with something of the solidity and menace of the Krak des Chevaliers, the great Crusader castle in Syria'.[87] Sadde Khan's armament included a gun that he had commissioned from the Kaniguram arms factories. It was a 'breech-loader of 2¾ ins bore, firing a 9-lbs solid iron shot about 9 inches long with a copper driving-band to take the barrel's rifling' and could be dismantled for transport. They had little hope of taking the fort, but they probably hoped to persuade the garrison to rise against their officers, as had happened at Wana in 1919.[88]

On the night of 7 July the Mehsuds attacked the khassadar posts in the area, and during the late evening of 8 July they fired Sadde Khan's gun at the fort.[89] When visibility permitted the RAF bombed their positions in the hills around Sora Rogha and Ahnai. The Mehsuds attacked again on the following evening. They fired the gun four times, one shot smashing into the wireless room; then the gun developed a problem which put it out of action.[90] An RAF plane attacked a large party in the Barari Tangi and killed some thirty men.[91] On 10 July, disheartened by the number of casualties and the problem with the gun, the lashkar withdrew north from Sora Rogha, burning the khassadar posts at Piazha and at Bibizai near Dwatoi. On the same day the Razmak Brigade moved down to Tauda China. On 11 May it was in action against small groups of Mehsuds and killed seventeen men.[92] In the meantime aircraft continued to bomb various villages, among them Mullah Gulin's village of Zadrana, Sadde Khan and Ramzan's village of Sultana, and Larakai, where Ghazi Mir Jan lived, as well as Kot Langar Khel.[93]

Some twenty Shabi Khels had been killed and thirty or forty men wounded, and both lashkars returned to what was left of their homes.[94] All the sections involved began to send representatives to negotiate with the British officials, while the RAF continued to bomb the villages. On 20 July the officials concluded an interim agreement with the Shabi Khels, who surrendered twenty British-made rifles as security. They agreed to the restoration of the previous *maliki* and khassadar arrangements and tribal and territorial responsibilities. Next day officials concluded a similar agreement with the Kikarais; the bombing had severely damaged their houses and spoiled their land.[95] By 25 July they had surrendered a number of rifles and provided hostages too.[96]

On 21 July Sadde Khan and Ramzan sent representatives to Razmak asking for peace, and on 29 July they accepted the terms offered. Sadde Khan surrendered his home-made gun (a 'degradation comparable with the surrender by a Pathan of his wife', one man said).[97] Checking and valuing the rifles was quite a complicated business. They were actually bought by the tribe from their owners and became tribal property before they were surrendered. Regimental armourers then had to inspect them before they could be accepted.[98] Sorting things out often took a long time and was accompanied by 'quarrels and bitter recriminations'.[99]

On 23 July the Razmak column went on to Ladha. After some further bombing, by 18 August the officials had reached agreements with all the groups whose members had participated in the lashkars – Shabi Khels (Alizais), Garrerais and Langar Khels (Manzai Alizais), Khalli Khels (Shaman Khels), Nazar Khels, Kikarais and Malikshahis (Bahlolzais).[100] Mullah Muhammad Yusuf escaped into Afghanistan.[101] In November the British announced the Mehsuds' punishment. This was a fine of Rs.85,010, comprised of Rs.56,088 in cash and rifles of a cash value Rs.28,922 (in addition fifty-nine rifles were taken as security). The money was to be recovered by cancelling six months of the allowances paid to the sections whose members had taken part in the lashkars and one month of their khassadari payments. Griffith explained that the fines were relatively moderate and that more could have been demanded, but that 'undue harshness' would aggravate the economic pressures which in his view the Mehsuds always experienced.[102] In December 1930 at Tank a jirga of Peshawar and Kohat men tried Mohan Lal and Chela Ram, the two men arrested after the May jirga, under the Frontier Crimes Regulations, and found them guilty. They recommended that nevertheless the men should be pardoned; instead they were given 'a deterrent sentence' – three years 'rigorous imprisonment' and fined Rs.2,000.[103]

The British might have taken a harder line with the Mehsuds had they not needed the troops elsewhere. Later in May, as the position in central Waziristan improved, the situation in Bannu and in Dera Ismail Khan became more difficult, with civil disobedience and hartals (shutdowns of shops) in both places.[104] Trouble continued in Bannu through the summer. Later in July two mullahs, Abdul Jalil and Fazal Qadir, were spreading the anti-British message among Bakka Khel and Jani Khel Wazirs living inside British territory in the Bannu District. The officials summoned both the tribes' jirgas and instructed them to arrest or expel the mullahs, which they did. Mullah Fazal Qadir went to the Hatti Khel country to the north of Bannu where he was able to hold meetings and encourage anti-British feeling.¹⁰⁵ On 22 August his supporters announced that a Congress meeting would be held at the Hatti Khel village of Mash Killi on 24 August. On 23 August the officials told them that the meeting must be cancelled, and the next day they sent troops out to destroy houses in the hamlets of two of its convenors. In the course of this a detachment of British troops confronted a large group of demonstrators. Some were armed and killed a British officer; soldiers fired at the crowd and killed as many as seventy men. The maliks burnt the houses of the men who had called the meeting, and not surprisingly after so many deaths, the agitation subsided.¹⁰⁶

Unrest also affected the Wazirs living in Shawal. Zar Khan Pipalai Kabul Khel and Gul Din Zilla Khel, who lived on the Afghan side of the border, encouraged the Kabul Khels to gather at Musa Nikka *ziyarat* (just on the British side of the Durand Line). Gul Din had helped Nadir Khan to establish himself in Kabul; one British report referred to him as a notorious hostile. They sent two men to see the resident, and they presented some of the same demands as had the Dawars and Mehsuds – repeal of the Sarda Act, non-interference with religion, modification of the post-mortem rules, and freedom to hold meetings and release of the Congress prisoners.¹⁰⁷

Nothing came of this, and although for a few weeks developments in Waziristan had alarmed the British, by the early autumn relative peace returned.¹⁰⁸ We have seen that the pro-British malik, Zangi Khan, had quickly regained his authority over the Madda Khels, and the *1931–32 Report on the Administration of the Border* stated optimistically that 'the rift in the Madda Khels is closing, very gradually'.¹⁰⁹ Moreover the Mehsud maliks had managed to limit the numbers of men joining the two lashkars, and thanks to the increased allowances and the presence of the troops at Razmak, it had for instance been possible to deal relatively easily with them; some of the Mehsuds had stopped others entering their territory, and some of the Mehsud khassadars had resisted the lashkars. Most British officials thought that this vindicated the introduction of the modified forward policy, and particularly the location of the garrison at Razmak.¹¹⁰ It is true that troops were on hand when anti-British resistance resurfaced, but it is possible that without the presence of the garrison and the associated road building and gashts by the Scouts, they might not have been needed at all. Contemporary observers also drew attention to the part that air power had played in forcing the Mehsud hostiles and Arsala Khan's Madda Khel supporters to surrender.¹¹¹

In January 1932 senior British officials held a conference in Peshawar to explore the reasons for the recent unrest along the frontier as a whole. Even though, for example, two Congress representatives had taken part in the

Mehsud jirga in May 1930, they concluded that sympathy with Congress ideals and solidarity with Pashtuns living in the settled areas had nothing to with it. Rather it was due to the tribes' 'virile and martial qualities and … predatory instincts'.[112] They also pointed to the tribes' 'geographical seclusion, their access to arms, and the relative prosperity of the settled districts of the N-WFP'.[113] In spite of all the talk of peaceful penetration, economic development was not the answer, they concluded; resistance must be met with 'swift and violent retribution', and regular troops should remain at Razmak and Wana.[114] Following this, on 29 March 1932 Maconachie discussed with the Afghan foreign and prime ministers their government's relations with the tribes on the Indian side of the frontier and 'called their attention to the points in which these relations were theoretically incorrect and on practical grounds objectionable'.[115] Afterwards Maconachie pointed out that just as their Afghan counterparts had links with tribes living on the British side of the Durand Line, British officials had their contacts among those living on the Afghan side. He concluded that the Afghan government's relations with the British frontier tribes, though technically incorrect, were not actually harmful. The GOA and the GOI did make some concessions to each other during 1932. For instance the GOA had always objected to the maintenance of units of Hazaras in the Indian Army, and the British disbanded them. On 2 November 1931 a Giga Khel Mehsud Khassadar named Zari had shot and killed two soldiers (Lieutenant Synge and Private Whawell) near Sarwakai. Zari escaped across the border and reportedly took refuge with Miralai, the Mehsud who had helped to incite the Mehsuds during the previous summer.[116] The GOA arrested Zari and sent him to northern Afghanistan.[117]

In Waziristan itself things remained reasonably quiet. Following the brief rising in the early summer of 1930, Ramzan himself went to Kabul and undertook military service with the GOA. Since the early 1920s, the Uzbek freedom fighter, Ibrahim Beg, had been fighting a guerrilla war against the Soviet Union, using Afghanistan as a base.[118] In June 1930 Soviet troops had followed him forty miles into Afghanistan in hot pursuit; by this time he was causing difficulties in northern Afghanistan as well as in the Soviet Union.[119] The rifles Nadir had requested from the British arrived in time for him to equip an irregular force and send it to drive Ibrahim Beg across the Soviet border in June 1931.[120] He was captured and executed by the Red Army.[121]

Ramzan distinguished himself in this action, and Nadir rewarded him for his services with an allowance of Rs.9,000 p.a., and he returned with horses and rifles to Waziristan early in 1932.[122] Every day he sat in front of his house 'guarded by

Afghan khassadar sentries of his company ... display[ing] ... his wealth and gorgeous uniform to admiring crowds'.[123] For various reasons the British officials continued to be anxious that relations with the Mehsuds might deteriorate again. Besides Ramzan's return, these included the continuing anti-British activities of Mullah Kundalai, and the Congress sympathizers whom the Mehsuds used to meet in Tank and whose appeals were, it was thought, bound to influence 'the untutored Mahsud "Kasharan" and minor maliks'.[124] Moreover, under pressure to reduce expenditure, the British announced in October 1931 that they would reduce the existing khassadars' pay (by 16 per cent) though they planned to recruit more of them.[125] They also cut back the road-building programme, which annoyed the Mehsud contractors.[126] Musa Khan returned from Kabul in January 1931. He announced that he intended to remain at peace with the British and did so.[127] Things never settled down completely. For example competition between Mehsuds and Wazirs for contracts and khassadari appointments relating to the road being built between Ladha and Tiarza led to a clash between Mehsud and Wazir lashkars in 1932.[128]

Afghanistan and the frontier

Supporters of the ex-king in Afghanistan and along the frontier continued to intrigue against Nadir Shah, who had many enemies. Prominent among these was the powerful Charkhi family, led by Ghulam Nabi Khan.[129] Late in 1932 Ghulam Nabi encouraged a man named Dauran Khan (referred to in one report as 'the agent of Amanullah Khan and Ghulam Nabi') to persuade the Dare Khel Zadrans who lived in Khost just across the Durand Line from the Madda Khels to revolt.[130] The Lewanai faqir, who had incited the attack by Zadrans and other Khost men on the Miranshah bazaar in November 1914, played a prominent role here, as did a Zadran man called the Tor (black) Malang.[131] The Afghan government successfully suppressed the rising.[132] The leaders took refuge at Anati, a village in the North Waziristan Agency, just on the British side of the Durand Line. In January 1933 the British tried to capture them in a joint operation with Afghan forces. The latter were to cover the border and stop anyone crossing it, while Zangi Khan with a lashkar of Madda Khels seized the wanted men.[133] The Afghans were not in position when Zangi made his move and the wanted men escaped. They remained in the area moving to and fro across the Durand Line and were able to persuade many men from Waziristan to join them. In February, encouraged by the Lewanai faqir, as many as 6,000 men from Waziristan, including Mehsuds and Wazirs, crossed into Afghanistan. They attacked the Afghan garrison at Matun. Abdur Rahman Madda Khel, who had been partly responsible for the North Waziristan militiamen's desertion in Miranshah in 1919, persuaded the Mehsud, Madda Khel and Khojul Khel militiamen in the Urgun Militia to desert and attack an Afghan army post.[134]

On 26 February 1933 the Matun garrison repulsed the lashkar, but it continued to attract recruits, and as many as 10,000 men renewed the attack a few days later. It seemed that the government might lose the town. The situation was very serious. The capture of Matun would have encouraged others to join the rebels, and a general rising in the Southern Province might well have followed. The Afghan garrison held out, and on 8 March George Cunningham, the acting chief commissioner flew to Wana and called the Waziristan maliks to a jirga. He warned them that if those in Afghanistan had not withdrawn within five days, their villages would be bombed. The Razmak Column moved to Tauda China and the Baddar Valley to increase the pressure on the Mehsuds. Most of the men from Waziristan went home.[135]

The GOA had naturally been alarmed by the British failure to stop thousands of men moving from Waziristan into Khost during the revolt; some members of it even suspected that the North-West Frontier Province government had encouraged British-side men to join in in order to pressure Afghanistan into adopting a more cooperative policy along the frontier.[136] In August 1933, to try and reassure the Afghans, Arthur Parsons, now the resident in Waziristan, visited Kabul. Shortly afterwards Mehsuds and Wazirs began to cross the border again, but this time the British stopped them. During the spring and summer the Lewanai faqir stayed on the Indian side of the line, but in October the GOA persuaded him to return to Afghanistan. He was forced to live in Kabul under surveillance, and the Tor Malang and three of his associates were executed.[137] In the summer a Joint Commission was also held with delegates representing the GOA and the GOI to sort out cases between the British and the Afghan tribesmen on the Kurram border. It marked, from the British point of view at least, 'a definite advance in cooperation between the two Governments in matters relating to their common frontier'.[138]

Antagonism between Nadir Shah's family and the Charkhis continued to destabilize the Afghan government. Nadir suspected Ghulam Nabi of being involved in the Zadran rising in Khost, and in November 1932, after an acrimonious meeting with him, he had him executed. In revenge, Ghulam Nabi's relatives arranged for an Afghan student to kill Nadir's brother Muhammad

Aziz, the Afghan ambassador in Berlin, in June 1933. The Charkhis were also blamed for arranging an attempt on Maconachie's life in the hope of provoking a crisis that would force the British to intervene and remove Nadir. On September 6 Muhammad Azem, a teacher at the Nejat school in Kabul, went into the British Legation in Kabul, aiming to find and kill Maconachie. He was away, but Muhammad Azem shot three other men before surrendering. To punish the Charkhis, Nadir had one of the other Charkhi brothers, Ghulam Gilani, as well as several influential pro-Amanullah prisoners executed.[139] In turn, the Charkhi family arranged for another student, Abdul Khaliq, to assassinate Nadir Shah himself on 8 November 1933. Muhammad Hashim, the prime minister was away touring the Northern Province, but another of Nadir's brothers, Shah Mahmud, assured a peaceful succession by quickly proclaiming Nadir's twenty-one-year-old son, Muhammad Zahir, king.[140]

In March 1932 the Afghan prime minister and the foreign minister had accepted that paying allowances to men from the British side of the Durand Line was 'wrong in principle and harmful in effect'.[141] But the 1933 rebellion showed how vulnerable the Afghan government was to tribal unrest. It decided not only to do more to placate its own tribes and keep them happy but also to rebuild its connections with the British-side tribes. Some British officials were already concerned about the payment of allowances to some men who had fought for Nadir Khan in 1929, including Shodi Khel Bhittani and Sher Zaman Khan Muhammad Khel.[142]

Maconachie was unhappy about them too, but as they were rewards for past services rather than current ones, and as the men did not cause any problems, 'it would be wise to keep the telescope to the blind eye'.[143] Neither Griffith nor the GOI were particularly concerned. The GOI accepted that reviving connections with the British-side groups was a kind of Afghan insurance policy; the GOA gave them allowances, because it knew that they were not fully under British control and feared that if trouble broke out in Afghanistan they would cross the border to take part again.[144] Moreover there was still, it was pointed out, an inclination to look upon the groups on the British side of the Durand Line 'as a useful buffer which on occasion might become an active military reinforcement'; there were therefore 'some misgivings at seeing them brought more under our control'. Payment of the allowances also enabled the government to show its critics that it was not doing everything the British demanded.[145] As a result it remained possible for the people of Waziristan to obtain allowances from both, one man receiving a British allowance, and a close relative, brother, cousin, or son, an Afghan one.[146]

The modified forward policy aka peaceful penetration

British officials had continued to argue that the modified forward policy, in practice the same thing as peaceful penetration, continued to be the best approach, although the GOI was not usually quite as anxious to pursue it as the local officials. For example, shortly after the reoccupation of Wana in 1929, the GOI had telegraphed the North-West Frontier Province government. It might perhaps have already considered, it said, the advisability of advising the resident not to do too much too quickly in the Wana area. If anything went wrong, it might not just be Waziristan that was affected.[147] But sending Scouts patrols into the more independent areas of Waziristan continued to be regarded as the 'most effective instrument of peaceful penetration', and Scouts began to carry out gashts in the hills and valleys around Wana, particularly to the north-west, in Dahna, Manra, Shawal and Upper Shakai.[148]

Adamec points out that the British continued with the modified forward policy even after it had become clear that India would eventually become independent. Hitherto control of the frontier had been seen as required for the defence of India, but during the 1920s, he suggests, control had become an end in itself.[149] It is true that by the early 1930s the British were pushing forward along various parts of the frontier not just Waziristan, building roads into remoter areas, including the Khajuri plain (south of Peshawar), Mohmand territory, Malakand and Bajaur. In June 1933 Griffith, now the lieutenant governor, stated that 'the new ideal which we must keep before us is definite administration and control throughout the tribal area up to the Durand Line'.[150] In 1934 it was even proposed to build a road into the Afridi sanctuary of Tirah (only once entered by British troops, in 1897). Opening roads facilitated troop movement and was associated with punitive military operations, and was therefore unwelcome to most people, and eventually the British abandoned the Tirah project.[151]

As regards relations with the Afghan government, early in 1934 Griffith pointed out that it had kept to its undertakings and obligations (Musa Khan's allowance appears to have been reduced in the summer). However, Maconachie (and his successor William Fraser-Tytler) continued to raise the question of Afghan relations with British-side men during the 1930s. But he requested that he should not be required to complain to the Afghan officials every time British officials in the North-West Frontier Province reported Afghan interference on the British side of the Durand Line. This might exasperate them and make them less cooperative. It would be better to put minor issues aside until a suitable occasion offered itself for presenting a number of them together. He was given permission for this; he need only protest when it appeared that 'Afghan interference [had]… exceeded the bounds of ordinary usage or … been actuated by unfriendly motives'.[152]

In the Wana area Abdullah Jan Zilla Khel (formerly a Brigadier in the Afghan army) and his cousin Firqa Mashar Angur continued to resist the extension of British influence.[153] Angur was the brother one of Major Finnis's murderers; in 1932 Abdullah Jan had sheltered Zari Giga Khel, the man who had murdered Synge and Whawell. Wazirs continued to snipe at troops and Scouts in and around the Dahna valley, and in 1934 Zilla Khels attacked a Scouts patrol at Manra.[154] During the summer of 1934 the Afghan governor of Khost, Firqa Mashar Muhammad Khan, met a jirga of British-side Wazirs. He told them that the GOI had no right to move into Dahna or Manra.[155] He visited the shrine of Musa Nikka and sacrificed some cattle there. He and other officials informed jirgas of British-side men that they were welcome in Afghanistan and would be given land if the British made them suffer for their opposition. He also announced plans to build roads near the border with South Waziristan.

British officials were concerned by this; they also accused the Afghans of encouraging the Madda Khel malik, Arsala Khan, to set himself up as a rival to Zangi Khan; this had weakened Zangi's position, they claimed.[156] For their part, after the failure of the siege of Matun in 1933, the Afghans wanted to get hold of Abdur Rahman Madda Khel, as well as a mysterious figure referred to in the British reports as 'the unknown individual'. The two men were reported to be living with the Madda Khels near the Durand Line and actively trying to arrange another incursion into Afghanistan in support of the former amir Amanullah.[157] 'The unknown individual' was rumoured to be a stepbrother of Amanullah's, but appears to have been Muhammad Amin, a nephew of the Lewanai faqir.[158] It was a difficult situation. The GOA was vulnerable to uprisings in Khost encouraged by its opponents both within and outside Afghanistan. By the 1930s it seems that in practice it began to welcome firmer British control over the people of Waziristan. Vulnerable to accusations that it was failing to uphold Islam and Pashtun nationalism, it called on the GOI to deal with the Madda Khels, but wanted this done as unobtrusively as possible.

In the event the British seized 135 Madda Khel men and 22 rifles in Bannu. The GOI proposed to present the Madda Khels with an ultimatum. If they did not deal with Abdur Rahman and Muhammad Amin, they would be blockaded and troops would be stationed in their country while a road was built into it.[159] Maconachie in Kabul was able to persuade the secretary of state that there was a real danger that this could lead to fighting along the Durand Line which would easily spill over into Afghanistan and pose a real threat to the Afghan government.[160] As the primary goal of British policy was to maintain stability in Afghanistan, not to extend its influence into Madda Khel country, it was decided to proceed carefully; the resident demanded that the Madda Khels give an undertaking to expel the agitators and surrender 100 hostages and 100 rifles as security.[161] This they did. After this Abdur Rahman's influence began to fade, and in August 1934 the hostages were released; Muhammad Amin was surrendered to the Afghan government in the autumn.[162] The threat of further incursions into Khost from the British side diminished. A complicating factor in all this was the rivalry between the Madda Khel malik Zangi Khan and his pro-Afghan rivals Dande Khan and Arsala Khan. It was a good example of how enmity within tribal groups could interfere with relations between the GOA and the GOI.[163]

10

Mirza Ali Khan's Insurgency, Mullah Sher Ali and the Shami Pir

Continuing problems for the British

Maconachie and senior Afghan officials continued to discuss frontier issues. Early in July 1934, for example, Maconachie talked things over with the Afghan foreign minister. He drew particular attention to the Afghans' contacts with Arsala Khan Madda Khel. Faiz Muhammad admitted that it was wrong for his government to pay allowances to the British-side men. But it should not, he said, be 'construed as one of ill-feeling or hostility towards the British Government'; 'when a state was as weak as Afghanistan was it was forced to pay blackmail all round.'[1] There was simply no alternative, he said. 'Afghanistan and the frontier tribes are neighbours possessing a common tongue and a common descent as well as a common religion and that on this account close relations have for centuries existed between the two. ... If at any time any interruption or weakening of them has occurred, grave dangers to Afghanistan and the frontier have occurred.'[2]

At about this time, however, Afghan officials invited eighteen Mehsud boys to attend the Habibia school in Kabul, among them the sons of Ramzan Khan and Sadde Khan Shaman Khel, who lived in Waziristan but received Afghan allowances.[3] This was not a traditional practice, Maconachie thought, and was therefore unjustified. He made a strong protest. The GOI commented that it was 'a particularly insidious form of cultural interference, the object of which can hardly be other than to suborn British tribesmen to the political influence of a country to which they do not owe allegiance'.[4] Somewhat reluctantly the GOA sent fourteen of the boys home, keeping two for a time so it could not be accused of caving in completely to British demands.[5]

In October 1934 Musa Khan went to Kabul again and stayed there for some months.[6] In November Maconachie and Harry Johnson, the South Waziristan political agent, discussed the situation with Muhammad Hashim, the prime minister. As regards the allowances, the prime minister explained that until 1933 Nadir Shah had resisted the Mehsuds' demands for allowances, but that the Khost incursion in that year showed that something needed to be done to placate them. It had been decided that those who had been paid allowances when Nadir had been commander-in-chief would be eligible for them in future if they had 'shown practical good will towards his Government' (presumably by supporting him in 1929–30).[7] At the meeting Johnson complained about the activities of Firqa Mashar Muhammad Khan, the governor of Khost, and later in the year the authorities in Kabul instructed him to cooperate with the British officials.[8] They also discussed the possibility of setting up a system of frontier commissars, to make it easier to sort out minor border issues, on the lines of those already appointed on Afghanistan's Iranian and Soviet frontiers.[9]

The British continued to experience problems with various Wazirs groups, including some of the Madda Khels, and the Hassan Khel Mohmit Khels from the Kaitu area of North Waziristan. According to the latter's agreement with the British, government forces were allowed to visit their country, and they disliked this. In June 1935 some of them fired on a Scouts patrol. Their jirga was summoned, but was uncooperative and was dismissed. They crossed the border into Afghanistan and tried to persuade the government and the local people to support them. In November 1935 the Afghans told them they must either return to Waziristan or move to northern Afghanistan. They crossed back into British territory in November and agreed to a settlement in 1936.[10]

Much more serious was the murder of the leading Madda Khel malik, Zangi Khan, in April 1935 by his cousin, Khan Habib's sons.[11] As we have seen, the British officials had tried to build up Zangi Khan as the leading Madda Khel representative, and he had been working, it seems quite successfully, to uphold British interests. It seems that the British did not find anyone to take his place (they did not think his eldest son, Khandan Khan, a suitable candidate): the feud between Zangi Khan's family and that of Arsala Khan grew worse, and the British found the Madda Khels more difficult to manage than ever.[12]

We saw in Chapter 8 that the Mehsuds had been encroaching for some years on the Tori Khels' land to the south of Razmak and that the Tori Khels had refused to give up their rights to this. Finally in 1934 the officials persuaded them to do so and accept the compensation of Rs.50,000.[13] Some Tori Khels lived in the Shaktu-Khaisora area to the east of Razmak, but after the First World War the British had experienced few problems with them, and they had largely escaped British attention. But the policy of peaceful penetration meant interference; in 1930–1, for example, the government created a new Scouts' post at Dosalli on the Razmak–Tochi road, and Scouts began to carry out gashts in the Shaktu.[14]

The British continued to have difficulties with the Zilla Khels in and around Wana, partly it would seem because the resident, Arthur Parsons, persisted in his plan to open up the Dahna area. Regular troops from Wana visited it and nearby Boza in June 1935, and at about this time the Afghans appear to have recruited some more Zilla Khel khassadars. Also in 1935 a Zilla Khel man named Base Gul murdered a clerk in the Wana camp and took refuge with Abdullah Jan, who was living in the Musa Nika area right on the Durand Line, and sheltered a number of other wanted men.[15] In 1936 British officials summoned the Zilla Khel jirga and demanded that they deal with him. Twice the jirga sent lashkars to bring him in; each time he undertook to surrender but backed out at the last moment, and the lashkars broke up.[16] By the summer of 1936 the Zilla Khels were reported to have fractured into 'wrangling factions' unable to fulfil government orders or exert any control over the Zilla Khels as a whole. They forfeited their security bond of Rs.5,000 on behalf of Abdullah Jan. The officials took hostages from all the sections and threatened air attacks.[17]

By October 1936 the NWFP (North-West Frontier Province) government judged that the situation was becoming more serious and that regular troops might be needed. The new resident, James Acheson, suggested that Afghan support for Abdullah Jan and his cousin Angur had made it more difficult for the British to control them. He imposed a blockade enforced by the Scouts and the Wana Brigade aided by the RAF. All the different sections, including the non-allowance holders, submitted, and they accepted responsibility for the good behaviour of the Zilla Khels as a whole. The officials decided to use the RAF to drive Abdullah Jan from his refuge on the border and requested the GOA to arrest him should he cross into Afghanistan. The Afghans persuaded him and Angur to come to Kabul. They eventually exiled him to the Koh Daman north of Kabul, but allowed Angur to return to Waziristan.[18] They also dismissed Angur's brother, Ali Jan, suspected of taking part in Finnis's murder, from the Khost Militia.[19] The other Zilla Khels were helpful when Suleiman Khel Powindahs attacked the Wana Column in February 1937.[20]

Issues like these continued to affect the Anglo-Afghan relationship. Indeed, owing to the difficulties with the Zilla Khels, the situation in South Waziristan was said at one point in 1936 to be approaching a crisis, with the British claiming that Afghanistan's recruitment of khassadars and militiamen had upset their system of tribal control.[21] The Afghans themselves were upset by other developments along the border, including British operations against the Mohmands from August to October 1935. These followed the construction of a road into their territory in 1933; there was some severe fighting and both sides suffered a number of casualties.[22] Tensions were also caused by the negotiations over the British's plan to build the Tirah road, mentioned above, as well as Afghan troubles in the Kunar area.[23]

As regards the Khost Militia, by 1936 it was reported to comprise 504 Ahmadzai Wazirs and 503 Mehsuds (103 Shaman Khels, 278 Bahlolzais and 122 Alizais).[24] It was still in existence in 1946, when it was reported to number more than 1,600 men in all including some 500 Ahmadzai Wazirs, some of whom lived in Afghan territory while many others remained in British territory, and 500 Mehsuds. The Badinzai Shaman Khel Mehsuds for instance had sixty appointments.[25] They spent most of the year on leave at home and were not 'actively hostile to [British] … interests'.[26]

Meanwhile there was continuing Afghan interest in the 'recalcitrant community' at Musa Khan Abdullai's settlement of Mandesh.[27] In 1936 for instance, the GOA reportedly gave Musa Khan and his son Firqa Mashar Ahmad Jan Rs.20,000, and Qazi Amir Khan Rs.2,000.[28] In that year Ahmad Jan asked Prime Minister Hashim Khan for additional khassadar appointments, but he was told there was no money for them. Hashim Khan told him that although Nadir Shah had agreed to bring the Mehsud numbers up to 500, times had changed, and the Mehsud khassadars were 'extremely slack and a constant source of trouble'.[29] Nevertheless at this point the GOA sent some money to Ramzan, Sadde Khan and a cousin, Madar, and some other Shaman Khel Afghan allowance holders and khassadars. It also paid the Mullah Powindah's son Fazal Din Rs.12,000.[30] We have already seen that it had become possible for families to be paid allowances by both the Afghan and British governments, and it became common for one man to receive a British allowance, and a close relative, brother, cousin, or son, an Afghan allowance.[31] Reportedly, in 1936 the Ahmadzai Wazirs received Rs.90,000 p.a. and the Madda Khels (Utmanzais) Rs.14,000 from Kabul. Dande Khan and his son Ghulam Muhiy-ud-din Khan Madda Khel each received a personal allowance of Rs.10,000, as did one of the late Zangi Khan Madda Khel's uncles.[32] Some Kabul Khels spent part of the year in Afghan territory and part of it in British territory; according to the same source they received Rs.48,000.[33] In spite of these difficulties with the Zilla Khels and the Madda Khels and the British grumbles about the payment of allowances by the GOA to British-side men, by 1937 Afghan–British relations were improving again. The Afghan prime minister, Muhammad Hashim, visited London in February, and the British government agreed to supply arms and ammunition and Hawker aircraft, as well as arranging credit facilities.[34]

Health, education and the economy

The British continued to take some modest steps towards improving health and education in Waziristan. By the early 1930s about a thousand children were attending school there. A system of scholarships had been introduced to make it possible for Mehsud boys to receive secondary education; the 1936–7 Administration Report noted that many Mehsuds welcomed access to education, although some Abdullais burned down a school in 1937 at Ashkar Kot in the Makin area.[35] A medical service was introduced too, which by 1932 was said to be within reach of more than half the population.[36]

There were also economic benefits from road-building contracts and khassadar service. Pears commented that the Mehsud men were 'energetic and adaptable'; they were said to be unsuited to clerical work but to possess considerable 'technical ability' and to be much more willing than the Wazirs to take advantage of new opportunities, such as those offered by the construction industry.[37] With British support some men also established a lorry service using the new roads to keep the posts in southern Waziristan supplied with essentials.[38] In the 1930s the government also made efforts to improve agriculture, horticulture and animal husbandry. For instance a trial of maize seeds was carried out in several areas in 1935, but it was not very successful. Nor was an attempt to improve the quality of the local cattle by bringing in a bull from outside (it is not clear why). There were also experiments with fruit trees. With government encouragement Mehsuds made a success of growing potatoes in the Kaniguram area; they were exported to Dera Ismail Khan and Bannu.[39]

As regards local manufacturing, it appears that since the mid-nineteenth century cheaper foreign imports had led to the decline of the export of iron to India. Workshops at Kaniguram turned to manufacturing guns (the barrels were imported from the Kohat Pass) and jewellery, as well as continuing to make knives and pots and pans which were exported to Afghanistan.[40] In addition growing sales of timber from trees felled in the forests in the mountains to the west may have some extent substituted for the export of iron and iron goods to the administered areas to the east.⁴¹

All this helped to make life in Waziristan and along its eastern border relatively peaceful between 1925 and 1935; the number of murders in the settled areas by transborder tribesmen fell from 153 in 1920–1 to an average of 5 in each of the years from 1926 to 1936.⁴² The road from Wana north to Tauda China was completed in 1933, and the 1935–6 *Report on the Administration of the Border* pointed out that during the previous year, 'from the Samana Range [to the north] to the Gumal Pass almost complete peace has prevailed … the fruits of the policy of peaceful penetration'.⁴³

These relatively peaceful conditions depended on the presence of a large number of troops and police relative to the size of the local population: the highest proportion of any region in the Indian Empire.⁴⁴ This was expensive – £3 to £4 million had been spent on military campaigns in Waziristan since 1919; per head the costs of maintaining security within it were 'almost unprecedented in the history of the British Empire'.⁴⁵ In 1930 getting on for three times as much was spent on keeping regular troops in Waziristan as on scouts, khassadars and the frontier constabulary, allowances and political staffs, and hospitals and schools.⁴⁶

The region was still not really pacified. Every year Scouts and Waziristani men skirmished somewhere in it and attacks on government personnel continued.⁴⁷ Many people continued to resent the British presence, objecting particularly to the stationing of Hindu troops at Razmak.⁴⁸ If British strategy no longer relied on old-fashioned punitive expeditions, it continued to be based on the threat of force, relying on the massive garrison at Razmak and the use of the troops and Scouts periodically to 'show the flag' and move through remoter areas of Waziristan. So for example, after minor disturbances in 1933 between some Tori Khels and Mehsuds living there, troops visited the upper Shaktu. It was the first time troops had done so since the Mehsud blockade in 1901. Arthur Parsons, the resident, decided that it was time to establish 'a loose control' over the lower Khaisora valley to the north of the Shaktu, and proposed to construct a road into it, and was given permission to open negotiations with the Tori Khel jirga in 1935. The maliks accepted the offer of an extra Rs.7,500 p.a. in return for recognizing the government's right to build roads and posts anywhere in their country. Brigades from Bannu and Razmak spent two nights camped at Bishe Kashkai in the Khaisora valley in February 1936. But the GOI decided it could not afford the proposed road, and the plan was shelved.⁴⁹

Mirza Ali Khan's insurgency

By this time developments in NWFP and Punjab, and in India as a whole, were helping to generate renewed opposition to British rule along the frontier as well as tensions between Muslims and Hindus. Indian politicians' attitudes towards the frontier varied considerably. As we saw in Chapter 9, Congress supporters tended to be critical of British policy in Waziristan, arguing that it was too repressive and did little to improve socio-economic conditions.[50] The Hindu nationalist Mahasabha party saw things differently. It wanted protection for the Hindus living along the frontier, who, as we have seen, were often targeted in raids from Waziristan. It demanded that either the government should establish full control of Waziristan or it should implement a real close-border policy, defending the administrative border properly and taking retaliatory action against the frontier men if they raided across it.[51]

In 1935 the Shiromani Gurdwara Parbandhak Committee, a group Sikhs had set up in 1920 to manage the historic gurdwaras in Punjab, destroyed a disused mosque in Lahore.[52] This also upset many Muslims and contributed to growing communal tensions. Waziristanis found the so-called Islam Bibi problem in 1936 particularly aggravating. According to what seems to be the most widely accepted version of events, early in 1936 a Pashtun schoolteacher, Sayyid Amir Noor Ali Shah, living in the Bannu district, married a young Hindu woman, Ram Kori, and she converted to Islam. Her family objected strongly, and as she was under sixteen she and her husband were both taken into custody. He was convicted of abduction and sentenced to imprisonment for two years. Ram Kori's family demanded that she come home, but she did not want to. It was decided therefore that she should live with a third party until she was legally an adult and could make up her own mind. While Ram Kori's family was unhappy and appealed against the decision, many Muslims were outraged, feeling that Hindus had pressured the government into making the wrong decision.[53]

On 11 April 1936 mullahs from Dawar met at Idak and decided to ask for the girl to be looked after by a Muslim family.[54] The British officials refused. As we have seen, there had already been some problems in Dawar in 1930, and a lashkar of discontented men now began to form. They were encouraged by Mirza Ali Khan, whom the British referred to as the Faqir of Ipi. A 'turbaned giant of a man, wearing baggy pants and a flowing robe', Mirza Ali Khan had been born in 1901 at a hamlet called Kurti near the Khajuri post at the western end of the Shinki defile.[55] His family came from the Haibatari section of the Tori Khels.[56]

His father and grandfather were both local religious figures and owned some land. He attended the government school at Idak in the Tochi valley as well as spending time in madrasahs there and in Bannu acquiring a traditional Islamic education. He visited Afghanistan too and became the disciple of a leading Afghan religious leader, the Naqib ('chief') of Chaharbagh near Jalalabad.[57] Returning to Waziristan he settled at Haipee (Ipi) in the Tochi valley where he gradually built up a following.[58]

Later in April 1936 he accompanied the Dawar lashkar when it crossed over into the Khaisora valley to try and persuade the Tori Khels to join it. The British officials ordered the Dawar maliks to recall the lashkar, but it would not disperse. They therefore destroyed Mirza Ali Khan's house and two other houses belonging to men they thought had been responsible for organizing the lashkar, blocked the routes between the lower Khaisora and the lower Tochi and blockaded villages in the Tochi valley between Khajuri and Idak. As a result the lashkar broke up.

In May 1936 Mirza Ali Khan went to Bishe Kashkai in the Khaisora valley, and he and his brother Sher Zaman built a house and mosque there. He tried to play on the anger caused by the Islam Bibi and Shahidganj cases to persuade the Utmanzai Wazirs and the Mehsuds to join him and rise against the government. He was in touch with Fazal Din, and the two men attended Friday prayers together on 10 July 1936. Warren sees Mirza Ali Khan as being motivated primarily by what he calls Islamic fundamentalism.[59] It is clear that he based his appeal largely on Islamic loyalties, though there was an ethnic aspect as well and even perhaps an element of Waziristani patriotism. He sent out a call for an anti-British rising, writing letters to representatives from the different Waziristan groups; it was time for them to 'choose between the Kufr [disbelievers] and Islam' and 'step into the battlefield for helping Islam'.[60] If his followers cut down trees, he promised he would turn the sticks into rifles. If they were 'true ghazi followers of Islam, and not mere plunderers and adventurers in search of private gain', God would protect them and British weapons would not harm them. Most people seem to have believed him. For example, the dropping of white warning leaflets from an aircraft a number of days before bombing, 'followed by red leaflets twenty-four hours before an attack was taken as evidence of his ability to turn bombs into paper'.[61]

In August 1936 the NWFP judicial commissioner ruled that because Islam Bibi was still a minor, her family was still responsible for her, and she was sent back to them. This further inflamed Muslim opinion and made some of the Wazirs readier to listen to Mirza Ali Khan. When the British officials learnt that he was now living in the Tori Khels' territory, they reminded the maliks that they had recently agreed not to harbour men hostile to the government.[62] The maliks tried but failed to persuade Mirza Ali Khan to call off his campaign. The resident, James Acheson, decided that a show of force was needed to assert British authority and compel the maliks to live up to their agreements. He therefore asked for a routine flag march by regular troops to be diverted through the lower Khaisora. Elsewhere along the frontier such movements were not customary and required the viceroy's permission, but it seems that in Waziristan this was not needed. The lieutenant-governor initially opposed the march, but changed his mind and authorized it on 17 November.[63] It looks like an overreaction since Mirza Ali Khan's activities had not so far had any very serious consequences, but Acheson was anxious lest Mirza Ali Khan's propaganda encourage the Mehsuds to join him and thought that British prestige was at stake – failure to deal firmly with him would suggest British weakness.[64]

On 25 November the British therefore despatched two troop columns to Bishe Kashkai, where they were to spend two nights. To their surprise, some Tori Khels, assisted by 'a formidable party of Mahsud badmashes', among them two prominent anti-British men, Khonia Khel Jalal Khel and Raji Gul Shabi Khel, as well as some Madda Khels, Bhittanis, Manzar Khels and Mohmit Khels, offered serious resistance to both columns.[65] One did not reach Bishe Kashkai until the following day. Both left on 27 November as planned, but it looked as though they had been forced to retreat by their opponents. Mirza Ali Khan's supporters saw it as a manifestation of his miraculous powers, and it encouraged others to join him.[66] He was reported to have 'acquired a halo not unlike that which once surrounded that warrior-saint, the Mullah Powindah. Prayers are offered for his success and long life in nearly every mosque in Waziristan and probably in some of those in Bannu also.'[67]

British casualties were twenty-nine men killed and 106 wounded. They had not expected such resistance, but Acheson had misjudged the extent of anti-British feeling among the ordinary Tori Khels and played into Mirza Ali Khan's hands.[68] As we have seen, across Waziristan there were hostile anti-government networks, consisting of men who drew allowances from Afghanistan; these were men who resented the fact that they had no allowances from either government and men who lived mostly from banditry. There were economic pressures too.[69] Employment on government contracts had been declining, the population was growing and the distribution of the new Khaisora allowances had caused tensions among the Tori Khels.[70] Another factor was political developments in the adjoining districts of the NWFP, in which Waziristanis were taking a growing interest.[71] The government had finally given the province its own legislature by the 1935 Government of India Act, and elections were to be held in 1937. In addition many of the younger men welcomed the opportunity to take part in some fighting for the first time.[72]

Madda Khels, and many Afghans, now joined Mirza Ali Khan; by early December around 1,200 men from outside the area had gathered in the Khaisora. Bhittanis also began to take part in raiding, instigated by Faqir Din Muhammad Bhittani, who became Mirza Ali Khan's chief lieutenant.[73] However, the political officers were able to persuade the Madda Khels to go home, and the Shabi Khels handed over twenty-two government rifles as security. It might therefore still have been possible to avoid a serious conflict, but the British were determined to deal severely with any opposition. On 29 November they handed over control of Waziristan to the army. Troops were sent back into the Khaisora valley, dispersed what remained of the lashkar and destroyed a number of villages.[74]

In the meantime Mirza Ali Khan had moved to Arsal Kot, an out-of-the-way settlement in the Shaktu valley on the southern edge of Tori Khel territory. The RAF began to bomb his camp there, and he withdrew into the nearby caves. At the end of January 1937 a representative Mehsud jirga met and handed over a number of British-made rifles and a machine gun to make amends for the fact that Khonia Khel and other Mehsuds had been involved in the Khaisora fighting.[75] The Tori Khel maliks also submitted.[76] The situation appeared to be improving, and Waziristan returned to civilian control. Educational, economic and medical assistance programmes continued; for example a new hospital was opened at Miranshah.[77]

Developments in 1937–8

Early in 1937 the situation began to deteriorate again. On 6 February 1937 two British officers, John Keogh and Roy Beatty, were killed in separate attacks. A Madda Khel man was responsible for Beatty's death, but the identity of Keogh's killer has never been established; Mirza Ali Khan could have been responsible. The murders signalled a revival of the insurgency, which began to spread. Near Wana, led by the anti-British Zilla Khel, Gul Din, men fired on a British column 'in a running fight that lasted several miles'.[78] Mehsud raiding gangs began to appear on the Derajat border. On 4 March Mirza Ali Khan himself called on all khassadars and maliks to stop supporting the government, warning them that if they continued to do so they would not be given a proper Muslim burial when the time came. The RAF bombed three Madda Khel villages suspected of harbouring wanted men.⁷⁹ The Army began to use the roads only on certain secretly selected days (Road-Opening Days), and all traffic went in convoy; troops were sent out from the camps and forts en route to picket the key positions beforehand.⁸⁰

Early in March 1937 Sir George Cunningham replaced Griffith as the NWFP governor. Harry Johnson, who had a great deal of experience of Waziristan, replaced Acheson as chief political officer. Utmanzai maliks visited Mirza Ali Khan to try and get him to settle with the government, but he would not. More men gathered at Mirza Ali Khan's headquarters at Arsal Kot. They also launched several raids on border villages, directed mainly at Hindus living in them, as well as attacking the bazaar at Idak in Dawar, and the camp at Damdil. On 29 March 1937 they attacked men from the first battalion of the Sixth Gurkha Rifles on picketing duty, killing thirty-four British and Gurkha soldiers and suffering ninety-two casualties themselves.⁸¹

The fact that Mirza Ali Khan did not receive much support from the Mehsuds was very important. Because Keogh had been murdered in their territory, the British demanded that they pay a fine of Rs.75,000. Early in March 1937 a large Mehsud jirga met at Sora Rogha, and even though it included many kashars, it agreed to pay the fine. Their maliks seemed to have the situation under control.⁸² The fact that in 1936 the British had awarded Fazal Din an allowance (so he was now getting money from them as well as the GOA) had helped to persuade him not to support Mirza Ali Khan. Some Mehsuds did take part nevertheless. Early in April, led by Khonia Khel, Jalal Khels, Abdur Rahman Khels and Bhittanis, carried out a very successful ambush on a British convoy in the Shahur Tangi. Forty-seven soldiers were killed and fifty wounded; sixteen tribesmen were killed and twenty-six wounded.⁸³

In response the British closed the Jandola–Razmak road. In April Mirza Ali Khan's followers also destroyed the road bridge between Razmak Narai and Razoni. This meant that the British could not use the northern route from Razmak to Bannu either. The base was therefore cut off from the plains. The garrison had ample supplies and was never really threatened. The insurgents did sever the pipeline from the base's main water reservoir, which meant that water had to be drawn from wells outside the perimeter fence; on 19 April they killed eight men during an attempt to do so. Water began to be rationed. Following the Shahur ambush, the British flew arms and ammunition into Wana instead of sending them by road; weekly convoys organized by cooperative Mehsuds delivered non-military stores.⁸⁴ Insurgents also stepped up their attacks on civilians in Waziristan and across the border, mostly concentrating on Hindus and Sikhs. They also began to attack the Scouts' posts.⁸⁵ In response the British bombed villages, took hostages and distributed rifles to vulnerable villages along the border. The rising was now spreading outside the Khaisora area and developing into a major insurgency. By the end of April 1937 the lashkar in North Waziristan had grown to nearly 3,000 strong. It comprised approximately 700 Tori Khels, 300 Madda Khels, 200 Bhittanis, 100 Dawars, 600 Mehsuds and 200 Bhittanis, and as many as 1,000 men from Afghanistan (in particular some 300 Kabul Khels living in Birmal and 300 Zadrans from Khost).[86]

The problems the GOI experienced with Mirza Ali Khan inevitably affected its relationship with Afghanistan. Participation by men from the Afghan side of the border had boosted the morale of his supporters in Waziristan and made them more willing to keep fighting.[87] William Fraser-Tytler, who succeeded Maconachie as the British minister in Kabul in 1935, complained to the Afghan government about this. It ordered the local officials to discourage men crossing the Durand Line, but it could only do so much, given that its authority on its side of the border was limited.[88] By July 1937 at least 5,000 Afghans had taken part in the fighting. The Afghan prime minister, Muhammad Hashim, who had visited London in the spring, expressed his willingness to try and remove or reach a settlement with Mirza Ali Khan, but the offer was rejected.[89]

Although the British position was a difficult one, it was never likely that the insurgents would be able to force them actually to withdraw from Waziristan. To do so they would have had to pose a real threat to the forts occupied by the Scouts, and to the Razmak base, and they lacked the weaponry and numbers to do this. Moreover many Wazir maliks saw Mirza Ali Khan as a threat to their own position and discouraged their supporters from supporting him; nor was he joined by many of their khassadars. The Mehsud Mullah Fazal Din used his influence to discourage the Mehsuds from joining in, and in May 1937 he actually offered to mediate between Mirza Ali Khan and the British.[90] Mirza Ali Khan's principal rival in North Waziristan was the Faqir of Shewa, a Kabul Khel; he did not support the insurgency either, despite pressure from Kabul Khels living in Afghan Birmal.[91] As a result Mirza Ali Khan's following was relatively small; 'only a comparatively small proportion of the tribal fighting strength has been actively involved', it was reported in 1937, 'the opposition consisting of a fluctuating collection of individuals from various tribes and sections (many of them foreign [i.e. Afghan]) rather than of complete tribal units'.[92]

Nevertheless it was humiliating that in spite of the establishment of the Razmak garrison and all the road building, the resistance was so difficult to crush. The GOI had to take it seriously. Rather than negotiating, it decided on further military action and returned Waziristan to military control.[93] By now General

Coleridge, the general officer commanding Northern Command (1936–40), had three infantry divisions at his disposal. His troops drove most of the insurgents out of the Shaktu-Khaisora area in May 1937 and almost succeeded in capturing Mirza Ali Khan, but he fled just in time. Troops also dispersed his Mehsud allies in Shawal.[94] Two brigades from Razmak moved south through Mehsud territory and halted at Ladha. Here the resident, Johnson, met jirgas from all the main Mehsud sections. They gave hostages and did not object when he announced that a road was to be built between the Tank Zam and the Shaktu.[95]

This appears to have been the insurgency's high point; subsequently the lashkars began to grow smaller, but Mirza Ali Khan was certainly not defeated. One argument for the introduction of the modified policy in Waziristan had been that it would prevent raiding into the administered areas, but it was no longer doing so.[96] Large gangs of from 50 to 100 men from Waziristan continued to raid in the settled districts, often attacking settlements a long way from the borders. For example seventy men attacked Paharpur on the night of 2/3 May. On the night of 23/24 May insurgents ambushed a train on the narrow-gauge railway to Tank in the Peyzu Pass north-west of the town. Meanwhile the British had repaired the bridge on the Razmak–Razoni road, and late in May 1937 they reopened it.[97] The Tori Khels sued for peace, and early in June an armistice was reached with their maliks. On the evening of 19 June 1937 troops tried to catch Mirza Ali Khan, but he had gone (dressed in a burka his enemies said).[98] In the meantime the Kikarai Mehsud Mullah Sher Ali had collected some 250 Mehsuds, Wazirs and Afghans at Tiarza south-west of Ladha. Troops destroyed his kot there and attacked his lashkar from different directions, and it dispersed.[99]

British officials held two conferences on 13 and 14 July 1937 in New Delhi to discuss future policy. They were reluctant to admit that the costly roads and cantonments that had been built since the early 1920s had not brought peace and stability and were not prepared to consider any major changes, let along withdrawing troops from Razmak.[100] Arthur Parsons, now officiating head of the External Affairs Department, and the lieutenant-governor, George Cunningham, for instance, thought that leaving Razmak would encourage the insurgents, expose Waziristan to Afghan intrigues and make Bannu and Dera Ismail Khan less secure.[101] The senior officials appear to have misled the viceroy, Linlithgow, into thinking that the Tori Khels were to blame for the problem; 'by their aggressive behaviour [they] have forced us to undertake an extension of our policy of penetration and control', he commented.[102] As we have seen, the reverse was true. The India Office was critical of the way Waziristan affairs had been handled, but nothing much changed, and the GOI continued to pursue the modified forward policy.[103]

In August 1937 the governor of Khost, Firqa Mashar Muhammad Khan, intervened. He instructed Musa Khan Abdullai, who, as we have seen, had continued to receive payments from Kabul, to organize a jirga to discuss the situation and see if Mirza Ali Khan could be persuaded to come to an agreement. The jirga met at Musa Khan's village of Mandesh in the Darra Algad, on the British side, only about eight miles from Razmak as the crow flies; it was attended by Mullah Fazal Din and thousands of other men, before moving to Manra. Mirza Ali Khan refused to call off his campaign.[104] The GOI was indignant about this Afghan interference; Prime Minister Hashim Khan explained that Muhammad Khan had acted without authority, but pointed out that his government could not ignore the unrest in Waziristan, which threatened to undermine its stability. He was also concerned about the activities of the Suleiman Khel Ghilzai Powindahs, who in June 1937 had risen and attacked a newly built Afghan post at Zargun Shahr in western Paktika. Moreover the ex-amir Amanullah's party was still active, and the arrest of an agent from Damascus in Afghanistan's Southern Province showed that it was still in touch with the frontier people.[105] The GOA requested the GOI to seize the Suleiman Khel Ghilzai ringleaders before they returned to Afghanistan in the spring of 1938, but only one was caught.[106] Nevertheless the Afghan government did make a real effort to stop its own subjects joining the insurgency. In August 1937 Zetland, the secretary of state, suggested to the GOI that it might benefit from Afghan help, but it ignored him. During August and September the British presented the Mehsud, Tori Khel, Bakka Khel, Jani Khel, Bhittani and Dawar maliks with demands for the payment of fines and the surrender of 2,060 rifles. As had happened so often in the past, the maliks paid the fines from their government allowances.[107]

For the rest of 1937 Mirza Ali Khan continued to move around, going first to Gumbakai in Shawal and then to a cave at Kaurai, twenty-one miles west of Miranshah. In the meantime, the Mehsud Mullah Sher Ali had established his headquarters and kitchen at Laswandai, north-west of Kaniguram. He collected a lashkar and raided a village in the Dera Ismail Khan district on 6 September 1937.[108] The Afghan government continued to work for a settlement. In September it arranged for the Karbogha Mullah to meet Mirza Ali Khan and tell him that 'he was acting contrary to Islamic law', but he was not persuaded.[109] In June 1937 the British began constructing a new set of Shaktu-Khaisora roads that would give access the upper reaches of the Shaktu valley. They hired some

5,000 Wazirs and 2,000 Mehsuds to work on them and more than a hundred miles were built; this provided some short-term employment in the area which may have helped to damp down anti-British feeling. Sporadic fighting continued nevertheless, and the British conducted a three-day operation in the Shaktu from 16 November to 18 November 1937.[110]

How important was the insurgency? It has been suggested that the events of 1936–7 were 'in terms of scale and cost, both human and matériel' not exceptional, and that they had little effect on British policy.[111] It is true that in the short term at least policy did not change and that the insurgency was never a really serious threat to the British position in Waziristan. But it had tied up large numbers of troops and led to many deaths; more than 40,000 soldiers had been involved, and 250 men killed and 687 wounded. (The insurgents it was calculated had lost 898 dead and 856 badly wounded.)[112] Repressing it was expensive too; the 1936–7 campaign had cost more than £1,500,000. Moreover as we have seen, the insurgency contributed to a serious deterioration in the security situation along the border with Waziristan, and this continued well into the 1940s, as well as complicating relations with Afghanistan. It was the main reason why British officials were persuaded to reassess the modified forward policy during the 1940s.

Mullah Sher Ali and the Shami Pir

As it had during the previous cold weather, Mirza Ali Khan's insurgency died down during the winter of 1937–8. When the weather turned warmer, his supporters began to form small lashkars again.[113] He had spent the winter living with the Madda Khels, and in February the British told them they should evict him or give security for him. They did neither, and the British subjected them to heavy bombing until 18 March, and then a land blockade.[114] The GOI finally decided that the situation was so bad that it would make sense to ask the GOA to cooperate in dealing with him, 'even at the cost of a temporary departure from the principle of non-interference by the Afghan government across the Durand Line'.[115] It therefore approached the prime minister, Muhammad Hashim, but he was reluctant to do much. He resented the fact that his earlier offer to help had been rejected, and he continued to blame the British officials for not doing more to control the Suleiman Khel Ghilzai Powindahs, who at that point were beginning to move back across the border from India into Katawaz in what is now the Afghan province of Paktika.[116]

In April 1938 Mullah Sher Ali also resumed the struggle. He assembled a lashkar near the Dargai Sar mountain, near the meeting of the Tank Zam and Shahur rivers and not far from Jandola, and attacked a picket and a road patrol. The British attacked the lashkar from the air and it dispersed; they also bombed the Splitoi, Maintoi and Upper Baddar valleys, from where the lashkar's members had mostly come. The Mullah collected another lashkar in early July, and on 12 July it brought down a low-flying aircraft; on 18 July it attacked a Scouts patrol. Meanwhile British relations with the Madda Khels continued to deteriorate; a village was attacked with anti-personnel and then delayed action bombs. Zetland was unhappy about this, but the RAF did not change its tactics. Insurgents in North Waziristan gathered a lashkar and on 10 May besieged the Datta Khel fort, and it was not relieved until 9 June.

In the spring of 1938 the so-called Shami Pir ('Sufi spiritual master from Damascus'), Muhammad Said Gilani, appeared on the scene.[117] Muhammad Said had inherited some of the *baraka* of the founder of the Qadiriyya Sufi order, Abd al-Qadir Gilani (d.1166); his family had long-established connections with Waziristan and were revered by many of its inhabitants who had connections with the Qadiriyya *tariqa*. The pir had already visited Afghanistan and Waziristan in the 1920s; he went to Wana in 1926 and was reported to have been a good influence.[118] At the beginning of June 1938 he told Major Humphry Barnes, the South Waziristan political agent, that 'he had lost property in Syria, and wished to make some money in Waziristan settling blood feuds'.[119] Many people would have willingly paid him *shukrana* (tithes), and this could have been one reason for his visit. But he was also a first cousin of Soraya, the wife of the former amir Amanullah (Amanullah and Soraya were now living in exile in Rome) and had married the daughter of a senior German police official. It is likely that the Italian government encouraged his visit to embarrass the British, if not to bring about regime change in Afghanistan itself.[120]

In January 1938 he went on to Tank where he stayed with the Nawab, and in March moved into Waziristan. The GOA asked for him to be removed, and on June 12 the political agent warned him that he might have to leave. The next day, he called a jirga at Kaniguram and denounced 'King Zahir Shah as a usurper and referred to Amanullah as the lawful King of Afghanistan', and the jirga issued a proclamation calling for the king's overthrow.[121] Large numbers of Mehsud and Wazir men joined the pir, and on 23 June he set out at the head of a large following for Afghanistan. He actually got within a day's march of the border, and some of his supporters moved into Afghanistan and clashed with Afghan irregulars.[122] The Afghan government was very concerned and several times asked the British to move him away from the frontier.[123] The lieutenant-governor, George Cunningham, flew to Razmak to discuss the situation with Barnes. On 26 June they managed to persuade the pir to come into Wana, and they offered him money to go back to Syria. He agreed to leave India in return for a payment of £25,000. This was quickly arranged, and he was flown out from Wana.[124] The Mehsud and Wazir men went home. At the request of the GOA, the British also removed another influential pir, Sayyid Yusuf, known as the Baghdadi pir. This reportedly upset one of his followers, Malik Hayat Khan Nazar Khel Bahlolzai.[125]

By now Mirza Ali Khan had established a base in the caves at Gorwekht in the mountains west of Datta Khel, near the Afghan border. In mid-July 1938 the British tried to capture him again. They seized or destroyed some stores and equipment, but he escaped, crossing the border into Tanni country in Khost. In August he met Afghan emissaries at Margha in Birmal who told him he must either surrender to the Afghan government or go back into British territory, so he returned to Gorwekht. Now that he was living in a remote area on the edge of Waziristan, the British no longer regarded him as such a threat. But neither he nor Mullah Sher Ali were finished. The latter raised a lashkar and attacked a permanent picket not far from the Splitoi post on 11 July 1938. The lashkar went on to Katskai near Sora Rogha where it attacked the Scouts send out to deal with them and then moved to Ladha where it killed two Scouts.[126]

Gorwekht remained Mirza Ali Khan's permanent residence for the rest of his life. His base consisted of 'a network of caves in the side of a deep canyon', which housed a mosque, an armoury, a granary, an office and a printing press.[127] If troops came for him he could easily slip across the border into Afghanistan. The *1940–41 Administration Report* concluded:

> Such is the nature of the country that probably only an attack by parachute troops will have any hope of success against any of his bases. He maintains in a series of caves (which are admirable air-raid shelters) stocks of ammunition and coins; a factory for the manufacture of weapons, reserve supplies of rations, and the headquarters of his administrative and intelligence system.[128]

In October 1938 he announced that he was determined to fight on, condemning the maliks and lambardars (landowners) as British lackeys, and he and his followers continued to wage a guerrilla war for another ten years at least.[129]

Following the departure of the Shami pir, the GOI gave a formal undertaking to the GOA to try and prevent similar incidents from occurring in future and expressed its willingness to have discussions on political and economic matters of mutual interest.¹³⁰ During the summer the GOA's relations with the Ghilzais in Katawaz in eastern Afghanistan appeared to be improving, and it began to take an interest in Mirza Ali Khan again. In October 1938 Sir Aubrey Metcalfe, the Indian government's foreign secretary, visited Kabul. They talked about Mirza Ali Khan, as well as discussing the British policy of peaceful penetration and partial occupation. The prime minister made no objection to the latter, but refused to make any concessions regarding the payment of allowances to British-side men, which he would not reduce any further.¹³¹ The British offered Mirza Ali Khan a free pardon, but he did not respond.¹³²

From the British point of view the situation in Waziristan itself was gradually improving, but during the summer of 1938 raiding into the settled districts along its eastern border grew more serious. The rugged Ahmadzai Salient to the north of Bannu became a refuge for insurgents and bandits.¹³³ Political developments contributed to the insecurity. The Frontier Congress administration in the NWFP had taken away the border village leaders' legal, financial and policing privileges. They resented this and saw no reason why they should bother to protect Hindus and Sikhs as they had done in the past. Since 1926 the strength of the Frontier Constabulary had been reduced by some 1,500 men, and this also made it more difficult to keep the villages safe.¹³⁴ It was not just villages that were under threat; more than 300 men, led by the Khattak Mehr Dil, one of Mirza Ali Khan's lieutenants, attacked Bannu City itself on 23 July 1938. They killed six Hindus and kidnapped others and did a great deal of damage, escaping with much valuable loot. This was particularly serious; it was the first time that Bannu itself had been attacked since 1849. In response the British authorities recruited 500 men for a special force to reinforce the police in the settled districts, and by 1939 they had distributed 4,000 rifles to border villagers.¹³⁵

11

Mirza Ali Khan, the Second World War and British withdrawal

Civil–military relations

During the interwar period the military often criticized the political officers for being too sympathetic to the frontier people. They saw them, for example, as having been responsible for the fact that during the campaigns against Mirza Ali Khan they had had to operate under what they saw as '"galling" political restrictions'; these, they argued, were responsible for their failure to deal effectively with him.[1] Relations between them and the civil or political authorities definitely became more difficult during the interwar period. The disagreement between Wigram and Bolton over the reasons for Zangi Khan's failure to take the officers to Maizar (and the appropriate response to it) is a good example. Indeed, Moreman suggests, the system of political and military control 'began to break down before the Second World War as growing inter-service rivalry and insufficient funds undermined its basis'.[2]

Civil officials had usually been primarily responsible for relations with the tribal groups living in Waziristan and along the Waziristan border, but the establishment of the Razmak base increased the influence of the military. During the 1930s some senior officers began to argue that the Indian army should play a bigger role. Some even called for the appointment of a military governor of Waziristan on French lines who 'would command all the regular and irregular forces and ... be responsible for the political work with the tribes'.[3] For example, an article in the *Journal of the United Services' Institution of India* claimed that the French army in southern Morocco was more successful than the Indian army on the North-West Frontier because a single military governor was in charge there.[4] In 1939 the viceroy initiated a review of policy in Waziristan.[5] In the memorandum he wrote as a result, he noted that in connection with Waziristan, 'the success of Marshal Lyautey in Morocco has been touched on', and that it had been suggested informally that 'the true solution of the problem … lies in the appointment of a Military Governor'.[6] He did not agree. Quite apart from 'any possible difference in the methods employed by the French', he said, 'I do not regard Morocco as a true parallel', because 'our' frontier 'abuts on another tribal area (not the sea or desert) only lightly under the control of its own government'.[7]

A related question was whether regular or irregular troops should have the primary responsibility for maintaining security in Waziristan. After the First World War, for example, the South Waziristan and North Waziristan Militias had been reformed as the South Waziristan and Tochi Scouts and put under the authority of the political agents, and the arrangement seems to have worked well. But in the early 1930s the Indian army's Northern Command suggested that regulars could police tribal territory more cheaply than the Civil Armed Forces. In 1932 trials were conducted to compare how well the Scouts and the Indian army did 'in terms of mobility and in the skills that made Scouts so effective in policing tribal territory'.[8] The Scouts did better, and some political officers began to suggest that the army was not playing a very effective role in tribal territory. For its part the army continued to resist 'any proposals that might leave the control of the frontier in the hands of irregulars', partly because service on the frontier offered combat experience unavailable elsewhere.[9] The creation of the RAF also complicated matters. In the later 1920s for example Trenchard had drawn up two schemes involving the use of aircraft rather than ground troops as the principal means of controlling Waziristan. Both were rejected.[10]

Developments in 1939

By the end of 1938 the British no longer considered Mirza Ali Khan to be such a serious threat, but there was still no peace in Waziristan and along its eastern border. Some Tori Khels (they were still under blockade), and the Mehsud Mullah Sher Ali's supporters, continued to resist the British occupation, as did some of the Madda Khels.[11] In order to increase the pressure on the Tori Khels, in January 1939 Coleridge sent troops back into their territory to destroy their mills and irrigation canals. A motor track was constructed along the lower Khaisora, east of Damdil, and in March regular troops were sent into the Tori Khel area east along the Shaktu valley past Arsal Kot, which the British had not previously visited. The column had to turn back because of the difficult terrain.[12] In March 1939 Khonia Khel Jalal Khel, who had led the Shahur Tangi ambush in April 1937, was killed in a shoot-out with men with whom he had a blood feud.[13] By now the British officials had raised two Mehsud Labour Battalions to keep the young men occupied and out of trouble (they were mainly employed on road-making).[14]

In March 1939 Mirza Ali Khan's supporters fired shells into the Datta Khel fort in Madda Khel territory, and the British blockaded the Madda Khels again. Zangi Khan was no longer there to represent them, and his son, Khandan Khan, had been jailed for anti-British activities. As many as 3,000 Madda Khels turned up to negotiate a surrender. 'No family could trust a member of any other family to report to them truthfully what really happened at the negotiations', it was reported, 'so each family sent at least one man, every one of whom had simultaneously to be admitted to the deliberations.'[15] In April the third settlement in three years was made with them, and once again they undertook to stop helping Mirza Ali Khan and his followers. Mirza Ali Khan remained at Gorwekht (which appears to have been in Madda Khel territory), and men continued to visit him to obtain his advice and his blessing. Clashes continued to take place between his followers and British troops.

From the British point of view, nevertheless, the situation in Waziristan itself continued to improve, and in April 1939 political authority was finally returned to Cunningham and the civil officers. Negotiations were still going on with the Tori Khels, and in May they complied with the government's demands.[16] But skirmishing and raiding from Waziristan into settled districts continued, and Muslims and Hindus began to attack each other.[17] Already in February 1939 there had been serious communal rioting in Dera Ismail Khan. On 10 August 1939 insurgents killed Lieutenant-Colonel May, deputy quartermaster-general Waziristan district, on the road between Bannu and Dera Ismail Khan. Kidnapping of Hindus for ransom became more frequent; in November 1939 for instance Mehsuds kidnapped Major Duggal, a Hindu in the Indian Medical Service. The maliks paid the ransom and obtained the major's release. The money was deducted from their allowances and those of the khassadars. The kidnappers told the assistant political agent at Sora Rogha just how much they detested the maliks and explained that initially they would have accepted Rs.3,000 for Duggal, but 'the more fuss that was made, the higher the price rose'.[18] During 1939 a column visited the Ahmadzai salient and left two detachments of Frontier Constabulary there.[19]

Waziristan policy

In spite of all the money spent on it, peaceful penetration and the Razmak policy had produced only a few relatively quiet years.[20] A minority of people in Waziristan had done well as a result of the growing British presence while the majority seem to have resigned themselves to it, though continuing to resent it. They disliked the establishment of the base at Razmak and the associated road-building, and the implementation of the policy of peaceful penetration, which involved troop movements and frequent gashts by the Scouts through their territory, the return of regular troops to Wana, further road-building into more or less independent areas, and sometimes ill-judged responses by officials when they judged people to have been insufficiently cooperative. Recalling the difficulties during the First World War, a major insurgency had developed in 1936 and continued until early 1939, with a recrudescence of serious raiding into the administered areas.[21] 'Once troops were brought in from outside, in an area as large as Waziristan', Elliott suggested, 'a variation of Parkinson's Law seemed to operate: the more troops there were the easier it was for the Fakir [Mirza Ali Khan] and his henchmen to recruit followers to fight them. Towards the end the presence of so many troops was unquestionably an irritating factor.'[22] Maffey's closed border policy was the 'more statesmanlike of the two', Elliott concluded, though he also wondered whether it would have made enough difference to prevent serious difficulties in Waziristan in 1943–4 when the Japanese were attacking India's eastern frontier.[23]

Mirza Ali Khan's insurgency helped to revive some of the controversies about frontier policy that had arisen in the early 1920s.[24] In his 1939 memorandum Linlithgow concluded tactfully that what he called the 1922 policy had been 'generally successful', but that at the same time there was scope for modification in the light of experience.[25] In particular he noted that problems were always likely to arise when troops moved freely through tribal areas, especially when they did so in large numbers. He therefore recommended the greater use of Scouts rather than regular troops where possible, beginning with the gradual replacement of a battalion at Wana, and possibly at Razmak; they would carry out 'the normal duties of watch and ward under the political authorities concerned'.[26] Where the 1922 policy had failed in his view was in respect of the economic and what he called 'the civilising side', and he also made some suggestions to address that.[27] The outbreak of the Second World War, however, made it impossible to introduce any changes in the short term, and two troop divisions were retained in Waziristan to ensure that the tribes did not exploit the situation.[28]

Linlithgow was right to point to the limited progress that had been made with 'nation-building' activities, such as constructing hospitals and schools and providing employment. Nevertheless, as we have seen, the government was giving some help with agriculture, education and medical care, and the region's economic development. Moreover, even before 1914 some Mehsud men had already been doing well as road and rail contractors, working as far away as Assam, and they and others prospered in the interwar period, not just as contractors, but for instance cattle-traders, lorry owners and shopkeepers. Malik Shahbatti's brother Shangui, for instance, had an emporium at Makin. He bought potatoes, hides, and wool and sold cloth, grain, oil and so on and was 'in a big way of business'.[29] Another business opportunity had come up when the British use of a lorry convoy to supply Wana after the attacks on the roads in the late 1930s mentioned earlier, although the convoy was not actually profitable until 1944 when the rates were raised. It was partly a way of maintaining Mehsud goodwill during Mirza Ali Khan's revolt, and Bhittanis and Ahmadzai Wazirs through whose territory it ran also had a share in them. The arrangements for it were quite complicated. Each tribe chose an agent, and he nominated a lorry to work for the period to which the section was entitled according to *nikat*. A deduction was made from each payment to the lorry's owner as commission for the agent, and a second one for the benefit of the section as a whole.[30]

Offering military service was another way the British attempted to win over the Mehsuds in particular. Among the families which prospered in the later British period was that of Mehr Dil Khan Manzai Alizai (not to be confused with the raider Mehr Dil Khattak) and his son Mir Badshah.[31] Mehr Dil Khan, formerly a successful raider, had, as we have seen, had gone to Kabul in 1919, and he played a major role in resistance to the British invasion and the subsequent occupation. He decided that it would make sense to work with the British government and made terms with it. In the meantime his son Mir Badshah had become a jemadar in the 127th Baluchis and served in Flanders and East Africa. He was badly wounded in the trenches at Ypres and lost an eye. He joined the Mesopotamian police and did not return to Waziristan until 1923, where he became one of the leading maliks.[32]

The larger allowances, and particularly the rise in the *maliki* or *khidmati* allowance to Rs.48,000, and the employment of khassadars, who were nominated by the maliks, were important too. Not that the system worked perfectly. The allowances were reduced in the early 1930s, and British attempts to ignore the *nikat* principle failed, so that by 1946 the maliki payments were regarded as more or less hereditary, and not dependent on service.[33] Although the British had to some extent succeeded in their aim of creating an elite of better-off maliks through whom it was possible to exert some control over the other Mehsuds, the maliks themselves continued to be divided. Whereas in the early 1900s Merk had seen the rivalry between maliks and mullahs as the principal feature of Mehsud politics, during the interwar period the mullahs' influence declined. In 1946 Curtis commented that it would 'not be correct to explain Mehsud politics as a struggle between the maliks and the mullahs. No mullah – not even Fazal Din – nowadays carries weight enough to rock the boat without the assistance or connivance of Mahsud maliks'.[34] There were, he noted, two main parties among the maliks, one led by Captain Mir Badshah Manzai and the other by M. Pir Rakhman Shabi Khel (Harap's son) (both Alizais), and each had his supporters among the Bahlolzais and the Shaman Khels.[35] The various Wazir groups were also divided; the Madda Khels for example, had pro- and anti-Kabul parties, and this made it more difficult to create leaders among them too. As we have seen, after Zangi Khan's murder, the Madda Khels became more difficult to manage.

1939–47

In August 1939 Germany had concluded an extensive financial and commercial agreement with Afghanistan, but it remained neutral during the Second World War.[36] The war helped to give Mirza Ali Khan's insurgency a new lease of life; Waziristan and the Derajat border were not very quiet at all.[37] Raiding continued; 'From fifty-seven and sixty-five raids in 1937-8 and 1938-9 respectively, the number of trans-border depredations in 1939-40 and 1940-41 rose to 119 and 98.'[38] In February 1940 insurgents killed eighteen men belonging to the Frontier Constabulary in an ambush in the Bannu district and wounded many others.[39] The Constabulary cleared the Ahmadzai salient in the spring, which did at least temporarily check the 'raiding epidemic'; instead the insurgents returned to attacking officers, troops and convoys in Waziristan itself.[40] On 6 July 1940 for example they wounded the resident himself in an ambush near Asad Khel; in August Tochi Scouts were attacked while searching the village of Tappi in Dawar.[41] In fact Dawars largely replaced the war-weary Tori Khels and Madda Khels as 'Ipi's crusaders'.[42] This was a concern for the British because the Bannu–Razmak road ran through their territory. In addition the Bhittani malik, Shodi Khel, turned against the authorities as a result of 'a fancied personal slight', and recruited a gang of Bhittanis who looted lorries and damaged roads and interrupted communications. They inflicted a number of casualties on the Tochi Scouts in August 1940, but Shodi Khel was killed by an RAF bomb in May 1941.[43]

Mirza Ali Khan remained the principal leader of anti-British resistance in Waziristan.[44] 'At the height of his prestige and power', he continued to draw in discontented men and offering them 'a roving life sanctified by the pseudo-religious blessing of a priest'; his influence enabled him to organize 'a regular system of subsidies from the adjoining districts of the N-WFP', and his income reportedly rose at time to more than Rs.5,000 a month.[45] Mirza Ali was also in touch with Hayat Khan Bahlolzai, who was still angry about the British's refusal to allow his *pir*, Sayyid Yusuf, to return to Wana. In November 1940 Hayat Khan raised a lashkar, and Mirza Ali's brother, Sher Zaman, with some Wazirs and Dawars joined it. The lashkar fired a cannon into the Tiarza and Ladha posts.[46] In response the British bombed Hayat Khan's village and despatched a column to the Ladha-Tauda China area on 6 December 1940. Mehsuds attacked it near Tauda China and kept it trapped there for more than a month. Additional troops had to be despatched to Razmak, and sixty-six soldiers were killed. The political agent commented that it was 'the worst incident in recent years'.[47] It may have prompted the GOI to allow Pir Sayyid Yusuf to return to Wana, from where he used his influence to restrain anti-British activity, for example reportedly persuading Hayat Khan not to join Mirza Ali Khan's attack on Datta Khel in May 1942.[48]

Walo Tangi, located in Wargara Bhittani territory in the lower Shaktu not far from the administrative border, was another rugged area that outlaws and bandits were able to use as a base because of its difficult terrain. In March 1941 the British enforced a blockade on the Wargara Bhittanis, and neighbouring Shabi Khel Mehsuds, Tori Khels and Jani Khels, and conducted a successful operation to clear it.[49]

At this point the British were concerned because the Axis legations in Kabul managed to make contact with Mirza Ali Khan.[50] In June 1941 Enrico Anzilotti, the secretary at the Italian embassy, visited Mirza Ali and spent three days with him in the Gorwekht caves.[51] In July the Afghan authorities intercepted two German agents and a small party of local men carrying arms and money for Mirza Ali; a shoot-out followed, and one German was killed and the other wounded.[52] Mirza Ali Khan continued to make things difficult. In March 1942 he was reported to be in Sheranna (the Madda Khels' largest village), and it was attacked by the RAF.[53] In May Mirza Ali Khan's followers cut the road to Datta Khel and besieged the fort. The British had to send two brigades to reinforce the Waziristan garrison, and regular troops relieved Datta Khel at the end of July.[54] The Madda Khels remained difficult to control partly because rivalry continued between Arsala Khan and Khandan. In 1942 there was also a problem at Makin. Malik Pir Gul Abdullai, who had a shop in the Razmak cantonment, had been evicted because he was accused of selling ammunition. The residents of Makin blocked the road in protest, and the army shelled their villages.[55]

In December 1943 their officers decided, against the advice of the Political Tehsildar, that Gurkha troops should carry out a training exercise on the slopes of Shuidar, only a few miles from Razmak. The Abdullais objected to them encroaching on their territory and attacked them; 'As night fell, the troops withdrew in disorder to Razmak cantonment. There was even fighting on the garrison's hockey field', and fifty soldiers were killed or wounded.[56] Towards the end of January 1944 Mirza Ali Khan returned to the Shaktu and renewed his insurgency, assisted by, among others, Mullah Gulin Kikarai, who had played a part in the 1930 Congress agitation.[57] At one point the RAF dispersed a lashkar a thousand strong. Mirza Ali Khan's men used their cannon to fire on the Ghariom post, and the army used howitzers at Razmak and Dosalli to shell his temporary base in the Shaktu in return. Gradually the British got a grip on the renewed insurgency, and in October Mirza Ali Khan went back to Gorwekht.[58]

By the end of the Second World War many officials were finally beginning to accept that a change was unavoidable. A Frontier Defence Committee (the Tuker Committee) had been set up in 1944, and it reported in the summer of 1945. It called for 'a new frontier-wide policy of self-administration and development', especially the latter.[59] It made various suggestions as to how this might be put into action; these included the withdrawal of most of the regular troops in Waziristan.[60] To fill the gap, it recommended that more Scouts should be recruited, and they should be better-armed.[61] By then most of the officials agreed that the occupation of Razmak had been a failure.[62] In 1947 Cunningham, for example, concluded that it had neither brought peace nor much economic development and tied up too many troops.[63] He conceded that 'the presence of regular troops has undoubtedly become an irritant. They cause many petty inconveniences to the tribes, and the tribesman magnifies them … I think the tribesmen feel that they are looked upon by regular troops, particularly by Hindu troops, simply as something to be killed.'[64] Arthur Parsons suggested that the brigade at Wana could be pulled back to Jandola and that Scouts might replace up to half the Razmak garrison. A plan for the gradual withdrawal of all the regular troops from Razmak and Wana (and the Khyber) was adopted.[65]

During 1946 men continued to snipe at troops and government officials along the roads and raid the border settlements; in June Shabi Khel Mehsuds kidnapped the South Waziristan political agent, Major Donald, though they soon released him.[66] The situation remained unsettled. In February 1947 for instance Din Faqir ambushed the North Waziristan political agent, Sir Benjamin Bromhead, killing Bromhead's bearer.[67] The Tochi Scouts thwarted another attempt to attack Bannu, but communal violence continued to increase. In April 1947 Mehsuds and Bhittanis looted and burned the Hindu bazaar at Tank (the first such attack since 1879). But Mirza Ali Khan instructed his followers not to molest the Hindus who lived in the agency (settled there for centuries, they dressed and spoke like Pashtuns). In fact Hindus from Bannu came and sheltered in the Wazir and Dawar villages and were allowed to stay provided they paid protection money to Mirza Ali Khan each month (a form of *jaziya* perhaps).[68]

British images of the Pashtuns and religion

Charles Lindholm has suggested that the colonial images of the frontier Pashtun changed and became more critical as British policy changed from a closed border to a forward one, and military confrontations became more frequent.[69] British appraisals of Pashtun character increasingly emphasized three characteristics in particular – 'jealousy of their independence, fanatical religion, and greed for gain'.[70] Sometimes they also regarded them as easily swayed by impulse and emotion. At the same time the British generally respected them for their determination to resist subjugation.

As regards religion, Robert Nichols has argued that the British tended to exaggerate its importance when it came to explaining events along the frontier: 'the notion that religious sensibilities were the primary Pakhtun motivation became entrenched in a body of authoritative imagery and analysis.'[71] This belief was often accompanied by the idea that their attachment to Islam meant that they easily became fanatical in its defence.[72] In some British eyes at least this supposed tendency to religious fanaticism helped to make them irrational, unpredictable and unwilling to compromise.[73] The British often regarded some groups as more liable to be affected by this than others, for instance the Dawars and people in Bannu. They usually thought of the Mehsuds as less fanatical, though they were still, Howell said, 'sufficiently so as to put a halo round the heads of all those who have been prominent in opposition to the Sirkar

[Government], whatever form their opposition may have taken'.[74] Some officials actually condemned the Mehsuds for not being religious enough and attributed what they saw as their materialism and hypocrisy to their failure to uphold Islamic values. In 1917 for instance Roos-Keppel described the Mehsuds as being fanatical but 'very slack in the observances of Islam, many of the adults [males] not even being circumcised'.[75] Nearly thirty years later, another British official, Curtis, said that 'religious fanaticism while it may excite momentary passion has no lasting influence with the Mehsud who is a materialist'.[76] But at the same time, he thought that 'economics do not explain Mahsudistan'.[77] The British could never quite make up their minds about how far poverty was responsible for the difficulties they experienced with the Mahsuds.

If the role of religion in frontier resistance should not be exaggerated, we should not underestimate its influence on the British themselves. They too were of course influenced by various ideologies or belief systems, one of which, especially in the nineteenth century, was evangelical Christianity.[78] The British civilizing mission was often explicitly associated with the spread of Christianity and 'Christian values'.[79] Henry Lawrence, the resident at the Sikh court from 1846 to 1848 and a member of the original Board of Administration set up to administer Punjab, for example, had strong evangelical beliefs.[80] He influenced many of the early frontier officers whose names have come up in earlier chapters, among them Reynell Taylor and John Nicholson (other well-known examples were Richard Pollock, Henry Lumsden, Henry Coxe, James Abbot and George Lawrence). Robert Sandeman too was deeply religious, as was Donald MacLeod (the lieutenant-governor of Punjab 1865–70).[81]

Herbert Edwardes, a 'firebrand evangelical fanatic' according to the historian Jeffrey Cox, was one of the most prominent frontier evangelicals.[82] A patron of the Church Missionary Society (CMS) in Peshawar, in the 1850s he lifted the ban on Christian missionary activity west of the Indus, although Christian preachers were not encouraged to proselytize outside Peshawar.[83] A CMS English language school was opened in Peshawar, and a church was built in the old city. Reynell Taylor was also convinced that it was his duty to do what he could to advance the cause of Christianity. He marked his departure from the Derajat with the establishment of a mission there and helped to pay for it.[84] In fact missionaries did not make many converts along the frontier. Nor were all the British officials in sympathy with Edwardes and Taylor's evangelical approach. In connection with the controversial Ambela expedition in 1863, for instance, the administrator Charles Trevelyan, referred to 'the partly military, partly fanatical Punjab Anglo-Indian spirit, with the praise of God in their mouths and a two-edged sword in their hands'.[85] At least in their reports, officials did not often refer explicitly to Christianity as an influence, but in one of his letters, however, Taylor referred to frontier tribal hostility towards 'the Christian dominant race'.[86] Crump was another official who specifically referred to the religious aspects of the encounter.

They may have been only one among various influences, but religious ideas and differences helped to shape the encounter between Britain and the frontier between 1849 and 1947 in various ways. The fact that the British came from a Christian background and that most of the inhabitants of the frontier were (mostly Sunni) Muslims was important; so too was the fact that a number of Hindus and Sikhs lived along the border. Because they tended to be shopkeepers, moneylenders and traders, they were quite often kidnapped for ransom.[87] After the establishment of the Razmak garrison, many people objected to the fact that there were Hindu soldiers in the regiments stationed there.

The future

Religious identities were of course deeply implicated in the partition of India in 1947. The initial draft of the plan proposed that all provinces, including the NWFP, were to be allowed the option of independence.[88] But in 1947, when the GOI announced that it intended to hold a referendum to decide the future of the NWFP, it restricted the choice to India or Pakistan. The people of Waziristan, and the other 'tribal areas', were not given a vote. Mirza Ali Khan advised visitors from the administered areas not to vote for Pakistan.[89] In his Bannu Declaration, issued in June 1947, Abdul Ghaffur Khan had called for the British to allow the choice of an 'independent Pashtunistan'; he advised his followers to boycott the referendum.[90] When the referendum was held in July, only 51 per cent of the electorate took part, the majority of them voting to join Pakistan.[91]

The question was a very difficult one. As in many other parts of the world colonial boundaries did not match realities on the ground. We have seen how close the connections between people living in Khost and Birmal and Waziristan were, and how the GOA continued to pay allowances to some men on the British side of the Durand Line and employ them in the Urgun militia. The simplest option was the choice between India and Pakistan, but there were other possibilities, though all had their drawbacks. One would have been to have created an independent NWFP (Pashtunistan or Pakhtunistan) that included the tribal areas. Abdul Ghaffar Khan, the 'Frontier Gandhi' and leader of the pro-Congress Muslims in the province, among others, was a prominent advocate of this.⁹² It has been suggested that this could have been the choice of many people in Waziristan.⁹³ Another alternative was the creation of an independent Waziristan; Mirza Ali Khan himself called for this, perhaps envisaging that he might become its head of state. But he did not have the support of everyone in the area; Leeson suggests that most of the Kabul Khels and Mehsuds were openly pro-Pakistan.⁹⁴ Nor did many outsiders see this as a serious option.

Another possibility was that the NWFP might be absorbed by Afghanistan. Much of it had after all been part of the Durrani Empire in the later eighteenth and early nineteenth centuries, and the 1921 Treaty had recognized the GOA's interest in Waziristan and other areas along the frontier. As we have seen people had continued to go freely to and fro across the Durand Line, sometimes in large numbers, and the GOA had continued to maintain connections with men living on the British side of the line. The Afghan government was concerned that British withdrawal might affect the stability of the frontier.⁹⁵ It pointed to the 'history, ethnology, and political loyalty' shared by Pashtuns on both sides of the Durand Line and continued to request that the NWFP, including Baluchistan, should be given the option not only of independence but also of reunification with Afghanistan. Afghan officials referred to something they called 'greater Pashtunistan', presumably to distinguish it from the 'lesser Pashtunistan' consisting of the NWFP and the tribal areas, envisaged by Abdul Ghaffur Khan. These arguments were dismissed by the GOI's External Affairs Department.⁹⁶

In fact the Afghan prime minister, Shah Mahmud, who had taken over from Muhammad Hashim in 1946, admitted that for various reasons it would really be impossible for Afghanistan to take responsibility for the NWFP and the tribal areas; for example it would not have the money to continue the allowances that the British were paying.⁹⁷ Nor would this have been popular with Afghanistan's non-Pashtun inhabitants, who collectively made up more than half its population. Incorporation of the NWFP into Afghanistan might even have encouraged the Soviet Union to claim sovereignty over the north of Afghanistan, with its largely Tajik and Uzbek population. The Afghan tendency to suggest that Baluchistan should be included in 'greater Pashtunistan' also complicated things, because the majority of people living in it were Baluchis, not Pashtuns. Presumably it was partly for these reasons that the Afghans were reluctant to define their claims precisely and publicly supported 'an independent Pashtunistan' rather than the NWFP's incorporation into Afghanistan.⁹⁸ Nevertheless before partition the Afghan government sent an official deputation across the border to Gorwekht to discuss the idea of an Afghan takeover with Mirza Ali Khan. He rejected the idea.⁹⁹

Late in June and early in July 1947 Mirza Ali Khan's lieutenant Din Faqir, attempted to shell Miranshah, Gardai and Datta Khel; the air force attacked the caves at Gorwekht.[100] In August 1947, following independence, experienced Muslim political officers replaced nearly all the British political agents. British troops were not withdrawn until September: during the withdrawal from Wana Mehsuds attacked a convoy of Sikh and Gurkha troops in the Shahur Tangi, causing a number of casualties.[101] On 30 September 1947 the GOA announced that it did not recognize the Durand Line as its frontier with Pakistan, and the Afghan press and radio began to support Mirza Ali Khan and Pashtunistan, signalling its intention to maintain Afghan influence along the frontier.[102] The GOA presumably continued to pay its allowances to Pakistan-side men, at least for a time.

In October 1947 the new Pakistani tribal adviser held a large jirga of Wazir and Dawar maliks and announced that the new Government of Pakistan (GOP) had decided to grant Mirza Ali Khan an amnesty. The offer implied that he and his *ghazi* followers were 'mere criminals hopeful of pardon', and he did not take it up.[103] A lashkar operating in the Idak-Isha area led by one of Mirza Ali Khan's followers, the Afghan, Mama the Tanni, moved to the Upper Tochi and blockaded the Miranshah–Boya road and sniped at the Miranshah Serai and fort. They fired two shells into the Razmak camp.[104] When the Tochi Scouts withdrew from Datta Khel in June 1948 Mirza Ali Khan sent a lashkar to occupy it. The GOP drove it out with bombing; aircraft also attacked the villages of his Shabi Khel Mehsud supporters.[105]

Meanwhile in the summer of 1947 a revolt had broken out in Jammu against the Maharajah of Kashmir. The rebels formed a provisional government and appealed for help from Pakistan. In the autumn many men from the frontier, including Mehsuds from Waziristan, answered the call. Mirza Ali Khan instructed the Wazirs that they should not join them (presumably because of his opposition to Pakistan). The Maharajah, who had been playing for time, promptly announced Kashmir's accession to India; Indian troops were rushed to his aid and secured his position.[106] Many Pakistanis believed that the Indians were sending money to Mirza Ali Khan and other insurgents in Waziristan via the Indian Embassy in Kabul, in order to tie up Pakistani forces so that they could not be used in Kashmir.[107] The GOP denounced him as a traitor.[108] Accusations that the Indian intelligence agency, R&AW (Research and Analysis Wing), is active along the frontier continue to be made to this day.[109]

Afghanistan reluctantly recognized Pakistan early in 1948. In 1949 the Pakistan authorities arrested more than 350 frontier leaders, including the

Khudai Khidmatgaran leader, Abdul Ghaffur Khan, and his son Wali Khan, who were imprisoned in Baluchistan for five years. In response Afghanistan recalled its ambassador and launched a propaganda campaign in support of Pashtunistan.[110] In March 1949 for example the Afghan embassy in Karachi sent a Radio Kabul commentary on Pakistani air action against Mirza Ali Khan as a press note to foreign missions in Pakistan.[111] The GOA also revived its policy of encouraging boys from the Pakistani tribal areas to attend schools in Kabul.[112] In June 1949 Pakistani planes bombed a hostile lashkar on the Afghan side of the border. In July a Loyah Jirga (a gathering of Afghan maliks and rural headmen) was held in Afghanistan and pronounced the Durand Line agreement and all treaties with the British null and void and declared an independent Pashtunistan with Mirza Ali Khan as its president.[113] During the 1950s the GOA continued to call for a lesser Pashtunistan that would comprise much of the NWFP and the tribal areas and encouraged Mirza Ali Khan to set up a 'Waziristan Branch of the Pakhtunistan National Assembly'.[114] Mirza Ali Khan was not the only influential man in Waziristan to refuse to recognize the new government. Fazal Din's son, Shahzada Taj-ud Din, was another.[115]

In the early part of the decade, with tacit support from the Afghan government, large tribal lashkars crossed from Afghanistan into Pakistan on several occasions, ostensibly in the Pashtunistan cause (for example there were Afridi incursions in 1950 and 1951).[116] All this was much resented in Pakistan, and relations between the two governments deteriorated. In 1955 for example a mob attacked the Pakistani embassy in Kabul, and Pakistan closed the border with Afghanistan for five months. In 1959 another revolt broke out in Paktia against the Afghan government, and people fleeing across the border received support from the Pakistan government.[117] In 1960 (and again in 1961) Afghan troops and Pashtun irregulars crossed into the Bajaur area of Pakistan to the north of Peshawar and were driven out.[118] Pakistan requested Afghanistan to close its consulates and trade agencies, and in August 1961 the Afghan Prime Minister Muhammad Daud closed the border between the two countries. It did not open again until 1963, following his resignation.

Mirza Ali Khan and Waziristan after 1947

The relationship between the tribal groups and the neighbouring states on the NWFP changed somewhat after the British left.[119] The GOP put into practice some of the ideas put forward by British planners after the war. They decided, for example, not to replace the regular British troops in Razmak, and the base was left empty. The South Waziristan Scouts took over the Wana cantonment, and the old Scouts' posts in central Waziristan were evacuated or handed over to khassadars.[120] This was a reversion to something more like Curzon's policy.[121] But gradually the GOP increased its presence. In 1960 it reformed the Mehsud Labour Battalions as combatant battalions, the 1st and 2nd Mehsud Scouts, and in 1973 it set up the Shawal Rifles and based them at Razmak.[122] The GOP also maintained the system of management by political agents inherited from the British, and new agreements were negotiated with the maliks, who continued to receive allowances and provide khassadars to protect the roads; Waziristan and the other Frontier Agencies (now called the Federally-Administered Tribal Areas) remained semi-autonomous, and the Frontier Crimes Regulations remained in force. One change was that the maliks were allowed to vote in elections for the provincial and national assemblies, though the other men were not (nor were women).

In the meantime, the outlaw, Mehr Dil Khattak had surrendered in 1954 to the Pakistani government; Mirza Ali Khan remained at Gorwekht and died there in 1960.[123] As they had done with the Mullah Powindah, opinions of Mirza Ali Khan differed considerably. Not surprisingly perhaps given his attitude to Pakistan, a leading Pakistani official referred to him as 'a vicious old man twisted with hate and selfishness, prone to treachery, and one who gave bonusses [sic] for the kidnapping or killing of the children of Political Agents'.[124] But the London *Times* in its obituary said he was 'a doughty and honourable opponent … a man of principle and saintliness … a redoubtable organizer of tribal warfare'. Certainly he seems to have been a determined, able and charismatic leader.[125]

There are some parallels between his career and that of his Mehsud predecessor, the Mullah Powindah. Both were charismatic leaders, who were believed to have miraculous powers. Both maintained a *langar*, 'kitchen', where followers and visitors were fed and could sleep, which were paid for by the donations of the faithful, as well as sometimes through protection money. Both had a retinue of followers – *khalifas*, *sheikhs* and *talibs*. Both were in competition with the maliks for influence. Both tried to build up influence by acting as mediators in feuds between different tribal groups and worked hard to create coalitions between them, though with mixed results. Mullah Powindah was never able to attract much Wazir support, and Mirza Ali Khan did not persuade many Mehsuds to support him.[126]

What were Mirza Ali Khan's aims? Some religious leaders of anti-British resistance on the frontier, like Saidullah (the so-called Mad Fakir) and the

Hadda Mullah, have been characterized as charismatic leaders 'mobilizing people towards millenarian objectives'.[127] Warren suggests that Mirza Ali Khan had 'a messianic dimension', but had no plans to reorder Wazir society and so did not fit the ideal of a millenarian prophet (nor it would appear did Mullah Powindah).[128] Until 1947, Warren argues, inspired by religious principles, his aim was simply to remove foreign influence from Waziristan – 'a traditional aim for a tribal insurgent leader'.[129] It is true that Mirza Ali Khan's aims were different from those of the mainstream nationalist movements in the subcontinent and that he does not seem to have had much of a political programme. After 1947, Haroon suggests, his aim was simply to establish his own status as intermediary between the Wazirs and the governments of Pakistan and Afghanistan.[130] There may have been more to it. As we have seen he had begun to talk the language of modern nationalism and refer to Pashtunistan.[131] The independence of Waziristan was obviously important to him, and if he did not manage to achieve it, he helped to keep anti-Pakistan sentiments alive. Indeed he had some influence on the policy the GOP pursued in Waziristan, because than anyone else he was responsible for convincing the British that it had been a mistake to have introduced the modified forward policy, and this influenced the GOP in turn.

As regards social and economic developments in Waziristan, with some success the GOP also continued with the kind of social and economic policies that had been tentatively pursued by the British in the 1920s and 1930s. For instance it extended educational and health provision and facilitated agricultural modernization in some parts of Waziristan. Land was offered to Mehsuds to encourage them to settle in Tank and Dera Ismail Khan, and they continued to develop their transport and light engineering businesses; many moving to the cities, especially Karachi.[132] Men from Waziristan worked as labourers, as well as joining the armed services and the professions and the cultural industries, and working as contractors, traders and wholesalers. Many worked for a time in the Gulf states.[133] For years some continued to resist integration into Pakistan, and some moved into Afghanistan, a number of Shabi Khel Mehsuds for example.[134] Overall it seems that the economic position of many Waziristanis did not improve very much, and a minority continued to carry out criminal activities including kidnapping, and arms and drug smuggling.[135]

A new chapter opened with the Saur Revolution in Afghanistan in April 1978, which established a left-wing pro-Soviet government there, followed by Soviet occupation at the end of the following year. In response the GOP began to set up new outposts nearer the Durand Line.[136] During the civil war in

Afghanistan that followed in the 1980s many Afghans took refuge in Waziristan as well as other frontier areas. In the earlier 1990s the GOP encouraged the formation of the Taliban, and by 1998 they had established their rule in most of Afghanistan. This had a significant impact in the frontier tribal areas too. Many men from Waziristan joined the Taliban and fought in Afghanistan. By the later 1990s 'the backwash from Afghanistan was leading to the "Talibanization" of Pakistan', as 'tribal groups imitating the Taliban sprang up across the Pashtun belt in NWFP and Baluchistan'.[137] This gained further momentum after the attack on the Twin Towers on 9/11 and the American-backed takeover of Kabul by anti-Taliban forces in November 2001. The Al-Qaida leader, Osama bin Laden, and several hundred of his followers, including Arabs, Chechens and Uzbeks from the Islamic Movement of Uzbekistan, who had been living in Afghanistan, fled across the border into Waziristan, where many of them stayed. The GOP came under enormous pressure from the US government to capture or kill them. However, the requirements of Pashtunwali and religious solidarity meant that the inhabitants, including the previously largely pro-government Mehsuds, mostly refused demands to hand them over. The fact that Al-Qaida refugees paid very well for local shelter and support was an additional incentive to keep them.[138]

As a result 'an undeclared war' broke out in Waziristan, beginning with a major Pakistani operation against Al-Qaida militants living at Azam Warsak, in South Waziristan between Wana and the Afghan border in June 2002.[139] In 2007 Beitullah Mehsud, a Shabi Khel Alizai, played a leading role in creating the Tehrik-i-Taliban, 'an umbrella organization of dozens of Taliban groups throughout Pakistan'.[140] In South Waziristan the Taliban more or less took over, setting up their own law courts and collecting taxes (just as Mirza Ali Khan had done in the mid-twentieth century).[141] In 2009 Pakistani forces went into the area again in force, where at the time of writing they remain; in 2014 they did the same in northern Waziristan. These offensives against the militants, coupled with drone attacks, had a major impact on ordinary people, and hundreds of thousands of them left their homes and moved down to the administered areas. Many Wazirs in particular crossed into Afghanistan to escape the fighting, demonstrating how porous the border between the two countries continues to be.[142]

Other important developments since the early 1970s include the increasing political importance of Islam in the region. As we have seen, this trend began in the later nineteenth century, and it gathered momentum after 1947. After Partition a number of new Deobandi *madrasahs* had been set up in and along the frontier, and following General Zia ul-Haq's *coup d'état* in 1978 the GOP supported the establishment of many more (with funding from the Gulf states).[143] The Deobandi scholar Muhammad Yusuf Binuri (d.1977) made a major contribution to this. He was a Pashtun from the Peshawar area who had received his early religious education in Kabul and gone on to study at Deoband itself.[144] He founded a *madrasah* in Karachi – the Jamiat-ul-Ulum-ul-Islamia, which became very influential.[145] Some of his close associates were also Pashtuns, for example Mufti Nizamudin Shamzai (assassinated in 2004), who came from Swat. The result was to increase the influence of Deobandi mullahs vis-à-vis the maliks, and the creation of many more mosque schools and madrasas in Waziristan and along the frontier generally, which have often offered the only available educational opportunities.[146] Militants established jihadi training camps in Waziristan too.[147]

In keeping with this, since the 1970s frontier resistance to the Pakistani government has mostly presented itself as being driven by Islamic ideals rather than, as Ghaffur Khan's Red Shirts had done for instance, those of Pashtun nationalism. Efforts to impose a conservative morality intensified: music and video shops and barbers were shut, girls prohibited from attending school and women subjected to very strict controls.[148] Taliban and Al-Qaida militants murdered many maliks and pro-government supporters, contributing to another important development – the breakdown of the system of political agents, maliks and payment of allowances which had developed since the late nineteenth century.[149] For some years the Pakistani government tolerated this and even accepted the de facto independence of Waziristan, especially in northern Waziristan where the so-called Islamic Emirate of Waziristan was set up in 2006. This was in order to enable it to concentrate on Afghanistan, where Pakistani Taliban continued to play an important part.[150] Contacts between the Pakistani Inter-Services Intelligence (ISI) and Jalaludin Haqqani, the founder of the Haqqani network, for example, went back to the early 1970s. The ISI continues to maintain a close relationship with the Haqqanis and allows the network to operate relatively freely because of its focus on Afghanistan; it is one way the Pakistani ISI can maintain its influence there. Always anxious about the potential threat from India, the Pakistani military see the maintenance of Pakistan's influence in Afghanistan as giving Pakistan 'strategic depth' in relation to India, and this takes priority over the question of peace on the frontier (much as it did for the British before 1947), which remains a 'volatile borderland'.[151]

12

Summary and conclusion

British approaches

We have seen that the British never possessed the military resources that would have enabled them to take full control of Waziristan. Officials therefore experimented with different ways of establishing at least some authority over it by combining the application of force (*barampta*, *bandish* and the punitive expedition) with various techniques for manipulating its people and putting indirect pressure on them. First, there was the use of soft power in various forms, such as offering people new opportunities to trade and use medical and educational facilities. This began to overlap with various forms of indirect subsidy. These included paying hostages to live in British territory, offering employment as khassadars (police), militiamen, soldiers and labourers on construction projects, as well as awarding transport and supply contracts and giving some families access to land to settle on in British territory. Third, there were direct payments to the people, at least in theory in return for some sort of service. In practice a very complicated structure of allowance payments (to the Mehsuds in particular) grew up, with the link between payments and reciprocal duties often disappearing. Payments included smaller ones made via the *wakils* and *mohtabars* to the heads of households, and larger ones to the men they regarded as being more influential (maliks) – in theory in return for helping the political agents. These were adjusted at several points depending on where successive political agents thought they could be most effectively applied. After the First World War, the proportion of the payments to the Mehsud maliks was raised considerably, to something like four-fifths of those to the tribe as a whole.

These payments, 'a colossal form of blackmail' according to some, were not a silver bullet.[1] If they addressed some problems, they also raised new questions, the most obvious being the difficulty of deciding who should receive them and how much they should be given. Competition for allowances became a new influence on politics. It encouraged men to make trouble for the political agents, hoping to be bought off with an allowance. Moreover the Afghan government began to try and buy people's cooperation too. It became possible for members of the same family to play the two governments off against each other and receive payments from both (and in some cases the same men, Mullah Powindah's son, Fazal Din, for example).

The extent to which channelling money to people was seen as a key to controlling them partly depended on how far the political officers regarded poverty as a reason for raiding. Initially there was a tendency to see it as the principal motivation. Later some British officials, Richard Bruce for example, came to appreciate that many people in Waziristan were not so poor that they could only survive by robbery and kidnapping. Other officials continued to ascribe the difficulties they faced in controlling Waziristan to people's inability to provide for themselves by peaceful means.

To help them manipulate them more effectively, some officers gave considerable attention to trying to understand the sociopolitical organization of the various groups living in Waziristan. Sometimes they drew interesting if not always convincing analogies with aspects of European social and political development. There are many references in the British reports to Mehsud 'democracy', for example, while, as we have seen, Johnston referred to the maliks as the Mehsud cabinet and the *mohtabars* as their parliament. As well as comparing the Mehsud cultivators to English yeomen, Merk suggested that the right of a single member of a jirga to prevent it reaching a decision on a particular issue resembled the way that during the seventeenth and eighteenth centuries legislation in the Polish sejm (legislative assembly) could be defeated by the vote of a single member (the *liberum veto*).[2]

As regards British efforts to get a grip on Waziristan by steering its society in a particular direction, there were two basic possibilities, though they could be used together. One was to try and create a sense of collective responsibility; the other was to look for potential leaders, men who with British support would control people on Britain's behalf. If the officials thought that the people of Waziristan lacked leaders but belonged to groups that they called tribes (or less often clans), they usually thought it made sense to make members of a particular group responsible for the behaviour of all those who belonged to that group. As we have seen, one problem was to identify a suitable group. While it seems that people did think of themselves as sharing patrilineal descent (it gave them a place in the tribal charter or *sarishta*), this was potentially the basis for different group identities, depending on how far back up the genealogical tree one went.

Moreover, rather than always identifying with one group in particular, people might identify with different ones at different times and in different situations. People might also cooperate and form networks and factions on the basis of cognatic links as well as agnatic ones.[3] Nor were they necessarily accustomed to the idea of collective, 'tribal', responsibility. There was also a further difficulty, of which at least some officials were aware. This was that the attempt to assign collective responsibility to particular groups tended to solidify the relationships encountered at a particular point in time and took no account of what were in practice constantly evolving configurations.[4]

Waziristanis could also be made collectively responsible for territory as well as other people. On the Bannu border, in the 1860s and 1870s for example, the British tried to allocate what they called pass responsibility to the tribal groups living along the passes leading into Bannu. Territorial responsibility was a development of this in that it made people living in a particular area responsible for its security. This meant that if men from group A attacked men from group B in territory belonging to group C, then the men from group C as well as the men from group A would have to contribute to making good any losses suffered by men from group B. Application of territorial responsibility was sometimes complicated by the fact that at least in the case of the Mehsuds, each section did not necessarily have a distinct territory of its own.

The alternative to collective responsibility was to try and create an oligarchy of more powerful men (maliks) through whom it would be possible to manage the rest (a form of indirect rule). This was the policy adopted by those who thought that there had been some kind of institutionalized authority in Waziristan in the past. For example, arguing that the Mehsuds had formerly recognized chiefly authority, in the late 1880s Richard Bruce began to pay some Mehsud maliks an allowance in return for providing levies and maintaining security. The officials returned to a more collective approach in the early 1900s and the payment of allowances to a much larger number of men. After the First World War they made another attempt to enhance the authority of the maliks in Waziristan by giving them the right to appoint khassadars in return for helping to control other members of their groups in the interests of the government.[5] An interesting example is the way that they tried to build up Zangi Khan's authority over the Madda Khel Wazirs in the 1920s and early 1930s. For a few years he apparently made some efforts to uphold British interests, before his enemies managed to kill him. It seems that the officials also had some success with the Mehsud maliks, who, for example, helped to ensure that relatively few Mehsuds joined Mirza Ali Khan's insurgency.

Afghan payments to British-side men were mentioned above, and the government in Kabul was also anxious to try and build up its influence in Waziristan. This was partly because it wanted to be able to use them as a defensive barrier against the British; it was also anxious to prevent the Waziristan tribes from invading Afghanistan. As we have seen, British-side men crossed the Durand Line in large numbers in the late 1920s and the 1930s to join uprisings against Amir Amanullah and his successors. Historical and cultural connections between eastern Afghanistan and Waziristan meant that there were opportunities for the GOA to try and win over its people by representing their interests to the GOI, offering them land to settle on, paying them allowances, enlisting them in militias, offering to educate their sons in Kabul and encouraging armed resistance by giving them money, weapons and ammunition. As a result, another feature of British policy eventually came to be efforts to discourage these activities and to win Afghan support for British efforts to control Waziristan. By the late 1930s they were enjoying some success with this.

Responses

As regards people's reactions to all this, judging by their behaviour few of them wholeheartedly welcomed British attempts to extend their influence into Waziristan, let alone the establishment of British forts and garrisons and road-building. The question was how to respond. Many men might take up arms when troops entered their territory, but only a minority consistently opposed the British directly. Not everyone was in a position to do so; men had to provide food and shelter for themselves and their families, and many of them had little choice but to cooperate with the British, if only for some of the time and up to a point. So for example, some men took part in Macaulay's hostage scheme or joined militias and the Indian army. They might also take advantage of the opportunity to become contractors. But, as in Zangi Khan's case, it could be dangerous for men to get too close to the British, as this could encourage others to kill them.[6] Alternatively they might resort to some of the weapons of the weak identified by the historian James Scott, including delaying tactics, dissimulation, desertion, false compliance, pilfering (such as stealing telephone wire) and sabotage (blowing up bridges and roads with IEDs).[7] Another tactic was to put pressure on the British officials by turning up to jirgas uninvited in very large numbers.

The point was made in Chapter 1 that Pashtun custom or Pashtunwali emphasized the importance of personal independence and maintaining honour and avoiding shame. In order to keep to Pashtunwali, a man might sometimes need to resort to violence – for example by taking revenge for an insult, or punishing a female member of his family for behaving dishonourably. *Tarburwali*, rivalry between patrilateral parallel cousins, also contributed to this. At the same time though there was an emphasis on hospitality and reconciliation rituals (*nanawatai*) and a willingness to meet and talk in councils or jirgas. Adherence to the tribal charter or *nikat* was important too. Their individualistic and competitive ethos, which was associated with the absence of leaders, certainly did not mean that people were unable to cooperate when it suited them. The Mehsuds, for example, were quite capable of organizing large tribal meetings, appointing *chalweshtis*, assembling lashkars and coordinating complex military manoeuvres, and coming to agreements about *nikat*.[8] Their highly individualistic ethos and reluctance to recognize maliks, as well as the development of internal factions, and inability to speak with one voice and agree on how they should respond to British demands may have been what Scott calls techniques of 'not being governed'.[9] It is important to note that in spite of Afghan attempts to win over the people of Waziristan, in practice they did not want to come under Afghan rule either.

As regards raiding and opposition to the British, the fact that some groups lived in areas with few resources does sometimes seem to have motivated them to take up raiding, although it was not just the result of poverty; it was exciting and enabled young men to demonstrate their manliness. Men from some groups in particular were more consistent raiders than others and were more difficult for the British to manage. Another factor was location; the further away people lived from the administered territory, the easier it was for them to resist British pressure, since they could always move further away from the Indian border (and after the demarcation of the Durand Line into the Afghan sphere of influence) if they came under attack. At some points the Afghans encouraged raiding by British-side men and supplied them with arms and ammunition. If habitual raiders lived relatively close to the administered areas, it helped if their territory was mountainous and difficult to access, and not near any important routes (such as the Shaktu and the Khaisara for instance). Whether or not a group was nomadic was also important, because it was easier for pastoral nomads to move out of trouble, and they did not have much in the way of buildings and agricultural infrastructure to be destroyed by troops.

From among the Mehsuds, raiders and men who resisted the British came mostly from the Abdullai, Abdur Rahman Khel and Jalal Khel Bahlolzai, and Shabi Khel Alizai sections. From among the Wazirs, the British most often experienced problems with some of the Zilla Khels, Kabul Khels and Madda Khels. At the same time it is important to remember that in those groups too there were men who were not so overtly hostile, and it seems to have been rare for them all to respond in the same way to British (or Afghan) demands. For example over time a division into pro-British and pro-Kabul parties or factions seems to have emerged. As well as a wish to continue raiding and to maintain their independence, there were other reasons for anti-British activities. There were internal tensions between older *mashar*s and younger *kashar*s; generally the latter were more willing to resort to violent opposition. This difference in attitudes between *mashar*s and *kashar*s seems to have overlapped to some extent with disparities of wealth, and there was hostility between the poor and the better-off, exacerbated during the British period by the fact that during it some men become a great deal wealthier than others. Religion could also motivate men to take up an anti-British stance. On the other hand religious loyalties were not necessarily strong enough to induce them willing to obey the Afghan government either.

Major and minor problems

There are many reference in the British records to what were called the major and the minor problems in relation to Afghanistan and the frontier, and the difficulty of harmonizing approaches to them.[10] The minor one was how to prevent raiding from Waziristan; as we have seen, this was difficult enough, given the independent and assertive ethos of the people (and the absence of leaders), the difficult landscape, the poverty of some sections and the competition for land between different groups, the Tori Khels and Mehsuds for instance, and their location on the border with Afghanistan. The major problem was the need to protect India by keeping Russian influence out of Afghanistan. There were different views on the extent to which this required intervention in Waziristan. Some policy-makers argued that the problems were quite distinct, and that therefore the major one could be solved without much interference in it. (They were the advocates of the close-border policy.) Sir John Maffey, for example, suggested that the major problem was 'as distinct, no more and no less, from the minor tribal problem as the Coast defence of India against piracy is from the Battle Fleet'.[11] Others (advocates of the forward policy), however, argued that to keep Afghanistan free from Russian or Soviet influence they needed to exert as much control over Waziristan as possible.

Each approach had its advantages and disadvantages. The close-border policy was cheaper, but theoretically opened the way for Afghanistan eventually to establish its authority over Waziristan, making the Derajat vulnerable to Afghan penetration. But the forward policy (quite apart from the additional cost) did not solve this problem either; by encouraging people to look for help to Afghanistan it also gave the Afghans an opportunity to interfere in it. Nevertheless, as we have seen, at several points, efforts to solve the major problem disrupted British attempts to deal with the minor one. This disruption began towards the end of the 1870s when the second British invasion of Afghanistan ruined Macaulay's efforts to win over the Mehsuds through settlement and military service. In the early 1890s British concern over continuing Russian expansion in Central Asia, as well as efforts by Britain's protégé, Amir Abdur Rahman Khan, to extend his authority into the still semi-independent frontier region, including Waziristan, prompted the extension of British outposts into Waziristan (as well as into areas to the north), the demarcation of the Durand Line, and the creation of the North and South Waziristan Agencies. In Waziristan this forward policy encouraged the Mullah Powindah's supporters to attack Bruce's camp and another punitive expedition, and it was discredited by the risings that erupted along much of the rest of the frontier in 1897. A return to a less interventionist approach, initiated by Lord Curzon, followed, and the Anglo-Russian Convention of 1907 reduced British worries about Russian influence in Afghanistan.

But there were still difficulties. First, powerful members of the Afghan elite, particularly Amir Habibullah's anti-British brother, Sardar Nasrullah, were able use the frontier mullahs to encourage anti-British activities among the groups living on the British side of the Durand Line. Even the relatively pro-British Amir expressed his indignation at the failure to consult him over the Convention by encouraging his brother to step up this interference for a time. The Curzon policy was nevertheless relatively effective until 1914 at least, and there were no military expeditions into Waziristan from 1902 until 1917. The First World War and its aftermath, however, severely eroded British authority, leading to more widespread and frequent raiding by Mehsuds, Wazirs and Bhittanis into the administered areas along its eastern border, encouraged by Sardar Nasrullah and Amanullah Khan.

After the First World War and their occupation of Mehsud territory (1919–23), the British returned to a forward policy, building the large Razmak base and constructing various roads, the rationale being that all this would prevent Afghan and Soviet interference, as well as facilitating the introduction of the policy of peaceful penetration and nation-building. This 'modified forward policy' involved 'showing the flag' by moving troops and Scouts through every part of Waziristan, as well as some limited economic development and education and health provision. The result was a major uprising in North Waziristan led by Mirza Ali Khan in 1936. The British failure to repress Mirza Ali Khan eventually helped to prompt another reassessment of policy, and officials came up with plans for the withdrawal of regular troops from Waziristan again, plans which were put into operation by the new GOP.

Perhaps we should not write off the British encounter with it as an entirely negative one. There were some positive features; by 1947 there had been some economic development, and the provision of some educational opportunities and some medical care, and some people from Waziristan had begun to engage constructively with the wider world and settle in the settled areas of the NWFP and in Afghanistan. But this had been achieved at a considerable cost in human life and the destruction of productive resources. As we have seen, the major problem made it difficult to deal with the minor one. If the objective of British policy was to keep out external influences altogether and stop Waziristanis fighting with each other and raiding the settled areas, it was a failure. When the British left, the Waziristan border was just as disturbed in 1947 as it had been nearly a century earlier, Waziristan itself was full of weapons, people continued to cross to and fro into Afghanistan in large numbers and serve in the Khost militia and receive payments from Kabul, and many people were unhappy with the prospect of becoming part of Pakistan and did not accept the new government's authority.

The GOP continued to face some of the same problems, in response to which it gradually increased its military presence in Waziristan, particularly after the Soviet occupation of Afghanistan and the anti-Soviet jihad. At the same time, in order to be able to maintain its influence in Afghanistan and hence ensure strategic depth, it permitted the Taliban and other militant Islamist groups such as the Haqqani network to operate from Waziristan, undermining its authority in the region. After a disturbed period following 9/11, the Pakistani armed forces invaded in strength in 2009 and 2014, suppressed the Tehrik-i-Taliban and established a degree of control over Waziristan, although it seems that militant Islamist groups continue to operate there (or in neighbouring areas like Kurram). The security of Afghanistan is still a major concern for the GOP today, and the situation in Waziristan is unlikely to improve as long as the Afghan civil war continues. The goal of developing and maintaining its influence in Afghanistan shaped British policy towards Waziristan (and the rest of the frontier); the same has been true of Pakistani frontier policy since the early 1970s.

Appendix 1: Timeline

1849 – British annexation of the Punjab.
1859 December – first British incursion into Kabul Khel territory.
1860 March – Mehsuds attempt to invade British territory.
1860 April – first British invasion of Mehsud territory; Mehsuds barred from British territory.
1861 – British lift Mehsud blockade.
1866 – Fredrick Graham implements small-scale Mehsud settlement scheme.
1868 – Sher Ali Khan becomes amir of Afghanistan.
1872 – introduction of Frontier Crimes Regulations.
1873 – Macaulay reaches agreements with Bahlolzai and Shaman Khel Mehsuds.
1878 July – Russian mission arrives uninvited in Kabul.
1878 November – British forces invade Afghanistan; Macaulay puts new Mehsud settlement scheme into operation.
1879 January – Mehsuds burn Tank bazaar and are barred from British territory.
1881 – British troops invade Mehsud territory.
1882 – Mehsud blockade lifted; new settlement scheme; experiment with *chalweshtis*.
1888 – Richard Bruce makes new settlement with Mehsuds, involving payments to the maliks in return for providing levies.
1890 – Appozai agreement – arrangements made with Mehsuds and Wazirs and other tribes for 'opening' the Gumal Pass route into Afghanistan.
1893 – autumn – Durand visits Kabul to negotiate with Amir Abdur Rahman over demarcation of British and Afghan spheres of influence along the frontier.
1894 November – encouraged by Mullah Powindah, Mehsuds attack Bruce's camp at Wana; British send retaliatory expedition. Troops remain at Barwand in Mehsud territory.
1895 – Bruce makes new *maliki* settlement with Mehsuds.
1895–7 – demarcation of most of Durand Line
1896 – British establish military posts in Waziristan (troops at Barwand moved to Sarwakai).
1897 June – some Madda Khels attack Major Gee and his escort at Maizar; British troops destroy their settlements at Sheranna and Maizar.
1897 July – anti-British risings break out along frontier north of Waziristan.
1900 December – Mehsuds barred from British territory.
1901 November – four British columns invade Mehsud territory.
1902 February – Mehsuds surrender; new settlement negotiated.

Early 1900s – new British militias raised in North and South Waziristan

1903 – British start to pay allowances to more than a thousand Mehsud elders (*mohtabar*s) rather than just the maliks.

1904 September – suicidal attacks on British officials begin with the murder of the South Waziristan political agent, Captain Bowring.

1906 – Leslie Crump alters Mehsud allowance arrangements, reducing the number of men receiving allowances.

1907 – signing of Anglo-Russian Convention upsets Amir Habibullah; his brother, Nasrullah Khan, steps up anti-British activities along the border.

1910 – John Donald changes allowance arrangements, increasing the number of Mehsud men receiving an allowance.

1913 November – death of Mullah Powindah.

1914 January – Sarfaraz Mehsud kills Major Dodd, the South Waziristan political agent, and two British officers (and three police) in his garden in Tank. Payment of Mehsud allowances is suspended.

1914 – Abdullai Mehsuds continue to encroach on Tori Khel Wazirs' land south of Razmak.

1915 November – British seize Mehsuds and impose blockade.

1917 February – first of several serious attacks on British troops in Waziristan by Mehsuds

1917 June – British launch retaliatory expedition.

1917 August – peace agreement.

1919 May – third Anglo-Afghan war breaks out; militiamen evacuated from posts west of Miranshah; Miranshah militiamen desert, and Wana militiamen mutiny; British lose control of much of Waziristan.

1919 June – Shah Daula and Haji Abdur Razaq occupy Wana on behalf of Amir Amanullah.

1919 August – interim Anglo-Afghan peace treaty signed at Rawalpindi.

1919 December – British invasion of Waziristan.

1920 – troops establish themselves at Ladha.

1920 – British reoccupy Wana; settlements reached with some Mehsuds.

1921 – negotiations in Kabul for permanent Anglo-Afghan treaty.

1921 spring – British begin to shell Makin with howitzers.

1921 November – Anglo-Afghan treaty signed in Kabul.

1922 April – Wana khassadars besieged and relieved by Scouts.

1922 – British open their first school in Mehsud territory.

1923 January – work begins on Razmak base.

1923 February – further bombing of settlements of hostile Mehsuds and ground attacks.

1923 April – Scouts withdrawn from Wana.

1923 November – most British troops leave Mehsud territory.

1923 – Tank Zam road completed.

1924 – rebellion against Afghan government in Khost.

Appendix 1

1925 March/April – air attacks on Mehsuds – first campaign on Frontier carried out entirely from the air.

1925 – troops and Scouts begin to 'show the flag' by moving through different parts of Waziristan.

1925 – skirmishing between Tori Khel Wazirs and Mehsuds.

1926 – attempt to resolve Tori Khel-Mehsud dispute fails.

1926 – Zangi Khan Madda Khel given title of Khan Sahib and bigger allowance.

1928 – difficulties with Zangi Khan resolved at the end of the year.

1928 November – Shinwari revolt sparks off a major insurrection in Afghanistan.

1929 – road from Sarwakai to Wana completed.

1929 January – King Amanullah leaves Kabul; Habibullah Kalakani takes over.

1929 October – Mehsuds and Wazirs who fought for Amanullah switch their support to Nadir Shah. Habibullah II is overthrown and Nadir Khan is proclaimed shah of Afghanistan.

1929 November – Manzai garrison relocated to Wana.

Early 1930s – the British continue with the modified forward policy or peaceful penetration.

1930 summer – 'hostile' Mehsuds raise lashkars and attack Sora Rogha.

1930 – around seventy demonstrators (mainly Hatti Khel Wazirs) killed by troops in Bannu district.

1930 – British troops show the flag in Dahna in south Waziristan, near Afghan border.

1931 – Ramzan Shabi Khel joins Nadir Shah's forces and they drive Ibrahim Beg out of northern Afghanistan.

1932 January – Zadrans in Khost rebel against Nadir Shah; in February several thousand Wazirs and Mehsuds join them and besiege Matun, but fail to take it.

1933 – Wana-Tauda China road completed.

1934 – British take hostages from Madda Khels, suspected of harbouring anti-GOA rebels. Madda Khel malik Zangi Khan murdered.

1935–6 – British experience difficulties with Zilla Khels.

1936 – Islam Bibi affair.

1936 November – serious opposition offered to British troops visiting Bishe Kashkai in the Khaisora.

1936 – Mirza Ali Khan's insurgency begins; Waziristan put under military command. Troops disperse insurgent lashkar.

1937 – lashkar reforms and insurgency revives.

1937 April – Razmak cut off by road.

1937 May – insurgents attack train on Lakki-Tank railway.

1937 August – Khost governor tries to persuade Mirza Ali Khan to settle with the British.

1938 January – so-called Shami Pir arrives at Tank.

1938 June – the Pir sets out with large number of Mehsuds and Wazirs for Afghanistan; the lieutenant-governor, Sir George Cunningham, persuades him to return to Italy with a large payment.

1938 July – insurgents and bandits attack Bannu City.

1938 – Sir Aubrey Metcalfe, Indian foreign secretary, visits Kabul.

December 1940/January 1941 – Mehsuds pin down column and kill sixty-six soldiers.

1942 May–July – Mirza Ali Khan's followers besiege Datta Khel.

1944 January – Mirza Ali Khan tries to revive insurgency in the Shaktu.

1946 May – Afghan prime minister Hashim Khan retires and Shah Mahmud succeeds him.

1947 April – Mehsuds loot and burn the Tank bazaar for the first time since 1879.

1947 July – majority of those who vote in the NWFP referendum opt to join Pakistan.

1947 October – Mehsuds and other frontier men take part in invasion of Kashmir.

1948 June – Mirza Ali Khan sends lashkar to occupy Datta Khel; it is dispersed with bombing.

1960–1 – Afghan troops and irregulars cross into Bajaur; border between Pakistan and Afghanistan closed until 1963

1978 April – Saor Revolution in Afghanistan.

1979 late December – Soviet troops begin to arrive in Afghanistan.

1996 – Taliban move into Kabul.

2001 November – Taliban government overthrown; Al-Qaeda fighters move into Waziristan.

2006 – proclamation of Islamic Emirate of North Waziristan.

2009 – Pakistani military occupy South Waziristan.

2014 – Pakistani military occupy North Waziristan.

Appendix 2: Brief relevant details of some personalities mentioned above

Abdullah Jan Zilla Khel – former Brigadier in Afghan army; leader of anti-British resistance in the Wana area during the 1930s.

Abdul Ghaffur Khan (Badshah Sahib) (1890–1988) – influenced by Gandhian ideas of non-violent political action, created the anti-British Khudai Khidmatgaran (Servants of God) movement in 1929.

Abdur Rahman Khan (d.1901) – amir of Afghanistan 1880–1901. Abdur Rahman Macha Madda Khel (known as 'Pak' – 'baldhead') joined North Waziristan Militia and became subahdar, but deserted 1919; enlisted in Urgun Militia and deserted from that in 1932 during the rising against Nadir Shah.

Abdur Razaq, Haji (d.1923?) – educated at the Deoband seminary, was the chief court mullah to Amir Habibullah and an ally of Sardar Nasrullah; anti-British; he played a major role in encouraging anti-British resistance in Waziristan from 1919 to 1922.

Acheson, Sir James (1899–1973) – political agent (PA) North Waziristan 1925–7; resident (R) Waziristan 1936–7.

Afzal Khan (1811–69) – son of Amir Dost Muhammad Khan, brother of Azem Khan, father of Abdur Rahman Khan, amir of Afghanistan 1866–7.

Aitchinson, Sir Charles (1832–94) – governor Punjab 1882–7.

Amanullah Khan (1892–1960) – amir of Afghanistan 1919–29.

Anderson, Henry – Deputy Commissioner (DC) Bannu 1887–8, DC Dera Ismail Khan 1892–4, Commissioner and Superintendent (C) Derajat 1899–1900.

Azem Khan, Sardar (d.1869) – brother of Afzal Khan, amir 1867–8.

Azem Khan Kundi – landowner in Tank district; Macaulay and then Bruce's principal intermediary with the Mehsuds in the 1870s, 1880s and 1890s.

Arsala Khan Madda Khel Wazir – pro-Afghan rival of Zangi Khan.

Bashir, Maulana, son of Haji of Turangzai, moved to Makin c.1919; murdered 1934.

Barnes, Humphrey, Major – PA South Waziristan 1934–9; murdered in Baluchistan 1941.

Bolton, Sir Norman (1875–1965) – Chief Commissioner North-West Frontier Province (CC NWFP) 1923–30.

Bowring, George Captain – PA South Waziristan, murdered by Kabul Abdur Rahman Khel in 1904.

Bray, Sir Denis (1875–1951) – Indian foreign secretary 1920–30.

Bruce, Sir Richard, Lieutenant-Colonel (1840–1926) – DC Dera Ismail Khan 1888–90; C Derajat 1890–6; in charge of Durand Line demarcation in Waziristan 1894–5.

Bruce, Charles, Lt.-Col. (1876–1950) – R Waziristan 1923–4, 1927–8.

Bugeaud, Thomas, Marshal (1784–1849) – played the leading role in the French conquest of Algeria in the later 1830s and 1840s (governor general 1841–7).
Charkhi, Ghulam Nabi (1830–1932) – influential supporter of Amanullah; suspected of involvement in the 1932 Khost rising and executed by Nadir Khan in the same year.
Chelmsford, Lord (1868–1933) – viceroy 1916–21.
Coleridge, Gen. Sir John (1878–1951) – general, Commanding Northern Command, 1936–40.
Crewe, Marquess of (1858–1945) – secretary of state for India 1910–15.
Copeland, Theodore – DC Dera Ismail Khan 1911–14, PA South Waziristan 1914–16.
Crump, Leslie – PA South Waziristan 1905–8.
Cunningham, Sir George (1888–1963) – governor NWFP 1937–46, 1947–8.
Curzon, Lord (1859–1925) – viceroy 1899–1905.
Deane, Lt.-Col. Sir Harold, (1854–1908) – CC NWFP 1901–8.
Dobbs, Sir Henry (1871–1934) – negotiated treaty with Afghanistan in Kabul in 1921.
Dodd, George, Major – PA South Waziristan from 1911; killed by Sarfaraz Mehsud in 1914.
Donald, Sir John (1861–1948) – R Waziristan 1908–1913; acting CC NWFP 1913–15.
Dufferin, Earl of (1826–1902) – viceroy 1884–8.
Edwardes, Sir Herbert, Major (1819–68) – C Peshawar 1853–9 (with break in 1857).
Edwards, Cosmo – PA North Waziristan 1926–9, DC Dera Ismail Khan 1929
Elgin, Earl of (1849–1917) – viceroy of India 1894–9.
Faiz Muhammad Zakaria (1892–1979) – foreign minister of Afghanistan 1929–38.
Fazal Din Shahzada (Mullah) – son and heir of Mullah Powindah; encouraged Mehsud resistance to the British during and after the First World War. Accepted a British allowance in 1936; did not recognize Pakistan in 1947.
Fitzpatrick, Sir Dennis (1837–1920) – governor Punjab 1892–7.
Fitzpatrick, James (1869–1937) – R Waziristan (and Political Adviser to Waziristan Field Force) 1916–22.
Fraser-Tytler, Sir William (1886–1963) – British representative in Kabul 1935–41.
Frere, Sir Bartle (1815–84) – commissioner Sind (1850–9), governor Bombay (1862–7).
Gee, Herbert, Major – first PA in North Waziristan; attacked by Madda Khels at Maizar in 1897.
Graham, Frederick, Major – DC Dera Ismail Khan 1862–6; C Derajat 1866–71.
Griffith, Sir Ralph – R Waziristan 1929–31, CC NWFP 1931–2 and governor 1932–7.
Habibullah Khan – succeeded his father as amir of Afghanistan in 1901, assassinated in 1919.
Habibullah Kalakani – ruler of Afghanistan from January to October 1929.
Hailey, Baron Sir Malcolm, (1872–1969) – member of Viceroy's Council in Finance and Home Departments 1919–24.
Haji of Turangzai (1858–1937) – an influential opponent of British rule in the NWFP.
Harman, Richard, Lt.-Col. (1864–1905) – commanding South Waziristan Militia; killed at Wana by Kabul Mehsud in 1905.

Harap Khan Shabi Khel Mehsud – a successful contractor.
Hayat Khan Manzi Alizai – until 1914 served in 130th Baluchis infantry regiment; a leading malik towards the end of the British period.
Heale, Robert, Lt. Col. – R Waziristan 1929
Howell, Sir Evelyn – PA Wana 1905, R Waziristan 1924–7, Indian Foreign Secretary 1930–3.
Humphrys, Sir Francis (1879–1971) – British representative in Kabul 1922–9.
Jangi Khan Salimi Khel Alizai – leading Mehsud malik; killed in attack on Tank 1860.
Johnson, Harry, Col. – PA South Waziristan 1930–4 and R Waziristan 1937–8.
Johnston, Frederick – DC Bannu 1900–1, PA South Waziristan 1902–4, 1909, R Waziristan 1910.
Lala Pir, Mullah Sayyid Lal Shah – later nineteenth and early twentieth century religious leader; lived in Khost.
Lansdowne, Marquess of (1845–1927) – viceroy 1888–94.
Lewanai Faqir – religious leader during the early twentieth century, lived in Khost; involved in 1932–3 Khost risings and their aftermath.
Linlithgow, Marquess of (1887–1952) – viceroy 1936–43.
Lyall, James, Sir (1838–1916) – governor Punjab 1887–92.
Lyautey, Marshal Louis-Hubert (1854–1934) – French colonial administrator, best known for his part in the French conquest of Morocco, and his popularization of the concepts of 'peaceful penetration' and 'indirect rule'.
Macaulay, Charles, Major – DC Dera Ismail Khan 1871–82.
Mackworth-Young, Sir William (1840–1924) – governor Punjab 1897–1902.
Maconachie, Sir Richard (1885–1962) – British representative in Kabul 1930–5.
Maffey, Sir John (1877–1969) – CC NWFP 1921–3.
Matheson, General Sir Torquil (1871–1963) – commanding Waziristan 1920–3.
Merk, William (1852–1925) – C Derajat 1900–2; in charge of Mehsud blockade 1901–2; CC NWFP 1909–10.
Minto, Earl of (1845–1914) – viceroy 1905–10.
Morley, Viscount (1838–1923) – secretary of state for India 1905–10, 1911.
Mir Badshah Manzai Alizai, Captain – a leading Mehsud malik in the interwar period and after.
Mirza Ali Khan, the so-called Faqir of Ipi – leader of an insurgency in North Waziristan in the later 1930s. He refused to recognize the new Government of Pakistan in 1947 and remained at Gorwekht near the Afghan border until his death in 1960.
Muhammad Hashim, Sardar (1885–1953) – younger brother of Nadir Shah; prime minister of Afghanistan 1929–46.
Muhammad Said Gilani, known as 'the Shami Pir' – he went to Waziristan in 1938, began to raise a Mehsud and Wazir lashkar to invade Afghanistan, but was persuaded to leave with a cash payment.
Mullah Hamzullah – the most influential religious leader among the Wazirs in the later nineteenth and early twentieth centuries.

Mullah Powindah – most influential Mehsud religious leader from the early 1890s until his death in 1913.

Musa Khan Abdullai – leader of Mehsud resistance to the British invasion of Mehsud territory in 1919–20; remained the leading Afghan allowance-holder.

Nabi Khan Shingi (d.1882) – had links with Sardar Azem Khan, and was Macaulay's principal Mehsud intermediary during the 1870s; discredited by Umar Khan's attack on Tank in 1879.

Nadir Shah (1883–1933) – commander-in-chief during the third Anglo-Afghan War in 1919 he led a column towards North Waziristan, sparking off desertions and mutiny in the Waziristan militias; minister of war 1919–24, king of Afghanistan 1929–3.

Nasrullah Khan, Sardar (1874–1920) – brother of Amir Habibullah; had contacts with Frontier mullahs including the Mullah Powindah and the Mullah Hamzullah.

Nicholson, John, Brigadier General (1821–57) – DC Bannu district 1852–5.

Obeidullah Sindhi (1872–1944) – convert to Islam and Indian revolutionary who went to Kabul in 1916, where he stayed until 1922.

Ogilvie, George – DC Dera Ismail Khan 1885–8, and C Derajat Division 1888–90.

Ommanney, Edward – C Derajat Division 1881–8.

Parsons, Sir Arthur (1884–1966) – PA South Waziristan 1919–22, DC Bannu 1928–30, R Waziristan 1931–5.

Pears, Sir Stuart – R Waziristan 1922–4, CC NWFP 1930–1.

Pashakai Shabi Khel Mehsud – anti-British relative of the Mullah Powindah.

Peel, Lord (1867–1937) – secretary of state for India, 1922–4.

Pir Rakhman Khaddar Khel Astanai Shabi Khel – Harap's son and a leading Mehsud malik in the 1930s and 1940s.

Ramzan Shaman Khel – one of the leaders of the Mehsud attack on Sora Rogha fort in 1930; took part in the Afghan operation to drive Ibrahim Beg out of northern Afghanistan in 1931.

Rawlinson, General Sir Henry (1864–1925) – commander-in-chief in India 1920–5.

Reading, Marquess of (1860–1935) – viceroy 1921–6.

Roos-Keppel, Sir George (1860–1921) – CC NWFP 1908–9, 1910–13, 1915–19.

Sadde Khan Shaman Khel – brother of Ramzan; held rank of colonel in Afghan service; one of the leaders of the Mehsud attack on the Sora Rogha fort in July 1930.

Sandeman, Sir Robert (1835–92) – CC Baluchistan 1877–92; introduced a new approach to tribal management, known as the Sandeman 'system'.

Shah Daula – Afghan cavalry commander; played a prominent role in encouraging anti-British resistance in Waziristan during 1919–21.

Shah Mahmud Khan (1890–1959) – prime minister of Afghanistan 1946–53.

Shah Nawaz Khan – tax-collector and then nawab of Tank (d.1881).

Sher Ali Khan (1825–79) – amir of Afghanistan 1863–6 and 1868–79.

Skeen, Andrew, Major-General (1873–1935) – commander of the invading British force in Waziristan 1919–20.

Tarzi, Mahmud Beg (1865–1933) – influential modernizer and writer; Afghan foreign minister 1919–22 and 1924–7.

Taylor, Reynell, Major-General (1822–66) – DC Bannu 1850–2, C Derajat 1860–2.

Thorburn, Septimus (1844–1924) – DC Bannu 1869–70; DC Dera Ismail Khan 1882–5.

Umar Khan Salimi Khel Manzai Alizai Mehsud – had links with the Afghan amir Sher Ali Khan; leader of attack on Tank at the beginning of January 1879; reached an agreement with Richard Bruce and was killed in 1888 trying to recover two British carbines stolen by relatives.

Watson, Hubert – PA South Waziristan 1899–1900.

Wigram, Sir Kenneth, General (1875–1949) – commander of Waziristan district 1926–31.

Zahir Shah (1924–2007) – king of Afghanistan 1933–73.

Zangi Khan Macha Khel Madda Khel, Khan Sahib – in the later 1920s the British began to treat him as the leading Madda Khel malik; murdered by a relative in 1935.

Zetland, Marquess of (1876–1961) – secretary of state for India 1935–7.

Appendix 3: Some genealogical links between Mehsud and Wazir lineages

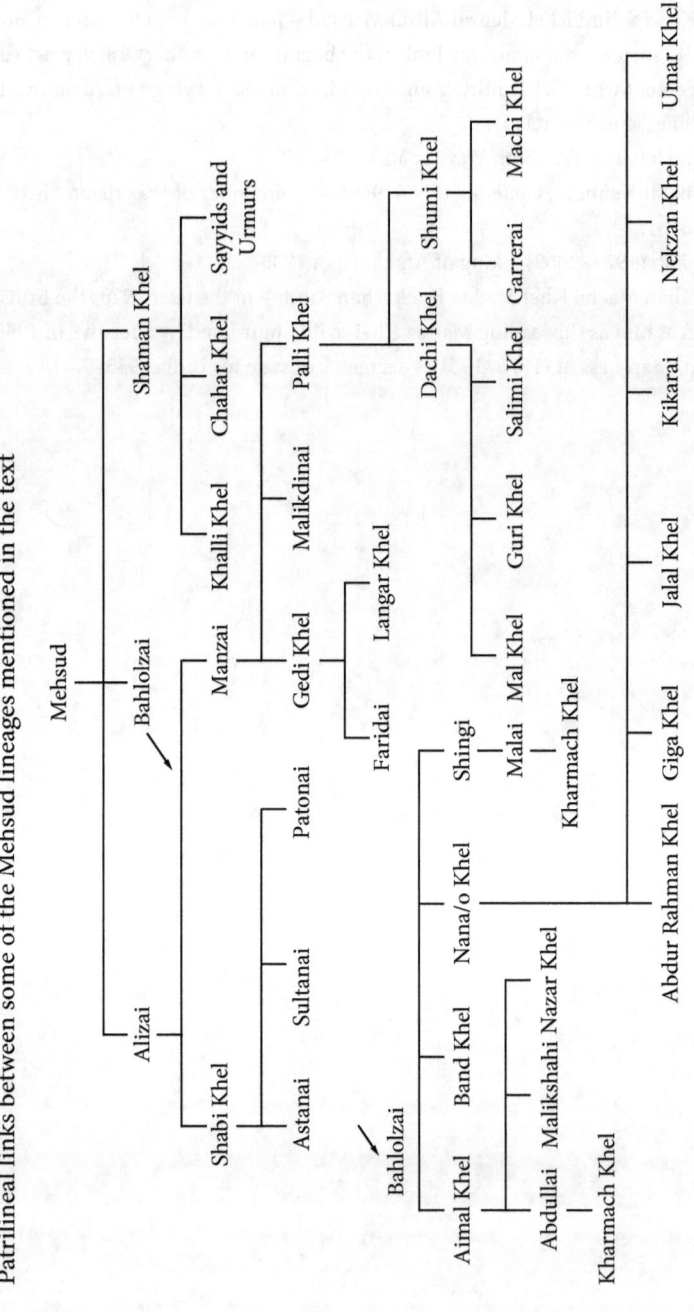

Patrilineal links between some of the Mehsud lineages mentioned in the text

Appendix 3

Patrilineal links between some of the Darwesh Khel Wazir lineages mentioned in the text

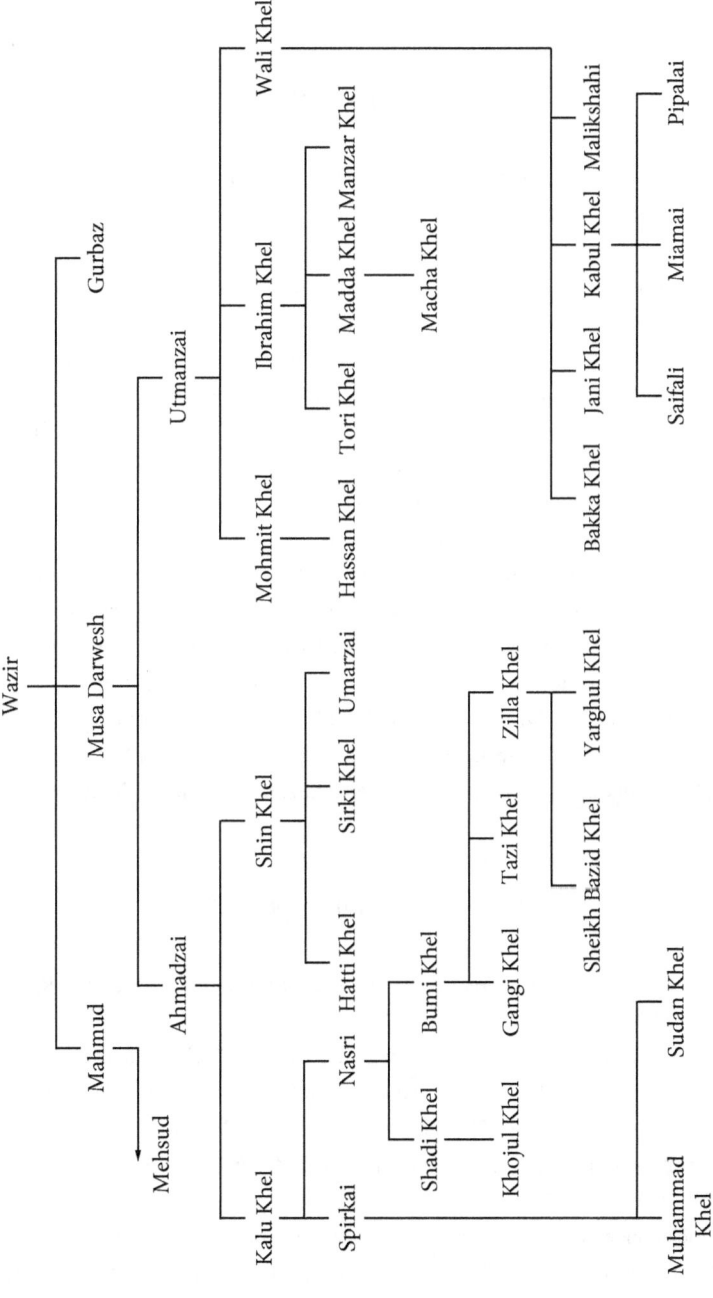

Notes

Introduction

1 Charles Chevenix-Trench's *The Frontier Scouts* (London, 1985), which drew extensively on British officers' private letters and diaries, is also worth mentioning in this connection.
2 Two useful studies of the movement towards independence in the North-West Frontier Province are Erland Jansson's *India, Pakistan or Pakhhtunistan: The Nationalist Movement in the North-West Frontier Province* (1981, Uppsala) and Stephen Rittenberg's *Ethnicity, Nationalism and the Pakhtuns: The Independence Movement in India's North-West Frontier Province* (1988, Durham, NC).
3 An important article is Milan Hauner, 'One Man against the Empire: the Faqir of Ipi and the British in Central Asia on the Eve of and during the Second World War', *Journal of Contemporary History*, Vol. 16 (1981), pp. 183–212.
4 Simon Potter and Jonathan Saha, 'Global History, Imperial History and Connected Histories of Empire', *Journal of Colonialism and Colonial History*, Vol. 16 (2015), No. 1, pp. 3–16, https://muse.jhu.edu/article/577738; Michiel Baud and Willem Schendel, 'Towards a Comparative History of Borderlands', *Journal of World History*, Vol. 8 (1997), No. 2, pp. 211–42 (p. 242); see also, for example, Willem Schendel, 'Making the Most of "sensitive" Borders', in David N. Gellner (ed.), *Borderland Lives in Northern South Asia* (2013, Durham, NC/London), pp. 266–72.

Chapter 1

1 Lal Baha, *North-West Frontier Province Administration under British Rule 1901-1919* (1978, Islamabad), p. 33.
2 Maira Hayat, 'Still "Taming the Turbulent Frontier"? The State in the Federally Administered Tribal Areas of Pakistan', *Journal of the Anthropology Society of Oxford (JASO)-online N.S.*, Vol. 1 (2009), No. 2, p. 201.
3 Thomas Barfield, *Afghanistan: A Cultural and Political History* (2010, Princeton, NJ/Oxford), pp. 24–5.
4 Social scientists have for some time questioned the analytical utility of the concept of tribe (see, for example, 'Tribe', p. 6, David Sneath in 'F. Stein et al (eds.) *The Cambridge Encyclopedia of Anthropology*, http://www.anthroencyclopedia.com/entry/tribe),

but it may be argued that 'named tribes with a self-consciousness of their identity do most certainly exist' and that 'as secondary formations tribes once created take on a life of their own' (James Scott, *The Art of Not Being Governed An Anarchist History of Upland Southeast Asia* [2009, New Haven, CT/London], p. 259). I have continued to use the term 'tribe' here rather than alternatives (for example peoples or nations) to refer to these largely self-governing groupings whose members deliberately lived beyond the direct control of expansionary states and state-governed people but had a relationship with them, the two in a sense forming a single system.

5 According, for example, to the *Makhzan-i-Afghani*, commissioned by the Mughal emperor Jahangir and completed about 1612 CE by Nematullah, a scribe at his court (Sir Olaf Caroe, *The Pathans 550 BC.-A.D.*, reprinted 1983 with a Foreword and an Epilogue on Russia [1957, Oxford], pp. 9, 15)

6 See, for example, Gerald Curtis, *Monograph on Mehsud Tribes* (MMT) (1947, Government of NWFP. Confidential), p. 9.

7 Hugh Beattie, *Imperial Frontier: Tribe and State in Waziristan* (2002, Richmond), Chapter 1, *passim*.

8 IOR: Ellington, Commanding RAF in India (C RAF India), to Jacob, commander-in-chief in India (CinC India), 23.6.1926, enclosure 2, Register (Reg.) P690, L PS/10/1142, p. 376.

9 Curtis, *MMT*, 1947, pp. 197–8, 346; Frank Leeson, *Frontier Legion: With the Khassadars of North Waziristan* (2003, Ferring, West Sussex), pp. 173–5, Major Charles Macaulay, Deputy-Commissioner (DC) to Punjab Government (PG), Final Report of the Mahsud Expedition, No. 99P, IOR: Punjab Foreign Proceedings, P1825 Appendix G. Chapter II p. 59, February 1882.

10 Leeson, *Frontier Legion*, 2003, pp. 174–5. Some Madda Khels also mined and smelted iron ore.

11 *Economist*, 17 February 2010, Vol. 394, No. 8663, pp. 17–20.

12 Beattie, *Imperial*, 2002, pp. 5, 9.

13 Akbar S. Ahmed, *Pukhtun Economy and Society Traditional Structure and Economic Development in a Tribal Society* (1983, London), pp. 116–25.

14 Scott, *The Art*, 2009, p. 1; IOR: Note by Captain Patterson, Political Agent (PA), Wana (W), no date, in Reg. 668, L/P&S/10/44.

15 IOR: Note, PA W, in Reg. 668, L/P&S/10/44.

16 From the word *chehel* – the number 40.

17 Richard Tapper, 'Studying Pathans in Barth's Shadow', in David Hopkins and Magnus Marsden (eds), *Beyond Swat: History, Society and Economy along the Afghanistan-Pakistan Frontier* (2013, London), p. 224.

18 Beattie, *Imperial*, 2002, p. 8; Sana Haroon, *Frontier of Faith: Islam in the Indo-Afghan Borderland* (2007, London), p. 67, Curtis, *MMT*, 1947, p. 346.

19 Capt. A.H. McMahon and Lieut. A. D. G. Ramsay, *Report on the Tribes of Dir, Swat, and Bajaour Together with the Utman-Khel and Sam Ranizai* (quoted David B. in Edwards, *Heroes of the Age Moral Fault Lines on the Afghan Frontier* [1996, Berkeley, CA], p. 266).

20 See, for example, Frederick Johnston, 1901, *Report on Waziristan and Its Tribes* (Lahore, 2005), p. 17, Caroe, *Pathans*, 1957, p. 23, Curtis, *MMT*, 1947, pp. 8, 117, 347. Well-known *ziyarat*s or shrines included Musa Nikka and Borak Nika (Akbar S. Ahmed, *Resistance and Control in Pakistan* [1991, London], pp. 113–14).

21 See, for example, Caroe, *Pathans*, 1957, p. 310.

22 Beattie, *Imperial*, 2002, p. 29.

23 The Multani Pathans were descendants of a group of Alizai Pashtuns from Kandahar (Sir Herbert Edwardes, *A Year on the Punjab Frontier, Vol. 2* [1851, London], pp. 16–17).

24 See, for example, Beattie, *Imperial*, 2002, pp. 34, 35.

25 Caroe, *Pathans*, 1957, pp. 323–4.

26 IOR: GOI to Board of Administration, No. 57, 27.8.50, No. 4 in No. 25, 23.9.1850, L/P&S/5/204. The correspondence began with a letter from Muhammad Azem in March 1850 (IOR: Muhammad Azem to Taylor, 9.3.1850 in BOA to GOI, 19.3.1850, No. 21 in No. 6, 15.5.1850, L/PS/5/204).

27 Lesley Hall, *A Brief Guide to Sources for the Study of Afghanistan in the India Office Records* (1981, London), Appendix 3.

28 Beattie, *Imperial*, 2002, pp. 67–8, 103.

29 Marshall Hodgson, *The Classical Age of Islam, The Venture of Islam Conscience and History in a World Civilization, Vol. 1* (1974, Chicago, IL/London), pp. 152–3.

30 Charles Lindholm, 'Models of Segmentary Political Action: the Usefulness of Colonial Ethnography', *Archives Européennes de Sociologie*, Vol. XXI (1982), No. 2, pp. 350–61.

31 See, for example, Scott, *The Art*, 2009, p. 257.

32 Richard Tapper, *Frontier Nomads of Iran: A Political and Social History of the Shahsevan* (1997, Cambridge), p. 344.

33 'Kurdish Tribes', Pierre Oberling, 2004. http://www.iranicaonline.org/articles/kurdish-tribes

34 Tapper, *Frontier Nomads*, 1997, p. 345.

35 Hugh Beattie, *Identidad y Etnicidad: Continuidad y Cambio* (2002, Mexico City), p. 92.

36 We might compare this with, for example, 'Romanization' in the Roman empire, and the 'Five Baits' offered to the Hsiung-nu by the Han government in China (Thomas Barfield, *The Perilous Frontier Nomadic Empires and China 221 BC to AD 1757* [1989, Cambridge, MA/Oxford], p. 51).

37 Scott, *The Art*, 2009, p. 123.

38   Beattie, *Imperial*, 2002, pp. 34–41.
39   Quoted in ibid., p. 39.
40   Some British officials criticized the expedition and argued that it was wrong to inflict indiscriminate punishment in this way, for example Sir Bartle Frere (at this point a member of the Viceroy's Council) (G.W. Forrest, *Life of Sir Neville Chamberlain* [1909, Edinburgh], p. 406).
41   In Beattie, *Imperial*, 2002, p. 174. See also, for example, Robert Nichols, *Settling the Frontier: Land, Law, and Society in the Peshawar Valley, 1500-1900* (2001, Karachi), pp. 6–9.
42   Richard Tapper, 'Introduction', in Richard Tapper (ed.), *The Conflict of Tribe and State in Iran and Afghanistan* (1983, Beckenham), p. 54. This meant maintaining a diffuse form of organization and refusing to recognize any leader, whether internal or externally imposed.
43   Beattie, *Imperial*, 2002, p. 48.
44   Evelyn Howell, *Mizh: A Monograph on Government's Relations with the Mahsud Tribe* (1979, Karachi), p. 3.
45   Beattie, *Imperial*, 2002, pp. 52–3.
46   Ahmadzais included Bizan Khels, Bodin Khels, Hatti Khels, Muhammad Khels, Painda Khels, Sirki Khels, Sudan Khels and Umarzais. The main Utmanzai settlers were Bakka Khels and Jani Khels (Beattie, *Imperial*, 2002, pp. 14–15).
47   Beattie, *Imperial*, 2002, pp. 55–62.
48   Ibid., pp. 69–72.
49   IOR: *Punjab Administration Report (PAR) 1876-77*, p. 5.
50   Beattie, *Imperial*, 2002, pp. 84–91.

Chapter 2

1   Beattie, *Imperial*, 2002, pp. 96–7.
2   Ibid., p. 292, note 36.
3   In 1872 officials reached an agreement with the Saifali Kabul Khels, and in 1874 they settled outstanding claims against the Miamai Kabul Khels on the Miranzai border.
4   Caroe, *Pathans*, 1957, p. 371.
5   Barfield, *Afghanistan*, 2010, pp. 136–7.
6   Howell, *Mizh*, 1979, pp. 3–4, Beattie, *Imperial*, 2002, p. 52.
7   Reynell Taylor, for example, did not believe that this was actually the case (Beattie, *Imperial*, 2002, pp. 109–10).
8   IOR: *PAR 1874-75*, p. 5, V/10/332.
9   For details see Beattie, *Imperial*, 2002, pp. 111–12.

10 IOR: DC DIK to Commissioner (C), Derajat Division (DD), No. 239, April No. 5, PP3620. Rivalry continued between his party and the supporters of the late nawab (IOR PP, C DD to DC, DIK, No. 860-4054, 29.8.1882, April, PP2012).
11 At this time Peshawar was regarded as being the most disturbed frontier district (see e.g. *PAR 1875-76*, p. 30).
12 Only by imposing tribal responsibility was 'control possible over the wild and fanatical tribes on the border', the lieutenant-governor, Davies, commented at about this time (IOR: Punjab to GOI, No., 774P, 21.4.1877, No. 78 July, India Proceedings [IP] P1035).
13 Beattie, *Imperial*, 2002, pp. 127–8.
14 IOR: *PAR 1876-77*, p. 15, Beattie, *Imperial*, 2002, p. 128.
15 Caroe, *Pathans*, 1983, pp. 373–4.
16 Barfield, *Afghanistan*, 2010, p. 140.
17 For an account of these developments see Jonathan Lee, *Afghanistan: A History from 1260 to the Present* (2018, London), pp. 330–60.
18 Beattie, *Imperial*, 2002, p. 135.
19 Ibid., pp. 130–3, 141, 146–50.
20 For details see Hugh Beattie, 'Hostages on the Indo-Afghan Border in the Later Nineteenth Century', *Journal of Imperial and Commonwealth History*, Vol. 43 (2015), No. 4, pp. 557–69.
21 Johnston, *Report*, 1901, pp. 70–1.
22 IOR: C DD to GP, No. 645, 24.12.1883, No. 14–16 January, PP2221; C DD to GOI Punjab, No. 505, 8.10.1883, No. 14–16 January, PP2221; Derajat and Peshawar Division Pol. Admin. Rep. 1882-3, No. 753, DC Bannu to C DD, 30.11.1883, No. 14–16 January, PP2221). Sardar Ghulam Sarwar Khan was appointed as the amir's representative with the Mehsuds.
23 IOR: C DD to GP, No. 333, 28.7.84, No. 30 August, PP P2222 1885.
24 IOR: GP to C DD, No. 283, 26.5.1884, No. 83 May, PP P2221; GP to GOI, No. 284, No. 84 May No. 43, PP P2221.
25 Ripon Papers, Vol. 43613, p. 59 quoted in D.P. Singhal, *India and Afghanistan 1876-1907: A Study in Diplomatic Relations* (1963, Brisbane), p. 104.
26 IOR: DC Kohat to C Peshawar Division (PD), No. 90 and a half, June 1885 PP P2742.
27 Johnston, *Report*, 1901, pp. 70/71.
28 'The example of what good management by a farmer can do [had] … fired the most intelligent Maliks with a desire to be once again entrusted with the management of the land', and they had begun to divide the land into three blocks, one for each section (ibid., p. 71).
29 Johnston, *Report*, 1901, p. 72.
30 Howell, *Mizh*, 1979, p. 97.
31 IOR: DC DIK to C DD, No. 84, 7.2.1884, No. 50 June, PP2221; DC DIK to C DD, No. 457, 11.7.1884, No. 30 August, P2222.

32 For instance some men saved up the money they were given to live on and used it to buy breech-loading rifles from arms dealers in Dera Ismail Khan (Beattie, 'Hostages', 2015, p. 8).
33 IOR: DC DI to C DD, No. 457, 11.7.1884, August No. 30, PP2222.
34 IOR: GP to C DD, 23.6.1884, No. 352, June No. 51, 23.6.1884, PP2221.
35 Leslie Harris, *British Policy on the North-West Frontier 1889-1901* (1960, PhD London University), p. 31.
36 Jonathan Parry, *Benjamin Disraeli* (2007, Oxford), p. 110.
37 Rob Johnson, '"Russians at the Gates of India" Planning the Defence of India, 1885-1900', *The Journal of Military History*, Vol. 67 (2003), No. 3, p. 710.
38 Harris, *British Policy*, 1960, p. 33.
39 Dufferin (Viceroy 1884-8), for example, commented that Russian advances in Central Asia made a close border policy less suitable (Charles Black, *The Marquess of Dufferin and Ava: Diplomatist, Viceroy, Statesman* [1903, London], p. 102).
40 IOR: GG to SofSI, No. 156, 4.10.1886, April No. 24, PP2923; Martin Ewans, *Afghanistan: A New History* (2001, Richmond), pp. 76-7.
41 Johnson, 'Russians', 2003, pp. 717, 724.
42 Sir Frederick Roberts, quoted in Johnston, *Report*, 1901, p. 2.
43 IOR: GG to SofS, No. 156, 4.10.1886, April No. 1 1887, PP2923; Johnston, *Report*, 1901, p. 43.
44 Johnson, 'Russians', 2003, p. 719.
45 IOR: SofS to GG, 27.1.1887, April No. 24, PP2923.
46 GOI to GP, 17.8.1887, quoted in C DD to GP, 28.2.1894, *House of Commons Parliamentary Papers*, Cd. 8713/4, p. 9.
47 Ibid.
48 IOR: Lt.-Governor quoted in Bruce, Mahsud Memo., in V. to SofS, No. 12, 28.1.1890, L/P&S/7/59, p. 62.
49 Ibid.
50 Johnston, *Report*, 1901, p. 44; Howell, *Mizh*, 1979, p. 10; Bruce, Mahsud Memo., in V. to SofS, No. 12, 28.1.1890, L/P&S/7/59, p. 115.
51 IOR: GP to GOI FD, No. 164, 21.4.1890, April No. 7, PP3620.
52 Johnston, *Report*, 1901, p. 17.
53 IOR: C DD to GP, No. 879, 31.7.1888, October No. 94, PP3194.
54 IOR: C DD to GP, No. 598, 7.6.1889, in No. 13, 28.1.90, GG to SofS, L/P&S/7/59.
55 Tucker's Settlement Report of DIK, Part 1, para 348, in C DD to GP, 24.7.1900, *Parliamentary*, Annexure 1, Cd. 496, p. 124.
56 IOR: C DD to GP, No. 598, 7.6.1889, in No. 13, 28.1.1890, GG to SofS, L/P&S/7/59.
57 Hugh Beattie, 'Negotiations with the Tribes of Waziristan 1849-1914 – The British Experience', *The Journal of Imperial and Commonwealth History*, Vol. 39 (2011), No. 4, pp. 571–87.

58 He thought that 'to be successful on the frontier a man has to deal with the hearts and minds of the people, and not only with their fears' (Thomas Thornton, *Colonel Sir Robert Sandeman: His Life and Works on Our Indian Frontier* [1895, London]).
59 Curtis, *MMT*, 1947, p. 175.
60 IOR: Bruce, Memo., p. 84, L/P&S/7/59.
61 IOR: C DD to GP, No. 598, 7.6.1889, in No. 13, GG to SofSI, 22.1.1990, L/P&S/7/59. Many other government officials have tried to create representative 'tribal' jirgas among Pashtuns during the past 200 years (see for example Antonio Giustozzi (*War, Politics and Society in Afghanistan 1978-1992* [2000, London], pp. 137, 139).
62 Richard Bruce, *The Forward Policy and Its Results* (1900, London) p. 117. According to Howell, he went ahead without full authority (*Mizh*, 1979, p. 10).
63 IOR: Translation (Trans.) of Agreement, in No. 24 October, PP 3396; Howell, *Mizh*, 1979, p. 10; Johnston, *Report*, 1901, p. 46.
64 Among the Abdur Rahman Khels was Mashak, who had been surrendered to the British in 1882 by other Mehsuds.
65 IOR: DC DIK to CDD, No. 237, 29.6.1889, No. 24 October, PP3396.
66 Quoted in Bruce, *Forward Policy*, 1900, p. 116. So did the Punjab Lt.-Governor (IOR: GP to GOI, No. 499, 21.10.1889, in No. 13, 28.1.1890, L/PS/7/59).
67 IOR: No. 598, C DD to GP, 7.6.1889, encl. in No. 13, 28.1.1890, GOI to SofS, L/PS/7/59. Ogilvie contrasted this with the 'Khyber system', according to which the Afridi men living along it were paid directly for irregular military service, and the maliks were remunerated separately.
68 Frederick Johnston, 1903, 'Notes on Wana', Appendix 4, reprinted in Robert Nichols, *Colonial Reports on Pakistan's Frontier Tribal Areas* (2005, Karachi), p. 49.
69 Harris, *British Policy*, 1960, p. 61.
70 Sandeman also suggested that one man should be responsible for dealing with Waziristan as well as the groups living to the south, but his proposal was rejected (IOR: Sandeman, Memo., 27.11.1889, April No. 7 Appendix, PP3620; GP to GOI FD, No. 164, 21.4.1890, April No. 7, PP3620).
71 It was essentially the scheme previously put forward by Graham and Macaulay (Beattie, *Imperial*, 2002, pp. 117, 154).
72 There were twenty-nine Zilla Khels, nine Tazi Khels, three Sirki Khels, two Dotanis, eleven Sayyids, four Urmurs and 104 Mehsuds (Bahlolzais 42, Alizais 30 and the Shaman Khels 33) (IOR: No. 7 April App. H, 1890 PP3620).
73 Howell, *Mizh*, 1979, p. 13; Johnston, 'Notes', 1903, p. 47.
74 IOR: GG to GOI FD, No. 164, 21.4.1890, April No. 7, PP3620.
75 IOR: Sandeman, Memo., 27.11.1889, April No. 7, App., PP3620; DC DIK to C DD, No. 426, 6.11.1889, April No. 7, PP3620.
76 Harris, *British Policy*, 1960, p. 61. He certainly had a good claim to Wana.
77 Ibid., 1960, p. 64.

78 Johnston, *Report*, 1901, pp. 48–9; Harris, *British Policy*, 1960, pp. 62–4.
79 GOI to SoSI, 10.7.1894, *Parliamentary*, Cd. 8713/4, p. 2; Johnston, *Report*, 1901, p. 49.
80 Johnston, *Report*, 1901, pp. 49–51.
81 Harris, *British Policy*, 1960, pp. 106, 163; Johnson, 'Russians', 2003, p. 22.
82 It appears that men from subsections for whom raiding had some importance, some of the Abdur Rahman Khels and Garrerais for example, feared that if they accepted the maliks' authority, they would have to give this up (Johnston, *Report*, 1901, pp. 117–18); see also Johnston, 'Notes', 1903, p. 48.
83 Johnston, *Report*, 1901, p. 117; GOI to GP, 24.9.1894, *Parliamentary* Cd. 8713/4, p. 36; Johnston, 'Notes', 1903, p. 47.
84 Howell, *Mizh*, 1979, p. 14, Johnston, *Report*, 1901, p. 118, Johnston, 'Notes', 1903, p. 48.
85 Johnston, *Report*, 1901, p. 119; GOR FD to SofSI, 11.9.1894, *Parliamentary*, Cd. 8713/4, p. 31.
86 GOI to SoSI, 10.7.1894, *Parliamentary*, Cd. 8713/4, p. 2, for details see Johnston, *Report*, 1901, pp. 51–2.

Chapter 3

1 Singhal, *India*, 1963, pp. 144–5, Harris, *British Policy*, 1960, p. 134.
2 Harris, *British Policy*, 1960, p. 135.
3 Bijan Omrani and Frank Ledwidge, 'Rethinking the Durand Line: The Legality of the Afghan-Pakistan Frontier', *The RUSI Journal*, Vol. 154 (2009), No. 5, p. 52.
4 Minute of Dissent, *Parliamentary*, Cd. 8713/4, p. 27.
5 Singhal, *India*, 1963, p. 159.
6 Charles E. Bruce, *The Tribes of Waziristan* (1929, London), pp. 17, 121, 125. Beattie, *Imperial*, 2002, p. 156.
7 C DD to GO, 28.2.1894, *Parliamentary*, Cd. 8713/4, pp. 4–5, 7; Harris, *British Policy*, 1960, p. 13. The outposts were to be at Jandola, in the Gumal, and in the neighbourhood of Spin south of Waziristan to protect the Powindahs in the Gumal and prevent raiding into the Zhob Agency, and also in Upper Dawar or Sheranna in the Tochi valley in the north of Waziristan.
8 C DD to GO, 28.2.1894, *Parliamentary*, Cd. 8713/4, p. 10.
9 *Parliamentary*, Cd. 8713/4, p. 10.
10 Harris, *British Policy*, 1960, pp. 174, 273.
11 Note, GP, 14.3.1894, *Parliamentary*, Cd. 8713/4, p. 20.
12 Ibid.

13 Rather as they did with the Mehsuds, the officials also disagreed among themselves as to whether the Afridis were really 'oligarchic' or 'democratic' (Beattie, *Imperial*, 2002, p. 179).
14 Note, GP, 14.3.1894, *Parliamentary*, Cd. 8713/4, pp. 14, 21.
15 The only good reason for occupying the Tochi and the Gumal was the strategic one, he said (Note, GP, 14.3.1894, *Parliamentary*, Cd. 8173/74, p. 16).
16 Harris, *British Policy*, 1960, p. 188; Note, GP, 14.3.1894, *Parliamentary*, Cd. 8713/4, p. 19.
17 Howell, *Mizh*, 1979, pp. 97–8.
18 GOI to SofSI, 10.7.1894, *Parliamentary*, Cd. 8713/4, p. 3.
19 In Harris, *British Policy*, 1960, p. 153.
20 Ibid., p. 156; see also GOI to SofSI, 10.7.1894, *Parliamentary*, Cd. 8713/4, p. 1.
21 *Parliamentary*, Cd. 8713/4, p. 14. In a dissenting minute three members of the Viceroy's Council strongly opposed the idea of establishing a garrison at Spin and urged 'abstention from aggressive activity on our north-west frontier' (*Parliamentary*, Cd. 8713/4, p. 28).
22 Quoted in Harris, *British Policy*, 1960, p. 153. Bruce, however, thought that 'the fair and square policy would obviously be for us to control our tribes and for the Amir to control his' (C DD to GOI, 28.2.1894, *Parliamentary*, Cd. 8713/4, p. 9).
23 In 1887 the mullah was suspected of complicity in the murder of the Darogha (manager) of the Bannu Jail and moved to Dawar and became a *murid* (disciple) of a well-known anti-British mullah, Gulabdin (Johnston, *Report*, 1901, p. 17).
24 Johnston, *Report*, 1901, p. 118.
25 IOR: Wana Political Diary (PD) week ending (w.e.) 31.5.1902, Reg. 1459A, L/P&S/7/149; Beattie, *Imperial*, 2002, p. 155; Howell quoted in Caroe, *Pathans*, 1957, p. 471. Fredrik Barth referred to men like these as Saints (Fredrik Barth, *Political Leadership* [1959, London], pp. 56–63).
26 Beattie, *Imperial*, 2002, p. 155; Howell quoted in Caroe, *Pathans*, 1957, p. 471.
27 Haroon, *Frontier*, 2007, p. 33.
28 Ibid., pp. 46, 49. Najmuddin settled at Hadda near Jalalabad; mullahs associated with him had established links with the famous Deoband seminary in northern India through Fazal Wahid (the Haji Sahib of Turangzai), who came from Turangzai in the Charsadda district north-west of Peshawar. In 1875 he met a party of Deobandi ulama on hajj and spent a few years at Deoband himself (Haroon, *Frontier*, 2007, pp. 53–5).
29 Johnston, *Report*, 1901, pp. 16–18; Haroon, *Frontier*, 2007, p. 81.
30 GOI FD to SofSI, 2.1.1895, *Parliamentary*, Cd. 8731/4, p. 35.
31 Ibid.; see also Johnston, *Report*, 1901, p. 119.
32 IOR: GOI to SofS, No. 1, 1895, L/P&S/7/78.
33 GOI FD to SoSI, 2.1.1895, *Parliamentary*, Cd. 8713/4, p. 35.

34 Howell, *Mizh*, 1979, pp. 15–16.
35 Johnston, *Report*, 1901, p. 58.
36 Harris, *British Policy*, 1960, p. 159.
37 Johnston, *Report*, 1901, pp. 17, 58–61, 124–7; Howell, *Mizh*, 1979, pp. 16–17; the maliks had arranged for Shahir Abdullai's murder because he had killed Karim Khan (Johnston, *Report*, 1901, pp. 126–7).
38 Howell, *Mizh*, 1979, p. 17; Harris, *British Policy*, 1960, p. 169; GOI FD to SofSI, 20.3.1895, *Parliamentary*, Cd. 8713/4, p. 41.
39 SofSI to GOI, 28.1.1898, *Parliamentary*, Cd. 8713/4, p. 173.
40 GOI FD to SofSI, 20.3.1895, *Parliamentary*, Cd. 8713/4, p. 43.
41 Harris, *British Policy*, 1960, p. 174.
42 IOR: Note by Sir D. Stewart on Letter from India, No. 96, 15.5.1895, L/P&S/7/79.
43 Johnston, *Report*, 1901, p. 67; GOI FD to SofSI, 20.3.1895, *Parliamentary*, Cd. 8713/4, p. 44.
44 IOR: *RAB 1938-39*, p. 15; Colin Davies, *The Problem of the North-West Frontier 1890-1908 second edition* (1975, London), p. 91.
45 A.H. Grant I.C.S. was the first PO at Wana and H.W. Gee I.C.S. the first in the Tochi.
46 Harris, *British Policy*, 1960, pp. 174, 179.
47 SofSI to GOI, 28.1.1898, *Parliamentary*, Cd. 8713/4, p. 173; Harris, *British Policy*, 1960, pp. 140–1.
48 Howell, *Mizh*, 1979, pp. 17–19; GP to GOI FD, 17.8.1900, *Parliamentary*, Cd. 1177, p. 120.
49 PO Wana, Note, 14.5.1900, *Parliamentary*, Cd. 1177, p. 136. Mistakes had inevitably been made, Watson said (PO Wana, Note, 14.5.1900, *Parliamentary*, Cd. 1177, p. 134).
50 PO Wana, 17.7.1900, Annexure 8, *Parliamentary*, Cd. 1171, p. 141.
51 IOR: Resident to CC NWFP, No. 101, 5.9.1910, Reg. 1811, L/PS/10/44.
52 Harris, *British Policy*, 1960, pp. 180–1.
53 Howell, *Mizh*, 1979, p. 19; IOR: C DD to GP, No. 177C, 26.5.95, in GP to GOI, 10.6.95, No. 58, L/P&S/7/85.
54 Howell, *Mizh*, 1979, p. 19.
55 Ibid., p. 17; Johnston, *Report*, 1901, p. 65; SofSI to GG, 8.5.1896, *Parliamentary*, Cd. 8713/4, p. 58, Harris, *British Policy*, 1960, p. 186.
56 Johnston, *Report*, 1901, p. 72.
57 Ibid., pp. 74–5.
58 IOR: Bruce, Memo., para. 60, L/P&S/7/59. The lieutenant-governor commented in 1890 that he had given valuable service for many years and that he was 'a remarkable instance of a frontier Pathan, who has been able to throw himself thoroughly in with our Government, and to adopt many English ideas without

losing the power of managing and influencing the hill tribes' (IOR: GP to GOI FD, 21.4.1890, April No. 7, PP3620.

59 The significance of this is not very clear; moieties were also found in other Pashtun groups – Samil and Gar in Miranzai for example.
60 PO Tochi Valley (TV), to C DD, 10.4.1896, *Parliamentary*, Cd. 8713/4, p. 70; Bruce, *The Tribes of Waziristan*, 1929, L/P&S/20/B290.
61 PO TV to C DD, 10.4.1896, *Parliamentary*, Cd. 8713/4, p. 70.
62 GOI FD to SofSI, 15.1.1895, No. 8, *Parliamentary*, Cd. 8713/4, pp. 43–4; GOI FD to SofSI, 1.1.1896, No. 13, *Parliamentary*, Cd. 8713/4, p. 50; GOI FD to SofSI, No. 16, 19.5.1896, *Parliamentary*, Cd. 8713/4, p. 59.
63 The Madda Khels shared equally with the Tori Khels, but it appears that the Manzar Khels had a smaller share (PO TV to C DD, 10.4.1896, *Parliamentary* Cd. 8713/4, p. 70).
64 Deputy Adjutant-General, Punjab Command to CP, *Parliamentary*, Cd. 8713/4, pp. 67–9.
65 PO TV to C DD, 10.4.1896, *Parliamentary*, Cd. 8713/4, p. 71; Sub-enclosure, in Bird to GOI FD, 25.9.1897, *Parliamentary*, Cd. 8713/4, p. 136.
66 PO TV to C DD, 10.4.1896, *Parliamentary*, Cd. 8713/4, p. 72.
67 Ibid.
68 Sub-enclosure in enclosure No. 1, 22.9.1897, *Parliamentary*, Cd. 8713/4, p. 136.
69 Sub-closure in enclosure No. 1, 22.9.1897, *Parliamentary*, Cd. 8713/4, p. 137.
70 PO TV to C DD, 19.6.1897, *Parliamentary*, Cd. 8713/4, pp. 93, 96.
71 Howell, *Mizh*, 1979, pp. 57–8. See also for example C DD to GOI, 16.6.1897, Encl. 2, *Parliamentary*, Cd. 8713/4, p. 84.
72 GP to GOI FD, 27.6.1897, *Parliamentary*, Cd. 8713/4, p. 91; also C DD to GOI FD, 16.6.1897, *Parliamentary*, Cd. 8713/4, p. 82.
73 Major-General Bird Commanding Tochi Field Force (OCTFF) to GOI FD, 13.10.1897, *Parliamentary*, Cd. 8713/4, p. 142.
74 GOI FD to SofSI, 4.11.1897, No. 36, *Parliamentary*, Cd. 8713/4, p. 130; PO TV, 19.7.1898, *Parliamentary*, Cd. 8713/4, p. 98.
75 GOI to OCTFF, 17.7.1897, *Parliamentary*, Cd. 8713/4, p. 103; OCTFF to GOI, 4.8.1897, *Parliamentary*, Cd. 8713/4, p. 111; OCTFF to FS, 17.8.1897, *Parliamentary*, Cd. 8713/4, p. 116.
76 Transl., 3.7.1897, *Parliamentary*, Cd. 8713/4, pp. 108–9.
77 Ludwig Adamec, *Historical and Political Who's Who of Afghanistan* (1975, Graz), p. 244; GOI FD to SofSI, 30.9.1897, *Parliamentary*, Cd. 8713/4, p. 115.
78 OCTFF to GOI FD, 25.8.1897, *Parliamentary*, Cd. 8713/4, pp. 133–4.
79 GOI FD to SofSI, 4.11.1897, *Parliamentary*, Cd. 8713/4, p. 131.
80 Harris, *British Policy*, 1960, p. 276.
81 Though there were a number of Mehsud raids (GP to GOI FD, 17.8.1900, *Parliamentary*, Cd. 8713/4, p. 120; C DD to GP, 27.1.1899, *Parliamentary*, Cd. 8713/4, p. 11; Howell, *Mizh*, 1979, p. 21).

82 Johnston, 1901, *Report*, pp. 65–6.
83 C DD to GP, 24.1.1900, *Parliamentary*, Cd. 1177, p. 55.
84 IOR: GOI to SofS, No. 182, 14.10.96, LP&S/7/88.
85 Howell, *Mizh*, 1979, p. 22.
86 Extract Police Diary, 13.1.1900, *Parliamentary*, Cd. 1177, pp. 79–80. By this time the Mehsuds had begun to buy the modern weapons which were becoming increasingly available from arms dealers via the Persian Gulf in the late nineteenth century, the Mehsud colony near Tank provided 'a meeting place for raiding gangs where they could store weapons and stolen property' (Note AC, 1.2.1902, *Parliamentary*, Cd. 1177, p. 274).
87 Note, AC, 1.2.1902, *Parliamentary*, Cd. 1177, pp. 273–5.
88 CC NWFP to GOI FD, 2.1.1902, *Parliamentary*, Cd. 1177, p. 256.
89 C DD to GP, 24.1.1900, *Parliamentary*, Cd. 1177, p. 55.
90 Note PO Wana, 14.5.1900, *Parliamentary*, Cd. 1177, p. 134. As Watson put it, 'Leading men come to see the Political Officer to air their grievances or to protest against their fines, as they had never done before.'
91 Tel. C DD to GP 26.1.1901, *Parliamentary*, Cd. 1177, p. 187.
92 GP to C DD, 26.1.1901, *Parliamentary*, Cd. 1177, p. 57; Howell, *Mizh*, 1979, p. 25.
93 Merk had previously managed relations with the Mohmands and Afridis.
94 C DD to GP, 30.3.1900, *Parliamentary*, Cd. 1177, p. 63.
95 Howell, *Mizh*, 1979, p. 26.
96 C DD to GP, 30.3.1900, *Parliamentary*, Cd. 1177, p. 62.
97 Ibid.
98 Ibid., p. 63.
99 Ibid.
100 Ibid., p. 58.
101 Ibid., p. 88; Note, C DD, 24.7.1900, *Parliamentary*, Cd. 1177, p. 127.
102 Harris, *British Policy*, 1960, pp. 285–8, 300. The forward policy had many critics, even in the military; Colonel Henry Hanna, for example, questioned its value in three essays he wrote in 1895–6 (James Hevia, *The Imperial Security State British Colonial Knowledge and Empire-Building in Asia* [2012, Cambridge], pp. 228–9).
103 Harris, *British Policy*, 1960, pp. 332, 390.
104 In ibid., p. 324.
105 Harris, *British Policy*, 1960, Ch. 9, *passim*.
106 The Punjab government objected strongly to the new arrangements, and the fact that it was not consulted about them before they were introduced led to considerable acrimony (Harris, *British Policy*, 1960, p. 376).
107 Howell, *Mizh*, 1979, pp. 29–30; GP to GOI FD, 17.8.1900, *Parliamentary*, Cd. 1177, p. 121.
108 Note, C DD, 24.7.1900, *Parliamentary*, Cd. 1177, p. 131.
109 IOR: CC NWFP to FD GOI, No. 47M, 7.9.1909, Reg. 1811, L/P&S/44.

110 C on Special Duty (SD), 20.3.1902, *Parliamentary*, Cd. 1177, p. 286.
111 C DD to GP, 18.5.1901, *Parliamentary*, Cd. 1177, p. 200.
112 IOR: CC NWFP to FD GOI, No. 1579, 7.9.1910. Reg. 1811, L/P&S/10/44; C on Special Duty (SD) to CC NWFP, No. 817 B, 20.3.1902, *Parliamentary*, Cd. 1177, p. 288.
113 IOR: CC NWFP to GOI FD, No. 1142, 9.11.1906, Reg. 2033, L/P&S/10/42.
114 Note, C DD, 24.7.1900, *Parliamentary*, Cd. 1177, p. 131.
115 Ibid.
116 Note, C DD, 24.7.1900, *Parliamentary*, Cd. 1177, p. 132; Harris, *British Policy*, 1960, p. 429.
117 Howell, *Mizh*, 1979, p. 31.
118 For example, an attack on the Kot Nasran Post in which two police were killed and several guns carried off; Lieutenant Hennessey was killed in pursuit of the raiders (*Parliamentary*, Cd. 1177, p. 155).
119 'The New Policy in Waziristan', *Times*, 17.8.1901, p. 13, *Times Digital Archive 1785-2010*, https://www.gale.com/intl/c/the-times-digital-archive.
120 GOI FD to SofSI, 30.1.1902, *Parliamentary*, Cd. 1177, p. 155.
121 C DD to GP, 17.6.1901, *Parliamentary*, Cd. 1177, p. 211.
122 GOI FD to SofSI, 30.1.1902, *Parliamentary*, Cd. 1177, p. 156.
123 Quoted in Baha, *Administration*, 1978, p. 37; see also Howell, *Mizh*, 1979, p. 22.
124 Tel. C DD to GP, 18.5.1901, *Parliamentary*, Cd. 1177, p. 195.
125 Ibid.
126 'The New Policy in Waziristan', *The Times*, 17.8.1901, p. 13, *Times Digital Archive 1785-2010*, https://www.gale.com/intl/c/the-times-digital-archive. Merk described the Mehsuds as 'seething' with 'political parties and … private feuds and quarrels' (C DD to GP, 18.5.1901, *Parliamentary*, Cd. 1177, p. 201).
127 C DD to GP, 28.5.1901, *Parliamentary*, Cd. 1177, p. 205.
128 C DD to GP, 8.5.1901, *Parliamentary*, Cd. 1177, p. 190; C DD to GP, 18.5.1901, *Parliamentary*, Cd. 1177, p. 195; GP to GOI FD, 20.5.1901, *Parliamentary*, Cd. 1177, p. 197, GOI FD to GP, 23.5.1901, *Parliamentary*, Cd. 1177, p. 198.
129 In 1900 the Punjab Land Alienation Act had been passed to prevent moneylenders acquiring land from their debtors.
130 C DD to GP, 8.10.1902, *Parliamentary*, Cd. 1177, p. 239; DC Bannu to C DD, 25.9.1901, *Parliamentary*, Cd. 1177, p. 241.
131 C DD to FS, 4.11.1901, *Parliamentary*, Cd. 1177, p. 24; Howell, *Mizh*, 1979, pp. 29–36.
132 Report Commandant South Waziristan Militia (SWM), 1.12.1901, *Parliamentary*, Cd. 1177, p. 266.
133 Howell, *Mizh*, 1979, p. 33.
134 AC SWM Column to C on SD, 27.11.1901, *Parliamentary*, Cd. 1177, p. 258.

135 Tel. C on SD to CC, 6.3.1902, *Parliamentary,* Cd. 1177, p. 280.
136 Howell, *Mizh,* 1979, p. 33. Mullah Powindah played a part; Crump later described it as the mullah's *bundobast* (agreement) (IOR: PA W to CC NWFP, 25.11.1905, Reg. 513, L/P&S/10/42).
137 Howell, *Mizh,* 1979, p. 34; CC NWFP to FS, 27.3.1902, *Parliamentary,* Cd. 1177, p. 283; Tel. No. 673B, C on SD, 6.3.1902, *Parliamentary,* Cd. 1177, p. 280.
138 Howell, *Mizh,* 1979, p. 43.
139 Baha, *Administration,* 1978, p. 39, Howell, *Mizh,* 1979, p. 34.
140 Tel. No. 673B, C on SD, 6.3.1902, *Parliamentary,* Cd. 1177, p. 280.
141 Howell, *Mizh,* 1979, p. 34.
142 Reportedly the khalifa Nur Muhammad of Margha (who had visited Jandola in 1893 on behalf of the amir) was also involved (Howell, *Mizh,* 1979, p. 36; IOR: V to Amir, 26.5.1902, No. 17, Reg. 1459A, L/P&S/7/149).
143 Howell, *Mizh,* 1979, p. 38.
144 Ludwig Adamec, *Afghanistan, 1900-1923: A Diplomatic History* (1967, Berkeley, CA), p. 78.
145 Howell, *Mizh,* 1979, pp. 38-9; IOR: Encl. to encl. No. 24, W PD, w/b 24.5.1902, Reg. 1459A, L/P&S/7/149, p. 19.
146 IOR: GOI to CC NWFP, No. 48, 30.9.1902, Reg. 1459A, L/P&S/7/149, p. 24; Howell, *Mizh,* 1979, p. 37.
147 IOR: CC NWFP to GOI FD, No. 627-N, 7.8.1902, Reg. No. 1448A, L/P&S/7/149.
148 IOR: PO Wana to CC NWFP, no day, 7.1902, IOR: Reg. 1448A, L/P&S/7/149; Howell, *Mizh,* 1979, p. 35.
149 IOR: PA W to CC NWFP, No. 693, 18.9.1906, Reg. 1756, L/P&S/10/43.
150 Baha, *Administration,* 1978, p. 40.
151 Howell, *Mizh,* 1979, p. 99.
152 According to Crump, in all but 231 cases each householder elected himself and took from the Rs.16,000 a share in proportion to his share in the Rs.54,000 list (IOR: PA W to CC NWFP, No. 693, 18.9.1906, Reg. 1756, L/P&S/10/43).
153 Johnston to Deane, quoted in Baha, *Administration,* 1978, p. 41.
154 Ibid.
155 Howell, *Mizh,* 1979, p. 36.
156 Ibid., p. 40.
157 IOR: PA W to CC NWFP, 25.11.1905, No. 25, Reg. 513, L/P&S/10/42.
158 Howell, *Mizh,* 1979, p. 39.
159 IOR: Gazetteer of the Bannu District Peshawar: NWFP Govt, 1907-13 Pt A (1907), p. 38; L/P&S/7/149, CC to GOI, 18.9.02.
160 Harris, *British Policy,* 1960, p. 336.
161 Beattie, *Imperial,* 2002, p. 157.

Chapter 4

1. IOR: Memo. PA W in CC NWFP to GOI FD, No. 359, 5.7.1907, Reg. 1756, L/P&S/10/43.
2. IOR: CC to FS. No. 407, 11.7.1906, Reg. 1684, L/P&S/10/42.
3. Ibid. We might compare him, at least in some respects, to the religious leaders in Swat, to whom Barth referred as Saints – according to him they took 'numerous variables into account' and had to be 'rather clever' (Barth, *Political Leadership*, 1959, p. 98).
4. IOR: CC to FD, 14.3.1905, Reg. 803, L/P&S/10/42; Memo. in CC NWFP to GOI FD, No. 359, 5.7.1907, Reg. 1756, L/P&S/10/43.
5. IOR: PA W, Memo. in, CC NWFP to GOI FD, No. 359, 5.7.1907, Reg. 1756, L/P&S/10/43; Howell, in Caroe, *Pathans*, 1957, pp. 471–2.
6. He was reported to have arranged for the murder, for example, of Maulvi Ghulam Muhammad (IOR: Memo. PA W, in CC NWFP to GOI FD, No. 359, 5.7.1907, Reg. 1756, L/P&S/10/43).
7. IOR: Extract S. Waz. Political Diary (SWPD), week beginning 8.9.1907, No. 32, Reg. 2015, L/P&S/10/43. Some contemporary jihadi groups encourage members to sing songs (*anashid*) extolling the virtues of violent jihad (Thomas Hegghammer, 'Non-military Practices in Jihadi Groups', in Thomas Hegghammer (ed.), *Jihadi Culture The Art and Social Practices of Militant Islamists*' [2017, Cambridge], pp. 188–9).
8. Howell quoted in Caroe, *Pathans*, 1957, p. 471.
9. IOR: PA W to CC NWFP, No. 234, 22.2.8, Reg. 254, L/P&S/10/44.
10. Hobsbawm, *Bandits*, 2000, p. 23.
11. Haroon, *Frontier*, 2007, p. 72.
12. IOR: PA W to CC NWFP, No. 25, 25.11.1905, Reg. 513, L/P&S/10/42.
13. Beattie, *Imperial*, 2002, pp. 203, 205.
14. IOR: CC to GOI FD, No. 716P, 3.5.1905, Reg. 1621, L/P&S/10/42.
15. IOR: CC NWFP to GOI FD, No. 1288, 10.10.1904, Reg. 498, L/P&S/10/42.
16. Charles Chevenix-Trench, *The Frontier Scouts* (1986, Oxford University Press), p. 18; also IOR: CC NWFP to GOI FD, No. 1288, 10.10.1904, Reg. 498, L/P&S/10/42. According to Chevenix-Trench, he was killed by his own brother (Chevenix-Trench, *The Frontier Scouts*, 1986, p. 18). The attacks appear in some ways to resemble the 'green on blue' attacks that have been carried out against NATO troops in Afghanistan (Bill Roggio and Lisa Lindquist, 'Green on Blue attacks in Afghanistan: The Data', *FDD's Long War Journal* [2017], https://www.rea lcleardefense.com/articles/2017/03/21/green-on-blue_attacks_in_afghanistan_ the_data_111015.html).
17. IOR: Lepel Griffin, Frontier Memo., Feb. No. 150, IP P1216.

18 Herbert Edwardes, *Political Diaries of Lieut. H.B. Edwardes* (1911, Allahabad), pp. 188–9.
19 Ibid., p. 223, see also Lady Edwardes, *Memorials of the Life and Letters of Major-General Sir Herbert Edwardes*, Vol. I (1886, London), p. 244.
20 IOR: DC DIK, No. 3, 19.1.1856, in CC Punjab (P), to GOI FD, No. 48, 21.1.1856, L/P&S/5/226, and DC DIK, No. 5, 21.1.56, in CC P to GOI FD, No. 52, 21.1.1856, L/P&S/5/226.
21 Lady Edwardes, *Memorials*, Vol. I, 1886, pp. 226–7.
22 Letter to James, 25.9.53, in Sir John Lawrence Papers, MSS Eur F.90 3 No. 1A, Demi-Official Correspondence (DOC), September 1850 to September 1853; Charles Allen, *God's Terrorists The Wahhabi Cult and the Hidden Roots of Modern Jihad* (2007, London), p. 24.
23 IOR: C PD to GP, No. 94, 7.10.65, October No. 91, IP P204/79; C PD to Judicial C P, No. 11, 28.1.1865, March 1865, IP 204/77; Qeyamuddin Ahmad, *The Wahhabi Movement in India* (1966, Calcutta).
24 IOR: *PAR 1866-67*, V/10/28, p. 34.
25 Edwardes ordered his first would-be assassin's body to be hung from a scaffold because he thought this would take away 'the virtue of Musulman martyrdom' (Edwardes, *Diaries*, 1911, p. 223). Usually British officials argued that it was important to burn a *shahid*'s body and scatter the ashes (see for example Bruce, *The Forward Policy*, 1900, p. 242). It is not clear that this was much of a deterrent.
26 IOR: PA W, Memo. in CC NWFP to GOI FD, No. 359, 5.7.1907, Reg. 1756, L/P&S/10/43.
27 Christopher Wyatt, *Afghanistan and the Defence of Empire Diplomacy and Strategy during the Great Game* (2011, London/New York), pp. 25–6.
28 Singhal, *India*, 1963, pp. 107–8.
29 Ewans, *Afghanistan*, 2001, pp. 81–2; Singhal, *India*, 1963, p. 167; Wyatt, *Afghanistan*, 2011, Ch. 4, *passim*.
30 Adamec, *Afghanistan*, 1967, pp. 61–2.
31 In Hall, *Brief Guide*, 1981, p. 23.
32 Harman had fallen out with Mullah Powindah's nephew, Faqir Muhammad, who felt that Harman had insulted him at the allowance jirga held at Jandola in December 1904 (IOR: PA W, Memo. in CC to GOI FD, No. 359, 5.7.1907, Reg. 1756, L/P&S/10/43).
33 Quoted by Howell in Caroe, *Pathans*, 1957, p. 473.
34 IOR: CC NWFP to GOI FD, No. 418P, 14.3.1905, Reg. 803, L/P&S/10/42.
35 Howell, quoted in Caroe, *Pathans*, 1957, p. 477.
36 See IOR: Tochi Political Diary (TPD), w.e. 31.3.1905, Reg. 1621, L/P&S/10/42.
37 IOR: Encl. No. 27, TPD, w.e. 28.2.1905, Reg. 803, L/P&S/10/42.

38 Baha, *Administration*, 1978, p. 41, Howell, *Mizh*, 1979, pp. 38–9, 42; see also Howell, 'Armon' (Appendix D in Caroe, *Pathans*, 1957, p. 477).
39 IOR: Officer Commanding Bannu to Adjutant-General in India, No. 835, 18.2.1905, Reg. 835, L/P&S/10/42.
40 IOR: CC NWFP to GOI FD, no. 418P, 14.3.1905, Reg. 803, L/P&S/10/42. According to Deane, they 'cherished that insensate greed which regards as a vested interest any reward once paid in return for services, quite irrespective of how these services were performed' (IOR: CC NWFP to GOI FD, No. 418P, 14.3.1905, Reg. 803, L/P&S/10/42).
41 IOR: CC NWFP to GOI FD, 14.3.05, Reg. 418P, L/P&S/10/42; W PD, 31.5.1902, Reg. 1459A, L/PS/7/149.
42 IOR: PA W, Memo, in CC NWFP to GOI FD, 5.7.1907, No. 359, Reg. 1756, L/P&S/10/43.
43 IOR: TPD, w.e. 26.11.1905, Reg. 513, L/P&S/10/42.
44 IOR: Extract TPD, w.e. 10.12.1905, Reg. 513, L/P&S/10/42.
45 IOR: DC Bannu to CC NWFP, Tel. 113, 16.11.1905, Reg. 513, L/P&S/10/42.
46 Baha, *Administration*, 1978, p. 42.
47 IOR: V to SofSI, 18.1.1906, Reg. 310, L/P&S/10/42; also PA W to CC NWFP, No. 488, 11.6.1906, Reg. 1684 in Encl. No. 35, L/P&S/10/42; CC, NWFP to GOI FD, No. 1142P, 13.12.1905, Reg. 513 in Encl. No. 8, L/P&S/10/42; Baha, *Administration*, 1978, pp. 42–3.
48 IOR: Tel. SofSI to V., Encl. No. 24, 30.1.1906, Reg. 513, L/P&S/10/42.
49 IOR: Tel. CC to FS, No. 97, Encl. No. 3, 2.3.1906, in Reg. 1684, L/P&S/10/42.
50 IOR: TPD, w.e. 10.6.1906, Encl. No. 3 in Reg. 1684, L/P&S/10/42.
51 IOR: Tel. CC to FS, 9.3.1906, No. 122, Encl. No. 9, Reg. 1684, L/P&S/10/42; Tel. FS to CC NWFP, 11.3.1906, No. 873, Encl. 11, Reg. 1684, L/P&S/10/42; W PD, w.e. 7.5.1906, Encl. No. 22, Reg. 1684, L/P&S/10/42.
52 IOR: PA W to CC, No. 488, 11.6.1906, Encl. No.35, Reg. 1684, L/P&S/10/42.
53 IOR: SWPD, w.e. 20.10.1906, Reg. 1830, L/P&S/10/43.
54 IOR: PA W to CC, No. 488, 11.6.1906, Encl. No. 35, Reg. 1684, L/P&S/10/42.
55 IOR: CC NWFP to FS, 11.7.1906, No. 407, Encl. No. 35, Reg. 1684, L/P&S/10/42.
56 IOR: FS to CC NWFP, 22.8.1906, No. 2703, Reg. 1684, L/P&S/10/42.
57 IOR: TPD, w.e. 27.5.1906, Reg. 1259, L/P&S/10/42. According to this report he showed up the Karbogha mullah for his lack of knowledge and denounced him as a Wahhabi (in other words a supporter of the Mujahidin colony founded by Sayyid Ahmed Bareilly and its supporters); he also accused him of having ordered Mullah Powindah to arrange the murder of another religious leader, Maulvi Ghulam Hussain. The missionary, Theodore Pennell, who spent twenty years on the frontier in the later nineteenth century, however, met the mullah and said that he excelled in 'the more abstruse theological speculations' (Theoodore Pennell, *Among the Wild Tribes of the Afghan Frontier* [1909, London], p. 123).
58 IOR: PA W to CC NWFP, No. 488, 11.6.1906, Encl. 35, Reg. 1864, L/P&S/10/42.

59 IOR: PA W to CC NWFP, No. 693, 18.9.1906, Reg. 1756, L/P&S/10/43.
60 Ibid.
61 Ibid. We might recall that Ogilvie and Bruce had also raised the possibility of creating such a jirga.
62 IOR: CC to FS, No. 407, 11.7.06, Encl. 35, 11.7.1906, L/P&S/10/42.
63 IOR: FS to CC NWFP, No. 2703, 22.8.1906, Reg. 2033, L/P&S/10/42.
64 IOR: CC NWFP to GOI FD, No. 1142, 9.11.1906, Reg. 2011, L/P&S/10/42.
65 IOR: Resident (R) Waziristan (W), to CC NWFP, No. 101, 5.9.1910, Reg. 1811, L/P&S/10/44.
66 Howell, *Mizh*, 1979, p. 45.
67 IOR: PA W to CC NWFP, No. 806, 15.10.1906, Reg. 1830, L/P&S/10/43.
68 IOR: SWPD, Reg. 1830, 6.10.1906, L/P&S/10/43. The feud between Kalagai's family and the mullah is described in Curtis, *MMT*, 1947, p. 38.
69 IOR: R W to CC NWFP, 1.12.1909, Reg. 1811, L/P&S/10/44.
70 Ibid.
71 IOR: Tel., CC to FS, 8.10.1906, Reg. 1830, L/P&S/10/43; Tel., Vic. to CC, No. 12, 11.12.06, , Reg. 1830, L/P&S/10/43.
72 IOR: Tel., 65C, FS to CC, 23.10.1906, L/P&S/10/43.
73 Wyatt, *Afghanistan*, 2011, p. 135; Ludwig Adamec, *Afghanistan's Foreign Affairs to the Mid-Twentieth Century Relations with the USSR, Germany, and Britain* (1974, Tucson), p. 14. The Sardar had visited Britain in 1898.
74 See for example Tochi PD (TPD), w.e. 22.9.1907, Reg. 2015, L/P&S/10/43; Senzil Nawid, *Religious Response to Social Change in Afghanistan 1919-29* (1999, Costa Mesa), pp. 33–4; Edwards, *Heroes*, 1996, p. 112; Ewans, *Afghanistan*, 2001, p. 80.
75 IOR: Note on the Afghan Project for Maintaining Afghan Khassadars in Waziristan, R W), in Memo. 7631-169-G. S., 23.5.1923, L/P&S/10/953, p. 196b. Safar was an official (Nazir) and keeper of Amir's Seal at Amir Abdur Rahman's Court and was 'a much-trusted officer' also said to have been in charge of intelligence, but he did not have so much influence with Amir Habibullah (Adamec, *Historical and Political*, 1975, p. 222).
76 Nawid, *Religious*, 1999, p. 34.
77 IOR: SW PD, 24.11.1906, Reg. 1830, L/P&S/10/43. Howell, *Mizh*, 1979, p. 46.
78 Curtis referred to him as the Shabi Khel 'general'; presumably the GOA had awarded him the title (Curtis, *MMT*, 1947, p. 38).
79 IOR: W PD w.e. 27.4.1907, Reg. 1000, L/P&S/10/43.
80 IOR: CC to FS GOI, No. 259P, 15.2.1907, Reg. 490, L/P&S/10/43.
81 IOR: Vic. to SofS, No. 167, 26.9.1907, Reg. 1830, L/P&S/10/43.
82 Baha, *Administration*, 1978, p. 45.
83 IOR: PA W to GOI FD, No. 200-W, 4.5.1907, Reg. 1036, L/P&S/10/43.
84 IOR: CC NWFP to PA W, No. 846P, 15.5.1907, Reg. 1036, L/P&S/10/43.
85 IOR: PA W to GOI FD, No. 200-W, 4.5.1907, Reg. 1036, L/P&S/10/43.

86 IOR: Note on the Afghan Project, in Memo. 7631-169-G. S., 23.5.1923, L/P&S/10/953, p. 196b; Nawid, *Religious*, 1999, p. 33; Ewans, *Afghanistan*, 2001, p. 83; 'Anglo-Russian Convention of 1907', F. Kazemzadeh, *Encyclopedia Iranica*, Vol. II, Fasc. 1, pp. 68–70. http://www.iranicaonline.org/articles/anglo-russian-convention-of-1907-an-agreement-relating-to-persia-afghanistan-and-tibet; Beattie, *Imperial*, 2002, p. 205.

87 IOR: SWPD No. 32, w.e. 14.9.1907, Reg. 2015, L/P&S/10/43.

88 Nawid, *Religious*, 1999, p. 35; Barfield, *Afghanistan*, 2010, p. 177.

89 IOR: PA W, Memo. in CC NWFP to GOI FD, No. 359, 5.7.1907, Reg. 1756, L/P&S/10/43; Baha, *Administration*, 1978, p. 45.

90 Minto quoted in Baha, *Administration*, 1978, p. 45.

91 Baha, *Administration*, 1978, pp. 45–6; IOR: PA W to CC NWFP, No. 234, 22.2.1908, Reg. 854, L/P&S/10/44.

92 IOR: TPD, No. XLI, w.e. 13.10.1907, Reg. 2063, L/P&S/10/43; also CC NWFP to GOI FD, No. 1461, 7.10.1907, Reg. 2063, L/P&S/10/43.

93 IOR: Appendix III. Transl. of statement of Gulband, son of Gul Imam, caste (*sic*) Langar Khel (Mehsud) of Kot Langar of Mehsud illaka, with No. 759, 25.9.1907, PA W to CC NWFP, Reg. No. 2015, L/P&S/10/43.

94 In Jamiat-Islami suicide attacks in Indonesia, 'Strong-willed seniors persuade younger men who seem somewhat vulnerable and marginalized that death for a cause bestows on life something sure and good' (Scott Atran, *Talking to the Enemy: Violent Extremism, Sacred Values, and What It Means to Be Human* [2010, London] p. 167).

95 Such as the Tori Khel Wazir, Mir Alam (IOR: Tochi (T) PD, no. XL1, 13.10.1907, Reg. 2063, L/P&S/10/43).

96 Stephen Dale, 'Religious Suicide in Islamic Asia: Anticolonial Terrorism in India, Indonesia, and the Philippines', *Journal of Conflict Resolution*, Vol. 32 (1988), No. 1, pp. 37–59 (p. 53).

Chapter 5

1 IOR: W PD w.e. 26.10.1907, Reg. 2063, L/P&S/10/43.

2 Curtis, *MMT*, 1947, pp. 38–40.

3 IOR: FS to CC NWFP, Tel. No. S-542. 6.12.1907, Reg. 2197, L/P&S/10/43.

4 Howell, *Mizh*, 1979, p. 47. During the autumn the influential pro-British Spirkai Wazir malik Mani Khan (grandson of Swahn Khan, mentioned in Chapter 1) also presented a petition - to the chief commissioner; in it he called on the government to establish posts in Waziristan and open a road through it from the Tochi to Wana.

5 IOR: PA W to CC NWFP, No. 234, 22.2.1908, Reg. 854, L/P&S/10/44. There are some parallels here with the bank robberies and kidnappings carried out by some of the Pakistani Taliban in the 2000s (see for example Arabinda Acharya, Syed Adnan Bukhari and Sadia Sulaiman, 'Making Money in the Mayhem: Funding Taliban Insurrection in the Tribal Areas of Pakistan', *Studies in Conflict & Terrorism*, Vol. 32 [2009], No. 2, p. 100).
6 IOR: PA W, No. 39, w.e. 2.11.1907, Reg. No. 2015, L/P&S/10/43.
7 IOR: PA W to CC N-WF, No. 234, 22.2.1908, Reg. 854, P L/P&S/10/44.
8 Quoted in Baha, *Administration*, 1978, p. 47; IOR: PA W to CC NWFP, No. 234, 22.10.1908, L/P&S/10/44.
9 Baha, *Administration*, 1978, p. 47.
10 IOR: Note by L.M. Crump on the Settlement of Waziristan, Reg. 633, in L/P&S/7/227.
11 Christian Tripodi, *Edge of Empire: The British Political Officer and Tribal Administration on the North-West Frontier 1877-1947* (2011, Farnham/Burlington, VT), p. 144; Baha, *Administration*, 1978, p. 47; Howell, *Mizh*, 1979, p. 49.
12 Howell, *Mizh*, 1979, p. 49.
13 Baha, *Administration*, 1978, p. 48; Howell, *Mizh*, 1979, p. 50.
14 IOR: Note by PA W, n.d., Reg. 668, L/P&S/10/44.
15 IOR: CC NWFP to GOI FD, No. A, 27.12.1909, Reg. 430, L/P&S/10/44.
16 Howell, *Mizh*, 1979, p. 52. It was equivalent to around £130,000 at the then current exchange rate of fifteen rupees to the pound sterling.
17 IOR: CC NWFP to GOI FD, No. A, 27.12.1909, Reg. 430, L/P&S/10/44.
18 IOR: CC NWFP (Merk) to FD GOI, No. 1579, 7.9.1910, Reg. 1811, L/P&S/10/44.
19 IOR: Extract Monthly Memo. June 1909, in letter from India No. 29M, 15.7.1909, Register No. 1105, L/P&S/10/44.
20 At this time the new political tehsildar was reported to have made a deal with the chief Abdur Rahman Khel raider, Muhammad Jan, according to which the Abdur Rahman Khels would be paid, unofficially, an extra allowance of Rs.6,000.
21 Howell, *Mizh*, 1979, pp. 51, 53.
22 'Khost Province District Studies', Audrey Roberts, www.tribalanalysiscenter.com/PDF-TAC/Khost Province District Studies (20 May 2013).pdf
23 In April 1909 a Bakka Khel Wazir sepoy in the North Waziristan militia shot and seriously wounded the commandant, Captain Keene (IOR: Tel. PA T to GOI FD, No. 150, 28.4.1907, Reg. 840, L/P&S/10/44).
24 Howell, *Mizh*, 1979, p. 54. In addition an Afghan Border Commission was set up to visit the Tochi and Kurram borders, on which Donald was the British representative (Wyatt, *Afghanistan*, 2011, p. 198; 'The North-West Frontier of India', *The Times*, 15.6.1910, https://www.gale.com/intl/c/the-times-digital-archive).

25 IOR: Memo. of information received, p. 3, Reg. 219, L/P&S/10/44.
26 Ibid.
27 IOR: CC NWFP to GOI FD, No. A, 27.12.1909, Reg. 430, L/P&S/10/44.
28 Ibid.
29 Howell, *Mizh*, 1979, pp. 36, 95.
30 IOR: CC NWFP to FD GOI, No. 1579, 7.9.1910 (para. 5), Reg. No. 1811, L/P&S/10/44.
31 IOR: Extract from N.-W. Frontier Provincial Diary, No. 53 for w.e. 31.12.1910, L/P&S/10/44.
32 IOR: Memo. of information received during December 1910, Reg. 219, L/P&S/10/44; Baha, *Administration*, 1978, p. 49; Howell, *Mizh*, 1979, p. 53.
33 Wyatt, *Afghanistan*, 2011, p. 197.
34 IOR: R W (Pears), Note on the Afghan Project, in Memo. 7631-169-G. S., 23.5.1923, L/P&S/10/953, p. 197b.
35 IOR: *North-West Frontier Province Administration Report (NWFP AR) 1911-12*, p. 5, V/10/371.
36 Howell, *Mizh*, 1979, pp. 52, 54.
37 Ibid., p. 54.
38 IOR: CC N-WFP to FS, Tel. P., No. 11 M, 6.3.1912, Reg. No. 1088, L/PS/11/14.
39 Howell, *Mizh*, 1979, p. 53. Montagu's Statement, *The Times*, 8.8.1913, *The Times Digital Archive 1785-2010*, https://www.gale.com/intl/c/the-times-digital-archive.
40 Rebels established themselves on the Kurram border and had to be persuaded to leave (IOR: *NWFP AR 1912-13*, p. i, V/10/371).
41 Ibid.
42 IOR: Tel., V to SofSI, No. 1071-S, 27.8.1923, L/P&S/S10/953, p. 109.
43 Howell, *Mizh*, 1979, p. 58. The British naval blockade had restricted the arms trade across the Persian Gulf, but enterprising men began to establish new workshops to manufacture arms in various places along the frontier, including Waziristan (IOR: *NWFP AR 1912-13*, p. ii, V/10/371).
44 IOR: *NWFP AR 1913-14*, p. i, V/10/372; CUL: Harding, Vol. 120, Part 2, pp. 21, 49.
45 Wyatt, *Afghanistan*, 2011, p. 199.
46 He is mentioned in No. 1C, 12.3.1917, PA SW to R W, L/P&S/10/373 (IOR).
47 Howell, *Mizh*, 1979, p. 60.
48 *Parliamentary*, Cd. 1177, p. 215.
49 Howell, *Mizh*, 1979, p. 60.
50 Wyatt, *Afghanistan*, 2011, p. 292.
51 While in some ways his career was comparable with theirs, he did not have the same influence as some of the better-known leaders of anti-European resistance such as Shamyl in the Caucasus, the so-called Mad Mullah in Somaliland, the Sanusi *sheikhs* in Libya, al-Muqrani in Algeria and Abd al-Qadir in Algeria.
52 IOR: *NWFP AR 1913-14*, p. i, V/10/371.

53 Howell, *Mizh*, 1979, p. 63; Baha, *Administration*, 1978, p. 51.
54 Howell, *Mizh*, 1979, p. 64; Baha, *Administration*, 1978, pp. 50–1.
55 Howell, *Mizh*, 1979, pp. 59–63.
56 IOR: No. 2017, PA W to CC NWFP, 2.11.1915, Reg. 4780, L/P&S/10/373; Memo. R W (Pears), No. 743, 2.8.1922, L/P&S/10/952; CUL: CC NWFP to V., 19.7.1914, in Hardinge, Vol. 120, Part 2, p. 125.
57 CUL: CC NWFP to V, 29.5.1914, Hardinge, Vol. 120, Part 2, pp. 90–1; V. to SofSI, 30.7.1914, Hardinge, Vol. 120, Part 2, p. 121; IOR: *NWFP AR 1914-15*, p. ii, V/10/372; also Howell, *Mizh*, 1979, p. 64.
58 CUL: CC NWFP to V, 19.7.1914, Hardinge, Vol. 120, Part 2, p. 126.
59 Alan Warren, *Waziristan, The Faqir of Ipi and the Indian Army: The North-West Frontier Revolt of 1936-37* (2000, Karachi), p. 37.
60 Howell, *Mizh*, 1979, p. 65.
61 CUL: Sir Beauchamp Duff to Hardinge, 21.1.1915, No. 50, Hardinge, Vol. 89, Part One, p. 43. The whole company was imprisoned in Rangoon Jail for the duration of the war (Curtis, *MMT*, 1947, p. 219).
62 Howell *Mizh*, 1979, p. 66.
63 Ibid., p. 68.
64 IOR: Kabul Diary (KD), 24.12.14, L/P&S/10/201.
65 See for example IOR: KD, 8.12.14, L/P&S/10/201.
66 Howell, *Mizh*, 1979, p. 69.
67 CUL: Roos-Keppel to Hardinge, 7.5.1915, No. 269, Hardinge Vol. 89, Part One, p. 339.
68 Haroon, *Frontier*, 2007, pp. 97, 100.
69 More than a hundred people were killed in the settled areas during 1915–16 (Howell, *Mizh*, 1979, p. 70).
70 CUL: Roos-Keppel to Hardinge, 7.5.1915, No. 269, Hardinge Vol. 89, Part One, p. 339.
71 Thomas Hughes, 'The German Mission to Afghanistan, 1915-16', *German Studies Review*, Vol. 25 (October 2002), pp. 447–76.
72 See Hugh Beattie, *Afghanistan*, 2016, https://encyclopedia.1914-18-online.net/article/afghanistan

   One important card held by the British was that several potential rivals to the amir's throne were living in British India, among them the sons of Ayub Khan, one of the deposed amir Sher Ali's sons, and the victor at Maiwand in 1880.
73 Adamec, *Afghanistan*, 1967, p. 88.
74 The Nawab of Tank was reported to be 'badly disposed' and intriguing with the troops or the tribesmen (CUL: Roos-Keppel to Hardinge, 31.1.1916, No. 68, Vol. 91, Part One, p. 65; see also R-K to H, 22.3.1915, No. 194, Vol. 89, Part One, p. 220.

75 Haroon, *Frontier*, 2007, p. 98.
76 Beattie, *Afghanistan*, 2016, p. 10.
77 Haroon, *Frontier*, 2007, p. 96; see also Ayesha Jalal, *Partisans of Allah: Jihad in South Asia* (2008, Cambridge, MA/London), pp. 203–4.
78 Jalal, *Partisans*, 2008, p. 206.
79 Saul Kelly, '"Crazy in the Extreme"? The Silk Letters Conspiracy', *Middle Eastern Studies*, Vol. 49 (2013), No. 2, pp. 162–78; Haroon, *Frontier*, 2007, p. 103.
80 IOR: North-West Frontier Provincial Diary No. 49 w.e. 5.12.1914, L/PS/10/202; CUL: Roos-Keppel to Hardinge, 2.12.1914, Hardinge, Vol. 88, Part One, p. 429. The Lewanai faqir was reported to be a Ghilzai from a village near Gardez, who had served in the army under Abdur Rahman, but 'got religion'; his real name was Sahib Din (IOR: L/PS/12/1571, p. 34).
81 IOR: CC NWFP to FS GOI, No. 345P, 7.4.1915, Reg. No. 1717, L/P&S/10/373.
82 Beattie, *Afghanistan*, 2016, p. 5. There was also some raiding on the frontier to the north of Peshawar. Early in December 1915 for instance Mohmands looted and burned the Charsadda bazaar, destroying more than 250 shops with all their contents; Roos-Keppel described it as 'the biggest thing done by any tribe since the Mehsuds' attack on the Tank bazaar in 1879' (Roos-Keppel to Hardinge, 10.12.1915, Hardinge, Vol. 90, Part One, p. 423). The Mohmands were barred from British territory from October 1916 to July 1917 (Beattie, *Afghanistan*, 2016, p. 11).
83 CUL: Roos-Keppel to Hardinge, 7.5.1915, Hardinge Vol. 89, Part One, p. 338.
84 IOR: Viceroy to Amir, No. 4-P, 8.6.1917, Reg. 2084, L/P&S/10/373.
85 Howell, *Mizh*, 1979, p. 70.
86 IOR: Tel. V. to SofSI, 25.5.1915, Reg. 2179, L/P&S/10/373. Markai, Mobin, Nambai and Silla Khan were not released until the early 1920s.
87 Howell, *Mizh*, 1979, p. 70; IOR: PA W to CC NWFP, No. 2017, 2.11.1915, Reg. 4780, L/P&S/10/373, p. 37.
88 CUL: Roos-Keppel to Hardinge, 22.3.1915, Vol. 89, Part One, Hardinge, p. 217.
89 The British found it difficult to send convoys through to Sarwakai and Wana (Tel. R W to GOI FD, No. 28-T, 30.11.1915, Reg. 4780, L/P&S/10/373, pp. 36–7).
90 CUL: Roos-Keppel to Hardinge, 31.1.1916, Vol. 91, Part One, Hardinge, p. 64.
91 IOR: Tel. R W to GOI FD, No. 28, 30.11.1915, Reg. No. 4780, L/P&S/10/373, p. 36; Howell, *Mizh*, 1979, p. 71.
92 IOR: Tel. CC NWFP to GOI FD, No. 1577-R, 6.6.1917, Reg. No. 2084, L/P&S/10/373.
93 IOR: R W, No. 108, 13.3.1917, Reg. No. 1896, L/P&S/10/373.
94 IOR: Report by Informer, Reg. No. 1896, L/P&S/10/373, p. 188.

95 Theodore Copeland had been DC DIK 1911-14, then PA S W (CUL: Roos-Keppel to Hardinge, 10.3.1915, Vol. 89, Part One, Hardinge, p. 164; 'Quelling the Mahsuds Fighting in Mountain Fastnesses', *Times* (London, England) 15.4.1918, https://www.gale.com/intl/c/the-times-digital-archive).
96 IOR: Minute Paper, Tel., V to SofSI, 3.5.1917, Reg. No. 1853, L/P&S/10/373, p. 196b.
97 Howell, *Mizh*, 1979, p. 72.
98 Ibid., p. 73.
99 IOR: Tel., CC NWFP to GOI FD, No. 213, 28.4.1916, Reg. 2341, L/P&S/10/373.
100 IOR: Minute Paper, Tel. from Viceroy, 3.5.17, Reg. No. 1853, L/P&S/10/373, p. 196b.
101 IOR: PA W to CC NWFP, No. 107-C, 11.5.1917, Reg. 2804, L/P&S/10/373; Howell, *Mizh*, 1979, p. 73.
102 IOR: Transl. letter from HM Habibullah Khan to V, No. 227, 11.6.1927, Reg. No. 2957, L/P&S/10/373, pp. 39–40; Tel., GOI FD to CC NWFP, No. 702-S, 11.6.1917, Reg. No. 2957, L/P&S/10/373, pp. 39–40; V to SofSI, no number, 1.6.1917, Reg. 2251, L/P&S/10/373, pp. 39–40.
103 IOR: Tel. V to SofSI, 11.5.1917, Reg. No. 1953, L/P&S/10/373, p. 175.
104 Ibid., p. 175; Tel. CC to D.M.I., 32123 cipher, 15.5.17, L/P&S/10/373.
105 'Quelling the Mahsuds Fighting in Mountain Fastnesses', *The Times* (London, England), 15.4.1918, https://www.gale.com/intl/c/the-times-digital-archive.
106 Howell, *Mizh*, 1979, p. 73; *Operations in Waziristan 1919-20* (1921, Calcutta), p. 45, https://archive.org/details/operationsinwaz00indi.
107 IOR: Tel. CC NWFP to GOI, No. 1561-R, 5.6.1917, Reg. 2804, L/P&S/10/373; Tel. V Army Dept., 2.6.1927, Reg. 2187, L/P&S/10/373; Tel. V AD, 18.5.1917, Reg. 2060, L/P&S/10/373; IOR: Tel., V to SofSI, 21.5.1917, Reg. P2081, L/P&S/10/373.
108 IOR: CC NWFP to FS GOI, No. 204-N, 26.5.1917, Reg. 2084, L/P&S/10/373.
109 IOR: Tel. V to SofSI, 11.5.1917, Reg. 1953, L/P&S/7/373; Brian Robson, *Crisis on the Frontier: The Third Afghan War and the Campaign in Waziristan 1919-20* (2004, Staplehurst), p. 163.
110 Howell, *Mizh*, 1979, p. 75.
111 Ibid.
112 Ibid., p. 76.
113 IOR: Memo. R W, No. 2238, 10.11.1921, L/P&S/10/952, p. 201b.
114 Howell, *Mizh*, 1979, p. 77.
115 IOR: Memo. R W, No. 2238, 10.11.1921, L/P&S/10/952, p. 201b.
116 He was imprisoned by Amanullah and died some years later (Barfield, *Afghanistan*, 2010, p. 181).

Chapter 6

1. Haroon, *Frontier*, 2007, pp. 109–10; Barfield, *Afghanistan*, 2010, p. 181.
2. Robson, *Crisis*, 2004, p. 98; Chevenix-Trench, *Scouts*, 1986, p. 37.
3. Robson, *Crisis*, 2004, pp. 166–7.
4. Chevenix-Trench, *Scouts*, 1986, pp. 37–8; Robson, *Crisis*, 2004, p. 168; Adamec, *Afghanistan's*, p.90.
5. Dyer had been responsible for ordering troops to fire on demonstrators at Amritsar in April 1919, which led to several hundred deaths.
6. Adamec, *Afghanistan*, 1967, p. 122.
7. Ewans, *Afghanistan*, 2001, p. 89.
8. Haroon, *Frontier*, 2007, pp. 109–10. The South Waziristan Militia had 8 British and 7 Pashtun officers, and 1,800 other ranks, including 230 Wazirs and 780 Afridis (Chevenix-Trench, *Scouts*, 1986, 38–9). Its headquarters were at Wana and there were six outposts.
9. Robson, *Crisis*, 2004, p. 169; Chevenix-Trench, *Scouts*, 1968, pp. 38–45.
10. Robson, *Crisis*, 2004, p. 171.
11. Chevenix-Trench, *Scouts*, 1968, p. 41.
12. Howell, *Mizh*, 1979, p. 79.
13. IOR: Memo, R W, No. 51, 5.1.1928, Reg. P2982, L/P&S/10/1142, p. 29.
14. Chevenix-Trench, *Scouts*, 1986, p. 46.
15. Robson, *Crisis*, 2004, pp. 171, 173.
16. Ibid., pp. 173–4; Howell, *Mizh*, 1979, p. 80.
17. Howell, *Mizh*, 1979, p. 75.
18. Ibid., p. 81. Sheranis lived to the south of the Gumal River.
19. Ewans, *Afghanistan*, 2001, p. 90; Adamec, *Afghanistan*, 1967, pp. 128–9.
20. Adamec, *Afghanistan*, 1967, p. 132.
21. Howell, *Mizh*, 1979, p. 80; Robson, *Crisis*, 2004, pp. 172–3.
22. Howell, *Mizh*, 1979, pp. 80–1.
23. IOR: Memo. R W to W Force, No. 2010-S, 20.10.1923, L/P&S/10/953, p. 37.
24. Howell, *Mizh*, 1979, p. 82; Robson, *Crisis*, 2004, pp. 175–6.
25. IOR: 'Mujahidin. Hindustani Fanatic Colony in Waziristan', L/PS/12/3122, pp. 197–8; Haroon, *Frontier*, 2007, p. 126.
26. IOR: R W DIK, No. 2586, 1.12.1921, L/P&S/10/951, p. 113.
27. Robson, *Crisis*, 2004, pp. 180–1.
28. IOR: R W DIK, No. 2586, 1.12.1921, L/P&S/10/951, p. 113; Howell, *Mizh*, 1979, p. 89.
29. Robson, *Crisis*, 2004, pp. 200–2.
30. Ibid., p. 223.
31. Ibid., pp. 203–29; Howell, *Mizh*, 1979, p. 84.

Notes

32 Robson, *Crisis*, 2004, pp. 230–6.
33 IOR: Memo. R W to General Officer Commanding Waziristan (GOCW), No. 2234, 9.11.1921, L/P&S/10/952, p. 200.
34 James Spain, *The Pathan Borderland* (1963, The Hague), p. 183.
35 Robson, *Crisis*, 2004, p. 235. In 2017 prices around £63 million. Howell says the force suffered 366 killed, 237 missing and 1,683 wounded; he estimates that between 1,500 and 2,000 Mehsuds were killed (Howell, *Mizh*, 1979, p. 83).
36 IOR: V to SofSI, 23.3.1920, Reg. 9794, L/P&S/10/951.
37 Robson, *Crisis*, 2004, p. 232.
38 IOR: Memo. R W to GOCW, No. 2234, 9.11.1921, L/P&S/10/952, p. 200.
39 Howell, *Mizh*, 1979, p. 85.
40 Ibid.
41 IOR: R W to GOCW, No. 1563-64, 7.10.1920, L/P&S/10/952, p. 370. Matheson and Fitzpatrick did not get on well (Mark Jacobsen, *Rawlinson in India* [2002, Stroud]), p. 93.
42 Robson, *Crisis*, 2004, p. 236.
43 IOR: Memo., R W to Headquarters, W Force, No. 1419-S, 14.10.1923, L/P&S/10/953, pp. 55b–56.
44 IOR: R W Note on the Afghan Project, in Memo. 7631-169-G. S., 23.5.1923, L/P&S/10/953, p. 196b.
45 Howell, *Mizh*, 1979, p. 86; IOR: Transl. of a proclamation issued from Shakin by Haji Abdurrazzaq in council against the British government, L/P&S/10/952, pp. 251–251b.
46 IOR: *Report on the Administration of the Border (RAB) 1921-22*, p. 7, V/10/390.
47 IOR: *RAB 1925-26*, p. 16, V/10/390; *RAB 1922-23*, p. 10, V/10/390; *RAB 1921-22*, p. 8, V/10/390.
48 IOR: *RAB 1922-23*, pp. 9, 13–14, 25, V/10/390.
49 Adamec, *Afghanistan*, 1967, Ch. 7, *passim*.
50 Robson, *Crisis*, 2004, 3, pp. 236–7, Howell, *Mizh*, 1979, p. 88.
51 IOR: R W, Memo., No. 1540, 3.10.1920, L/P&S/10/952, pp. 368b–9; Howell, *Mizh*, 1979, p. 85.
52 In the autumn Wazirs attacked a regular army post between Manzai and Tank and carried off the soldiers' rifles (Robson, *Crisis*, 2004, p. 237).
53 Howell, *Mizh*, 1979, p. 80.
54 Robson, *Crisis*, 2004, pp. 238–9, 243; Howell, *Mizh*, 1979, pp. 87–8; see 'Maffey' in *Dictionary of National Biography*.
55 IOR: *RAB 1921-22*, p. 2, *RAB 1922-23*, p. 2, V/10/390; Howell, *Mizh*, 1979, p. 86.
56 Adamec, *Afghanistan*, 1967, p. 157.
57 Dobbs had been sent to Herat in 1903–4 in connection with the boundary pillars on the Afghan border with Russia, some of which needed repair; he was also

a member of the Dane Mission to Kabul in 1904–5 (Wyatt, *Afghanistan*, 2011, Chapter 1).
58 Adamec, *Afghanistan*, 1967, p. 160.
59 Saikal suggests that during the First World War the GOI had promised that it would allow the Afghans to take over Waziristan, but advances no evidence for this (Amin Saikal, *Modern Afghanistan: A History of Struggle and Survival* [2012, London], p. 65).
60 Adamec, *Afghanistan*, 1967, p. 160.
61 IOR: R W, Memo., No. 15-L, C., 13.10.1921, L/P&S/10/952, pp. 215b–6.
62 Adamec, *Afghanistan*, 1967, p. 160.
63 IOR: British Rep., Kabul Mission, Tel. P, No. 212-C, 19.7.1921, to FS GOI, L/P&S/10/952, p. 234b.
64 Rhea Talley Stewart, *Fire in Afghanistan 1914-1929: Faith, Hope and the British Empire* (1973, Garden City, NY), pp. 167–8.
65 David E. Omissi, *Air Power and Colonial Control: The Royal Air Force 1919-1939* (1990, Manchester/New York), p. 13.
66 Ibid.; IOR: Memo., No. 6997-G, 29.5.1922, OCWF, to CofGS, Simla, L/P&S/10/952, p. 81b.
67 Robson, *Crisis*, 2004, p. 236.
68 'Action of Spinchilla Pass', Supplement to the London Gazette, 4.12.1922, https://www.thegazette.co.uk/London/issue/32773/supplement/8600.data.pdf; Howell, *Mizh*, 1979, p. 87.
69 Gambier Parry, *Reynell Taylor A Biography* (1888, London), pp. 96–7.
70 IOR: Memo. R W (Pears), No. 743, 2.8.1922, L/P&S/10/952; MSS IOR: Eur. E238/24, p. 387.
71 See for example Howell, *Mizh*, 1979, p. 97.
72 IOR: *RAB 1938-39*, p. 39.
73 The raiders got away with twenty-six rifles and a number of horses and mules (Howell, *Mizh*, 1979, p. 87).
74 Tripodi suggests that the 'ferocity of the Pashtun' was a reflection of the ferocity of the British themselves (Tripodi, *Edge*, 2011, p. 13).
75 See for example Mark Condos, 'Licence to kill: The Murderous Outrages Act and the Rule of Law in Colonial India, 1867-1925', *Modern Asian Studies*, Vol. 50 (2015), No. 2, *passim*.
76 War and International Humanitarian Law', *International Committee of the Red Cross* (2010), https://www.icrc.org/eng/war-and-law/overview-war-and-law.htm
77 James Hevia, *The Imperial Security State: British Colonial Knowledge and Empire-Building in Asia* (2012, Cambridge), pp. 215–22.
78 David Omissi, 'The Hendon Air Pageant, 1920-37', in John Mackenzie (ed.) *Popular Imperialism & the Military: 1850-1950* (1992, Manchester), p. 213.
79 Con Coughlin, *Churchill's First War Young Winston and the Fight Against the Taliban* (2013, London), p. 214.

80 See for example Caspar Erichsen and David Olusoga, *The Kaiser's Holocaust: Germany's Forgotten Genocide and the Colonial Roots of Nazism* (London, 2010).

81 Omissi, *Air Power*, 1990, pp. 166, 171. Trenchard even said of the frontier tribesmen 'they have no objection to being killed' (quoted in Omissi, *Air Power*, 1990, p. 170).

82 Mumford quoted in Andrew M. Roe, *Waging War in Waziristan: The British Struggle in the Land of Bin Laden, 1849-1947* (2010, Lawrence, KS), p. 276. 'Elaborate restrictions' were imposed on the use of airpower 'for a mixture of military, political and ethical reasons' (Tim Moreman, '"Watch and Ward": The Army in India and the North-West Frontier, 1920-1939', in David Killingray and David Omissi (eds), *Guardians of Empire* [1999, Manchester], p. 145).

83 Gray quoted in Michael Finch, *A Progressive Occupation? The Gallieni-Lyautey Method and Colonial Pacification in Tonkin and Madagascar 1885-1900* (2013, Oxford), p. 12.

84 Quoted in Beattie, *Imperial*, 2002, p. 33.

85 Thomas Rid, 'The Nineteenth Century Origins of Counterinsurgency Doctrine', *Journal of Strategic Studies*, Vol. 33 (2010), No. 5, pp. 727–758; Finch, *A Progressive*, 2013, p. 40.

86 Brian Ferguson and Neil Whitehead, 'Preface to the Second Printing', in Ferguson and Whitehead (eds), *War in the Tribal Zone Expanding States and Indigenous Warfare* (1999, Santa Fe NM, Oxford), p. xxiii.

87 Anton Blok suggests that we should 'hesitate before defining violence as "senseless" or "irrational"' (*Honour and Violence* [2001, Cambridge], p. 111); see also Bettina Schmidt and Ingo Schröder, 'Introduction', in Schmidt and Schröder (eds), *Anthropology of Violence and Conflict* (2001, London/New York), p. 5.

88 Finch, *A Progressive*, 2013, pp. 24–5.

89 Al-Qaida's fighters have described their attacks as a language, 'the only one that America or the West understands. In other words these men define violence as a mode of conversation and persuasion, the common language they share with their enemies' (Faisal Devji, *Landscapes of the Jihad: Militancy, Morality, Modernity* [2008, London], p. 42).

90 'An unseen death is, in the end, a meaningless death' (Jack Eller, *Cruel Deeds, Virtuous Violence: Religious Violence across Culture and History* [2010, New York] p. 151).

91 See for example IOR: Donald, R W, Note on Affairs in Waziristan at the present time, 20.8.1909, Reg. 1811, L/P&S/10/44. French and observers noted what was described as the great 'moral effect of a well-executed razzia' (Rid, 'The Nineteenth Century', 2010, p. 735).

92 Benjamin Brower, *A Desert Named Peace: The Violence of France's Empire in the Algerian Sahara, 1844-1902* (2010, New York), p. 36.

93 Alex Tickell, *Terrorism, Insurgency and Indian-English Literature, 1830-1947* (2013, London/New York), p. 7.

94 IOR: Tel. Wazirforce (WF) to Chief of General Staff (CofGS), No. 6901-22.G, 5.10.1921, L/P&S/10/952, p. 225; CC NWFP to GOI FD, Tel. P., no number, P.A.-Camp 12, 27.7.1921, L/P&S/10/952, p. 234b.
95 Supplement to the London Gazette, 4.12.1922, https://www.thegazette,co.uk/London/issue/32773/supplement/8600.data.pdf https://trove.nla.gov.au/newspaper/article/84498152.
96 IOR: *RAB 1921-22*, p. 2, V/10/390, IOR: Tel. CC NWFP to FS in GOI, No. 51P. N., 5.9.1921, L/P&S/10/952, p. 239b.
97 IOR: Statement in GOCW, No. 7196-G. S-32, 1.11.1923, L/P&S/10/953, p. 42.
98 IOR: *RAB 1921-22*, p. 2, V/10/390.
99 IOR: GOC Wazirforce to CofGS, Tel. No. 6901-21G, 5.10.1921, L.PS/10/952, p. 225; Tel. P, Wazirforce to CofGS, No. 6901-22.G, 5.10.1921, L.PS/10/952, p. 225.
100 Stewart, *Fire*, 1973, pp. 167–8, 180–2.
101 Adamec, *Afghanistan*, 1967, p. 164; IOR: Tel. V to SofSI, P. No. 21-C. 23.10.1921, L/P&S/10/952, pp. 215b-6.
102 IOR: Tel. British Representative (BR), Kabul to FS to GOI, No. 212-C, 19.7.1921, L/P&S/10/952, p. 234b; Stewart, *Fire*, 1973, p. 179.
103 They included for instance the stipulations that 'women cases' should not interfered with by the government (1) and that they should not be expected to pay land revenue (3). For the full list see IOR: R W to GOCW, No. 1583, 7.10.1920, L/P&S/10/952, p. 370b.
104 IOR: R W to GOCW, No. 1583, 7.10.1920, L/P&S/10/952, pp. 370b-71.
105 IOR: Tel. CC NWFP to FS to GOI, No. 563-P, 24.10.1921, L/P&S/10/952, p. 216b.
106 Howell, *Mizh*, 1979, p. 87.
107 IOR: Tel. V to SofSI, No. 21-C, 23.10.1921, L/P&S/10/952, p. 215b.
108 IOR: Announcement made to the Mahsuds on 5 November 1921, L/P&S/10/952, p. 223.
109 IOR: Memo. R W to GOCW, No. 2234, 9.11.1921, L/P&S/10/952, 200b.
110 IOR: Tel. FS to GOI to GOCW, No. 34-C., 30.10.1921, L/P&S/10/952, p. 217.
111 Both quotations from IOR: Memo., R W to GOCF, No. 2238, 10.11.1921, L/P&S/10/952, p. 202; see also IOR: R W to GOCW, 9.11.1921, L/P&S/10/952, pp. 200–1.
112 IOR: Memo., R W to GOCF, No. 2238, 10.11.1921, L/P&S/10/952, p. 202.
113 Vartan Gregorian, *The Emergence of Modern Afghanistan: Politics of Reform and Modernization, 1880-1946* (1969, Stanford, CA), p. 238.
114 Abdul Arghandawi, *British Imperialism and Afghanistan's Struggle for Independence 1914-21* (1989, New Delhi), p. 295; Stewart, *Fire*, 1973, p. 179; Adamec, *Afghanistan*, 1967, pp. 160–1.
115 Adamec, *Afghanistan*, 1967, p. 187.

116 Treaty between the British and Afghan governments, signed Kabul, 22 November 1921, in L/P&S/10/951.
117 L/PS/10/952, pp. 188, 215.
118 Stewart, *Fire*, 1973, p. 189.
119 IOR: Note, Pears, 9.4.1922, L/P&S/10/952, p. 159; Stewart, *Fire*, p.197, 'A Wazir Raid British Column Overwhelmed on Frontier', *Straits Times*, 12.12.1921, p. 2, http://eresources.nlb.gov.sg/newspapers/digitised/issue/straitstimes19211212-1. In 1919 Amanullah had settled 700 Wazir families at Shahjui across the Durand Line, north of Hindubagh. The men were armed with .303 rifles, and 'from this sanctuary, immune to retaliation and too far away for easy surveillance, they were ideally placed to cross the border anywhere in six hundred miles' (Chevenix-Trench, *Scouts*, 1986, p. 80; IOR: PZ 2834/34 redraft of paper by Arnold Toynbee [c.1926/7], L/P&S/12/3208, p. 44; Leeson, *Frontier*, 2003, p. 69). As we have seen, since the turn of the century the GOA had offered shelter in Afghanistan to various groups of people from Waziristan. Many influential men from Waziristan moved to Afghanistan in 1919, where they were given land. By the 1940s, for example, Khalli Khel Shaman Khels had forty houses in Nalband in Logar (Curtis, *MMT*, 1947, p. 330).
120 IOR: V to SofSI, Tel., 1.12.1921, P5291, L/P&S/10/1019, p. 266.
121 Leon Poullada, *Reform and Rebellion in Afghanistan, 1919–1929, King Amanullah's Failure to Modernize a Tribal Society* (1973, London), p. 244. The British also objected to the way that Amanullah had taken up the cause of Indian Muslims and worked with Indian nationalists like Mahendra Pratap, Barkatullah and Obeidullah Sindhi and his aide Zafar Hussain (Poullada, *Reform*, 1973, p. 246).
122 Poullada, *Reform*, 1973, p. 244; Poullada blames the first British minister, Sir Francis Humphrys, for this, saying that he had little if any sympathy for Amanullah; he describes the 1920s as a 'decade of tension' in Afghan-British relations (Poullada, *Reform*, 1973, p. 237).

Chapter 7

1 IOR: Transl. in L/P&S/10/952, pp. 251–51b.
2 They had, he said, incited the Arabs of the Hejaz to rise against the Ottoman caliph; they had taken control of Mecca and Medina for a time and even bombed the tomb of the Prophet, as well as occupying Jerusalem and Baghdad and keeping the caliph under surveillance in Constantinople (IOR: Proclamation of Jehad in the Way of God ... to All the followers of Islam, L/P&S/10/1019, pp. 14–15).
3 IOR: Transl., 15.3.1922, in L/P&S/10/1019, p. 303.
4 For instance 'Faith in God and his Prophet is the best of deeds, after that ranks jehad in the way of God', and 'The feet which are covered with dust in the way of

God even for an hour on them shall the fire of hell not fall'; for a slightly different translation see, for example, Reuven Firestone, *Jihad: The Origins of Holy War in Islam* (1999, Oxford/NY), p. 100.

5 IOR: Proclamation of Jehad in the Way of God ... to All the followers of Islam, L/P&S/10/1019, pp. 314–15.
6 Ibid., p. 317.
7 IOR: Note, Pears, L/P&S/10/952, p. 159.
8 IOR: Extract from Diary of Intelligence Bureau, NWFP, February 1923, L/P&S/10/1019, p. 343.
9 IOR: Memo., R W to GOCW, No. 597, 31.5.1922, L/P&S/10/952, p. 86; Note, Pears, L/P&S/10/952, p. 158b.
10 IOR: V to SofSI, Tel., P1439, 7.4.1922, L/P&S/10/1019, p. 225.
11 Stewart, *Fire*, 1973, p. 191.
12 IOR: Tel. V to SofSI, 9.4.1922, L/P&S/10/1019, p. 221; V to SofSI, 7.4.1922, L/P&S/10/1019, p 225.
13 IOR: PA W, Report – Events in Wana April 1922, L/P&S/10/952, pp. 85–85b.
14 IOR: Memo. GOCW to CofGS, 15.4.1922, L/P&S/10/952, p. 163b. When British planes crashed, local Mullahs usually claimed that it was their prayers that had brought them down.
15 IOR: CinC, The Occupation of Waziristan, Memo., L/PS10/952, p. 61.
16 IOR: *RAB 1922-23*, p. 18, V/10/390.
17 IOR: Note on the situation in Wana, PA W, 25.5.1922, L/P&S/10/952, p. 86b.
18 IOR: GOCW to FS to GOI, No. 7631-G.s., 11.5.1922, L/P&S/10/952, p. 157b.
19 IOR: *RAB 1923-24*, p. 14, V/10/390.
20 IOR: Tel. FS to GOI to CC NWFP, No. 2460-S, 26.10.1921, L/P&S/10/952, p. 216b.
21 'Action of Spinchilla Pass', *Supplement to London Gazette*, 4.12.1922, p. 8602, https://www.thegazette.co.uk/London/issue/32773/supplement/8602/data.pdf. IOR: Tel. V. to SofSI, 16.12.1921, L/P&S/10/1019, p. 259.
22 IOR: V to SofSI, Tel., 18.4.1922, L/P&S/1019, p. 219; *RAB 1921-22*, p. 19, V/10/390; *RAB 1922/23*, p. 9, V/10/390; Howell, *Mizh*, 1979, p. 82.
23 IOR: Answer to the Mahsud petition by the resident in Waziristan (Pears), L/P&S/10/952, p. 30; see also Memo. R W, No. 743, 2.8.1922, L/P&S/10/952, pp. 28b–29; Howell, *Mizh*, 1979, p. 87.
24 To show that he was serious he insisted that the Shaman Khels pay a fine for an attack on a British convoy that occurred near their settlement at Ahmadwam on 1 July 1922 (IOR: Memo. R W, No. 743, 2.8.1922, L/P&S/10/952, p. 28b). Howell suggests that 'the principles of local, sectional and tribal responsibility were stated and their application defined' (Howell, *Mizh*, 1979, p. 89).
25 IOR: Memo. R W, No. 743, 2.8.1922, L/P&S/10/952, p. 28 (also Curtis, *MMT*, 1947, p. 7). This memo also has a reference to the possible release of the men imprisoned after Dodd's murder, including Sarfaraz's brother Silla Khan.

26 Warren, *Waziristan*, 2000, p. 58. Charles Bruce described them as practically *chalweshtis* or tribal police, recalling Macaulay and Thorburn's efforts to turn the hostages into tribal police in the 1880s (*The Tribes of Waziristan*, 1929, p. vii).
27 Curtis, *MMT*, 1947, pp. 6–7.
28 IOR: Memo. R W, No. 743, 2.8.1922, L/P&S/10/952, p. 29b; Tel. GOCW, No. 6013-R. G., 4.9.1922, L/P&S/10/952, p. 3.
29 Howell, *Mizh*, 1979, p. 90; IOR: *RAB 1922-23*, p. 9, V/10/390.
30 Robson, *Crisis*, 2004, p. 241. Rawlinson's father had been an influential advocate of the 'forward policy' on the frontier (F. Sir Maurice, *Life of Lord Rawlinson 1862-25* [1928, London], p. 276).
31 Warren, *Waziristan*, 2000, p. 52.
32 IOR: Tel. SofSI to V Army Dept., 11.1.1923, L/P&S/10/951, p. 28; Adamec, *Afghanistan*, 1967, p. 163.
33 Robson, *Crisis*, 2004, p. 242.
34 IOR: V to SofSI, 23.3.1920, L/P&S/10/951, pp. 2–3; Robson, *Crisis*, 2004, p. 232; Howell, *Mizh*, 1979, p. 81.
35 Robson, *Crisis*, 2004, p. 241; see also Tripodi, *Edge*, 2011, p. 134.
36 'India and her Budget', *The Times*, 8.8.1913, *The Times Digital Archive, 1785-2010*, https://www.gale.com/intl/c/the-times-digital-archive
37 In Maurice, *Life*, 1928.
38 The Committee's other members were Sir John Maffey, Sir Armine Dew (the agent to the governor general in Baluchistan 1919–22), Sir Henry Dobbs, Sir Denis Bray, Sir Stuart Pears (the new resident in Waziristan) and General Sir Andrew Skeen (IOR: Tel. P., No. 118-S, 30.1.1922, V to SofSI, L/P&S/10/952, p. 166).
39 In addition Hailey proposed to double the Wazir and Mehsud allowances, build roads from Thal to Idak and inside administered territory along the Waziristan border from Draband to Ghazni Khel, and pay the border villages to organize their own defence. Rather as Fitzpatrick had done, Pears talked about involving the maliks and the *tuman* through the khassadar scheme 'so deeply in one common advantage and one common responsibility that they will thereby combine to create a single tribal machine (or Sarishta), capable of organising and controlling the affairs of the whole tribe' (IOR: R W to GOC W, No. 125, 25.2.1922, L/P&S/10/952, p. 181b). Details of the khassadar scheme are in IOR: R W to GOC W, No. 125, 25.2.1922, L/P&S/10/952, pp. 179–82.
40 IOR: Memo, No. 12355 (G.S.-M.O.1), 18.2.1922, L/P&S/10/952, p. 167b.
41 IOR: V to SofSI, Tel. P., No. 118-S, 30.1.1922, L/P&S/10/952, pp. 166–7.
42 IOR: SofSI to V AD, Tel. P, No. 1538, 12.4.1922, L/P&S/10/952, pp. 101–2. To reduce expenditure the viceroy wanted to reduce the numbers of British troops in India in a year's time, but the secretary of state refused to commit himself to a timetable for this (IOR: SofSI to V AD, Tel. P, No. 807, L/P&S/10/952, pp. 182b-183). See also IOR: V to SofSI, 7.4.1922, L/P&S/10/1019, p. 225; Jacobsen, *Rawlinson*, 2002, pp. 98–9).

43 IOR: SofSI to V, Tel. P. No. 807, L/P&S/10/952, p. 183b.
44 'Lord Reading and India', *Times*, 4.5.1922, https://www.gale.com/intl/c/the-times-digital-archive
45 IOR: SofSI to V, Tel. No. 1538, 12.4.1922, L/P&S/10/952, p. 101b.
46 'Lord Reading and India', *Times*, 4.5.1922, https://www.gale.com/intl/c/the-times-digital-archive
47 IOR: V to SofSI, Tel. P, No. 551, 25.4.1922, L/P&S/10/952, pp. 102b–103b.
48 In Jacobsen, *Rawlinson*, 2002, pp. 100–1.
49 Jacobsen, *Rawlinson*, 2002, pp. 107–8.
50 IOR: Sir John Maffey, Unsolicited Views on an Unsolved Problem, in No. 350, 2/8/1922, MSS Eur.E. 238/24, p. 387.
51 In fact, Robson suggests, by implication he left out the Tochi Valley as far as Miranshah, the Kurram, Khyber and Malakand (Robson, *Crisis*, 2004, p. 243).
52 IOR: Sir John Maffey, Unsolicited Views, in No. 350, 2/8/1922, MSS Eur.E. 238/24, p. 387.
53 At about the same time, Air Vice Marshal Sir John Salmond, after touring part of the frontier with Maffey, put forward another scheme according to which the RAF would take primary responsibility for controlling Waziristan. But, unlike Maffey, he envisaged that the regular army would still play a role. Robson (*Crisis*, 2004, p. 243–4).
54 IOR: V to SofSI, Tel. P, No. 1247-S, 20.10.1922, L/P&S/10/952, p. 126.
55 IOR: Note, R W (Pears), L/P&S/10/953, pp. 399–400.
56 Some Garrerais seem to have been responsible for Dickinson's murder, though some officials blamed Musa Khan (Howell, *Mizh*, 1979, p. 90; IOR: R W to CC NWFP, 2.9.1923, L/P&S/10/953, p. 102b).
57 IOR: Note, L/P&S/10/953, p. 448.
58 IOR: Memo, R W, 29.12.1922, L/P&S/10/1019, p. 119.
59 IOR: SofSI to GOI, 30.1.1923, L/P&S/10/951, p. 244.
60 IOR: SofSI, 11.1.1923, L/P&S/10/951, p. 254; see also Howell, *Mizh*, 1979, p. 84.
61 IOR: Tel. V AD to SofSI, 3.2.1923, L/P&S/10/951, p. 399; Jacobsen, *Rawlinson*, 2002, pp. 121–2.
62 IOR: Tel. V F&P to SofSI, 5.1.1923, L/PS/10/951.
63 IOR: Reproduced in L/P&S/10/953, pp. 66–66b; Haroon, *Frontier*, 2007, pp. 126–7, 129. *Al Mujahid* also noted that the Mehsuds 'never shrink from the defence of their country's and nation's honour and independence on account of the lover of martyrdom' (L/P&S/10/953, p. 65b). Reportedly the paper's editor received an allowance from the GOA (IOR: L/P&S/12/1571, p. 285).
64 IOR: V AD to SofSI, 15.2.1923, L/P&S/10/951, p. 233; SofSI to GOI, 30.1.1923, L/P&S/10/951, p. 22. Major Parsons was seriously wounded by friendly fire and was replaced as PA by Major Thompson Glover in March 1923 (Howell, *Mizh*, 1979, p. 91).

65 IOR: V AD to SofSI, 12.1.1923, L/P&S/10/951, p. 248. Brigadier Adam Khan arrived at Shakin in December to summon the Wazirs and Mehsuds who belonged to Haji Abdur Razaq's levies (IOR: R W, 21.12.1922, Memo., L/P&S/10/1019, p. 119).
66 IOR: GOCW to CofGS, Tel. No. 6846-386-G., 22.1.1923, L/P&S/10/953, p. 375; GOCW to FS to GOI, Tel. 6846-387-G., 24.1.1923, L/P&S/10/953, 377b. Flying in Waziristan was challenging. The weather was unpredictable, the mechanical condition of the planes was sometimes poor and places for emergency landings were few and far between.
67 IOR: GOCF to FS GOI, Memo. No. 6850-G.S.-121, 9.1.1923, L/P&S/10/953, p. 363b; FS to GOI to GOCW, 3.1.1923, no number, L/P&S/10/953, p. 354.
68 IOR: GOCW to FS to GOI, Tel. No. 8-G., 10.2.1923, L/P&S/10/953, p. 308; V AD to SofSI, 8.2.1923, L/P&S/10/951, p. 237.
69 Robson, *Crisis*, 2004, p. 245.
70 In Beattie, *Imperial*, 2002, p. 39.
71 IOR: Transl. Letter, 28.1.1923, FM GOA to His Majesty's minister, Kabul (HMMK), L/P&S/10/953, p. 264.
72 IOR: Tel., HMMK to SofS for Foreign Affairs (SofSFA), 12.2.1923, L/P&S/10/951, p. 118; Howell, *Mizh*, 1979, p. 91; W. Fraser-Tytler, *Afghanistan*, third edition (1967, London), pp. 263–4.
73 IOR: V to SofSI, Tel., P516, 7.2.1923, L/P&S/10/951, p. 119. The paper had been founded by Nadir Khan (Saikal, *Afghanistan*, 2012, p. 87).
74 Abdul Hadi, a poet, had been an assistant editor of the first Afghan newspaper, *Siraj-ul-Akhbar* (Light of the News), worked in the Afghan Foreign Office and was the minister in London from 1922 to 1924. A supporter of Amanullah Khan, he joined him in Kandahar during Habibullah Kalakani's uprising. He returned to Kabul in 1932 and was imprisoned from 1933 until 1949 (Adamec, *Historical and Political*, 1975, pp. 95–6).
75 Haroon, *Frontier*, 2007, p. 116.
76 Ewans, *Afghanistan*, 2001, p. 91.
77 Haroon, *Frontier*, 2007, p. 126; Benjamin Hopkins, 'A History of the "Hindustani Fanatics" on the Frontier', in Benjamin Hopkins and Magnus Marsden (eds), *Beyond Swat: History, Society and Economy along the Afghanistan-Pakistan Frontier* (2013, London), pp. 84, 88. In 1927 the Soviet legation in Kabul reportedly tried to send £300 in gold to the Mujahidin colony in Waziristan, but this was intercepted by the Afghan authorities (Hopkins, 'A History', 2013, p. 85).
78 Haroon, *Frontier*, 2007, pp. 115–18. Curtis refers to Amir Shah, 'a mullah of note', receiving Rs.1,000 p.a. (Curtis, *MMT*, 1947, 220); another report refers to him as 'fanatically hostile' (IOR: GOC W to CofGS, Tel. 7866-1-G, 11.7.1923, L/PS/10/953, p. 150b).

79 According to the *1940-1 Report on the Administration of the Border*, Haji Mirza Ali Khan and others feared that 'the coming of enlightenment in whatever guise [would] … lead to a decrease of their influence and prestige' (IOR: L/P&S/12/3148, p. 29).
80 Haroon, *Frontier*, 2007, pp. 126–7, 129.
81 IOR: R W to HW, Memo. No. 245-S, 24.5.1923, L/PS/10/953, p. 171; IOR: R W to HW, Memo. No. 6 4-S, 6.4.1923, L/PS/10/953, pp. 265b/1–265b/2. Traditionally, Curtis noted, the khan of all the Mehsuds had come from the family of Jangi Khan, Salimi Khel; he thought that during the nineteenth century Jangi Khan and Umar Khan had indeed been regarded as tribal leaders (Curtis, *MMT*, 1947, p. 176).
82 IOR: HMMK to SofS FA, 6.4.1923, L/P&S/10/953, p. 262.
83 'When we introduced the Khassadar scheme on a generous scale, the Afghan Government decided to revive the Haji's levies in the guise of Afghan Khassadars' (IOR: R W, Note on the Afghan Project, Memo. 7631-169-G. S., 23.5.1923, p. 197b).
84 Fraser-Tytler, *Afghanistan*, 1967, p. 263; IOR: SofSI to GOI FD, No. P.-2967, L/P&S/12/1142, p. 74.
85 Fraser-Tytler, *Afghanistan*, 1967, p. 262.
86 Ibid.
87 Jacobsen, *Rawlinson*, 2002, p. 137; IOR: Paraphrase Tel., SofSI to V AD, 29.1.1923, L/P&S/10/951, p. 23; SofS to GOI, 30.1.1923, L/P&S/10/951, p. 244.
88 IOR: V AD to SofSI, 3.2.1923, L/P&S/10/951, p. 239.
89 IOR: V AD to SofSI, 16.2.1923, L/P&S/10/951, p. 228; SofSI AD to V, 7.2.1923, L/P&S/10/953, p. 302.
90 IOR: *RAB 1924-25*, p. 9, V/10/390.
91 IOR: Extract from Legislative Assembly Debates, Vol. III, No. 49, FS, 5.3.1923, in L/P&S/10/951, p. 90; IOR: PA W to R W, No. 342, 21.11.1921, L/P&S/10/952, p. 215.
92 IOR: Extract from Legislative Assembly Debates, Vol. III, No. 49, FS, 5.3.1923, in L/P&S/10/951, p. 89; Robson, *Crisis*, 2004, p. 175.
93 IOR: L/PS/12/1571, p. 27; Fraser-Tytler, *Afghanistan*, 1967, p. 263.
94 Adamec, *Afghanistan*, 1967, p. 86; Fraser-Tytler, *Afghanistan*, p. 263. The Afghan historian Abdul Samad Ghaus claims that British deliberately provoked opposition along the border to the amir (Saikal, *Modern Afghanistan*, 2012, pp. 64–5).
95 See for example Robson, *Crisis*, 2004, pp. 167–8.
96 Jacobsen, *Rawlinson*, 2002, p. 130.
97 Robson, *Crisis*, 2004, 244.
98 They did not have British officers, and had to build their own outposts (Brandon Marsh, *Ramparts of Empire: British Imperialism and India's Afghan Frontier, 1918-1948* [2015, Basingstoke/New York], p. 50, footnote 61). So the description of the Wana khassadar scheme as 'a bold experiment … in effect the Militia scheme as originally proposed by Lord Curzon' was not quite correct (IOR: No. 88, 4.10.1921, PA W to R W, L/PS/10/952, p.213).

99   Chevenix-Trench, *Scouts*, 1968, pp. 50–1; Tripodi, *Edge*, 2011, pp. 192–3, 199; IOR: OCW to CofGS, Memo. No. 6997-G, 29.5.1922, L/P&S/10/952, p. 84b.
100 IOR: *RAB 1924-25*, pp. 29/30, V/10/390; Leeson, *Frontier*, 2003, p. 20.
101 Howell, *Mizh*, 1979, p. 89; Warren, *Waziristan*, 2000, p. 54.
102 James Spain, *Pathans of the Latter Day* (1995, Karachi), p. 86.
103 Warren, *Waziristan*, 2000, p. 69.
104 IOR: R W to CC NWFP, Memo., No. 1006-T, 29.9.1926, L/P&S/10/1142, pp. 309–309b.
105 IOR: CC, Tel. P. No. 2551-R., 12.9.1923, LPS/10/953, p. 76.
106 IOR: R (Pears) W, Note on the Afghan Project, in Memo. 7631-169-G. S., 23.5.1923, L/P&S/10/953, p. 195b.
107 IOR: FS to GOI to HMMK, Tel. P. No. 1100-S, 4.9.1923, L/P&S/10/953, p. 118b.
108 IOR: V to SofSI, Tel. P., No. 1017S, 7.8.1923, L/P&S/10/953, pp. 125–6.
109 Nawid, *Religious*, 1999, p. 88; Stewart, *Fire*, 1973, pp. 218, 221–2.
110 Stewart, *Fire*, 1973, pp. 231, 242.
111 IOR: Agent to GG Baluchistan to FS GOI, Tel. No. 2-P, 2.12.1923, L/P&S/10/953, pp. 12–13b.
112 IOR: GOCW to FS to GOI, Tel. No. 6846-206.G, 12.11.1923, L/P&S/10/953, p. 46b; *RAB 1929-30*, p. 26.
113 IOR: Encl. 1, in HMMK, No. 14, 16.6.1923, L/P&S/10/953, p. 164.
114 See for example Leeson, *Frontier*, 2003, p. 75; IOR: *RAB 1923-24*, p. 13, V/10/390; IOR: R W to GOCW, Memo. No. 228-C, 24.8.1923, L/P&S/10/953, p. 103b; Howell, *Mizh*, 1979, p. 85; Ahmed, *Resistance*, 1991, p. 224.
115 IOR: GOCW DIK, No. 6846-490-G, 24.9.1923, L/P&S/10/953, p. 82.
116 IOR: R W to FS to GOI, No. 1011-S., 10.11.1923, L/P&S/10/953, pp. 44b–45.
117 Howell, *Mizh*, 1979, p. 92.
118 IOR: Memo., R W to GOCW, Memo. No. 125-C., 2/3.8.1923, L/P&S/10/953, p. 126b.
119 Stewart, *Fire*, 1973, p. 237.
120 Ibid., p. 239.
121 Ibid., pp. 246–8.
122 Fraser-Tytler, *Afghanistan*, 1967, p. 263.
123 Poullada, *Reform*, 1973, p. 94; Haroon, *Frontier*, 2007, p. 117.
124 Steward, Fire, 1973, pp. 252–5. Muhammad Wali Khan replaced Nadir as the commander in chief (Gregorian, *Emergence*, 1969, pp. 282–3).
125 IOR: HMMK, No. 183–3, 2.9.1925, Reg. 690 (No. 207), L/P&S/10/1142; Adamec, *Foreign Affairs*, 1974, p. 89. In 1924 the GOI did the Afghan government a favour by capturing at Parachinar the two younger sons of the ex-amir of Afghanistan, Yaqub Khan, who had escaped from internment at Dehra Dun and were on their way to join the rebels. In July another of Yaqub Khan's sons, Abdul Karim, born to a slave mother, broke parole in Benares/Varanasi and was able to cross into

Khost. He returned to India as soon as it seemed the rebellion would fail (IOR: PZ 2834/34, Toynbee (c.1926/7) L/P&S/12/3208).
126 Saikal, *Modern Afghanistan*, 2012, p. 72.
127 Gregorian, *Emergence*, 1967, p. 238; in 1926 the GOI commented that since 1923 'objectionable Afghan intrigue in Waziristan' had largely ceased (IOR: Memo. to HMMK, No. 240-F, 18.10.1926, L/P&S/10/1142).

Chapter 8

1 The chief commissioner reported that anti-British 'hostiles' living in Afghanistan were responsible for 75 per cent of all offences committed in 1923–4 (Howell, *Mizh*, 1979, p. 92).
2 IOR: *RAB 1924-25*, p. 11, V/10/390. In July 1924 Faridais from Dre and Kachari Algads ambushed Scouts at Sora Rogha and killed three of them and carried off their rifles (IOR: Wazirdist to Northern Command, Tel. No. 16083-G, 3.11.1924, L/P&S/10/1142, p. 509).
3 IOR: *RAB 1924-25*, pp. 11–12, V/10/390.
4 IOR: R W to NWF, No. 527-T, 10.12.1924, L/P&S/10/1142, p. 143; PA W to R W, Tel. H-999, No. 552-T, 14.2.1924, L/P&S/10/1142,, p. 144.
5 Reportedly he paid up in gold (Curtis, *MMT*, 1947, pp. 45-6; *RAB 1925-26*, p. 14, V/10/390; L/P&S/1142, p. 148). He was one of eleven maliks who took responsibility for the security of the road between Sora Rogha and Razmak in 1924 (Ahmed, *Resistance*, 1991, pp. 156–7).
6 IOR: R W to N-WF, Tel., No. 573-T, 16.12.1924, L/P&S/10/1142, pp. 144–5.
7 IOR: Air vice-marshal commanding RAF in India (AV-MC RAFI) to commander-in-chief in India (CinCI), 23.6.1926, Report on RAF operations in Waziristan 9.3.1925 to 23.6.1925 (enclosure 2), L/P&S/10/1142, p. 376–83; Chaz Bowyer, *RAF Operations 1918-38* (1988, London), p. 170.
8 Robson, *Crisis*, 2004, p. 246; Omissi, *Air Power*, 1990, p. 48. The campaign is sometimes referred to as Pink's War after the name of the wing commander in charge.
9 IOR: AV-MC RAFI to CinCI, 23.6.1926, Report on RAF op.s in Waziristan 9.3.1925 to 23.6.1925 (encl. 2), L/P&S/10/1142, pp. 376–83; Howell, *Mizh*, 1979, p. 93.
10 On 21 March 1925 rifle fire brought down a plane in Guri Khel territory. One man was killed instantly, and the other died shortly afterwards, though the Guri Khels did their best to save him (IOR: AV-MC RAFI to CinCI, 23.6.1926, Report RAF op.s, 9.3.1925 to 23.6.1925 (encl. 2), L/P&S/10/1142, pp. 376–83). Aircrew carried 'safety certificates', colloquially referred to as 'goolie chits', documents printed

in Urdu and Pashto, promising ransom for 'the return unharmed of any British personnel' (Bowyer, *RAF Operations*, 1988, p. 161).
11 Bowyer, *RAF Operations*, 1988, p. 175.
12 Howell, *Mizh*, 1979, p. 92.
13 IOR: AV-MC RAFI to CinCI, 23.6.1926, Report RAF op.s, 9.3.1925 to 23.6.1925 (encl. 2), L/P&S/10/1142, pp. 376–8.
14 IOR: CinCI, 29.6.1925 (encl. 1), L/P&S/10/1142, p. 375.
15 See Jacobsen, *Rawlinson*, 2002, pp. 109–10; Tim Moreman, 'Watch and Ward': The Army in India and the North-West Frontier, 1920-1939', in David Killingray and David Omissi (eds), *Guardians of Empire* (1999, Manchester), pp. 137–56.
16 IOR: *RAB 1923-24*, p. 13, V/10/390.
17 See for example, Enquiry into the Extended Use of the RAF on the North-West Frontier of India, in L/MIL/17/13/37.
18 Warren, *Waziristan*, 2000, p. 56. In the summer of 1923 Charles Bruce took over from Pears as the Waziristan resident (IOR: GOI FD to CC, NWFP, Memo. No. 484–412 (1)-F., 7.6.1923, L/P&S/10/953, p. 155).
19 IOR: *RAB 1925-26*, p. 15, V/10/390.
20 Ibid.
21 Fraser-Tytler, *Afghanistan*, 1967, p. 267; IOR: *RAB 1926-27*, p. 12, V/10/390.
22 Curtis, *MMT*, 1947, pp. 175–6.
23 IOR: R W to CC NWFP, C.E. Bruce, Note on Waziristan Affairs, Sub-encl. No. 1, Tel. P, No. 212-C, 19.7.1921, L/P&S/10/1142, pp. 274–6. In June 1929 two British personnel were shot and killed at Bibizai (IOR: *RAB 1929-30*, p.16, V/10/390).
24 IOR: *RAB 1927-28*, p. 38, V/10/390.
25 IOR: *RAB 1927-28*, p. 13, V/10/390.
26 IOR: *RAB 1925-26*, pp. 22, 26–17, V/10/39; *RAB 1927-28*, p. 27, V/10/39.
27 IOR: V to SofSI, 16.12.1926, L/P&S/10/1142, p. 301.
28 Ghulam Nabi's father, Ghulam Haider Khan, had been one of Amir Abdur Rahman's favourite generals, and the family was an influential one (Saikal, *Modern Afghanistan*, 2012, p. 91).
29 The resident thought that Musa Khan had received some money from Kabul, but not as much as a lakh; Humphrys was not sure that any money reached him at all (IOR: CC NWFP, Tel. No. 196-P, 26.10.1926, L/P&S/10/1142, pp. 311–16; No. 1140-T, 24.11.1926, and enclosures, IOR: CC NWFP, Tel. No. 196-P, 26.10.1926, L/P&S/10/1142, pp. 314–14b, Memo. HM Min. Kabul, No. 183–8, 9.10.1926, L/P&S/10/1142, p. 310).
30 IOR: Memo. to HMM Kabul, No. 240-F, 18.10.1926, L/P&S/10/1142, p. 74. Amanullah also sent money to set up schools on the Indian side of the Durand Line (Haroon, *Frontier*, 2007, p. 117).
31 Finch, *Progressive*, 2013, p. 58.

32 In ibid., p. 60.
33 Finch, *Progressive*, 2013, p. 59.
34 Ibid., p. 60.
35 Rid, 'The Nineteenth Century', 2010, pp. 751–2.
36 Finch, *Progressive*, 2013, p. 138.
37 Ibid., pp. 63–4.
38 Gallieni quoted in Finch, *A Progressive*, 2013, pp. 59, 65.
39 William A. Hoisington Jr., *Lyautey and the French Conquest of Morocco* (1995, Basingstoke), p. vii.
40 Benjamin C. Brower, *A Desert*, 2011, p. 54.
41 Quoted in Rid, 'The Nineteenth Century', 2010, p. 740.
42 Finch, *A Progressive*, 2015, p. 35.
43 Quoted in Douglas Porch, *Counterinsurgency: Exposing the Myths of the New Way of War* (2013, Cambridge/New York), p. 54; Finch, *A Progressive*, 2015, p. 36.
44 William A. Hoisington Jr., *Lyautey and the French Conquest of Morocco* (1995, Basingstoke), p. 92; Porch, *Counterinsurgency*, 2013, pp. 54–5.
45 Beattie, *Imperial*, 2002, pp. 189/90.
46 Bartle Frere argued that collective punishments were uncivilized and inefficient (Beattie, *Imperial*, 2002, pp. 125–6).
47 See for example Christian Tripodi, '"Good for one but not the other"; The "Sandeman System" of Pacification as Applied to Baluchistan and the North-West Frontier, 1877-1947', *The Journal of Military History*, Vol. 73 (July 2009), pp. 784–6. Charles Bruce, the Waziristan resident in the mid-1920s, suggested that Lyautey had actually drawn on Sandeman's experience (Bruce, *Waziristan*, 1938, p. 1).
48 André Singer, *Lords of the Khyber: The Story of the North-West Frontier* (1984, London), p. 132; see also for example Simanthi Dutta, *Imperial Mappings: In Savage Spaces Baluchistan and British India* (2002, Delhi).
49 IOR: R W to CC NWFP, No. 244-S, 20.7.1927, Reg. No. 4999, Note on Waziristan Affairs, L/P&S/10/1142, p. 274.
50 IOR: Extract from the Legislative Assembly Debates, Vol. III, No. 49, FS, 5.3.1923, in L/P&S/10/951, p. 90.
51 IOR: R W to CC NWFP, Memo., No. 664-T, 15.7.1926, L/P&S/10/1142, pp. 336b–337.
52 IOR: GOI to CC NWFP, No. 181-F, 18.9.1926, L/P&S/10/1142, p. 311.
53 IOR: 11.3.1940, Indian Legislative Assembly debate, p. 1100, L/PS/12/3265, p. 32.
54 IOR: *RAB 1921-22*, p. 8, V/10/390; *RAB 1922-23*, p. 9, V/10/390; *1923-24*, p. 10; *RAB 1924-25*, p. 13, V/10/390.
55 IOR: R W to CC NWFP, No. 244-S, 20.7.1927, Reg. No. 4999, Note on Waziristan Affairs, L/P&S/10/1142, pp. 274–6.
56 IOR: *RAB 1925-26*, p. 12, V/10/390.

57 IOR: *RAB 1928-29*, p. 15, V/10/390.
58 For instance a confrontation between a large number of Mehsuds and Wazirs between Ladha and Tiarza (Chevenix-Trench, *Scouts*, 1986, pp. 116–7); for another example see IOR: *RAB* 1933-34, p. 37, V/10/390.
59 IOR: *RAB 1927-28*, p. 15, V/10/390; also p. 25; *RAB 1926-27*, p. 10, V/10/390.
60 IOR: Lt.-Col. C.E.Bruce, Memo on Policy in Waziristan, 23.1.1929, L/P&S/12/3151, pp. 268–9.
61 Tripodi, *Edge*, 2011, p. 197.
62 William Barton, *India's North-West Frontier* (1939, London), p. 222; IOR: R W to CC NWFP, Memo., No. 664-T, 15.7.1926, L/P&S/10/1142, pp. 336b–37.
63 Akbar S. Ahmed, *Religion and Politics in Muslim Society* (1983, London), p. 184; IOR: *RAB 1925-26*, V/10/390, pp. 15–16.
64 IOR: *RAB 1927/28*, p. 19, V/10/390; Barton, *India's*, 1939, p. 222; R W to CC NWFP, No. 664-T, 15.7.1926, L/P&S/10/1142, pp. 336b–337.
65 IOR: *RAB 1924-25*, p. 14, V/10/390; *RAB 1927-28*, p. 19, V/10/390; *RAB 1928-29*, p. 23, V/10/390.
66 Daniel Neep, *Colonising Violence: Space, insurgency and subjectivity in French Mandate Syria* (2009, PhD London University), p. 141.
67 To show that you have power at your disposal so as not to have to use it (Neep, *Colonising Violence*, 2009, p. 142).
68 Neep, *Colonising Violence*, 2009, p. 144. The French also practised the *politique des races* in Syria.
69 Lyautey, quoted in Finch, *A Progressive*, 2013, p. 67; see also Hoisington, *Lyautey*, 1995, p. 50. Bartle Frere had also argued that on the Punjab frontier one official should exercise both military and political powers.
70 They had four main sections, Haibatari, Dreplarai, Khushalai and Shogi, and numbered about 3,400 fighting men in all (Warren, *Waziristan*, 2000, p. 88), so perhaps a total population of 13,000.
71 IOR: R W to CC NWFP, No. 162-5, 14.5.1927, L/P&S/10/1142, pp. 261–2.
72 IOR: R W to CC N-WFO, Memo., No. 597, 14.3.1925, L/P&S/10/1142, pp. 531b–33b; R W to NWFP, No. 822-T, 8.8.1925, L/P&S/10/1142, p. 401b; R W to CC NWFP, No. 880-T, 14.10.1925, L/P&S/10/1142, p. 416b.
73 IOR: Note, Barrett Commanding Razmak, L/PS/10/1142, p. 412.
74 R W to NWFP, No. 822-T, 8.8.1925, L/P&S/10/1142, p. 403b.
75 They included Sir Abdul Qaiyyum Khan, formerly PA in the Khyber, who became the first minister of the NWFP in 1937 (IOR: R W to CC, NWFP, No. 578-T, 10.8.925, L/P&S/10/1142, p. 399). The kashars were reported to be difficult (L/PS/10/1142, p. 428).
76 IOR: CC NWFP to R W, No. 3923-P, 18.3.1926, L/P&S/10/1142, p. 366.
77 IOR: R W to CC NWFP, No. 96-C, 6.3.1926, L/P&S/10/1142, p. 364.

78 It appears that because of the ongoing boundary dispute the Tori Khel allowances had not been paid after the 1923 agreement (IOR: N-WF AR 1936-37, L/P&S/12/3148).
79 IOR: CC NWFP to FS GOI FP., No. 3621-P.S./652-11, 10.10.1928, L/P&S/10/1142, p. 138; IOR: R W, Note on K.S Zangi Khan, 12.5.1928, L/P&S/10/1142, pp. 193–200.
80 IOR: *RAB 1924-25*, p. 9, V/10/390.
81 IOR: PA Tochi to R W, No. 215-P, 11.5.1928, L/P&S/10/1142, p. 193.
82 IOR: letter CC NWFP, No. 1938-P.S./362-P.S., 6.10.1926, L/P&S/10/1142, pp. 308–9.
83 IOR: R W, Note on K.S Zangi Khan, No. 3621-P.S./652-11, 10.10.1928, L/P&S/10/1142, pp. 193–200.
84 IOR: *RAB 1925-26*, p. 12, V/10/390; IOR: CC NWFP to GOI FP, No. 830 P.C.N., 26.5.1928, L/P&S/10/1142, pp. 209–10.
85 IOR: N-WF to F, Tel., No. 82-P.N., 26.5.1928, L/P&S/10/1142, p. 204.
86 IOR: R W to CC NWFP, No. 317-C, 22.5.1928, L/P&S/10/1142, p. 211.
87 IOR: *RAB 1927-28*, p. 17, V/10/390.
88 IOR: PA Tochi to R W, No. 185-P, 11.4.1928, L/P&S/10/1142, pp. 224–35.
89 IOR: Memo. No. 6729/79/G.1, 22.5.1928, from Hdqtrs, WD to R, Report about visit to Sheranna 29.3.1928, L/P&S/10/1142, p. 211.
90 IOR: Memo. No. 6729/79/G.1, 22.5.1928, from Hdqtrs, WD to R, Report about visit to Sheranna 29.3.1928, L/P&S/10/1142, p. 212.
91 IOR: R W to CC NWFP, No. 317-C, 22.5.1928, L/P&S/10/1142, p. 219. The Razmak officers were already exasperated by the political officers' failure to resolve the Abdullai-Tori Khel boundary dispute (see for example Minute Paper, No. 317-C, 22.5.1928, L/P&S/10/1142, p. 388).
92 IOR: CC to GOI FD, No. 3621-F.S./652-11, 10.10.1928, L/P&S/10/1142, p. 138; CC NWFP to GOI FP, No. 830 P.C.N., 26.5.1928, No. 3621-F.S./652-11, L/P&S/10/1142, p. 209; PA Tochi [Edwards] to R W, No. 185-P, 11.4.1928, L/P&S/10/1142, pp. 224–35.
93 IOR: Memo. No. 6729/79/G.1, 22.5.1928, from Hdqtrs, WD to R, Report about visit to Sheranna 29.3.1928, L/P&S/10/1142, p. 212.
94 IOR: CC, NWFP to FS GOI FP.; No. 3621-P.S./652-11, 10.10.1928, L/P&S/10/1142, p. 140.
95 IOR: Statement Khan Sahib Zangi Khan in R W, 12.5.1928, L/P&S/10/1142, p. 201; PA N W to CC, Tel. 200-P, 30.4.1928, L/P&S/10/1142, p. 201.
96 IOR: R W to CC NWFP, No. 317-C, 22.5.1928, L/P&S/10/1142, p. 219.
97 IOR: F to NWFP, Tel. No. 1082-S., 29.5.1928, L/P&S/10/1142, p. 205.
98 IOR: Tel. No. 81-P, 26.5.1928, Norwef (N-WF) to Foreign (F), L/P&S/10/1142, p. 204; CC, NWFP to GOI FP, 10.10.1928, No. 3621-P.S./652-11, L/P&S/10/1142, p. 140.

99 IOR: R to NWFP, encl. 1, Memo No. 887-S, 16.11.1928, L/P&S/10/1142, p. 115; PA N W to CC NWFP, Memo. No. 3197/P, 27.10.1928, L/P&S/10/1142, p. 120; *RAB 1928-29*, pp. 2, 16, V/10/390.
100 IOR: R W to CC NWFP, Memo. No. 2200-P.N.[37]10, 23.8.1929, L/P&S/10/1142, p. 52; P3521 R W to NWFP, Memo, re Utmanzai situation, No. 334-S, 24.3.1929, L/P&S/10/1142, pp. 57–60; Memo. R to CC NWFP, 24.11.1928, L/P&S/10/1142, p. 94.
101 IOR: Minute Paper 1928, L/P&S/10/1142, pp. 100–100b.
102 IOR: R W to CC, NWFP, Memo. No. 51, 5.1.1928, L/P&S/10/1142, p. 29.
103 The Dotani Powindahs and Zilla Khels living around Wana had for a long time been on bad terms with each other, and enmity flared up again in October 1926, with Suleiman Khel Powindahs and Tazi Khel Wazirs also taking part in the resulting clashes (IOR: Memo, CC N-WFP, No. 7038, 4.5.1927, Fighting Between Wana Wazirs and Powindahs, L/P&S/10/1142).
104 IOR: *RAB 1926-27*, p. 10, V/10/390; R to CC, No. 52-R, 5.9.1924, L/P&S/12/3151, p. 297; R W to CC, NWFP, Memo. No. 51, 5.1.1928, L/P&S/10/1142, p. 29.
105 IOR: R W to CC, NWFP, Memo. No. 51, 5.1.1928, L/P&S/10/1142, p. 29; CC NWFP to GOI FP, No. 3640 P.S./583, 31.12.1927, L/P&S/10/1142, p. 54; Stewart, *Fire*, 1973, p. 243.
106 IOR: Bray quoted in GOI FPD to SofSI, 12.7.1934, No. 3, L/P&S/12/3151, p. 41. Maffey had earlier commented in his 'Unsolicited Views' that Wana was 'a grim possession' and that he would rather 'prove his title to the name of Englishman by saving [his] … save his fellow-countrymen from going to Wana than by sending them' (IOR: Maffey, 'Unsolicited Views, MSS Eur.E. 238/24 Reading Collection, Letters and Telegrams to and from Persons in India, Vol. II, 1922, No. 350, p. 384).
107 Warren, *Waziristan*, 2000, p. 61
108 IOR: R W CC NWFP, Memo. No. 1117-S, 20.11.29, L/P&S/10/1142, p. 29.
109 Warren, *Waziristan*, 2000, pp. 61–2.
110 IOR: GOI, Tel. GOI FD to SofSI, No. 3740-S., 14.11.1930, L/P&S/12/3123, p. 97.
111 IOR: Letter No. 2 To Tahsildar Sahib, from All the maliks of Toji [Tazi] Khel, Gangi Khel, Zilli [Zilla] Khel and Khojal Khel of Dahna, L/P&S/12/3123, p. 85; PA SW to R W, Memo. No. 319-S, 21.11.1930, L/P&S/12/3123, p. 91.
112 IOR: PA S W to R W, Memo. No. 395-S, 22.11.1930, L/P&S/12/3123, p. 88.
113 On 18 January 1928 Mehsuds fired shots over the heads of the political agent and his party as they returned from a visit to Qutab Khan Salimi Khel Alizai's kot at Nano (IOR: *RAB 1927-28*, p. 17, V/10/390).
114 IOR: PA S W to CC, N-WFP, No. 341, 25.10.1928, L/PS/10/1142.
115 The RAF was reported to have 'correctly picked out the villages and the very houses of those most deeply concerned' (IOR: R W to CC, NWFP, Memo,

7.12.1928, L/P&S/10/1142, pp. 40–1; CC NWFP, No. 459-P, 9.11.1928, L/P&S/10/1142, p. 376).

116 IOR: Report of Air Op.s against the Giga Khel and Nekzan Khel-Nov. 1928, L/P&S/10/1142, pp. 45–47b.
117 IOR: R W, No. 624-T, 6.7.1926, L/P&S/10/1142, p. 345b; GOI to CC NWFP, No. 181-F/26, 17.7.1926, L/P&S/10/1142, p. 348.
118 IOR: *RAB 1923-24*, p. 10, V/10/390.
119 IOR: *RAB 1925-26*, p. 12, V/10/390; see also *RAB 1924-25*, p. 9, V/10/390, *RAB 1927-28*, p. 16, V/10/390.
120 An unmetalled road, it crossed the Kaitu by a new bridge at Spinwam (Warren, *Waziristan*, 2000, p. 54; Robson, *Crisis*, 2004, p. 245; IOR: *RAB 1927-28*, p. 16, V/10/390; *RAB 1926-27*, p. 11, V/10/390).
121 IOR: *RAB 1925-26*, p. 11, V/10/390; *RAB 1928-29*, p. 16, V/10/390.
122 Charles Bruce, *Waziristan 1936-37 The Problems of the North-West Frontier of India and their Solutions* (1938, Aldershot), p. 5; IOR: Sub-encl. No. 1 R W (C.E. Bruce) Note on Waziristan Affairs, L/P&S/10/1142, p. 55.
123 Warren, *Waziristan*, 2000, p. 58, IOR: *RAB 1928-29*, p. 34, V/10/390.

Chapter 9

1 Barfield, *Afghanistan*, 2010, pp. 188–90. See Poullada (*Reform*, 1973, pp. 160–4) for the background to the Shinwari revolt.
2 Poullada, *Reform*, 1973, pp. 170–1.
3 Bowyer, *RAF Operations*, 1988, p. 193.
4 Stewart, *Fire*, 1973, p. 516.
5 Saikal, *Modern Afghanistan*, 2012, p. 92.
6 Hall, *A Brief Guide*, 1981, p. 31. Adamec, *Afghanistan's*, 1974, pp. 173, 176; Stewart, *Fire*, 1973, p. 517.
7 Adamec, *Afghanistan's*, 1974, pp. 176–7; Saikal, *Modern Afghanistan*, 2012, p. 93.
8 IOR: Summary of events from 4.5.1930, L/P&S/12/3122, pp. 235–6b.
9 Gregorian, *Emergence*, 1969, pp. 282–5; Adamec, *Afghanistan's*, 1974, pp. 177–8; Saikal, *Modern Afghanistan*, 2012, p. 99; Barfield, *Afghanistan*, 2010, p. 195.
10 'Hitler of the N.W. Frontier Rise and Fall of an Outlaw', *Times* (London, England), 13.4.1941, *The Times Digital Archive, 1785-2010*, https://www.gale.com/intl/c/the-times-digital-archive
11 Barfield, *Afghanistan*, 2010, p. 195; Saikal, *Modern Afghanistan*, 2012, p. 108.
12 Saikal, *Modern Afghanista*, 2012, pp. 106, 116.
13 IOR: *RAB 1928-29*, p. 16, V/10/390. Some secret GOI political files may have been destroyed subsequently (Poullada, *Reform*, 1973, p. 161; Adamec, *Afghanistan's*, 1974, p. 154).

14 Adamec, *Afghanistan's*, 1974, pp. 150–2.
15 Poullada, *Reform*, 1973, p. 295; Adamec, *Afghanistan's*, 1974, p. 150.
16 Roberts, *The Origins*, 2003, p. 53, Adamec, *Afghanistan's*, 1974, p. 185, Ewans, *Afghanistan*, 2001, p. 102.
17 IOR: L/P&S/12/1571, p. 29. In April 1931 the GOI introduced a temporary regulation which enabled it censor most of the pro-Amanullah articles which had been appearing in newspapers published in Lahore.
18 Marsh, *Ramparts*, pp. 175–7. Tripodi suggests that during the 1930s, in pursuit of the policy of peaceful penetration, the frontier officials failed to recognize that their forward moves along the border put the GOA in a difficult position. If the GOA failed to respond vigorously to them, it laid itself open to accusations of being too friendly to the British. In the case of the Madda Khels in 1933, however, it was the GOI that wanted to adopt an aggressive approach rather than the NWFP government (IOR: Minute Paper, 14.2.1934, L/PS/12/3206, p. 364; Christian Tripodi, '"Politicals", Tribes and Musahibans: The Indian Political Service and Anglo-Afghan Relations 1919-39', *The International History Review*, Vol. 34, No. 4, 2012, pp. 865–86).
19 See for example IOR: L/P&S/12/1571, pp. 260b, 292b, 363.
20 IOR: HMMK to GOI FD, Demi-Official (D.O.) No. 595, 31.1.1934, L/PS/12/3206, p. 356.
21 IOR: L/P&S/12/1571, pp. 257–7b.
22 Jeffrey Roberts, *The Origins of Conflict in Afghanistan* (2003, Westport, CO/London), p. 54.
23 Faiz Muhammad had a long career as a diplomat and minister, becoming ambassador in Ankara, London, and Jeddah, and then minister of education in the 1950s (Adamec, *Historical and Political*, 1975).
24 IOR: HMMK, Encl. 1 to Kabul dispatch No. 162, 29.12.1933, L/P&S/3208, p. 41.
25 Ibid.
26 IOR: HMMK, Kabul, to FO London, No. Katodon-109, 18.8.1930, L/PS/3122 p. 250b.
27 IOR: L/P&S/12/1571, p. 232; Dupree, *Afghanistan*, 1978, p. 460; Barfield, *Afghanistan*, 2010, p. 197.
28 IOR: L/P&S/12/1571, p. 385b; also p. 223b para. 104.
29 Barnett Rubin, *The Fragmentation of Afghanistan: State Formation and Collapse in the Internal System*, (1995, New Haven, CT), p. 62. Nadir encouraged the use of the Pashto language, though he did not speak it himself (Private communication, Dr Muhammad Jamil Hanifi); IOR: L/P&S/10/1571, p. 233b.
30 IOR: R W to CC NWFP, No. 665-S., 29.5.1930, L/P&S/12/3122, p. 235b.
31 IOR: CC NWFP, No. 631-S. 26.5.1930, L/P&S/10/3122, p. 232.
32 IOR: Agent to GG Baluchistan to Governor Kandahar, 7.1.1923, L/P&S/10/1019, p. 163; NWFP to FS to GOI, No. 513 P.C./1086(4)-II, 20.2.1934, L/P&S/10/1019, p. 39; L/P&S/10/1571, p. 364b.

33. One British official described him as 'a well-known intriguer of former days' (IOR: L/P&S/10/1571, p. 364b).
34. IOR: N-WFP to GOI, No. 513 P.C./1086(4)-II, 20.2.1934, L/PS/12/3208.
35. For details of this, see for example Lee, *Afghanistan*, 2018, *passim*.
36. Mukulika Banerjee, *The Pathan Unarmed: Opposition and Memory in the North-West Frontier* (2000, Oxford/Karachi/New Delhi/Santa Fe, NM) pp. 48–56.
37. Ibid., p. 57.
38. Marsh, *Ramparts*, 2015, pp. 96–117. Thirty is almost certainly too low (Banerjee, *Unarmed*, 2000, p. 57); see also the letter by Sir Olaf Caroe's son, Michael Caroe, in *Asian Affairs*, 2001, Vol. 32, Part 1, pp. 114–19.
39. Roberts, *The Origins*, 2003, pp. 55–6; Rittenberg, *Ethnicity, Nationalism and the Pakhtuns*, 1988, p. 80.
40. Chevenix-Trench, *Scouts*, 1986, pp. 120–7.
41. In addition it was hoped that the roads would facilitate economic development (Tim Moreman, 'Watch and Ward', 1999, pp. 141, 146).
42. IOR: R W to CC NWFP, No. 2054-S., 17.11.1930, L/P&S/12/3123, p. 71.
43. Gregorian, *Emergence*, 1967, p. 330; IOR: R W to CC NWFP, Memo. No. 458-S., 9.5.1930, L/P&S/12/3122, p. 199.
44. IOR: R W to CC NWFP, 30.8.1930, L/P&S/12/3123, pp. 178–8b.
45. IOR: CC NWFP to GOI FP, Memo. No. 312-S.S., 5.3.1931, L/P&S/12/3122, p. 121b.
46. Ibid.
47. IOR: Memo, Griffith, 26.5.1930, L/PS/12/3122, pp. 231b–2.
48. IOR: No. 632-S., Summary of events in Waziristan from 4.5.1930, L/P&S/12/3122, p. 233b.
49. IOR: Minute Paper, Reg. No. P. 3001/30, Secret PD, L/P&S/12/3123, p. 355; IOR: No. 632-S.; L/P&S/12/3122, p. 233b.
50. IOR: NWFP, Tel. No. 485 P, L/P&S/12/3123, p. 315.
51. IOR: No. 632-S., Summary, L/P&S/12/3122, p. 233b; IOR: Memo. No. No. 604-S. 17.4.1931, p. 73; CC NWFP, 28.5.1930, L/P&S/10/3123, p. 304; V to SofSI, 16.5.1930, L/P&S/10/3123, p. 339.
52. IOR: No. 632-S., Summary, L/P&S/12/3122, p. 233b.
53. IOR: Transl. of the statement of Madda Khel maliks, L/P&S/12/3122, p. 74b.
54. IOR: No. 632-S., Summary 4.5.1930, L/P&S/12/3122, p. 234; R W to CC, D.-O., 24.6.1930, L/P&S/12/3122, p. 254; *RAB 1930-31*, p. 24, V/10/390.
55. IOR: PA, North W, No. 600-P., 17.6.1930, L/P&S/12/3123, p. 74.
56. IOR: PA SW to R W, No. 139-S, 19.5.1930, transl., Shah Mahmud, 14.5.1930, L/P&S/12/3122, p. 251b.
57. IOR: L/P&S/12/1571, p. 294; R W to CC NWFP D.O., No. 859-S., 24.6.1930, L/P&S/12/3122, p. 254; R W to CC NWFP, D.O., No. 896-S., 27.6.1930,

L/P&S/12/3122, p. 259; Gregorian, *Emergence*, 1973, p. 294; Poullada, *Reform*, 1973, p. 200.
58   IOR: GOI to SofSI, No. 5.130-F. 30, 23.8.1930, L/P&S/12/3122, p. 251. Britain was entitled, the Indian foreign secretary thought, to object to the Afghans supporting these men, as well as Gul Din and Mullah Gulin (IOR: GOI to SofSI, No. 5.130-F. 30, 23.8.1930, L/P&S/12/3122, p. 251).
59   IOR: PA SW to R W, No. 139-S, 19.5.1930, L/P&S/12/3122, pp. 230–1.
60   He had formerly been a clerk in the Tochi Agency Headquarters at Miranshah (IOR: CC NWFP to GOI FP, Memo. No. 312-S.S., 5.3.1931, L/P&S/12/3122, p. 121b).
61   IOR: No. 632-S., Summary of events in Waziristan from 4.5.1930, L/P&S/12/3122, p. 234.
62   Some Congress party members from the administered areas, including some Hindus, even crossed into Khost (Barton, *India's*, 1939, pp. 222–3).
63   IOR: Statement Khaisor Khan, L/P&S/12/3122, p. 96; CC NWFP, No. 631-S. 26.5.1930, L/P&S/12/3122, p. 231b.
64   IOR: CC NWFP, No. 631-S. 26.5.1930, L/P&S/12/3122, p. 231b.
65   IOR: CC NWFP, No. 631-S. 26.5.1930, L/P&S/12/3122, pp. 231–2; No. 632-S., Summary, 4.5.1930, L/P&S/12/3122, p. 234b.
66   The mullahs were not all anti-British (Haroon, *Frontier*, 2007, pp. 125–6).
67   IOR: Order, Assistant PA, 10.12.1930, L/P&S/12/3122, p. 106.
68   IOR: PA South W to R W, No. 139-S., 19.5.1930, L/P&S/12/3122, p. 230; No. 632-S., Summary, 4.5.1930, L/P&S/12/3122, pp. 234–4b.
69   IOR: Tel., V to SofSI, 19.5.1930, L/P&S/12/3123, pp. 322–3.
70   Ibid.
71   As well as the INC, another nationalist group, the socialist Nau Jawan Bharat Sabha (literally 'new young India group') was reported to have attempted to influence some of the trans-border tribes in 1930–1 and to have been active again the following year (IOR: *RAB 1931-32*, p. 1).
72   IOR: Order, L/P&S/12/3122, p. 105; jirga statement, Order, L/P&S/12/3122, p. 106b; No. 632-S., Summary, 4.5.1930, L/P&S/12/3122, 234b.
73   IOR: R W to CC NWFP, No. 729-S., 7.6.1930, L/P&S/12/3122, pp. 237–7b; Tel. 1788, 1.6.1930, L/P&S/12/3123, p. 300; *RAB 1930-31*, p. 25, V/10/390; Curtis, *MMT*, 1947, p. 239.
74   IOR: R W to CC NWFP, Memo., No. 898-S., 27.6.1930, L/P&S/12/3122, p. 241b.
75   IOR: V to SofSI, No. 2035-S, 19.6.1930, L/P&S/12/3123, p. 283.
76   IOR: R W to CC N-WFP, Tel., No. 964-S, 5.7.1930, L/PS/3122 pp. 24–5.
77   IOR: R W to CC NWFP, No. 665-S., 29.5.1930, L/P&S/12/3122, p. 235b.
78   IOR: Marginal note on L/P&S/12/3122, p. 40, Marsh, *Ramparts*, 2015, pp. 178–9.
79   IOR: R W to CC NWFP, No. 964-S., 5.7.1930, L/P&S/12/312, p. 240b.

80 IOR: V to SofSI, No. 2301-S, 16.7.1930, L/P&S/12/3123, p. 239; V to SofSI, No. 2212-S., 8.7.1930; L/P&S/12/3123, p. 277, Chevenix-Trench, *Scouts,* 1986, p. 139.
81 Chevenix-Trench, *Scouts,* 1986, p. 139; IOR: V to SofSI, No. 2212-S., 8.7.1930 L/P&S/12/3123, p. 267.
82 IOR: V to SofSI, No. 2301-S, 16.7.1930, L/P&S/12/3123, pp. 239–40.
83 IOR: Statement Khaisor Khan, L/P&S/12/3122, p. 98b.
84 IOR: V to SofSI, No. 2301-S, 16.7.1930, L/P&S/12/3123, p. 239.
85 Fraser-Tytler, *Afghanistan,* 1967, p. 276.
86 IOR: V to SofSI, No. 2212-S., 8.7.1930, L/P&S/12/3123, p. 267; V to SofSI, No. 2197-S, 5.7.1930, L/P&S/12/3123, p. 277.
87 Chevenix-Trench, *Scouts,* 1986, p. 139.
88 Ibid., p. 142.
89 Ibid., pp. 139, 141; IOR: V to SofSI, No. 2301-S, 16.7.1930, L/P&S/12/3123, p. 237.
90 IOR: V to SofSI, No. 2301-S, 16.7.1930, L/P&S/12/3123, p. 239.
91 Ibid., p. 250.
92 IOR: V to SofSI, Tel.No. 2301-S., 16.7.1930, L/P&S/12/3123, p. 238; V to SofSI, number unreadable, 13.7.1930, L/P&S/12/3123, p. 243, Chevenix-Trench, *Scouts,* 1986, p. 142.
93 IOR: R W to N-WF, No. 1319-S, 25.7.1930, L/P&S/12/3123, p. 218.
94 IOR: V to SofSI, 16.7.1930, L/P&S/12/3123, p. 238.
95 IOR: R W to CC NWFP, 22.7.1930, L/P&S/12/3123, pp. 160–1.
96 IOR: Maulvi Muhammad Gulin to Nadir Khan, L/P&S/12/3122, p. 206; V to SofSI, No. 2387-S., 25.7.1930, L/P&S/12/3122, p. 216.
97 IOR: IOR: R W to CC NWFP, No. 1441-S, 18.8.1930, L/P&S/12/3123, p. 148.
98 IOR: V to SofSI, Tel. No. 1319-S, 25.7.1930, L/P&S/12/3123, p. 218.
99 IOR: R W to CC NWFP, No. 1441-S, 18.8.1930, L/P&S/12/3123, p. 147.
100 For details see IOR: R W, Endorsement, No. 1415-S, 13.8.1930, L/P&S/12/3123, p. 154.
101 IOR: IOR: CC NWFP to GOI FP, Memo. No. 312-S.S., 5.3.1931, L/P&S/12/3122, p. 121b.
102 IOR: CC NWFP, No. 2054-S., 17.11.1930, L/P&S/12/3123, p. 71; CC NWFP, Memo. No. 4995-P./22/29, 17.12.1930, L/P&S/12/3123, p. 70.
103 IOR: Order, Assistant PA, 10.12.1930, L/P&S/12/3122, pp. 106–6b.
104 IOR: R W to CC NWFP, No. 1441-S., 18.8.1930, L/P&S/12/3123, p. 149; Tel. 1788-S., L/P&S/12/3123, pp. 300–2.
105 IOR: Tel. 1788-S., L/P&S/12/3123, p. 300.
106 IOR: DC Bannu to CC NWFP, Memo. No. 148, 30.8.1930, L/P&S/12/3123, pp. 124–30; Haroon, *Frontier,* 2007, p. 161.
107 IOR: R W to Foreign, Tel. No. 1502-S., 12.9.1930, L/P&S/12/3123, p. 170; GOI FD to SofSI, No. 2930-S., 29.8.1930, L/P&S/12/3123, p. 182.

108 Fraser-Tytler, *Afghanistan*, 1967, p. 276.
109 IOR: *RAB 1931-32*, p. 19, V/10/390.
110 Bowyer, *RAF Operations*, 1988, p. 205; Rittenberg, *Ethnicity*, 1988, p. 80; Warren, *Waziristan*, 2000, pp. 63–4.
111 Warren, *Waziristan*, 2000, p. 64.
112 Report of the Tribal Control and Defence Committee, 1931 (Delhi, 1931), quoted in Marsh, *Ramparts*, 2015, p. 206).
113 Marsh, *Ramparts*, 2015, p. 206.
114 Ibid.
115 IOR: LPS/12/1571, p. 292.
116 IOR: L/P&S/12/1571, p. 364b.
117 For details see IOR: 12/1571, pp. 292b, 231.
118 Its origins are obscure, but the word 'basmachi' came to mean bandits because it was used pejoratively by the Soviet Union to refer to the opposition to their rule in Central Asia ('Basmachis', Daniel E. Schafer, Encyclopedia of Russian History. *Encyclopedia.com*, http://www.encyclopedia.com/history/asia-and-africa/central-asian-history/basmachi).
119 He had supported Habibullah Kalakani (Adamec, *Afghanistan's*, 1974, p. 202).
120 IOR: PA S W to R W, 26.1.1932, L/P&S/12/3122, p. 32. Some Mehsuds and Wazirs were killed in the fighting (IOR: CC NWFP, Memo., No. 1950-S., 3.11.1930, L/P&S/12/3122, p. 102b; CC NWFP, Memo., No. 100/783-P.S., 6.1.1931, L/P&S/12/3122, p. 103).
121 IOR: L/P&S/12/1571, p. 29.
122 On his return to Kabul, Ramzan was instructed not to have any dealings with the Soviet Embassy (IOR: PA S W to R W, L/P&S/12/3122, p. 21; L/P&S/12/1571, pp. 294, 342b).
123 IOR: PA S W to R W, 26.1.1932, L/P&S/12/3122, pp. 32–3.
124 Ibid., p. 32.
125 Four Mahsud khassadar companies refused to accept the reduced rates of pay (IOR: *RAB 1931-32*, pp. 2, 24; Adamec, *Afghanistan's*, 2012, p. 209). In addition, it was suggested early in 1932 that with the approach of spring 'the young Mahsud's fancy naturally turns to thoughts of fighting' (IOR: PA S W to R W, 26.1.1932, L/P&S/12/3122, p. 32).
126 IOR: *RAB 1931-32*, p. 3, V/10/390.
127 IOR: L/P&S/12/1571, p. 364b.
128 Chevenix-Trench, *Scouts*, 1968, p. 116.
129 Ghulam Nabi had been governor of the Southern Province and ambassador in Moscow.
130 IOR: L/P&S/12/1571, p. 231b.
131 Ibid.
132 Ibid.

133 Ibid.; *RAB 1932-33*, p. 16, V/10/390.
134 IOR: NWFP to GOI FP, No. 2116, 6.7.1934, L/P&S/12/3208, p. 308; L/P&S/12/1571, pp. 223, 231b–2b; Roberts, *The Origins*, 2003, p. 60; Haroon, *Frontier*, 2007, p. 173; Curtis, *MMT*, 1947, p. 303.
135 IOR: *RAB 1932-33*, p. 20; L/P&S/12/1571, p. 232; Warren, *Waziristan*, 2000, p. 67.
136 IOR: D.O. Maconachie to GOI FP, No. 97, 20.7.1934, L/P&S/12/3208, p. 298; L/P&S/12/1571, p. 231. See also IOR: L/P&S/12/1571, p. 298; Tel. F to Min. Kabul, 15.7.1936, L/P&S/12/1571, p. 31.
137 IOR: L/P&S/12/1571, p. 233.
138 Ibid., p. 234b.
139 Adamec, *Afghanistan's*, 1974, p. 197, Dupree, *Afghanistan*, 1978, pp. 475–6.
140 Adamec, *Afghanistan's*, 1974, p. 198, Saikal, *Modern Afghanistan*, 2012, p. 109.
141 IOR: NWFP to GOI, No. 513 P.C., 20.2.1934, L/P&S/12/3208, p. 39.
142 IOR: Memo, No. 1776-S, 21.12.1935, PA NW to RW, L/PS/12/3208.
143 Ibid.
144 IOR: N-WFP to GOI FP, No. 2116, P.C.N., 6.7.1934, PZ 5271, L/PS/12/3208, pp. 307–9; see also Curtis, *MMT*, 1947, p. 1.
145 IOR: Minute Paper, L/P&S/12/1571, p. 89.
146 Curtis, *MMT*, 1947, p. 218.
147 IOR: FS to NWFP, No. 3417-S, 22.11.1929, L/P&S/10/1142, p. 32.
148 IOR: *RAB 1930-31*, p. 21; see also Warren, *Waziristan*, 2000, p. 67, Leeson, *Frontier*, 2003, p. 80.
149 Adamec, *Afghanistan's*, 1974, p. 211.
150 In 'Policy on the North-West Frontier', IOR: L/PS/18/A216.
151 Tripodi, *Edge*, 2011, p. 232.
152 IOR: F to N-WFP, 18.6.1936, PZ5934, L/PS12/3208; Southwaz Tank to R W, No. 1045-S., 27.11.1935, L/P&S/12/3208, pp. 178–9.
153 IOR: N-WF to F, No. 2901 P.C. 1721-P.S., 8/10.8.1936, L/P&S/12/3247.
154 IOR: HMMK, No. 97, 31.7.1934, L/P&S/12/3208, p. 281; D.O., 22.2.1935, No. 113-P.S., N-WFP to R W, L/P&S/12/3208, p. 27.
155 IOR: PA S W to R W, No. 457-P.S., 27.8.1934, L/P&S/12/3208, p. 257; PA S W to R W, No. 476-S, 9.7.1934, L/P&S/12/3208, p. 294.
156 Ibid.; N-WFP to GOI FP, No. 2116, 6.7.1934, L/P&S/12/3208, pp. 307, 309.
157 IOR: *RAB 1932-33*, p. 15, V/10/390.
158 IOR: *Times of India*, 21.4.1934, extract in L.P&S/12/3206, p. 265.
159 IOR: Minute Paper, 14.2.1934, L/P&S/12/3206, p. 363–4.
160 IOR: SofSI to GOI FPD, Tel., L/P&S/12/3206, p. 323.
161 IOR: Minute Paper, 10.3.1934, L/P&S/12/3206, p. 301.
162 IOR: Minute Paper, L/P&S/12/3206, p. 154.
163 IOR: IOR: HMMK, No. 97, 31.7.1934, L/P&S/12/3208, p. 281; as regards Pak, see also L/P&S/12/1571, pp. 208–8b.

Chapter 10

1. IOR: HMMK D.O., to GOI FP, No. 97, 20.7.1934, L/P&S/12/3208, p. 298.
2. IOR: FM GOA, Encl. II to HMMK, No. 162, 29.12.1933, L/P&S/12/3208, p. 43.
3. Eighteen of them according to the 1934 *Annual Report on Afghanistan* (L/P&S/12/1571, p. 210, but thirteen according to the Military Attaché, Kabul (Extract from Diary, No. 35, 30.8.1934, L/P&S/12/3208, p. 253). Reportedly they attended the Habibia School rather than the so-called Tribal School, the Izharia (IOR: Counsellor (C), British Legation (BL) K to GOI FD, Memo. No. 936, 25.8.1936, L/P&S/12/3208; also PZ 1893 Memo., L/P&S/12/3208; CBLK to GOI FP, Memo., 20.11.1935, L/P&S/12/3208).
4. IOR: GOI FP to HMMK, No. F364-F/34, 24.8.1934, L/P&S/12/3208, p. 279. At this time the British were also concerned about visits by Soviet officials to tribal areas (Tripodi, *Edge*, 2011, pp. 199–200).
5. They were still there in 1936 it appears (CBLK to GOI FD, Memo. No. 936, 25.8.1936, L/P&S/12/3208).
6. IOR: L/P&S/12/1571, p. 210.
7. IOR: PZ5415 Memo. HMMK, No. 97 IX, 31.7.1934, L/P&S/12/3208, pp. 287–8.
8. IOR: L/P&S/12/1571, p. 210b. The prime minister also raised the issue of RAF planes overflying the Afghan side of the border (IOR: L/P&S/12/1571, p. 208b).
9. IOR: L/P&S/12/1571, p. 208b. In December 1934 Mullah Bashir, publisher of the anti-British paper, *Al Mujahid*, was murdered, at the instigation of a rival, probably Fazal Din (IOR: L/PS/12/1571, p. 32).
10. IOR: *RAB 1935-36*, p. 19; *RAB 1936-37*, pp. 16–17.
11. IOR: L/P&S/12/1571, pp. 142, 169b, 180–80b; *RAB 1935-36*, p. 18, V/10/390; Warren, *Waziristan*, 2000, pp. 93–4.
12. In 1938 Khandan Khan was jailed for anti-British activities (IOR: *RAB 1938-39*, p. 17).
13. Warren, *Waziristan*, 2000, p. 89. Mehsuds were also trying to encroach on Tori Khel land in the 'rich Shawal uplands west of Razmak', and in August Wazirs mobilized to resist them by motor-lorry – 'a curious sign of the times' commented the *RAB 1936-37* (pp. 16–17, V/10/390).
14. Warren, *Waziristan*, 2000, p. 91.
15. Reportedly he killed a Muslim groom and a Hindu shopkeeper as well (IOR: Peshawar Intelligence Summary (S), 29.7.1935, L/P&S/12/3208, p. 20; Minute Paper PZ 4019/35, L/P&S/12/3208, p. 213; L/P&S/12/1571, p. 180b).
16. IOR: L/P&S/12/3148, p. 21.
17. IOR: Exp. Norwef to F, No. 2901, L/P&S/12/3247.
18. Members of his gang remained at Musa Nika (Memo. No. 10/Ar/36/4141-43, 2.11.1936, Deputy Director, Intelligence (DDI), GOI Peshawar to NWFP, L/P&S/12/3247).

19. IOR: L/P&S/12/1571, p. 142b.
20. IOR: *RAB 1936-37*, L/P&S/12/3148, p. 21.
21. IOR: Secret PD Minute, D.O. No. 3775-P.C., 8/9.10.1936, FS to GOI, L/P&S/12/3208, pp. 77–80.
22. IOR: L/P&S/12/1571, p. 169, also pp. 163b, 175–6.
23. IOR: L/P&S/12/1571, pp. 178–9.
24. IOR: 1937 NWFP D.O., No. 4358-P.C.-1083, 24/25.11.1936, L/P&S/12/3208, p. 59; see also L/P&S/12/1571, p. 180b.
25. Curtis, *MMT*, 1947, p. 318.
26. Warren, *Waziristan*, 2000, p. 68.
27. IOR: Memo No. 10/Ar/36/24-50, 16.1.1936, DDI, GOI Peshawar to NWFP, L/P&S/12/3208, pp. 171–2.
28. It is not clear whether Musa Khan and his son received Rs.20,000 each or in total (IOR: Extract K Intelligence Summary, No. 13, w.e. 27.3.1936, P2865, L/P&S/12/3208, p. 110).
29. IOR: Memo No. 10/Ar/36/24-50, 16.1.1936, DDI, GOI Peshawar to NWFP, L/P&S/12/3208, pp. 171–2.
30. Ibid.; Extract K Intelligence Summary, No. 13, w.e. 27.3.1936, P2865, L/P&S/12/3208, p. 110.
31. Curtis, *MMT*, 1947, p. 218.
32. IOR: Extract K Intelligence Summary, No. 13, w.e. 27.3.1936, L/P&S/12/3208, P2865, p. 110.
33. In 1935 the Saifali and Pipalai Kabul Khels were each reported to have received 50 new enlistments in the Urgun Militia and Rs.3,000 (IOR: Memo. No. 4/Afg./25/9315-18, 3.12.1935, DDI, GOI, Peshawar to NWFP, L/P&S/12/3208. PZ 929, Brit. Legation K, 15.1.1937 to GOI FD, L/P&S/12/3208, pp. 71–2.
34. IOR: L/P&S/12/1571, pp. 95, 102; Ewans, *Afghanistan*, 2001, p. 104.
35. IOR: *RAB 1936-37*, p. 24; see also Barton, *India's*, 1939, pp. 221–2; Curtis, *MMT*, 1947, p. 410.
36. Warren, *Waziristan*, 2000, pp. 60–1.
37. IOR: Officer on Special Duty to GOI FP, L/P&S/10/953, p. 114. For some details of the Pioneers see Chevenix-Trench, *Scouts*, 1968, p. 180; *RAB 1934-35*, p. 19, V/10/390.
38. Barton, *India's*, 1939, pp. 221–2. The new roads were definitely making travel through Waziristan easier; for example, the *Report on the Administration of the Border 1934-35* noted that a Wazir could now travel from Shakai to Bannu by buying a seat on a lorry, rather than having to walk (*RAB 1934-35*, p. 19, V/10/390).
39. IOR: *RAB 1936-37*, pp. 11, 24.

40 Curtis, *MMT*, 1947, p. 344; for details see Leeson, *Frontier*, 2003, pp. 174–5.
41 Beattie, *Imperial*, 2002, p. 152.
42 Warren, *Waziristan*, 2000, p. 69.
43 IOR: L/P&S/12/3148, p. 2.
44 Warren, *Waziristan*, 2000, p. 62.
45 Barton, *India's North-West*, 1939, p. 251; Warren, *Waziristan*, 2000, p. 286.
46 Warren, *Waziristan*, 2000, p. 62.
47 Ibid., p. 69.
48 IOR: Cunningham MSS Eur.D 670/13, Recommendations to GOP, 10.9.1947.
49 Warren, *Waziristan*, 2000, pp. 89, 92.
50 Barton, *India's*, 1939, p. 247.
51 Ibid., p. 248; IOR Cunningham MSS Eur.D 670/13, 'Interaction between Indian politics and tribal territory', 20.6.1939. According to Cunningham, Pandit Krishna Kant Malaviya, Ganpat Rai, Bhandari and Bhai Parmanand were among the Hindu nationalist politicians in favour of an aggressive frontier policy (see e.g. Christophe Jaffrelot, *Hindu Nationalism A Reader* [2007, Princeton, NJ] p. 364).
52 It was at a site called the Shahidganj (place of martyrs).
53 Warren, *Waziristan*, 2000, pp. 80–2.
54 Ibid., p. 82.
55 'Frontier Firebrand', *Time Magazine*, 4.3.1940, http://www.time.com/time/magazine/article/0,9171,763573,00.html
56 Warren, *Waziristan*, 2002, p. 84; J.G. Elliott, *The Frontier 1839-1947 The Story of the North-West Frontier of India* (1968, London), p. 271.
57 Poullada, *Reform*, 1973, p. 179; Haroon, *Frontier*, 2007, p. 41. The Hazrats of Chaharbagh belonged to one of the three major (Naqshbandi) Mujaddidiyya lineages in Afghanistan descended from the great Indian Sufi reformer, Ahmad Sirhindi (1564–1624) (Haroon, *Frontier*, 2007, p. 41).
58 Warren, *Waziristan*, 2000, p. 85.
59 Ibid., 82–7, 94–95, p. 97.
60 Ibid., pp. 97–8.
61 Roe, *Waging*, 2010, p. 208; IOR: L/L/MIL/5/1065, Suppl. 3 to Intelligence Summary 6, 17–23/6/1937, app. A, quoted in Warren, *Waziristan*, 2000, p. 98.
62 Warren, *Waziristan*, 2000, pp. 99–101.
63 Ibid., pp. 101–3.
64 Warren, *Waziristan*, 2000, pp. 104–5; Tripodi, *Edge*, 2011, p. 245.
65 IOR: *RAB 1936-37*, p. 22.
66 Warren, *Waziristan*, 2000, p. 129.
67 Frontier Intelligence summary 30.11.1936, in Warren, *Waziristan*, 2000, p. 129. Edwards describes another occasion when British troops were believed to have been turned back by the miraculous powers of a holy man, in this case the Hadda Mullah (Edwards, *Heroes*, 1996, p. 201).

68. Warren, *Waziristan*, 2000, pp. 119–20.
69. Marsh, *Ramparts*, 2015, p. 219.
70. IOR: *RAB 1936-37*, p. 17, V/10/390.
71. Ibid., p. 29.
72. Warren, *Waziristan*, 2000, pp. 120–1, IOR: *RAB 1936-37*, p. 17, V/10/390.
73. Warren, *Waziristan*, 2000, p. 122. Din Faqir Muhammad Ali Khel had been born in 1892 and had been a Havildar of khassadars. He left khassadar service in the 1920s and became a faqir himself early in the 1930s (though according to the *RAB 1936-37* (p. 13), he was 'not a Mulla in the strict sense').
74. Warren, *Waziristan*, 2000, pp. 129–31.
75. IOR: *RAB 1936-37*, p. 22, V/10/390.
76. Warren, *Waziristan*, 2000, p. 135.
77. IOR: *RAB 1936-37*, p. 1, V/10/390.
78. Warren, *Waziristan*, 2000, p. 138.
79. Ibid., p. 137.
80. Leeson, *Frontier*, 2003, p. 85.
81. Warren, *Waziristan*, 2000, pp. 144–5, 152.
82. IOR: *RAB 1936-37*, V/10/390, p. 23.
83. Warren, *Waziristan*, 2000, pp. 157–8.
84. Ibid., pp. 158–9, also Leeson, *Frontier*, 2003, p. 89.
85. For instance on 16 to 17 April, some Mehsuds, led by Mullah Sher Ali Khan Umar Khel, attacked the Tiarza post. Bhittanis joined in these attacks as well, firing into the Tajori police station on the nights of 17 and 18 April 1937 (Warren, *Waziristan*, 2000, pp. 159–61; Barton, *India's*, 1939, p. 23).
86. IOR: L/P&S/12/1571, p. 97.
87. Ibid., p. 97b.
88. Warren, *Waziristan*, 2000, p. 133.
89. Ibid., pp. 161–2; IOR: L/P&S/12/1571, p. 41.
90. Curtis, *MMT*, 1947, p. 64.
91. IOR: *RAB 1936-37*, p. 10, V/10/390; also Warren, *Waziristan*, 2000, p. 178, and Haroon, *Frontier*, 2007, p. 172.
92. IOR: *RAB 1936-37*, pp. 1–2, V/10/390; also Warren, *Waziristan*, 2000, p. 163.
93. Warren, *Waziristan*, 2000, p. 161.
94. Leeson, *Frontier*, 2003, p. 89; Warren, *Waziristan*, 2000, p. 181.
95. Leeson, *Frontier*, 2003, p. 88; Warren, *Waziristan*, 2000, pp. 186, 193.
96. Adamec suggests that the tribes were 'effectively contained' during the interwar period (1974, p. 211), but this was not the case in Waziristan.
97. Warren, *Waziristan*, 2000, pp. 186–9.
98. Leeson, *Frontier*, 2003, p. 88; Warren, *Waziristan*, 2000, pp. 190, 194–5.
99. Warren, *Waziristan*, 2000, pp. 196–7; Curtis, *MMT*, 1947, p. 551; Leeson, *Frontier*, 2003, p. 90.

100 Warren, *Waziristan*, 2000, p. 191.
101 Ibid. The Foreign and Political Department had been replaced by the External Affairs Department in the mid-1930s.
102 The only House of Commons Parliamentary Paper to be published on the fighting in Waziristan blamed it entirely on Mirza Ali Khan and repeated the fabrication that the Tori Khel maliks had requested government intervention (Warren, *Waziristan*, 2000, pp. 190–1).
103 Ibid., pp. 201–2. Sir Arthur Parsons claimed that the Malik-cum-Khassadar system had prevented 'a much greater disturbance' (in Warren, *Waziristan*, 2000, p. 199). There are some details of schools in Waziristan in the *RAB 1936-37* (p. 13).
104 Leeson, *Frontier*, 2003, pp. 92–3, Warren, *Waziristan*, 2000, pp. 203–6.
105 Warren, *Waziristan*, 2000, p. 205; IOR: L/P&S/12/1571, p. 102. Johnson thought that Afghans taking part in the fighting were led by supporters of Amanullah in the Southern Province (Warren, *Waziristan*, 2000, pp. 203–6).
106 IOR: L/P&S/12/1571, pp. 38b, 95b. Later in the year the prime minister, Muhammad Hashim, was upset by a series of articles in a journal published in Rawalpindi called the *Rahnuma*, in which it was claimed that the GOA was cooperating with the GOI in repressing the Frontier tribes.
107 Warren, *Waziristan*, 2000, p. 206.
108 Leeson, *Frontier*, 2003, pp. 93–4.
109 Warren, *Waziristan*, 2000, p. 207. Mirza Ali Khan held a well-attended meeting at Musa Nika on 10 September, to try and encourage more men to join him (Warren, *Waziristan*, 2000, p. 207).
110 Warren, *Waziristan*, 2000, pp. 198, 209–10; Leeson, *Frontier*, 2003, p. 98.
111 Tripodi, *Edge*, 2011, p. 171.
112 Warren, *Waziristan*, 2000, pp. 210, 212, Leeson, *Frontier*, 2003, pp. 95–6, 98.
113 The British attributed Mirza Ali Khan's continuing resistance partly to 'the misplaced sympathy with [his cause] … expressed by a section of political opinion in India' which saw the Wazirs as 'innocent victims of aggression, animated only by patriotic sentiments' (IOR: *RAB 1937-38*, p. 4, V/10/390).
114 Warren, *Waziristan*, 2000, p. 213.
115 IOR: L/P&S/12/1571, p. 41.
116 Ibid.; Adamec, *Afghanistan's*, 1974, pp. 227–8.
117 Bowyer, *RAF*, 1988, pp. 229, 231.
118 IOR: L/P&S/12/1571, p. 42.
119 Warren, *Waziristan*, 2000, pp. 216–17.
120 Though Hauner is not convinced (Hauner, 'One Man', 1981, pp. 194–5); see also Caroe, *Pathans*, 1957, p. 408; Chevenix-Trench, *Scouts*, 1986, p. 206).
121 IOR: L/P&S/12/1571, p. 42b; Warren, *Waziristan*, 2000, p. 217.
122 IOR: L/P&S/12/1571, p. 42b.

123 Ibid., p. 38b; Adamec, *Afghanistan's*, 1974, p. 228.
124 Norval Mitchell, *Sir George Cunningham: A Memoir* (1968, Edinburgh/London), p. 70; IOR: GOI External Affairs Department (EAD) to Minister Kabul, 8.6.1941, L/PS/12/3265, p. 32. Asked what he would have done if he had been able to enter Afghanistan, he said he 'could have established himself and his family as rulers of the country and that, as Qadria [Qadiriyya] adepts represented a very large majority of the Afghans, he would have been able to bring peace and good Government to that country' (in Adamec, *Afghanistan's*, 1974, p. 229).
125 Curtis, *MMT*, 1947, p. 2; IOR: Tel. GOI to H.M.M. Kabul, 8.6.1941, L/PS/12/3256.
126 Chevenix-Trench, *Scouts*, 1986, pp. 189–90.
127 Warren, *Waziristan*, 2000, p. 262; see also IOR: *RAB 1940-41*, p. 30, Leeson, *Frontier*, 2003, p. 99.
128 IOR: *RAB 1940-41*, V/10/390, p. 28.
129 Leeson, *Frontier*, 2003, p. 99.
130 IOR: L/P&S/12/1571, p. 38b.
131 Ibid., pp. 39b, 41b.
132 Leeson, *Frontier*, 2003, pp. 100–1.
133 Ibid., p. 99.
134 Warren, *Waziristan*, 2002, pp. 234–6.
135 Ibid., pp. 234, Leeson, *Frontier*, 2003, p. 99.

Chapter 11

1 Moreman, 'Watch and Ward', 1999, pp. 150–1. In this context we might recall the accusation that the *bureaux Aarabes* in Algeria upheld the interests of the Arabs rather than the settlers (Rid, 'The Nineteenth Century', 2010, p. 742).
2 Moreman, 'Watch and Ward', 1999, pp. 150, 153; see also Tripodi, *Edge*, 2011, pp. 185–90.
3 Moreman, 'Watch and Ward', 1999, p. 149.
4 Ibid.
5 Warren, *Waziristan*, 2000, p. 248.
6 IOR: V to SofSI, Memo., 22.1.1939, L/PS/12/3265, p. 22; Moreman, 'Watch and Ward', 1999, p. 149; Fraser-Tytler, *Afghanistan*, 1967, pp. 269–70.
7 IOR: Memo. L/PS/12/3265, p. 22. Members of the Viceroy's Council agreed with him (GOI to SofSI, No. 1, 22.7.1939, pp. 84–7).
8 Ibid., p. 149.
9 Ibid., p. 148. The trials also contributed to making army and political officers more competitive and suspicious of each other.
10 Omissi, *Air Power*, pp. 48–9; Moreman, 'Watch and Ward', 1999, p. 147.
11 Warren, *Waziristan*, 2000, pp. 232, 237–8; Mitchell, *Cunningham*, 1968, p. 72.

12 Warren, *Waziristan*, 2000, pp. 208, 222, 238–40.
13 IOR: *RAB 1937-38*, p. 20, V/10/390; for more details see Warren, *Waziristan*, 2000, pp. 240–1.
14 Chevenix-Trench, *Scouts*, 1986, p. 281.
15 IOR: *RAB 1938-39*, p. 17, V/10/390.
16 Warren, *Waziristan*, 2000, p. 241, Mitchell, *Cunningham*, 1968, p. 71.
17 Mitchell, *Cunningham*, 1968, p. 71.
18 Quoted in Warren, *Waziristan*, 2000, pp. 242–3.
19 Leeson, *Frontier*, 2003, p. 99.
20 Warren, *Waziristan*, 2000, p. 244. Moreover, the establishment of the Razmak base exacerbated tensions between the military officers and the political ones.
21 Other forms of resistance included blowing up bridges and culverts with IEDs and stealing telephone wire (Curtis, *MMT*, 1947, p. 66).
22 Elliott, *The Frontier 1830-1947*, p. 280.
23 Ibid., p. 281; Robson, *Crisis*, 2004, p. 249.
24 Moreman, 'Watch and Ward', 1999, p. 150.
25 IOR: Linlithgow, Memo. in No. 1, GOI EAD to SofSI, 22.7.1939, L/PS/12/3265, p. 19.
26 IOR: Memo., L/PS/12/3265, p. 25. Already in 1932, only three years after their return, the possibility of withdrawing troops from Wana had been raised as an economy measure (FPD to SofSI, No. 3, 12.7.1934, L/PS/12/3151, p. 41).
27 IOR: Memo, L/PS/12/3265, p. 19; see also pp. 29–31. The Memo. also brought up the possibility of disarming Waziristan, but did not think it practical (IOR: Memo, L/PS/12/3265, p. 18).
28 Warren, *Waziristan*, 2000, pp. 248–9.
29 Curtis, *MMT*, 1947, p. 419. Curtis mentions several other successful entrepreneurs, contractors, shopkeepers and lorry owners (see e.g. pp. 93, 130, 417).
30 Ibid., p. 14.
31 Ibid., p. 186.
32 Ibid., pp. 46, 186.
33 Ibid., pp. 7–8.
34 Ibid.
35 Ibid., pp. 4, 22.
36 Gregorian, *Emergence*, 1967, pp. 380, 382–3; Adamec, *Afghanistan's*, 1974, p. 243.
37 The North-West 'remained a large military liability during the Second World War' (Moreman, 'Watch and Ward', 1999, p. 151).
38 Warren, *Waziristan*, 2000, p. 249.
39 Mitchell, *Cunningham*, 1968, p. 76.
40 IOR: Linlithgow to Amery, 29.8.1940, private letter, L/P&S/12/3265: Warren, *Waziristan*, 2000, pp. 249–50.

41 Warren, *Waziristan*, 2000, pp. 250–1; Leeson, *Frontier*, 2003, pp. 103–4.
42 Leeson, *Frontier*, 2003, p. 103.
43 'Hitler of the N.W. Frontier Rise and Fall of an Outlaw', *Times* (London, England), 13.4.1941, *The Times Digital Archive, 1785-2010*, https://www.gale.com/intl/c/the-times-digital-archive
44 Chevenix-Trench, *Scouts*, 1986, p. 241.
45 IOR: *RAB 1940-41*, pp. 28–9.
46 Ibid., p. 31.
47 Mitchell, *Cunningham*, 1968, p. 76; Warren, *Waziristan*, 2000, pp. 251–2.
48 IOR: Norwef to Foreign, No. 22225-26/376, 6.8.1942, L/PS/12/3265; also see *RAB 1941-42*, p. 2, L/PS/V/390. The fact that Sayyid Yusuf was allowed to return to Wana was an example of Cunningham's more tolerant attitude towards the frontier religious leaders during the war; he encouraged them to speak out against the Soviets, and the Axis Powers as enemies of Islam (Haroon, *Frontier*, 2007, p. 174).
49 IOR: *RAB 1940-41*, pp. 24–5, V/10/390.
50 Hauner, 'One Man', 1981, p. 197.
51 Ibid., p. 199.
52 The British claim that the German legation succeeded in sending Mirza Ali Khan some money remains unproven (Adamec, *Afghanistan's*, 1974, p. 251, Stewart, *Fire*, 1973, p. 189, Hauner, 'One Man', 1981, p. 201). The Soviet Embassy in Kabul is also reported to have sent money to him, but no evidence has been produced for this either (see for example Arthur Swinson, *The North-West Frontier* [London, 1967], p. 321).
53 Some Zadrans and Kabul Khels from Khost joined the Faqir at this point, having reportedly been in touch with the Italian Legation in Kabul (IOR: HMMK to Foreign, No. 690, 14.5.1942, L/P&S/12/3208, pp. 35–6; *RAB 1941-42*, p. 11, V/10/390).
54 Warren, *Waziristan*, 2000, pp. 253–4.
55 Curtis, *MMT*, 1947, p. 417. In 1945 he was readmitted; it turned out that he had been falsely accused by Wazirs who wanted to get his trade.
56 Warren, *Waziristan*, 2000, pp. 256–7.
57 Curtis, *MMT*, 1947, p. 499.
58 Warren, *Waziristan*, 2000, p. 257.
59 Tripodi, *Edge*, 2011, p. 215.
60 Chevenix-Trench, *Scouts*, 1986, p. 263.
61 Warren, *Waziristan*, 2000, p. 258.
62 IOR: Cunningham, MSS Eur. D 670/13, p. 29.
63 Warren, *Waziristan*, 2000, p. 260.
64 Ibid., pp. 246–7.

65 Marsh, *Ramparts,* 2015, p. 252; see also p. 248.
66 Warren, *Waziristan,* 2000, p. 259. In October 1946 the Indian Congress Party leader, Jawaharlal Nehru, toured the Frontier Agencies; in Waziristan he was not made welcome (see for example Leeson, *Frontier,* 2003, p. 111).
67 Leeson, *Frontier,* 2003, pp. 136–7.
68 Ibid., p. 143; Chevenix-Trench, *Scouts,* 1986, p. 266.
69 Charles Lindholm, *Perspectives: Essays in Comparative Anthropology* (1996, Karachi/New York) p. 9.
70 Alfred Hamilton Grant, 'The North-West Frontier of India', *Asiatic Review,* N.S. Vol. 19 (1923), p. 628. We might recall Fitzpatrick's comment that the Mehsuds were 'sensitive beyond words'.
71 Nichols, *Settling,* 2001, pp. 91, 227; see also, for example, Marsh, *Ramparts,* p. 127.
72 Coughlin refers to the British fighting against 'Wahhabi-inspired fanatics' during the Ambela campaign in 1863 (Coughlin, *Churchill's,* 2013) p. 136.
73 See for example Edwards, *Heroes,* 1996, p. 181.
74 Howell, *Mizh,* 1979, p. 98.
75 IOR: CC NWFP to FS GOI, No. 204-N, 26.5.1917, L/P&S/10/373.
76 Curtis, *MMT,* 1947, p. 2.
77 Ibid., p. 4.
78 Darwin, 'Imperialism and the Victorians: The Dynamics of Territorial Expansion': *The English Historical Review,* Vol. 112 (1997), No. 447, p. 627.
79 See for example Jeffrey Cox, *Imperial Fault Lines Christianity and Colonial Power in India, 1818-1940* (2002, Stanford, CA), pp. 32–3.
80 See for example Herbert Edwardes, *Life of Sir Henry Lawrence,* 2 vols (1872, London) also Peter Lumsden and George Elsmie, *Lumsden of the Guides* (1899, London), p. 20.
81 Singer, *Lords,* 1984, p. 126.
82 Cox, *Imperial Fault,* 2001, p. 32.
83 Nichols, *Settling,* 2001, p. 160.
84 Parry, *Reynell Taylor,* 1888, p. 256.
85 Quoted in Michael Kasprowicz, '1857 and the fear of Muslim rebellion on India's North-West Frontier', *Small Wars and Insurgencies,* Vol. 8 (1997), No. 2, p. 13.
86 Quoted in Ibid., p. 8.
87 Though it seems that the Hindus and Sikhs living in Waziristan itself were not usually badly treated.
88 Roberts, *Origins,* 2003, p. 104.
89 Leeson, *Frontier,* 2003, pp. 143, 160, 164–5.
90 Roberts, *Origins,* 2003, p. 108; Feroz H. Khan, 'The Durand Line', in Thomas J. Johnson and Barry S. Zellen (eds), *Culture, Conflict, and Counterinsurgency* (2014, Stanford, CA), p. 154.

91 Abubakar Siddique, *The Pashtun Question: The Unresolved Key to the Future of Pakistan and Afghanistan* (2014, London).
92 Roberts, *Origins*, 2003, p. 106.
93 Zahid Hussain, *Frontline Pakistan: The Struggle with Militant Islam* (2007, London/New York), p. 147.
94 Leeson, *Frontier*, 2003, p. 165.
95 Elisabeth Leake, *The Defiant Border: The Afghan-Pakistan Borderlands in the Era of Decolonization, 1936-1965* (2017, Cambridge), p. 86.
96 Roberts, *Origins*, 2003, p. 107. The GOA was also concerned about access to the sea for its land-locked country and tried but failed to persuade Britain to ensure this (Roberts, *Origins*, 2003, p. 84).
97 Roberts, *Origins*, 2003, p. 122.
98 Ibid., p. 122.
99 Leeson, *Frontier*, 2003, pp. 164–5. Another visitor at this point was a 'Kandahari Mullah' who joined the Kabul Khels for a time and called for the restoration to the Afghan throne of ex-amir Amanullah (Leeson, *Frontier*, 2003, p. 165).
100 Leeson, *Frontier*, 2003, pp. 161–4.
101 Chevenix-Trench, *Scouts*, 1986, pp. 268–9.
102 Leeson, *Frontier*, 2003, p. 187; Caroe, *Pathans*, 1957, pp. 436–7; Robert Wirsig, *The Baluchis and Pathans, Minority Rights Group Report No. 48* (1981, London), p. 15.
103 Leeson, *Frontier*, 2003, pp. 191.
104 Ibid., pp. 190–1.
105 Warren, *Faqir*, 2000, pp. 262–3.
106 Leeson, *Frontier*, 2007, pp. 204–5, 207.
107 Haroon, *Frontier*, 2007, p. 182.
108 Ibid., pp. 182, 186.
109 Jawad R. Awan, 'Interaction between Indian Politics and Tribal Territory', *The Nation*, (2015), 28.9.2015, https://nation.com.pk/28Sep-2015/nds-raw-nexus-fuelling-terrorism-in-pakistan
110 Roberts, *Origins*, 2003, p. 168.
111 Haroon, *Frontier*, 2007, pp. 187, 189; Warren, *Waziristan*, 2000, p. 263.
112 Raghav Sharma, *Nation, Ethnicity and the Conflict in Afghanistan: Political Islam and the Rise of Ethno-Politics 1992-1996* (2017, Abingdon/New York).
113 Haroon, *Frontier*, 2007, p. 191; Erland Jansson, *India, Pakistan or Pakhtunistan* (1981, Uppsala), p. 237; Roberts, *Origins*, 2003, p. 168.
114 Haroon, *Frontier*, 2007, pp. 191–2.
115 Singer, *Lords*, 1984, p. 172; see also Ahmed, *Resistance*, 1991, pp. 115–27.
116 Dupree, *Afghanistan*, 1978, pp. 492–3.
117 Vahid Brown and Don Rassler, *Fountainhead of Jihad: The Haqqani Nexus, 1973-2012* (2013, London), p. 35.

118 Leake, *Defiant*, 2017, p. 221.
119 Haroon, *Frontier*, 2007, pp. 178, 194–5.
120 Hassan Abbas, 'Transforming Pakistan's Frontier Corps', *Terrorism Monitor*, Vol. 5 (2007), No. 6, https://jamestown.org/program/transforming-pakistans-frontier-corps/
121 Leeson, *Frontier*, 2003, p. 177.
122 Chevenix-Trench, *Scouts*, 1986, p. 281.
123 Warren, *Waziristan*, 2000, p. 269.
124 In Bowyer, *RAF Operations*, 1988, p. 232. Roe describes him as 'a brutal and treacherous man' (Roe, *Waging War*, 2010, p. 233).
125 Warren, *Waziristan*, 2000, p. 276.
126 Ibid., pp. 278–9.
127 Edwards, *Heroes*, 1996, p. 185; see also Akbar S. Ahmed, *Millennium and Charisma among Pathans* (1976, London), pp. 104–6.
128 Warren, *Waziristan*, 2000, p. 276.
129 Ibid., p. 277.
130 Haroon, *Frontier*, 2007, p194.
131 He was in touch with Abdul Ghaffur Khan and even wrote to Nehru in 1937, addressing him as 'the distinguished Head of the Indian Nation' (Hauner, 'One Man', 1981, pp. 191, 207).
132 Beattie, *Imperial*, 2002, p. 21; Malcolm Yapp, 'Waziris and Waziristan', In P. Bearman et al. (eds), *Encyclopedia of Islam*, Second Edition, http://dx.doi.org.libezproxy.open.ac.uk/10.1163/1573-3912_islam_SIM_7906
133 Singer, *Lords*, 1984, p. 172.
134 Ahmed, *Resistance*, 1991, p. 115. Faiz Muhammad Mahsud was one of the boys from Waziristan who was given a scholarship by the GOA to study in Kabul; he became the minister of the interior in President Daud's government in 1973; he was relegated to the Ministry of Border and Tribal Affairs in 1975 and died in an ambush in Paktia in 1980 (Siddique, *Pashtun Question*, 2014, pp. 163–5).
135 Mariam Abou Zahab, '*Kashar*s against *Mashar*s: *Jihad* and Social Change in the FATA', in Benjamin Hopkins and Magnus Marsden (eds), *Beyond Swat* (2013, London), pp. 53–4.
136 Haroon, *Frontier*, 2007, pp. 204, 207; Roe, *Waging War*, 2010, p. 242.
137 Ahmed Rashid, *Islam, Oil and the New Great Game in Central Asia* (2000, London/New York), pp. 187, 194.
138 Ibid., p. 148.
139 Hussain, *Frontline*, 2007, p. 145.
140 Mahsud, Mansur Khan, 'The Taliban in South Waziristan', in Peter Bergen (ed.) with Katherine Tiedemann, *Talibanistan: Negotiating the Borders between Terror, Politics, and Religion* (2013, Oxford/New York), p. 169.

141 Ibid., p. 170.
142 'Waziristan Refugees Hail Afghan Gvnt. Hospitality', https://www.pajhwok.com/en/2017/03/27/waziristan-refugees-hail-afghan-govt-people-hospitality
143 Ian Talbot, *Pakistan A New History* (London, 2012), pp. 130–2; Ahmed Rashid, *Descent into Chaos How the War against Islamic Extremism Is Being Lost in Pakistan, Afghanistan and Central Asia* (2008, London), p. 111.
144 Muhammad Qasim Zaman, 'Tradition and Authority in Deobandi Madrasas of South Asia', in Robert W. Hefner and Muhammad Qasim Zaman (eds), *Schooling Islam The Culture and Politics of Modern Muslim Education* (2007 Princeton, NJ/Oxford), pp. 71–3; also Mariam Abou Zahab and Olivier Roy, *Islamist Networks: The Afghan-Pakistan Connection* (London, 2004), pp. 27, 29.
145 Talbot, *Pakistan*, 2012, p. 132.
146 Rashid, *Descent*, 2008, p. 277; Zahab, *Islamist*, 2004, p. 111; Shaukat Qadir, 'Pakistan's Waziristan Problem', *RUSI*, Vol. 153 (2008), No. 2, pp. 42–5.
147 Rashid, *Taliban*, 2000, p. 89.
148 Haroon, *Frontier*, 2007, p. 215.
149 *Economist*, 2.1.2010, p. 4; Hussain, *Frontline*, 2007, p. 152.
150 Antonio Giustozzi, *Koran, Kalashnikov and Laptop The Neo-Taliban Insurgency in Afghanistan,* (2007, London), p. 35; Marvin G. Weinbaum and Jonathan B. Harder, 'Pakistan's Afghan Policies and Their Consequences', *Contemporary South Asia*, Vol. 16 (2008), No. 1, p. 32.
151 Brown and Rassler, *Fountainhead*, 2013, pp. 156–7. See also for example 'The Genesis of Pakistan's "Strategic Depth" in Afghanistan', Arni Anand and Tondon Abhimanyu, https://www.fairobserver.com/region/central_south_asia/the-genesis-of-pakistans-strategic-depth-in-afghanistan-88910/

Chapter 12

1 Bruce, *Tribes*, 1929, p. viii.
2 C on Special Duty to CC NWFP, 20 March 1902, in No. 28, *Parliamentary* Cd. 1177, 1902, p. 288.
3 IOR: *RAB 1938-39*, p.12.
4 See for example IOR: *RAB 1940-41*; L/PS/12/3148, p. 17.
5 IOR: *RAB 1940-4,* p. 1, V/10/390. In the Khyber the political agent organised the enlistment of the khassadars.
6 Many maliks who have been seen as being too close to the Pakistani government have been murdered in recent years.
7 James Scott, *Weapons of the Weak: Everyday Forms of Peasant Resistance* (1985, New Haven, CT/London), p. xvi; Tripodi, *Edge*, 2011, p. 36.

8 Chevenix-Trench points out that little has been written about the military organization and chain-of-command of the tribes, which was sophisticated enough to control lashkars numbering thousands. 'It was', he says, 'similar to the Scottish Highlanders' system, each family, sept and clan following some proven war-leader who was not formally elected, but was nevertheless the tribe's choice' (Chevenix-Trench, *Frontier*, 1968, p. 48).
9 As he argues, in acephalous societies resisting states, 'Far from being sociological and cultural givens, lineage practices, genealogical reckoning, local leadership patterns, household structures, and perhaps even the degrees of literacy have been calibrated to prevent (and in rare cases to facilitate) incorporation into the state' (Scott, *The Art*, 2009, p. 32).
10 See, for example, *Annual Report on Afghanistan* (IOR: L/P&S/12/571, p. 207) and the *RAB 1936-37* (p. 12 V/10/390).
11 As Maffey saw it, 'We have got ourselves involved in the minor area on some vague theory that our position there should strengthen our arm against the major and more distant danger' (IOR MSS EUR 238/24, pp. 373–4).

Glossary

Algad valley, ravine.
badmash hooligan, trouble-maker.
bandish blockade.
barampta seizure of people to put pressure on relatives, and of animals and property to put pressure on their owners.
chalweshti group of men selected to act as temporary police.
chigha a village pursuit party.
gasht patrol.
ghaza fighting for Islam.
ghazi fighter for Islam.
jangal uncultivated area.
jehad [jihad] striving or struggle; often understood (incorrectly) to refer only to fighting for Islam.
jemadar military rank equivalent to lieutenant.
jirga meeting, assembly.
kashar young man, 'have not'.
khassadar tribal policemen.
khel lineage.
khidmati allowance in return for service.
kot walled hamlet.
lambardar landowner usually with police and other powers.
langar kitchen.
lashkar war-party.
malik/maliki leader/payment in return for leader's service.
mashar wealthier man, elder.
mohtabar elder.
muharrir clerk.
mulla/h a man trained in Muslim law and theology.
nanawatai reconciliation procedure.
nikat charter of hereditary entitlement and responsibility.
pir Sufi master, holy man.
raghza table-land, plateau.
sarishta thread, link.
shahid witness; someone who witnesses for the faith by dying for it.
sheikh/shaikh follower or deputy of a Sufi teacher.

shukrana tithe paid to a holy man.
subahdar captain.
talib-ul-ulm religious student.
tangi narrow passage through hills.
tarburwali rivalry with father's brother's son.
tehsildar an official in the political administration.
toi stream.
tuman/tumani tribe/tribal.
ulus tribe.
wakil representative.
wam field.
zam stream.
ziyarat shrine.

Sources and bibliography

IOR: British Library

L/P&S Political and Secret Department Records, 1756-1950

L/P&S/7 – Political and Secret Correspondence with India, 1875-1911
L/P&S/10 – Departmental Papers: Political and Secret Separate (Subject) Files, 1902-31.
L/P&S/11 – Departmental Papers: Political and Secret Annual Files, 1912-1930
L/P&S/12 – Departmental Papers: Political (External) Files and Collections c. 1931-50.
L/P&S/18 - Political and Secret Memoranda, c. 1840-1947.
L/P&S/20 - Political and Secret Department Library, c. 1800-1947.

Proceedings of the Government of India and of the Presidencies and Provinces, 1702-1942

India (Political and Foreign)
Punjab Foreign, 1871-1901

Private Collections

Lord Chelmsford - MSS Eur E264
Lord Curzon Collection - MSS Eur F111–112
Sir George Cunningham Collection 1911-68 MSS Eur D670
Sir John Lawrence - MSS Eur F90
Marquess of Reading - MSS Eur E238

University of Cambridge Library

Lord Hardinge Private and Political Papers ca.1880-1941.

Official publications

Bruce, Charles E. (1929) *The Tribes of Waziristan* (H.M. Stationery Office for the India Office, London).
Curtis, Gerald (1947) *Monograph on Mahsud Tribes* (Government of North-West Frontier Province). Confidential.
Edwardes, Herbert (1911) *Political Diaries of Lt. H.B. Edwardes 1847-1849* (Pioneer Press, Allahabad).
Johnson, Harry H. (1934) *Mahsud Notes* (Government of India, Simla).
Johnston, Frederick (1901) *Report on Waziristan and Its Tribes* (Punjab Government Press, Lahore, reprinted Sang-e-Meel Publications, 2005).
Johnston, Frederick (1903) 'Notes on Wana', reprinted in R. Nichols, ed., *Colonial Reports on Pakistan's Frontier Tribal Areas* (Oxford University Press, Karachi, 2005).
Operations in Waziristan 1919-20 (1921), (Superintendent Government Printing Press, Calcutta, https://archive.org/details/operationsinwaz00indi).
Reports on the Administration of the Border of the North-West Frontier Province, Government of the North-West Frontier Province.
Reports on the Administration of the Punjab, Government of the Punjab.
Taylor, Reynell (1865) *District Memorandum Dera Ismail Khan 1852* (Government Press, Lahore).
Tucker, Louis and Hill, W. *Report on the Traffic in Arms on the North-West Frontier*, in IOR Curzon Collection F.111/315A.

Parliamentary papers

British relations with the neighbouring tribes on the north-west frontier of India, and the military operations undertaken against them during the year 1897-1898, Cd8713/Cd8714.
Mahsud-Waziri Operations, Cd1177, 1902.
Papers regarding British relations with the neighbouring tribes on the north-west frontier of India and Punjab frontier administration, Cd496, 1901.

Other printed sources

Abou Zahab, Mariam (2013) '*Kashar*s against *Mashar*s: Jihad and Social Change in the FATA', in Benjamin Hopkins and Magnus Marsden (eds), *Beyond Swat: History, Society and Economy along the Afghanistan-Pakistan Frontier* (Hurst, London), pp. 51–60.
Abou Zahab, Mariam and Roy, Olivier (2004) *Islamist Networks: The Afghan-Pakistan Connection*, trans. J. King (Hurst, London).

Acharya, Arabinda, Bukhari, Syed Adnan and Sulaiman, Sadia (2009) 'Making Money in the Mayhem: Funding Taliban Insurrection in the Tribal Areas of Pakistan', *Studies in Conflict & Terrorism*, Vol. 32, No. 2, pp. 95–108.

Adamec, Ludwig (1967) *Afghanistan, 1900-1923: A Diplomatic History* (University of California Press, Berkeley and Los Angeles).

Adamec, Ludwig (1974) *Afghanistan's Foreign Affairs to the Mid-Twentieth Century: Relations with the USSR, Germany, and Britain* (The University of Arizona Press, Tucson).

Adamec, Ludwig (1975) *Historical and Political Who's Who of Afghanistan* (Akademische Druck-u. Verlaganstalt, Graz).

Ahmad, Qeyamuddin (1966) *The Wahabi Movement in India* (Firma K.L. Mukhopadhyay, Calcutta).

Ahmed, Akbar S. (1976) *Millennium and Charisma among Pathans* (Routledge, London).

Ahmed, Akbar S. (1980) *Pukhtun Economy and Society: Traditional Structure and Economic Development in a Tribal Society* (Routledge & Kegan Paul, London).

Ahmed, Akbar S. (1991) *Resistance and Control in Pakistan* (Routledge, London). First published as *Religion and Politics in Muslim Society* (Cambridge University Press, London, 1983).

Allen, Charles (2007) *God's Terrorists: The Wahhabi Cult and the Hidden Roots of Modern Jihad* (Abacus, London).

Arghandawi, Abdul A. (1989) *British Imperialism and Afghanistan's Struggle for Independence 1914-21* (Munshiram Manoharala, New Delhi).

Atran, Scott (2010) *Talking to the Enemy: Violent Extremism, Sacred Values, and What It Means to Be Human* (Penguin, London).

Baha, Lal (1970) *N.-W.F.P. Administration under British Rule 1901-1919* (National Commission on Historical and Cultural Research, Lahore).

Banerjee, Mukulika (2000) *The Pathan Unarmed: Opposition and Memory in the North-West Frontier* (James Currey, Oxford; Oxford University Press, Karachi and New Delhi; School of American Research Press, Santa Fe, NM).

Barfield, Thomas (1989) *The Perilous Frontier: Nomadic Empires and China 221 BC to AD 1757* (Blackwell, Cambridge, MA).

Barfield, Thomas (2010) *Afghanistan: A Cultural and Political History* (Princeton University Press, Princeton, NJ).

Barth, Fredrik (1959) *Political Leadership among Swat Pathans* (Athlone Press, London).

Barton, William (1939) *India's North-West Frontier* (John Murray, London).

Baud, Michiel and van Schendel, Willem (1997) 'Towards a Comparative History of Borderlands', *Journal of World History*, Vol. 8, No. 2, pp. 211–42.

Beattie, Hugh (2002) *Imperial Frontier: Tribe and State in Waziristan* (Curzon, Richmond).

Beattie, Hugh (2002) 'Etnicidad, nationalism y el Estudo en Afghanistan', in Devalle, Susana (ed.), *Identidad y Etnicidad: Continuidad y Cambio* (El Colegio de Mexico, Mexico City), pp. 83–117, English translation available at oro.2002.beattie.

Beattie, Hugh (2011) 'Negotiations with the Tribes of Waziristan 1849-1914 – The British Experience', *The Journal of Imperial and Commonwealth History*, Vol. 39, No. 4, pp. 571–87.

Beattie, Hugh (2013) 'Custom and Conflict in Waziristan: Some British Views', in Benjamin Hopkins and Magnus Marsden (eds), *Beyond Swat: History, Society and Economy along the Afghanistan-Pakistan Frontier* (London, Hurst), pp. 209–20.

Beattie, Hugh (2015) 'Hostages on the Indo-Afghan Border in the Later Nineteenth Century', *The Journal of Imperial and Commonwealth History*, Vol. 43, No. 4, pp. 557–69.

Black, Charles (1903) *The Marquess of Dufferin and Ava: Diplomatist, Viceroy, Statesman* (Hutchinson, London).

Blok, Anton (2001) *Honour and Violence* (Polity, Cambridge).

Bowyer, Chaz (1988) *RAF Operations 1918-38* (William Kimber, London).

Brower, Benjamin C. (2011) *A Desert Named Peace: The Violence of France's Empire in the Algerian Sahara, 1844-1902* (Columbia University Press, New York).

Brown, Vahid and Rassler, Don (2013), *Fountainhead of Jihad: The Haqqani Nexus, 1973-2012* (Hurst, London).

Bruce Charles (1938) *Waziristan 1936-37: The Problems of the North-West Frontier of India and their Solutions* (Gale & Polden, Aldershot).

Bruce, Richard (1990) *The Forward Policy and Its Results* (Longman Green, London).

Caroe, Michael (2001) letter in *Asian Affairs*, Vol. 32, No. 1, pp. 114–19.

Caroe, Sir Olaf (1957) *The Pathans 550 BC.-A.D.*, reprinted 1983 with a Foreword and an Epilogue on Russia (Oxford University Press, Oxford).

Chevenix-Trench, Charles (1986) *The Frontier Scouts* (Jonathan Cape, London).

Condos, Mark (2015) 'Licence to Kill: The Murderous Outrages Act and the Rule of Law in Colonial India, 1867-1925', *Modern Asian Studies*, Vol. 50, No. 2, pp. 479–517.

Condos, Mark (2016) 'Fanaticism and the Politics of Resistance along the North-West Frontier of British India', *Comparative Studies in Society and History*, Vol. 58, No. 3, pp. 717–45.

Coughlin, Con (2013) *Churchill's First War: Young Winston and the Fight against the Taliban* (Macmillan, London).

Cox, Jeffrey (2002) *Imperial Fault Lines: Christianity and Colonial Power in India, 1818-1940* (Stanford University Press, Stanford, CA).

Dale, Stephen F. (1980) *Islamic Society on the South Asian Frontier: The Mappilas of Malabar* (Oxford University Press, Oxford).

Dale, Stephen F. (1988) 'Religious Suicide in Islamic Asia: Anticolonial Terrorism in India, Indonesia, and the Philippines', *Journal of Conflict Resolution*, Vol. 32, No. 1 (March), pp. 37–59.

Darwin, John (1997) 'Imperialism and the Victorians: The Dynamics of Territorial Expansion', *The English Historical Review*, Vol. 112, No. 447, pp. 614–42.

Davies, Colin (1975) *The Problem of the North-West Frontier 1890-1908*, second edition (Curzon, London). First published Cambridge University Press, Cambridge, 1932.

Devji, Faisal (2005) *Landscapes of the Jihad: Militancy, Morality, Modernity* (Hurst, London).

Dupree, Louis (1978) *Afghanistan* (Princeton University Press, Princeton, NJ).

Dutta, Simanthi (2002) *Imperial Mappings: In Savage Spaces Baluchistan and British India* (B.R. Publishing. Delhi).

Edwards, David B. (1989) 'Mad Mullahs and Englishmen: Discourse in the Colonial Encounter', *Comparative Studies in Society and History*, Vol. 31, No. 4, pp. 649–70.

Edwards, David B. (1996) *Heroes of the Age: Moral Fault Lines on the Afghan Frontier* (University of California Press, Berkeley).

Edwardes, Herbert (1851) *A Year on the Punjab Frontier*, Vol. 2 (Richard Bentley, London).

Edwardes, Herbert (1872) *Life of Sir Henry Lawrence*, Vol. 1 (Smith, Elder & Co, London).

Edwardes, Lady Emma (1886) *Memorials of the Life and Letters of Major-General Sir Herbert Edwardes*, Vol.1 (Kegan Paul, Trench, London).

Eller, Jack D. (2010) *Cruel Deeds, Virtuous Violence: Religious Violence across Culture and History* (Prometheus, London).

Elliott, J.G. (1968) *The Frontier 1839-1947: The Story of the North-West Frontier of India* (Cassell, London).

Erichsen, Caspar and Olusoga, David (2010) *The Kaiser's Holocaust: Germany's Forgotten Genocide and the Colonial Roots of Nazism* (Faber & Faber, London).

Ewans, Martin (2001) *Afghanistan: A New History* (Curzon, Richmond).

Ferguson, R. Brian and Whitehead, Neil L. (1999) 'Preface to the Second Printing', in R. Brian Ferguson and Neil L. Whitehead (eds), *War in the Tribal Zone Expanding States and Indigenous Warfare* (School of America Research Press, Santa Fe, NM; James Currey, Oxford), pp. xi–xxxv.

Finch, Michael, P.M. (2013) *A Progressive Occupation? The Gallieni-Lyautey Method and Colonial Pacification in Tonkin and Madagascar 1885-1900* (Oxford University Press, Oxford).

Firestone, Reuven (1999) *Jihad: The Origin of Holy War in Islam* (Oxford University Press, Oxford/New York).

Forrest, G.W. (1909) *Life of Field Marshall Sir Neville Chamberlain* (Blackwood, Edinburgh)

Fraser-Tytler, W. (1967) *Afghanistan*, third edition (Oxford University Press, London).

Giustozzi, Antonio (2000) *War, Politics and Society in Afghanistan 1878-1992* (Hurst, London).

Giustozzi, Antonio (2007) *Koran, Kalashnikov and Laptop: The Neo-Taliban Insurgency in Afghanistan* (Hurst, London).

Grant, Alfred (1923) 'The North-West Frontier of India', *Asiatic Review*, N.S. Vol. 19, pp. 625–33.

Gregorian, Vartan (1969) *The Emergence of Modern Afghanistan: Politics of Reform and Modernization, 1880-1946* (Stanford University Press, Stanford, CA).

Hall, Lesley (1981) *A Brief Guide to Sources for the Study of Afghanistan in the India Office Records* (India Office Library and Records, London).

Haroon, Sana (2007) *Frontier of Faith: Islam in the Indo-Afghan Borderland* (Hurst, London).

Hauner, Milan (1981) 'One Man against the Empire: The Faqir of Ipi and the British in Central Asia on the Eve of and during the Second World War', *Journal of Contemporary History*, Vol. 16, No. 1, pp. 183–212.

Hegghammer, Thomas (2017) 'Non-military Practices in Jihadi Groups', in Thomas Hegghammer (ed.), *Jihadi Culture: The Art and Social Practices of Militant Islamists* (Cambridge University Press, Cambridge), pp. 171–201.

Hevia, James (2012) *The Imperial Security State: British Colonial Knowledge and Empire-Building in Asia* (Cambridge University Press, Cambridge).

Hobsbawm, Eric (2000) *Bandits* (Abacus, London).

Hodgson, Marshall (1974) *The Classical Age of Islam: The Venture of Islam Conscience and History in a World Civilization*, Vol. 1 (University of Chicago Press, Chicago, IL/London).

Hoisington, William A. Jr. (1995) *Lyautey and the French Conquest of Morocco* (Macmillan, Basingstoke).

Hopkins, Benjamin (2013) 'A History of the "Hindustani Fanatics" on the Frontier', in Benjamin Hopkins and Magnus Marsden (eds), *Beyond Swat: History, Society and Economy along the Afghanistan-Pakistan Frontier* (Hurst, London), pp. 39–49.

Howell, Evelyn (1957) 'Appendix D', in Sir Olaf Caroe, *The Pathans 550 BC.-A.D.*, reprinted 1983 with a Foreword and an Epilogue on Russia (Oxford University Press, Oxford), pp. 468–78.

Howell, Evelyn (1979) *Mizh: A Monograph on Government's Relations with the Mahsud Tribe* (Oxford University Press, Karachi). First published Government of India Press, Simla, 1931.

Hughes, Thomas (2002) 'The German Mission to Afghanistan, 1915-16', *German Studies Review*, Vol. 25 (October), 447–76.

Hussain, Zahid (2007) *Frontline Pakistan: The Struggle with Militant Islam* (I.B. Tauris, London/New York).

Jacobsen, Mark (2002) *Rawlinson in India* (Stroud Publishing Ltd., for Army Records Society, Stroud).

Jaffrelot, Christophe (2007) *Hindu Nationalism: A Reader* (Princeton University Press, Princeton, NJ).

Jalal, Ayesha (2008) *Partisans of Allah: Jihad in South Asia* (Harvard University Press, Cambridge, MA/London).

Jansson, Erland (1981) *India, Pakistan or Pakhtunistan: The Nationalist Movement in the North-West Frontier Province* (Acta Universitatis Upsaliensis, Uppsala).

Johnson, Robert (2003) '"Russians at the Gates of India"? Planning the Defence of India, 1885-1900', *The Journal of Military History*, Vol. 67, No. 3, pp. 697–743.

Kasprowicz, Michael D. (1997) '1857 and the Fear of Muslim Rebellion on India's North-West Frontier', *Small Wars and Insurgencies*, Vol. 8, No. 2, pp. 1–15.

Kelly, Saul (2013) '"Crazy in the Extreme"? The Silk Letters Conspiracy', *Middle Eastern Studies*, Vol. 49, No. 2, 162–78.

Khan, Feroz H. (2014) 'The Durand Line: Tribal Politics and Pakistan-Afghanistan Relations', in Thomas J. Johnson and Barry S. Zellen (eds), *Culture, Conflict, and Counterinsurgency* (Stanford University Press, Stanford, CA), pp. 148–75.

Laithwaite, Gilbert (2004) 'Maffey, John Loader', in *Dictionary of National Biography* (Oxford University Press, Oxford), pp. 104–5.

Leake, Elisabeth (2017) *The Defiant Border: The Afghan-Pakistan Borderlands in the Era of Decolonization, 1936-1965* (Cambridge University Press, Cambridge).

Lee, Jonathan (2018) *Afghanistan: A History from 1260 to the Present Day* (Reaktion Books, London).

Leeson, Frank (2003) *Frontier Legion: With the Khassadars of North Waziristan* (The Leeson Archive, Ferring, West Sussex).

Lindholm, Charles (1980) 'Images of the Pathan: the Usefulness of Colonial Ethnography', *Archives Européennes de Sociologie*, Vol. 21, No. 2, pp. 350–61.

Lindholm, Charles (1982) *Generosity and Jealousy: The Swat Pukhtuns of Northern Pakistan* (Columbia University Press, New York).

Lindholm, Charles (1982) 'Models of Segmentary Political Action: the Usefulness of Colonial Ethnography', Archives Europeénnes de Sociologie, vol. XXI, No. 2, pp. 350–61.

Lindholm, Charles (1996) *Frontier Perspectives: Essays in Comparative Anthropology* (Oxford University Press, Karachi/New York).

Lumsden, Peter and Elsmie, George (1899) *Lumsden of the Guides* (John Murray, London).

Mahsud, Mansur Khan (2013) 'The Taliban in South Waziristan', in Peter Bergen (ed.), with Katherine Tiedemann, *Talibanistan: Negotiating the Borders between Terror, Politics, and Religion* (Oxford University Press, London/New York), pp. 164–201.

Marsden, Magnus and Hopkins, Benjamin (2012), *Fragments of the Afghan Frontier* (Hurst, London).

Marsh, Brandon (2015) *Ramparts of Empire: British Imperialism and India's Afghan Frontier, 1918-1948* (Palgrave Macmillan, Basingstoke/St. Martins, New York).

Maurice, F. Sir (1928) *Life of Lord Rawlinson 1862-1925* (Cassell, London).

Metcalfe, Thomas R. (1995) *Ideologies of the Raj: The New Cambridge History of India III.4* (Cambridge University Press, Cambridge).

Mitchell, Norval (1968) *Sir George Cunningham: A Memoir* (Blackwood, Edinburgh/London).

Moreman, Tim (1999) '"Watch and Ward": The Army in India and the North-West Frontier, 1920-1939', in David Killingray and David Omissi (eds), *Guardians of Empire* (Manchester University Press, Manchester), pp. 137–56.

Nawid, Senzil (1999) *Religious Response to Social Change in Afghanistan 1919-29* (Mazda, Costa Mesa, CA).

Nichols, Robert (2001) *Settling the Frontier: Land, Law, and Society in the Peshawar Valley, 1500-1900* (Oxford University Press, Karachi).

Nichols, Robert (2005) 'Introduction', in R. Nichols (ed.), *Colonial Reports on Pakistan's Frontier Tribal Areas* (Oxford University Press, Karachi), pp. ix–xiv.

Omissi, David E. (1990) *Air Power and Colonial Control: The Royal Air Force 1919-1939* (Manchester University Press, Manchester/New York).

Omran, Bijan and Ledwidge, Frank (2009) 'Rethinking the Durand Line: The Legality of the Afghan-Pakistan Frontier', *The RUSI Journal*, Vol. 154, Issue 5, pp. 48–56.

Parry, Gambier (1888) *Reynell Taylor A Biography* (Kegan Paul and Trench, London).

Parry, Jonathan (2007) *Benjamin Disraeli* (Oxford University Press, Oxford).

Pennell, Theodore (1909) *Among the Wild Tribes of the Afghan Frontier* (Seeley, London).

Porch, Douglas (2013) *Counterinsurgency: Exposing the Myths of the New Way of War* (Cambridge University Press, Cambridge/New York).

Potter, Simon and Saha, Jonathan (2015) 'Global History, Imperial History and Connected Histories of Empire', *Journal of Colonialism and Colonial History*, Vol. 16, No. 1, https://muse.jhu.edu/article/577738.

Poullada, Leon B. (1973) *Reform and Rebellion in Afghanistan, 1919-1929: King Amanullah's Failure to Modernize a Tribal Society* (Cornell University Press, Ithaca, NY/London).

Rashid, Ahmed (2000) *Islam, Oil and the New Great Game in Central Asia* (I.B. Tauris, London/New York).

Rashid, Ahmed (2008) *Descent into Chaos: How The War against Islamic Extremism Is Being Lost in Pakistan, Afghanistan and Central Asia* (Penguin, London).

Rid, Thomas (2010) 'The Nineteenth Century Origins of Counterinsurgency Doctrine', *Journal of Strategic Studies*, Vol. 33, No. 5, pp. 727–758.

Rittenberg, S. A. (1988) *Ethnicity, Nationalism and the Pakhtuns: The Independence Movement in India's North-West Frontier Province* (Carolina Academic Press, Durham, NC).

Roberts, Jeffery J. (2003) *The Origins of Conflict in Afghanistan* (Praeger, Westport, CO/London).

Robson, Brian (2004) *Crisis on the Frontier: The Third Afghan War and the Campaign in Waziristan 1919-20* (Spellmount, Staplehurst).

Roe, Andrew M. (2010) *Waging War in Waziristan: The British Struggle in the Land of Bin Laden, 1849-1947* (University Press of Kansas, Lawrence).

Rubin, Barnett (1995) *The Fragmentation of Afghanistan: State Formation and Collapse in the Internal System* (Yale University Press, New Haven, CT).

Saikal, Amin (2012) *Modern Afghanistan: A History of Struggle and Survival* (I.B. Tauris, London/New York).

Schröder, Ingo W. and Schmidt, Bettina E. (2001) 'Introduction', in Bettina E. Schmidt and Ingo W. Schröder (eds), *Anthropology of Violence and Conflict* (Routledge, Abingdon), pp. 1–24.

Scott, James (1985) *Weapons of the Weak: Everyday Forms of Peasant Resistance* (Yale University Press, New Haven, CT/London)

Scott, James (2009) *The Art of Not Being Governed: An Anarchist History of Upland Southeast Asia* (Yale University Press, New Haven, CT/London).

Sharma, Raghav (2017) *Nation, Ethnicity and the Conflict in Afghanistan: Political Islam and the Rise of Ethno-Politics 1992-1996* (Routledge, Abingdon).

Siddique, Abubakar (2014) *The Pashtun Question: The Unresolved Key to the Future of Pakistan and Afghanistan* (Hurst, London).

Singer, André (1984) *Lords of the Khyber: The Story of the North-West Frontier* (Faber and Faber, London and Boston, MA).

Singhal, D. P. (1963) *India and Afghanistan 1876-1907: A Study in Diplomatic Relations* (University of Queensland Press, Brisbane).

Spain, James (1963) *The Pathan Borderland* (Mouton, The Hague).

Spain, James (1995) *Pathans of the Latter Day* (Oxford University Press, Karachi).

Stewart, Jules (2014) *The Kaiser's Mission to Kabul: A Secret Expedition to Afghanistan in World War I* (I.B. Tauris, London/New York).

Stewart, Rhea Talley (1973) *Fire in Afghanistan 1914-1929: Faith, Hope and the British Empire* (Doubleday & Company, Garden City, NY).

Surridge (2008) 'The Ambiguous Amir: Britain, Afghanistan and the 1897 North-West Frontier Uprising', *Journal of Imperial and Commonwealth History*, Vol. 36, No. 3, pp. 417–34.

Swinson, Arthur (1967) *The North-West Frontier* (Hutchinson, London).

Talbot, Ian (2012) *Pakistan: A New History* (Hurst, London).

Tapper, Richard (1983) 'Introduction', in Richard Tapper (ed.), *The Conflict of Tribe and State in Iran and Afghanistan* (Croom Helm, Beckenham), pp. 1–82.

Tapper, Richard (1997) *Frontier Nomads of Iran: A Political and Social History of the Shahsevan* (University of Cambridge Press, Cambridge).

Tapper, Richard (2013) 'Studying Pashtuns in Barth's Shadow', in David Hopkins and Magnus Marsden (eds), *Beyond Swat: History, Society and Economy along the Afghanistan-Pakistan Frontier* (Hurst, London), pp. 221–37.

Thornton, Thomas (1895) *Colonel Sir Robert Sandeman: His Life and Works on Our Indian Frontier* (John Murray, London).

Tickell, Alex (2013) *Terrorism, Insurgency and Indian-English Literature, 1830-1947* (Routledge, London/New York).

Tripodi, Christian (2009) '"Good for one but not the other"; The "Sandeman System" of Pacification as Applied to Baluchistan and the North-West Frontier, 1877-1947', *The Journal of Military History*, Vol. 73 (July), pp. 767–802.

Tripodi, Christian (2011) *Edge of Empire: The British Political Officer and Tribal Administration on the North-West Frontier 1877-1947* (Ashgate, Farnham/Burlington, VT).

Tripodi, Christian (2012) '"Politicals", Tribes and Musahibans: The Indian Political Service and Anglo-Afghan Relations 1919-39', *The International History Review*, Vol. 34, No. 4, pp. 865–86.

Warren, Alan (2000) *Waziristan, The Faqir of Ipi and the Indian Army: The North-West Frontier Revolt of 1936-37* (Oxford University Press, Karachi).
Weinbaum, Marvin G. and Harder, Jonathan B. (2008) 'Pakistan's Afghan Policies and Their Consequences', *Contemporary South Asia*, Vol. 16, No. 1, pp. 25–38.
Wirsig, Robert G. (1981) *The Baluchis and Pathans, Minority Rights Group Report No. 48* (Minority Rights Group, London).
Wyatt, Christopher M. (2011) *Afghanistan and The Defence of Empire: Diplomacy and Strategy During the Great Game* (I.B. Tauris, London/New York).
Yapp, Malcolm (1983) 'Tribes and States in the Khyber 1838-42', in Richard Tapper (ed.), *The Conflict of Tribe and State in Iran and Afghanistan* (Croom Helm, Beckenham), pp. 150–91.
Zaman, Muhammad Qasim (2007) 'Tradition and Authority in Deobandi Madrasas of South Asia', in Robert W. Hefner and Muhammad Qasim Zaman (eds), *Schooling Islam: The Culture and Politics of Modern Muslim Education*, (Princeton University Press, Princeton, NJ/Oxford), pp. 61–86.

Theses

Harris, Leslie (2008) *British Policy on the North-West Frontier 1889-1901*, PhD, London University, 1960.
Neep, Daniel (SOAS) (2009) *Colonising Violence: Space, insurgency and subjectivity in French Mandate Syria*, PhD, London University.

Internet

'Action of Spinchilla Pass', *Supplement to London Gazette*, 4.12.1922, https://www.thegazette.co.uk/London/issue/32773/supplement/8602/data.pdf to check, accessed 31.5.2017.
'Afghanistan', Hugh Beattie, in *International Encyclopedia of the First World War*, https://encyclopedia.1914-1918-online.net/article/afghanistan.
'Anglo-Russian Convention of 1907', Encyclopædia Iranica, *Vol. II, No. 1, pp. 68–70*, F. Kazemzadeh, http://www.iranicaonline.org/articles/anglo-russian-convention-of-1907-an-agreement-relating-to-persia-afghanistan-and-tibet, accessed 21.6.2017.
'Basmachis', Daniel E. Schafer, https://www.encyclopedia.com/history/encyclopedias-almanacs-transcripts-and-maps/basmachis, accessed 8.4.2019.
'Frontier Ambush', 26.7.1921, *Zeehan and Dundas Herald*, https://trove.nla.gov.au/newspaper/article/84498152, accessed 8.4.2019.
'Frontier Firebrand', *Time Magazine*, 4.3.1940, http://www.time.com/time/magazine/article/0,9171,763573,00.html, accessed 3.2.2009.
'The Genesis of Pakistan's "Strategic Depth" in Afghanistan,' Arni Anand and Tondon Abhimanyu, 2.6.2014, https://www.fairobserver.com/region/central_south_asia/the-genesis-of-pakistans-strategic-depth-in-afghanistan-88910/, accessed 2.6.2014.

'Green on Blue Attacks in Afghanistan: The Data', Bill Roggio and Lisa Lindquist, *FDD's Long War Journal*, https://www.realcleardefense.com/articles/2017/03/21/green-on-blue_attacks_in_afghanistan_the_data_111015.html, accessed 23.10.2017.

Hayat, Maira (2009) 'Still "Taming the Turbulent Frontier"? The State in the Federally Administered Tribal Areas of Pakistan', *JASO-online N.S.*, Vol. 1, No. 2, pp. 179–206, https://www.anthro.ox.ac.uk/sites/default/files/anthro/documents/media/jaso1_2_2009.pdf, accessed 28.10.2013.

'Hitler of the N.W. Frontier Rise and Fall of an Outlaw', *Times* (London, England), 13.4.1941, *The Times Digital Archive, 1785-2010*, https://www.gale.com/intl/c/the-times-digital-archive, accessed 8.6.2018.

'India and her Budget', *Times* (London, England), 8.8.1913, *The Times Digital Archive, 1785-2010*, https://www.gale.com/intl/c/the-times-digital-archive, accessed 28.1.2014.

'Interaction between Indian Politics and Tribal Territory', Jawad R. Awan, *The Nation*, 28.9.2015, https://nation.com.pk/28Sep-2015/nds-raw-nexus-fuelling-terrorism-in-pakistan, accessed 14.9.2018.

'Khost Province District Studies', Audrey Roberts, 20.5.1913, Tribal Analysis Centre, www.tribalanalysiscenter.com/PDF-TAC/Khost Province District Studies, accessed 3.4.2014.

'Kurdish Tribes', Pierre Oberling, *Encyclopedia Iranica,* (2004), http://www.iranicaonline.org/articles/kurdish-tribes, accessed 21.9.2016.

'The Last Frontier', *Economist*, 31.12.2009, https://www.economist.com/node/15173037, accessed 27.5.2010.

'Lord Reading and India', *Times* (London, England), 4.5.1922, *The Times Digital Archive 1785-2010*, https://www.gale.com/intl/c/the-times-digital-archive, accessed 28.1.2014

'The New Policy in Waziristan', *Times* (London, England), 17.8.1901, p. 13. *The Times Digital Archive 1785-2010*, https://www.gale.com/intl/c/the-times-digital-archive, accessed 24.8.2011.

'The North-West Frontier of India', *Times* (London, England), 15.6.1910, *The Times Digital Archive 1785-2010*, https://www.gale.com/intl/c/the-times-digital-archive, accessed 30.11.2013.

'House of Commons Mr Montagu's Statement', *Times* (London, England), 8.8.1913, *The Times Digital Archive 1785-2010*, https://www.gale.com/intl/c/the-times-digital-archive, accessed 3.12.2018.

'The North-West Frontier', *Times* (London, England) 22.5.1922, p. 19. *The Times Digital Archive 1785-2010*, https://www.gale.com/intl/c/the-times-digital-archive, accessed 28.1.2014.

'Quelling the Mahsuds Fighting in Mountain Fastnesses', *Times* (London, England), 22.5.1922, *The Times Digital Archive 1785-2010*, https://www.gale.com/intl/c/the-times-digital-archive, accessed 30.11.2013.

'Transforming Pakistan's Frontier Corps', *Terrorism Monitor*, Vol. 5, No. 6, 2007, Hassan Abbas, https://jamestown.org/program/transforming-pakistans-frontier-corps/, accessed 14.10.2017.

'Tribe', David Sneath in F. Stein, Andrew Sanchez, Hildegard Diemberger, Joel Robbins, Matei Candea, Rupert Stasch, and Sian Lazar (eds), *The Cambridge Encyclopedia of Anthropology*, http://www.anthroencyclopedia.com/entry/tribe, accessed 6.5.2018.

'War and International Humanitarian Law', *International Committee of the Red Cross* (2010), https://www.icrc.org/eng/war-and-law/overview-war-and-law.htm, accessed 19.7.2012.

'A Wazir Raid British Column Overwhelmed on Frontier', *The Straits Times*, http://eresources.nlb.gov.sg/newspapers/digitised/issue/straitstimes19211212-1, accessed 30.3.2015.

'Waziristan Refugees Hail Afghan Gvnt. Hospitality', https://www.pajhwok.com/en/2017/03/27/waziristan-refugees-hail-afghan-govt-people-hospitality, accessed 11.4.2017.

'Waziristan: Terror Destination', South Asia Intelligence Review/IBNS, 16.6.2014. http://www.indiablooms.com/ibns_new/news-details/M/2047/waziristan-terror-destination.html, accessed 4.5.2017.

'Wazīrīs and Wazīristān', M. E. Yapp, in *Encyclopaedia of Islam*, second edition, P. Bearman, Th. Bianquis, C.E. Bosworth, E. van Donzel, W.P. Heinrichs (eds). Consulted online on 3.12.2018, http://dx.doi.org.libezproxy.open.ac.uk/10.1163/1573-3912_islam_SIM_7906. First published online: 2012, accessed 3.12.2018.

Index

Abbas Khan Salimi Khel Alizai Mehsud 131, 132
Abdul Ghaffur (Akhund of Swat) 11, 36
Abdul Ghaffur Khan (Badshah Sahib) 149, 150, 151, 193, 194, 196, 279 n.131
Abdul Hadi 119, 253 n.74
Abdul Khaliq 161
Abdullah Jan Zilla Khel Ahmadzai Wazir 163, 167
Abdullai Bahlolzai Mehsuds 15, 31, 37, 49, 76, 81, 97, 102, 112, 137–8, 154, 169, 190
Abdullai-Tori Khel conflict 137
Abdur Qaiyyum Khan 259 n.75
Abdur Rahim (Haji Abdur Razaq's son) 96
Abdur Rahman, Macha Madda Khel Utmanzai Wazir (also known as Pak) 89, 91, 149, 160, 163, 164
Abdur Rahman Khan. *See* Amir Abdur Rahman
Abdur Rahman Khels, Bahlolzai Mehsuds 7, 15, 23, 28, 31, 37, 51, 57, 71, 76, 77, 79–80, 83, 86, 94, 97, 104, 112, 129, 130, 205, 239 n.20
Abdurrashid, Qais 6
Acharya, Arabinda 239 n.5
Acheson, James 167, 173, 175
action lente (slow action) 133, 136
action vive (quick action) 133
Adamec, Ludwig 162, 253 n.74, 254 n.94, 255 n.125, 263 n.23, 267 n.125, 272 n.96, 274 n.124
Adam Khan, Brigadier 117, 120, 125, 253 n.65
Adam Khan, Madda Khel Utmanzai Wazir 42
Afghan government (GOA) 14, 21–2, 33, 51, 60, 67, 76, 87, 125, 145–7, 194–6. *See also* militias Khost/Urgun
opposition to in Khost 74, 77, 127, 159–61
relations with men living on British side of the Durand Line 20–3, 27, 95, 110, 119–20, 132, 138, 148–9, 158, 161–5, 167–8, 176, 178, 180, 182, 196, 204
Afghanistan
British invasion 22
gains full independence 89
Independence Day 119
neutral status in WWI and WW2 80–1, 188
Afridis 34, 47, 75, 196, 226 n.67, 228 n.13
Afzal Khan, Sardar 20, 21
Ahmad Jan Abdullai, Firqa Mashar 168
Ahmad Shah Bareilly 59
Ahmadzai Wazirs 6, 17–18, 20, 143, 168, 223 n.46
Ahmed, Akbar S. 3, 8, 222 n.20
Aimal Khels, Bahlolzai Mehsuds 15
air attacks and bombing, British 85, 90, 92, 100–1, 112, 117–19, 126, 129–31, 143, 151, 154–5, 174, 179–80, 189, 249 n.2. *See also* Royal Air Force
Afghans and Shinwaris 145
Jalalabad and Kabul 90
Air Power and Colonial Control (Omissi) 2
Aitchinson, Charles 24
Ajab Khan 124–5
Akhund of Swat. *See* Abdul Ghaffur (Akhund of Swat)
Algeria 14, 101, 132
Alizais Mehsuds 6, 16, 20, 21, 23, 28, 66, 81, 112, 143
allowances and payments to tribes 25, 27, 38, 47, 120, 123, 131, 148–9, 157, 161, 166, 173, 187, 201–2, 251 n. 39
competition for 31, 45
Mehsuds 28, 29, 39–41, 47–8, 50–2, 65–6, 73, 79, 83, 86–7, 156, 158, 170
Al Mujahid (newspaper) 118, 269 n.9

Al-Qaida 247 n.89
Amanullah Khan. *See* Amir Amanullah
Amir Abdur Rahman 14, 20, 24–5, 27, 51, 60, 76, 207
Amir Amanullah 87, 89, 97, 106, 118–19, 121, 124, 127, 145–9, 153, 163, 180, 249 nn.119, 121–2, 257 n.30, 273 n.105
Amir Dost Muhammad Khan 12, 20, 146
Amir Habibullah 14, 51, 60, 67–9, 76, 80–1, 84, 87
Amir Sher Ali Khan 20, 21, 22
Anderson, Henry 42, 43, 44, 45–6
Anglo-Afghan Treaties
 (1855) 13
 (1857) 13
 (1919) 91
 (1921) 97, 102–3, 105–6, 109
Anglo-Russian Convention (1907) 68–9, 75, 113
Angur, Bazid Khel Zilla Khel Ahmadzai Wazir, Firqa Mashar 125, 163, 167
Anzilotti, Enrico 189
Appozai agreement 29, 30, 31
Ardali 124, 125, 126
Arnawai 106
Arsala Khan, Madda Khel Utmanzai Wazir 138, 141, 151, 157, 163, 164
Ashiq, Palli Khel Manzai Alizai Mehsud 50, 51
Asmat Khan, Yarghul Khel Zilla Khel Ahmadzai Wazir 90, 142
Atran, Scott 238 n.94
Ayambe, Khan Madda Khel Utmanzai Wazir 42–3
Ayub Khan, Madda Khel Utmanzai Wazir 42
Azem Khan, Muhammad, Sardar 12, 13, 20–1
Azem Khan Kundi 21, 23, 28–9, 31, 41
Aziz Khan, Shingi Bahlolzai Mehsud 91
Azmat, Shingi Bahlolzai Mehsud 22–4

Badr Din, Umar Khel Alizai Mehsud 30, 51
Badshah Khan, Salimi Khel Alizai Mehsud 30, 51
Bahlolzai (Mehsuds) 6, 7, 15–16, 20, 23, 66, 81, 93, 97, 123

Baluchistan 22, 27, 31, 90, 106, 134, 194, 199
bandish (blockade) 15, 19, 45–6, 48–53, 167, 189, 201
Band Khels, Bahlolzai Mehsuds 102, 104, 123
Banerjee, Mukulika 3, 264 n.38
Bangash 6
Bannu 6, 12, 17–19, 53, 58, 62–3, 90, 131, 151, 156, 169, 182, 191, 203
Bannuchi Mullah, Muhammad Yusuf 152, 154, 156
Bannuchis (Karlanri Pashtuns) 6
Bannu Declaration (1947) 193
Barak, Abdur Rahman Khel Bahlolzai Mehsud 50, 51
Barakis. *See* Urmurs
barampta (seizing people and/or property 15, 19, 45, 72, 74, 76, 83, 141, 143–4, 150, 201
Barfield, Thomas 222 n.36
Barnes, Humphrey 180, 181
Barth, Fredrik 3, 228 n.25, 234 n.3
Bashir, Maulana, son of Haji of Turangzai 92, 102, 104, 119, 269 n.9
Basmachis 267 n.118
Bat, Zilla Khel Ahmadzai Wazir 142
Beattie, Hugh 3, 224 n.20, 225 n.57, 226 n.71, 241 n.72, 242 n.82
Bedouin Arabs 14
Beitullah, Shabi Khel Alizai Mehsud 199
Benyon, G. W., Major-General 86
Beyond Swat (Hopkins and Marsden) 3
Bhittanis 6, 16, 20, 23, 45, 96, 174, 188, 272 n.85
 occupation of 8
bin Laden, Osama 199
Bird, Wilkinson, Major-General 43
Birmal 8, 21, 33, 50, 95, 125, 176, 181, 193
blockade. *See bandish* (blockade)
Blok, Anton 247 n.87
Bolan Pass 46
Bolton, Norman 122, 132, 138, 140, 141, 183
border/frontier situations 13–15
Bostan, Madda Khel Utmanzai Wazir 50
Bowring, J. B. 52, 57, 59, 61, 63
Bowyer, Chaz 257 n.11

Boyak, Abdullai Bahlolzai Mehsud 22–4
Brag, Abdur Rahman Khel Bahlolzai Mehsud 71, 79, 83
Bray, Denys 105, 121, 135, 141, 251 n.38, 261 n.106
British anxiety over Russian and Soviet influence 22, 25–6, 60, 97–8, 106, 113, 154
British Foreign Office 98
British representatives in Kabul and meetings with Afghan officials 126, 128, 165–6
British withdrawal from Frontier (1947) 19, 120, 193–5, 208
Bromhead, Benjamin 191
Brown, Captain 79
Browne, Captain 61
Bruce, Charles, Lieutenant-Colonel 126, 135, 140, 144, 251 n.26, 258 n.47
Bruce, Richard, Lieutenant-Colonel 27–31, 34, 36–41, 42, 44–5, 47, 62, 65–6, 76, 202, 203, 228 n.22, 235 n.25
Bugeaud, Thomas-Robert 101, 132–4
Bunny, A. C., Lieutenant-Colonel 43
Butler, Captain 78

Canning, Lord, governor-general and Viceroy 15
Caroe, Michael 264 n.38
Caroe, Olaf 2, 221 n.5
chalweshtis (tribal police) 9, 28, 50, 251 n.26
Chamberlain, Austen 85
Chamberlain, Neville, Field Marshal 16, 93
Charkhi, Ghulam Nabi 132, 145, 159–61
Chela Ram 152, 153, 156
Chelmsford, Viscount, Viceroy 85, 94, 97, 113, 114
Chevenix-Trench, Charles 220 n.1, 234 n.16, 249 n.119, 259 n.58, 270 n.37, 281 n.8
Child Marriage Restraint Act (Sarda Act) (1930) 150, 151
chillas 10
civil–military relations 139–40, 183–4
close border policy 24, 29, 46, 52, 116
Coleridge, General 177, 184

collective responsibility 16, 18, 46, 202, 203
Committee of Imperial Defence 26
  subcommittee 115
Conciliation Committees 76, 96
Congress Party. *See* Indian National Congress
Copeland, Theodore 84, 242 n.95
Coughlin, Con 277 n.72
Cox, Jeffrey 192
Crisis on the Frontier (Robson) 2
Crewe, Marquess of, Secretary of State for India 79
Crosthwaite, Major 94
Crump, Leslie 55, 62–6, 71–2, 75, 76, 152, 193, 233 n.136
  Mullah Powindah and 62–6, 69–71
  strategy failure of 68–70
Cunningham, George 175, 177, 181, 185, 190, 271 n.51, 276 n.48
Curtis, Gerald 188, 192, 237 n.68, 253 n.78, 254 n.81, 256 n.5, 275 n.29, 276 n.55
Curzon, Lord, Viceroy 4, 46–8, 48, 51–2, 60, 63, 78, 102, 113, 122, 207, 254 n.98

Dalagai, Shabi Khel Alizai Mehsud 63–4
Dale, Stephen 70
Dalhousie, Lord, governor general 13
Dande Khan, Madda Khel Utmanzai Wazir 164, 168
Dane, Louis 60
Darwesh Khels. *See* Wazirs
Datta Khel 39, 43, 89, 111, 135, 136, 139, 140, 151, 180, 185, 189, 195
Daud Shah 124–6
Dauran Khan 159
Davies, Colin 2
Dawagar, Mehsud malik 31, 37
Dawars 6, 16, 34, 42, 44, 151, 188
  occupation of 8
Deane, Harold 45, 47, 50, 52, 62–9, 72, 236 n.40
Defiant Border, The (Leake) 3
democracy 27, 40, 47, 87, 202, 228 n.13
Deoband seminary, influence of 36, 82, 149, 228 n.28
  madrasahs 199–200

Derajat   5–6, 29, 49, 174, 188, 192, 207
Devji, Faisal   247 n.89
Dew, Armine, Lieutenant-Colonel   251 n.38
Disraeli, Benjamin   25
Dobbs, Henry   96–8, 103, 105–6, 115, 245 n.57, 251 n.38
Dodd, George, Major   75, 79, 86
Donald, John   72, 73–6, 79, 83
Donaldson, Captain   62–4, 66
Dotani Ghilzai Powindahs   6, 29, 261 n.103
Dufferin, Marquess of, Viceroy   27, 225 n.39
Durand, Mortimer   33
Durand Line   2, 33 42, 50, 76, 114, 124, 195
Durrani, Ahmad Shah   11
Dyer, Reginald, Colonel   90, 244 n.5

economic-organizational action   133, 134
Edge of Empire, The (Tripodi)   3
Edwardes, Herbert, Major   12, 13, 17, 58, 192, 222 n.22, 235 n.25
Edwards, Cosmo   139, 141
Edwards, David B.   3, 271 n.67
Elgin, Lord, Viceroy   35, 36, 38
Ellington, Edward, Marshal   130, 221 n.8
Elliott, James G., Major-General   2, 186
expeditions, punitive   14–15, 21, 31, 40, 46, 49, 63, 100, 101–2, 115, 118, 130, 134, 136–7, 162, 170, 192, 201, 207, 223 n.40

Faiz Muhammad Mahsud   279 n.134
Faiz Muhammad Zakaria   147–8, 165, 263 n.23
Faqir Din, Muhammad Ali Khel Bhittani   174, 195, 272 n.73
Faqir of Ipi and the Indian Army, The (Warren)   2
Fazal Din. *See* Mullah Fazal Din
Federally-Administered Tribal Areas (FATA), Pakistan   19
Finnis, Major, murder and murderers   125, 142, 163
Firestone, Reuven   250 n.4
First World War   1, 4, 80–4, 89, 100, 113, 115, 119, 130, 186, 207, 246 n.59
Fitzpatrick, Denis   34–5, 38, 43
Fitzpatrick, James   84, 86–7, 94–5, 102, 103–4, 105, 245 n.41, 277 n.70

forward policy   26–9
   modified   162–4, 207
Fragments of the Afghan Frontier (Hopkins and Marsden)   3
Fraser-Tytler, William, Lieutenant-Colonel   120, 162, 176
French colonial policy   132–4, 136–7
Frere, Bartle, Baronet   134, 223 n.40, 258 n.46, 259 n.69
Frontier 1839–1947, The (Elliott)   2
Frontier Constabulary   122, 188
Frontier Crimes Regulations (1872)   19, 156, 197
Frontier Defence Committee   190
Frontier Legion (Leeson)   2
Frontier of Faith (Haroon)   3
Frontier Perspectives (Lindholm)   3

Gallieni, Joseph   133, 134, 136, 137
Gandapurs   24
Gandhi, Mahatma   110, 150
Gangi Khel Ahmadzai Wazirs   142
Garrerais (Alizai Mehsuds)   37, 51, 252 n.56
Gee, Herbert   42–4
Generosity and Jealousy (Lindholm)   3
George V, King of England   69, 81
Ger Madda Khel Utmanzai Wazirs   41–2
German mission to Afghanistan 1915–16   81
Ghalib Pasha   82
ghaza   68–9
Ghazah (newspaper)   92
ghazi (fighter for Islam)   55–6, 67, 109, 172
Ghazi Mir Jan   152, 155
Ghulam Haider Khan   257 n.28
Ghulam Hyder Khan, son of amir Dost Muhammad   13
Ghulam Muhiy-ud-din Khan, Madda Khel Utmanzai Wazir   168
Ghulam Muhammad Charkhi. *See* Charkhi, Ghulam Nabi
Giga Khels (Bahlolzai Mehsuds)   94, 129, 143, 262 n.116
Giustozzi, Antonio   226 n.61
Gorezais   20
Government of India (GOI)   19, 24–7, 30, 35, 37, 39, 47, 49, 51, 60, 90–1, 96, 97, 100, 103, 105, 106, 115–6,

135, 143, 158, 160–5, 170, 176, 178–9, 181, 189, 193, 204, 246 n.59, 255 n.125, 256 n.127, 263 n.17
Government of India Act 1935   173–4
Government of Pakistan (GOP)   195, 196–9, 200, 208
Graham, Frederick   16, 25, 226 n. 71
Grant, Alfred Hamilton   97, 114, 229 n.45
Griffin, Lepel   58
Griffith, Ralph   151, 154, 156, 162, 175
Gulband, Langar Khel Alizai Mehsud   69–70
Gul Din, Zilla Khel Ahmedzai Wazir   146, 157, 174
Gullajan, Sultanai Shabi Khel Mehsud   62–3, 69
Gul Muhammad Khan, Sardar   30, 42, 44
Gumal Pass (route, road)   17, 26–7, 29–31, 34–5, 46, 79, 170
Gumal river   5, 27
Gurbaz Wazirs   6, 33
Guri Khels, Alizai Mehsuds   44, 126, 129, 130, 256 n. 10
Gwaleri Pass   29, 84

Habibullah Kalakani   145, 147, 253 n.74
Habibullah Khan. *See* Amir Habibullah
Hadda Mullah   11, 36, 198, 228 n.28, 271 n.67
Haibat Khels (Bahlolzai Mehsuds)   94, 95
Hailey, Malcolm, Baron   114, 116–7, 251 n.39
Haji Abdur Razaq   67, 68, 89–91, 95, 96–7, 117, 125, 127, 149
   and Wana   109–11
Haji of Turangzai   92, 149, 228 n.28
Hanna, Henry   231 n.102
Harap Khan, Shabi Khel Alizai Mehsud   125–6, 129, 131, 188
Hardinge Lord, Viceroy   75, 79
Harman, Richard, Lieutenant-Colonel   57, 60, 61, 63, 235 n.32
Haroon, Sana   3, 198, 228 n.28, 244 n.8, 252 n.63, 253 n.n.77, 78, 271 n.57, 275 n.48
Harris, Leslie   227 n.7, 228 n.22, 231 nn.102–106
Hassan Khel, Mohmit Khel Utmanzai Wazirs   166

Hatti Khels, Ahmadzai Wazirs   17–18, 156–7
Hauner, Milan   220 n.3, 276 n.52, 279 n.131
Hayat Khan, Nazar Khel Bahlolzai Mehsud   153, 181, 189
Hayat Khan, Manzai Alizai Mehsud   80, 91, 120
Heale, Robert, Lieutenant-Colonel   143
health, education, and economy   136, 169–70, 187
Hentig, Werner Otto von   81–2
Heroes of the Age (Edwards)   3
Hevia, James   231 n.102
Hickie, Lieutenant   79
Hindu nationalists   171, 271 n.51.
   See also Mahasabha party
Honda Ram   42, 43
honour and shame   8, 51, 68, 124, 150, 204, 252 n.63
Hopkins, Benjamin   3, 253 n.77
hostages   20, 23–5, 27, 38, 50, 79, 86, 151, 155, 164, 167, 176, 177, 201, 251 n.26
Howell, Evelyn   52, 61, 100, 143, 147, 191, 226 n.62, 245 n.35, 246 n.73, 250 n.24, 256 n.1
Hughes, Major   84
Humphrys, Francis   110, 118, 125, 132, 146–7, 249 n.122, 257 n.29

Ibrahim Beg   158
Inayatullah Khan   145
India   75, 81–2, 136, 145, 146, 200, 206
India's North-West Frontier (Barton)   2
Indian National Congress (Congress party)   149–53, 265 n.62, 277 n.66
Indian Penal Code (1861)   19
insurgencies   1, 4, 49, 84–7, 150–1, 171–80, 182, 185–6, 188, 190, 195, 203
Irwin, Lord, Secretary of State for India   138
Islam Bibi problem   171, 172
Ittihad-i-Mashriqi (newspaper)   119, 125

Jaffrelot, Christopher   271 n.51
Jaggar, Abdur Rahman Khel Bahlolzai Mehsud   37, 51, 67
Jalal Khels, Nana Khel Bahlolzai Mehsuds   7, 15, 23, 94, 97, 102, 104, 112–13, 117, 153

Jalaludin Haqqani   200
Jamaat-i-Mujahidin   82, 92, 119, 154.
Jambil, Abdur Rahman Khel
    Bahlolzai   31
Jandola   30, 38–9, 49, 50, 52, 61, 73,
    90–2, 96, 103, 136, 142, 190,
    227 n. 7, 235 n.32
Jangi Khan, Salimi Khel Alizai
    Mehsud   15, 21, 28, 254 n.81
Jansson, Erland   220 n.2
Jats   6
jihad   68–9, 109, 116, 234 n.7
jirgas (councils)   9, 19, 24–5, 27, 31, 37,
    45, 48–52, 64–5, 72–3, 83, 92, 95,
    102–4, 120, 126, 167, 178
  manageable representative   28, 75,
    226 n. 61
Johnson, Harry   165, 166, 175, 273 n.105
Johnston, Frederick   28, 51–2, 65–6, 76,
    87, 202, 227 n.82, 228 n.23,
    229 n.37
Juma Khan, Nekzan Khel Bahlolzai   30

Kabul (city)   5, 13, 20, 22, 24, 33, 41,
    51, 56, 73, 81, 98, 102, 105–6, 118,
    125–6, 142, 145, 152, 182, 187, 196,
    199
Kabul, Abdur Rahman Khel   57, 60, 61,
    69
Kabul Khels (Utmanzai Wazirs)   17, 33,
    36, 143, 276 n.53, 278 n.99
Kabul party   148, 152
Kalagai, Patanai Shabi Khel Alizai
    Mehsud   62–4, 67
Kamil, Alizai Shabi Khel Alizai
    Mehsud   74
Kaniguram   6, 7, 10, 27, 37, 64, 72, 77,
    80, 83, 91, 93–4, 120, 152, 155, 169,
    180
Kaniguram Sayyids   11
Karbogha Mullah. *See* Mullah Karbogha
Karim Khan, Guri Khel Alizai
    Mehsud   123
Karlanri   6
Karram, Abdur Rahman Khel   31
kashars   9, 175, 206, 259 n.75
Kazha Madda Khel Utmanzai
    Wazirs   41–2, 139, 151
Keene, Captain   239 n.23
Keogh, John   174–5

Khaisor Langar Khel Alizai
    Mehsuds   148, 152
Khaisora valley   16, 170, 172–4, 184
khalifas (deputies)   11, 56, 197
Khalli Khels, Shaman Khel Mehsuds
    249 n.119
khanaqas (Sufi lodges)   10
Khanate of Kalat (Baluchistan)   14, 22,
    134
Khandan Khan, Madda Khel Utmanzai
    Wazir   166, 185, 269 n.12
Khan Sahib, Dr   149
Khan Sahib Marwat Khan, Shaman Khel
    Mehsud   135
Khan Sahib Muhammad Hayat
    Khan   113
Kharotis   6
khassadars   74, 95–6, 102, 106, 110–12,
    122–3, 144, 154–5, 169, 187, 201,
    251 n.39, 254 n.83, 254 n.98
Khattaks   6
Khizr Khels, Kabul Khel Utmanzai Wazirs
    Wazirs   42, 92
Khonia Khel, Jalal Khel Bahlolzai
    Mehsud   173, 175, 185
Khost   5, 53, 74, 77, 82, 84, 121, 126–7,
    139, 160, 163, 164, 166–8, 193, 208
Khudai Khidmatgaran (Servants of
    God)   149–50
Khyber Pass   34, 46, 47
Khyber system   226 n.67
Kikarais, Bahlolzai Mehsuds   132, 143,
    153–6
Kimberley, Lord, Secretary of State for
    India   26
Kitchener, Herbert, Lord, Commander In
    Chief   69, 78
Kundis   6

Lala Pir, Mullah Sayyid Lal Shah   36,
    67–8, 76, 80–1, 120
Lanessan, Jean de   133
langar (kitchen)   11, 56, 178, 197
Langar Khels, Alizai Mehsuds   37
Lansdowne, Lord, Viceroy   29–30, 33, 35
Lawrence, Henry, Brigadier-General
    192
Lawrence, John, Lord, Viceroy   59, 101
Lawrence, T. E. (Lawrence of
    Arabia)   146

Leake, Elizabeth 3
Leeson, Frank 2, 194, 277 n.66, 278 n.99
Leia Division 12
Lewanai Faqir 82, 159–60, 163, 242 n.80
Lindholm, Charles 3, 191
Linlithgow, Marquess of, Viceroy 177, 186–7
Lockhart, William, General 37–8
Lohani Marwats 6
Lyall, James 29, 34
Lyall, R. A., Captain 72
Lyautey, Hubert, Marshal 133–4, 137, 184, 258 n.47, 259 n.69
Lytton, Lord, Viceroy 22, 24

Macaulay, Charles, Major 20–5, 41, 45, 204, 251 n.26
Mackeson, Frederick, Lieutenant-Colonel 59
Mackworth-Young, William 45–7
Maconachie, Richard 146–8, 154, 158, 161–3, 165
Madar, Shaman Khel Mehsuds 168
Madda Khels, Utmanzai Wazirs 33, 41–4, 52, 61, 89, 91–2, 137, 151, 157, 163–4, 166, 174, 180, 185, 190, 263 n.18
  and Zangi Khan 138–41
madrasah (seminary) 10, 36, 151, 199, 200
Maffey, John 97, 99, 113, 116–17, 122, 186, 206, 251 n.38, 252 n.53, 261 n.106, 281 n.11
Mahasabha party 171
Mahmud, Mufti Shah 21
Maizar 43–4, 138, 139, 140, 151
Makin 5, 7, 16, 49, 92–3, 95, 97–8, 100, 102, 114, 118–19, 154, 190
  Makin Abdullai Bahlolzais 102
Malik Hayat Khan, Nazar Khel Bahlolzai Mehsud 153, 181
maliki allowances 39–41, 47, 51–2, 65–7, 103, 105, 112, 155, 187
maliki policy 50, 58
Malik Pir Gul, Abdullai Bahlolzai Mehsud 190
maliks 9, 10, 28, 30–1, 39, 42–3, 46, 66–7, 86, 105, 141, 151, 251 n.39
  Mehsud 24, 37, 72, 135, 157, 201, 203
  Wazir 17–18, 21, 24, 38, 176

Malik Shahbatti, Abdullai Bahlolzai Mehsud 187
Malikshahis, Bahlolzai Mehsuds 79, 83
Malikshahis, Utmanzai Wazirs 143
Mamia Khel, Shingi Bahlolzai Mehsuds 15
Mando Khels 29
Mangals 6, 74, 77, 127
Mani Khan, Spirkai Wazir 238 n.4
Manzai Alizai Mehsuds 6, 96, 143
Manzar Khels, Utmanzai Wazirs 8, 42, 92
Markai, Malikshahi Bahlolzai Mehsud, brother of Sarfaraz 79, 83, 242 n.86
Marsden, Magnus 3
Marsh, Brandon 3, 254 n.98, 267 n.112
Marwats 6
Marwat, Shaman Khel Mehsud, Khan Sahib 91, 135
Mashak, Abdur Rahman Khel Mehsud 22–4, 226 n.64
mashars 9, 206
Matheson, Torquil, General 94–5, 102, 111, 113, 117–20, 245 n.41
Matin, Langar Khel Alizai Mehsud 22–4
Maulana Husain Ahmad Madni 82
Maulana Mahmudul Hasan 82
May, Lieutenant-Colonel 185
Mecham, Robert, Captain 17
Mehmed V, Sultan 80
Mehr Dil Khan, Manzai Alizai Mehsud 91, 187
Mehr Dil Khattak 197
Mehsudland and Wana, occupation of 92–6
Mehsuds 6, 8–10, 12, 15–17, 20–3, 25, 27–30, 34–41, 48–50, 55–7, 68, 77–8, 83–6, 91–2, 102, 205, 231 n.86, 252 n.63, 277 n.70
  in 1930 152–9
  air campaign against 129–1
  attacks on British officials 44, 57–62, 68, 71–2
  British efforts to settle on land in British territory 16, 22, 24–5
  British occupation 92–4
  British punitive expeditions against 15–16, 23, 37, 49–50, 85–6
  early British relations with 15–17
  invade British territory in force 15, 22–3, 191

maliks including 'old maliks'   24,
    27–8, 37, 51, 65–6, 72, 135, 157,
    201, 203
Mullah Powindah and   44–8, 55–6,
    71–4
occupations of   7–8
resistance   93–4, 98, 111–13, 118
Tori Khels and   137–8
Merk, William   45, 47–8, 49–52, 65, 74,
    76, 78, 188, 202
Metcalfe, Aubrey, visits Kabul   182
Miamai Kabul Khel Utmanzai
    Wazirs   143, 223 n.3
Miani Pashtuns   6, 20
Mianji, Abdur Rahman Khel Bahlolzai
    Mehsud   37, 50–1, 67, 72
Michan Khels   11
militias   1, 16–17, 20, 23, 46, 48, 50,
    68–9, 74, 82, 113, 167, 254 n.98,
    270 n.33; See also chalweshtis
    Khost/Urgun   120, 124, 138, 149, 160,
        168, 204, 208
    North Waziristan   85, 89–91, 111,
        138
    South Waziristan   57, 60, 62, 67, 75,
        78, 90
Millennium and Charisma among Pathans
    (Ahmed)   3
Minto, Earl, Viceroy   63, 64, 69, 72
Miralai, Nekzan Khel Bahlolzai
    Mehsud   143, 154
Miranshah   39, 42, 46, 82, 89, 116, 130,
    135–6, 141, 146, 151, 159–60, 174
Mirat Khel, Jalal Khel Bahlolzai
    Mehsud   132
Mir Badshah, Manzai Alizai Mehsud,
    Captain   136, 187, 188
Mir Dil, Mal Khel Manzai Alizai
    Mehsud   63
Mirkabul, Giga Khel Bahlolzai
    Mehsud   143
Mirza Ali Khan (Faqir of Ipi)   4, 171–7,
    181–91, 194–8, 208, 254 n.79, 273
    n.n.102, 109, n.113, 276 n.52
    Afghans try to win him over   178
    establishes himself at Gowekht   181
    his aims and achievements   197–8
    influence on British policy in
        Waziristan   179

insurgency of   171–4, 179, 186, 203
miraculous powers   172–3
and Waziristan after 1947   196–9
Mirza Khan, Abdur Rahman Khel
    Bahlolzai Mehsud   79, 86
Misri, Sheikh Bazid Khel Zilla Khel
    Ahmadzai Wazir   125
Mobin, Malikshahi Bahlolzai Mehsud,
    brother of Sarfaraz   79, 83,
    242 n.86
Mohan Lal   152–3, 156
Mohmands   33, 127, 162, 242 n.82
Mohmit Khel Utmanzai Wazirs   151
mohtabars (elders)   38, 40, 51, 65, 75,
    105, 201
Montagu-Chelmsford reforms
    (1919)   149
Montgomery, Archibald   113
Moreman, Tim   183, 247 n.82, 264 n.41
Morley, Viscount, Secretary of State for
    India   60, 63, 69, 72, 75
Morocco   133–4, 183–4
Mufti Nizamudin Shamzai   200
Muhammad Afzal Khan   37
Muhammad Akbar Khan, governor of
    Khost   76–7
Muhammad Amin, nephew of Lewanai
    Faqir   163–4
Muhammad Aziz, Nadir Shah's
    brother   160–1
Muhammad Barakatullah   82
Muhammad Daud, Sardar   196
Muhammad Hashim Khan   146, 161,
    166, 168–9, 176, 178, 273 n.106
Muhammad Hayat Khan Sahib, Extra
    Assistant Commissioner   113
Muhammad Jan, Abdur Rahman Khel
    Bahlolzai Mehsud   239 n.20
Muhammad Khan, Firqa Mashar   163,
    178
Muhammad Khel Ahmadzai Wazirs
    18–19
Muhammad Said Gilani. *See* Shami Pir
Muhammad Shafi   117
Muhammad Wali Khan   98, 102, 255
    n.124
Muhammad Yusuf. *See* Bannuchi Mullah
Muhammad Yusuf Binuri   200
Muhammad Zahir   161

Muhiy-ud-Din Shabi Khel Alizai Mehsud, Mullah Powindah   4, 35–8, 43, 51–2, 55–6, 59–61, 66–7, 69, 71, 76, 124, 173, 197, 233 n.136, 236 n.57, 240 n.51
   British officials try to win him over   48, 62
   Crump and   62–5, 69–70
   death of   76–8
   his achievements assessed   78
   Mehsuds and   44–8, 55–6, 71–4
   and Mirza Ali Khan compared   197–8
   and suicidal attacks   59–60, 69–70
   Mullah Abdul Hakim   77–9, 91
Mullah Abdul Jalil   156
Mullah Abdul Sarir   153
Mullah Adakar   22–3
Mullah Fazal Din, Shabi Khel Bahlolzai Mehsud   77, 79, 84, 90–1, 93, 126, 154, 168, 172, 175–6, 178, 202
Mullah Fazal Qadir   156–7
Mullah Ghain-ud-Din   151
Mullah Gulabdin, Shabi Khel   27, 30, 85
Mullah Gulin Kikarai   152–5, 190
Mullah Hamzullah, Bizan Khel Ahmadzai Wazir   36, 43, 56, 64–5, 67–8, 76–7, 80–1, 84, 110
Mullah Karbogha   36, 65, 67, 236 n.57
Mullah Kundalai   151–2, 154, 159
Mullah Mahmud Akhundzada   125
   Mullah Sher Ali Khan, Umar Khel Bahlolzai Mehsud   177–8, 180, 184, 272 n.85
Multani Pathans   12, 15,   233 n.3
Munro, Alexander, Lieutenant-Colonel   23
Muqbils   6
murids (disciples)   11
Musa Khan, Abdullai Bahlolzai Mehsud   85, 93, 102–3, 117–8, 120, 124, 125–6, 132, 145, 146, 148, 159, 162, 165, 168, 178, 252 n.56, 257 n.29

Nabi Khan, Shingi Bahlolzai Mehsud   20–1
Nadir Khan   89, 90–1, 125, 127, 142, 146–9, 152–3, 157–60, 166, 168, 253 n.73, 263 n.29
Nadir Shah. *See* Nadir Khan
Nambai, Malikshahi Bahlolzai Mehsud, cousin of Sarfaraz   79, 83, 242 n.86

Nana Khels, Bahlolzai Mehsuds   15, 23, 28, 81, 84
nanawatai (reconciliation procedure)   71, 205
Nander, Langar Khel Alizai Mehsud   148
Nasrullah Khan, Sardar   67–8, 74, 76–7, 80–1, 84, 87, 119, 148, 207
Nau Jawan Bharat Sabha   265 n.71
Nawab Foujdar Khan   13
Nawab Sir Ahmad Nawaz Khan   135
Nazar Din, Shabi Khel Alizai Mehsud, Kalagai's cousin   67
Neep, Daniel   136, 259 nn.67–8
Nehru, Jawaharlal   277 n.66, 279 n.131
Nekzan Khels, Bahlolzai Mehsuds   76, 104, 143
Nichols, Robert   3, 191
Nicholson, John, Brigadier-General   17, 58, 100, 192
Niedermayer, Oskar von, Lieutenant-Colonel   81, 82
nikat   10, 28, 29, 51, 66, 75, 187, 205
Nineteen-twenty-two (1922) policy   186
Northbrook, Viceroy   22
North-West Frontier Province (NWFP)   149–50, 162, 167, 171–3, 182, 193–4, 196, 208, 263 n.18
Nur Muhammad, Qazi Khalifa   30

Obama, Barak   1
Obeidullah Sindhi   82
Ogilvie, George   25, 27–8, 226 n.67
oil spot theory   133
Omissi, David E.   2, 247 n.81
Ommanney, Edward   24
Ommanney, Lieutenant A.   59
Ottomans   14, 81

Pakistan   193, 195, 196, 200
Parsons, Arthur, Major-General   106, 111–2, 132, 160, 167, 170, 177, 190, 252 n.64, 273 n.103
Pashakai, Shabi Khel Alizai Mehsud   37, 62–4
Pashtunistan   193–4, 196, 198
Pashtuns   6, 14, 99, 127, 148, 158
   British images of   191–3
Pashtunwali   8, 199, 204

Pathan Borderland, The (Spain) 2
Pathans 43
Pathans 550 BC.-A.D, The (Caroe) 2, 221 n.5
Pathan Unarmed, The (Banerjee) 3
Patterson, Captain 73
peaceful penetration 1, 4, 106, 132–7
 modified forward policy and 162–4, 207
Pears, Stuart 111–12, 117, 122–3, 131, 137, 169, 251 nn.38–9
Peel, Lord, Secretary of State for India 113, 115–17, 120
Pennell, Theodore 236 n.57
Pennequin, Theophile 133
Peshawar 5, 12, 13, 31, 47, 56, 59, 99, 119, 146–7, 150, 157, 192, 224 n.11
Pink, Richard, Air Commodore 130, 256 n.8
Pipalais, Kabul Khel Utmanzai Wazirs 270 n.33
pir (Sufi master) 10–11, 14
Political Leadership among Swat Pathans (Barth) 3
politique des races (divide and rule) 133, 136
Porch, Douglas 134
Potter, Simon 4
Poullada, Leon 249 nn.121–2, 262 n.13
Powindahs 7, 21, 23, 27, 30, 227 n.7, 261 n.103. *See also* Dotani Ghilzai Powindahs and Suleiman Khel Ghilzai Powindahs
Problem of the North-West Frontier 1890–1908, The (Davies) 2
Protected Areas 37, 39, 42, 92
Pukhtun Economy and Society (Ahmed) 3
punitive expeditions 14–15, 31, 37, 40, 46, 69, 72, 80, 92, 101–2, 115, 118, 130, 136–7, 162, 170, 201, 207, 223 n.40, 258 n.46
Punjab Land Alienation Act (1900) sw232 n.129
Punjab Murderous Outrages Act (1867) 57, 59, 62, 73, 100

qalang Pashtuns 8
Qazi Amir Khan 168

Qutab Khan, Salimi Khel Manzai Alizai 120, 131, 261 n.113

RAF. *See* Royal Air Force
Rahmat Badshah, Kaniguram Sayyid 11
Rajah Mahendra Pratap 82
Raji Gul Shabi Khel 67, 71, 173
Ramparts of Empire (Marsh) 3
Ramzan, Shaman Khel 131, 142, 148–9, 152, 154–6, 158–9, 168, 267 n.122
Rawlinson, Henry, General, Commander-in-Chief 111, 113, 115–16, 120, 131
Razmak Military Column 135
Razmak policy 117, 120–7, 186
razzia (surprise attack) 101
Reading, Marquess of, Viceroy 114–7, 120–1
Resistance and Control in Pakistan (Ahmed) 3
Rid, Thomas 247 n.91, 274 n.1
Ripon, Lord, Viceroy 24
Rittenberg, Stephen 220 n.2
roads and road-building 26–7, 75–6, 86, 103, 114–17, 126, 135–6, 142–3, 159, 162, 178–9
 contracts for work on 79, 103–4, 126, 131
Roberts, Frederick, Earl, Field Marshal 25, 29
Roberts, Jeffrey 278 n.96
Robson, Brian 2, 94, 121, 245 nn.35, 52, 252 nn.51, 53
Roe, Andrew M. 2, 247 n.82, 279 n.124
Roos-Keppel, George, Lieutenant-Colonel 72–3, 79, 83, 86, 114, 192, 242 n.82
Royal Air Force (RAF) 110, 116, 126, 129–31, 145, 151, 154–5, 174, 189, 195–6, 252 n.53, 261 n.115. *See also* air attacks and bombing, British
Russia and Afghanistan 22, 26, 60

Sabir, Astanai Shabi Khel Alizai Mehsud 60–1, 69
Sadde Khan, Madda Khel Utmanzai Wazir 42–3, 138
Sadde Khan, Shaman Khel Mehsud 131, 142, 146, 148, 152–6, 168

Safar the Nazir, Afghan official   67, 237 n.75
Safavids   14
Saha, Jonathan   4
Sahib Din, one of Mullah Powindah's sons   74, 77
Saidullah (so-called Mad Fakir)   197
Saifali Kabul Khel bandits   50
Saifali Kabul Khel Utmanzai Wazirs   143, 270 n.33
Saikal, Amin   246 n.59, 254 n.94, 257 n.28
Salisbury, Lord, Secretary of State for India   22, 26
Salmond, John   252 n.53
Sandeman, Robert   22, 27–31, 134, 192, 226 n.70
Sandeman system, of tribal management   28, 31, 134
Sandemanization   144
Sarda Act. See Child Marriage Restraint Act (1930)
Sarfaraz, Malikshahi Aimal Khel Bahlolzai (Dodd's killer)   79
Sarwakai   41, 44, 51, 57, 59, 66, 72, 76, 84–6, 90, 96, 117
Sayyid Lal Shah, Mullah. *See* Lala Pir
Sayyids   11, 50
Sayyid Yusuf (Baghdadi Pir)   181, 189, 276 n.48
scientific frontier   25, 26
Scott, James   204–5, 221 n.4, 281 n.9
Scouts   114–15, 122, 135–6, 144, 170
    South Waziristan Scouts   111, 122, 197
    Tochi Scouts   188–9, 191
Second World War   186, 188–90, 275 n.37
segmentary lineage theory   9
settlement schemes (British)   16–17, 21–5, 41, 201
Settling the Frontier (Nichols)   3
Shabi Khels, Alizai Mehsuds   37, 67, 81, 83–4, 93, 132, 155, 174, 191
Shah Ali Akbar (Naib Tehsildar)   142
Shah Daula, Colonel   91, 93, 96, 149
Shah Mahmud Khan (Nadir Shah's brother)   146, 152, 161, 194
Shah Nawaz Khan, nawab of Tank   12, 14–15, 21

Shah Pasand, Langar Khel Alizai Mehsud   135
shahpirai (king of fairies)   61
Shah Wali Khan (Nadir Shah's brother)   146
shahidi (suicidal violence)   57–62
Shahi Khan, Masti Khel Zilla Khel Ahmadzai   125, 142
Shahir, Abdullai Bahlolzai Mehsud   31, 37, 229 n.37
Shahjui Wazirs   106, 110–11, 148
Shahur Shaman Khels   20
Shahzada (brother of Ajab Khan)   124, 125
Shahzada Taj-ud Din, Mulla Powindah's grandson   196
Shaktu   8, 49, 132, 137, 153–4, 166–7, 170, 174, 177–9, 184, 189, 190, 205
Shaktu-Khaisora   166, 177, 178
Shaman Khels (Mehsuds)   6, 11, 16–17, 20, 23, 28, 51, 66, 93, 100, 112, 143, 250 n.24
Shami Pir   180, 181
sheikhs (deputies)   11, 14, 36, 44–5, 48, 56, 69
Sherani Pashtuns   6, 29, 90–1, 244 n.18
Sheranna   8, 40–1, 43, 139, 141, 189
Sherdad, Abdur Rahman Khel Bahlolzai Mehsud   79, 86
Sher Dil, Abdur Rahman Khel Bahlolzai Mehsud   85
Sher Dil Khan, Sardar   43
Sher Zaman, Mirza Ali Khan's brother   172, 189
Sher Zaman Khan, Muhammad Khel   161
Shingi Bahlolzai Mehsuds   7, 15–16, 21, 44, 93, 102
Shinwaris   127, 145, 148
Shiromani Gurdwara Parbandhak Committee   171
Shodi Khel, Hamzoni Bhittani   146, 161, 188–9
Shondakas   11
shukrana (regular offerings/tithes)   11, 56, 180
Siddique, Abubakar   279 n.134
Silla Khan, Malikshahi Mehsud, brother of Sarfaraz   79, 242 n.86, 250 n.25
Singh, Chattar (Sikh general)   13
Singh, Gurmukh   147
Singh, Mitha   147

Singh, Rattan 147
Sirki Khels, Ahmadzai Wazirs 29, 223 n.46, 226 n.72
Skeen, Andrew, General 93, 98, 100, 251 n.38
Sneath, David 220 n.4
soft power 15
Soviet Union 103, 106, 127, 145, 147, 158, 267 n.118
Spain, James 2, 94
Starr, Lilian 125
Stewart, Donald 38
Stirling, Captain 74
Stolietov, Nikolai, General 22
Subahdar Baluch Khan, Nazar Khel Bahlozai Mehsud 153
Sufis 10–11
suicidal attacks 57–60, 63–4, 70–1, 78
Suleiman Khel Ghilzai Powindahs 6, 44, 90, 167, 178–9, 182, 261 n.103
Sultan Akbar Shah (Kaniguram Sayyid) 11
Sultan Muhammad Khan 146
Swahn Khan, Sudan Khel Ahmadzai Wazir 17
Swinson, Arthur 276 n.52
Synge, Lieutenant 158, 163
Syria 136, 155, 181–2

Taliban/Tehrik-i-Taliban 36, 199, 200, 208, 239 n.5
talibs/taliban 11, 36, 42, 56
Tank 6–8, 11–12, 14, 17, 20–3, 44–5, 72, 77, 83–4, 129–30, 151, 156, 159, 180
Tank raid, nawab's party and Afghanistan 20–3
  further attack on 97
Tannis 6, 82
Tapp, Lieutenant 129
Tapper, Richard 221 n.16, 223 n.42
tarburwali 9, 205
Tarin, Tori Khel Utmanzai Wazir 89, 111
Tarzi, Mahmud 89, 98
Taylor, Reynell, Major 12–13, 16–18, 99–100, 118, 134, 192, 193, 223 n.7
Tazi Khel Ahmadzai Wazirs 29, 142–4, 261 n.103
Thorburn, Septimus 24, 25, 251 n.26
Thornton, Thomas 226 n.58
Times (newspaper, London) 114, 122, 144, 197

Tochi river and valley 6, 8, 38–42, 74, 82, 122, 172, 227 n.7, 252 n.51
Tochi route 26–7, 34, 35, 46, 140
Tochi Wazirs 143
Tokhi Ghilzais 148
Tori Khel Utmanzai Wazirs 42, 77, 81, 123, 137, 141, 166, 170, 172–8, 184, 188, 259 n.70
  Mehsuds and 137–8
Toynbee, Arnold 249 n.119, 256 n.125
Trenchard, Hugh, viscount 100, 184, 247 n.81
Trevelyan, Charles 192
tribal responsibility 14, 16, 21, 23, 46, 52, 112, 153, 202–3, 224 n.12, 250 n.24
tribe, significance of 10, 220–1 n.4
Tripodi, Christian 3, 246 n.74, 258 n.47, 263 n.18
tuman (Mehsuds as a whole) 55, 65, 86, 251 n.39
tumani (tribal) allowances 51, 65–6, 103, 105, 112
Turis 6

Umar Khan, Salimi Khel Manzai Alizai Mehsud 20–4, 28, 254 n.81
Umarzais, Ahmadzai Wazirs 17
Urmurs (Barakis) 6
Utmanzais (Wazirs) 6, 17, 41, 81, 123, 137, 138–9, 141, 154, 168, 172, 175, 223 n.46

Vincent, William 117
violence 57–60, 99–102
von Kaufman, Constantine 22

Waging War in Waziristan (Roe) 2
wakils (representatives) 51–2, 65–6, 73, 86, 105, 201
Wali Khan (Abdul Ghaffur Khan's son) 196
Wana 6, 8, 24–5, 27–30, 33, 36–40, 46, 61–3, 70, 85, 90–2, 96–8, 104, 106, 110–11, 142–3, 162, 261 n.106, 275 n.26
Waris Khan, Madda Khel Utmanzai Wazir 42
Warren, Alan 2, 172, 198, 259 n.70, 262 n.120

Warza Shingi Bahlolzai Mehsuds 102
Watson, Hubert 40, 44, 231 n.90
Waziristan. *See also individual entries*
   and Afghanistan, during First World
      War 80–4
   after 1947 196–200
   and British, in 1850s 12–13
   British policy in 113–20, 186–8
   discontent in 1930 150
   geography of 5
   people of 6
   political and social organization
      of 8–10
   political position in 1849–50 11–12
   religion of 10–11
   socio-economic development in 136,
      169, 198
   Wazirs 6, 10, 16, 17, 34, 45, 68, 78, 91,
      96–7, 199, 205
   early British relations with 17–18
   occupations of 8
Webster, Lieutenant, Royal
      Engineers 125
Whawell, Private 158, 163
Wigram, Kenneth, General 139–40, 183
women 8, 99, 100, 135, 154
Woodhouse, N. S., Frontier
      Constabulary 111

World War I. *See* First World War
World War II. *See* Second World War
Wyatt, Christopher M. 245–6 n.57

Yaqub Khan 255 n.125
Yarghul Khels, Zilla Khel Ahmadzai
      Wazirs 90
Yarik Khan, Langar Khel Alizai 12, 15,
      21–4

Zadrans 6, 41, 82, 159, 276 n.53
Zahir Shah 148
Zaimukhts 6
Zangi Khan, Madda Khel Utmanzai
      Wazir 138–41, 151, 157, 159,
      163–4, 166, 183, 185, 203, 204
Zar Khan, Pipalai Kabul Khel Utmanzai
      Wazir 157
Zariband, Malikshahi Bablolzai
      Mehsud 50
Zari, Giga Khel Bahlolzai Mehsud
      Khassadar 158, 163
Zetland, Marquess of, Secretary of State
      for India 178, 180
Zia ul-Haq, General 200
Zilla Khel Ahmadzai Wazirs 17, 20, 23,
      27, 29–30, 34, 41, 90–1, 96, 106,
      110, 125, 142, 163, 167, 261 n.103

www.ingramcontent.com/pod-product-compliance
Lightning Source LLC
Chambersburg PA
CBHW070016010526
44117CB00011B/1595